AN ECONOMIC HISTORY
OF WESTERN EUROPE
1945–1964

M. M. POSTAN

An Economic History of Western Europe

1945–1964

METHUEN & CO LTD
11 New Fetter Lane, London EC4

First published 1967 by Methuen & Co Ltd,
11 New Fetter Lane, London EC4
© *1967 by M. M. Postan*
University Paperback published 1967
Printed in Great Britain by
Richard Clay (The Chaucer Press), Ltd,
Bungay, Suffolk

Distributed in the USA by Barnes and Noble Inc.

CONTENTS

TABLES

Chart

PREFACE

The history of this book carries with it its own apology. A few years ago I accepted an invitation to contribute an economic section to a popular book on the history of Europe after 1945. It was only later, while equipping myself for the enterprise that I discovered how greatly was the way ahead beset with 'difficult' problems which could not be surmounted without recourse to the manner and matter of modern economics. The discovery opened before me two courses. One was to avoid the difficult stretches altogether and, in this way, produce a wholly popular account (which I may still do); the other was to take all the obstacles, but to do this as lightly mounted as the field would permit. I have chosen the second, the compromise, course and have produced a semi-popular treatise: simple to the full extent of my ability to simplify, yet bristling with passages which the uninitiated may find too technical. For their benefit, however, some of the chapters – especially those on investment and innovation – have been so composed as to make it possible for the more difficult passages to be skipped. These passages have been indicated by appropriate footnotes.

The other limitation for which an apology is due is that of geographical scope. The area ostensibly covered by the book is that of Western Europe; but the nature of the subject and the need for uniform treatment required that I should confine myself to the problems of the more advanced and more fully industrialized regions of Western Europe and leave out such countries as Spain, Portugal, Greece, Finland or Turkey, whose economic systems and economic histories differ radically from those of the main core in Western Europe. Yet even within the more restricted circle of the latter, I found it necessary to concentrate on countries best served by evidence and by secondary authorities, and to devote a disproportionate amount of space to the United Kingdom, Germany and France. It is because the geographical area has been so narrowly circumscribed *ab initio*, I also allow myself the further convenience of simplified geographical apellations, and used the term 'Germany' whereas only West-Germany was dealt with, 'European' where only Western-Europe was meant, referred to Belgium, where Belgium-cum-Luxembourg were implied and did not always make the necessary allowances for the inclusion of the Saar into Germany.

My main apologies, however, concern the material and the concepts with which I had to operate. Many of my concrete illustrations deal with the experiences of firms and governments too recent to have found their way into authoritative publications or works of scholarship. Some of them come from current periodicals and have been assembled through several years of preparatory browsing in the ephemeral reportage of the financial press. Most of them have therefore been cited without proper footnote references, and must be taken in the spirit in which they are offered – as mere illustrations and not as crucial evidence. On the few occasions in which they happen to provide an essential ingredient of the argument they have been verified and appropriately footnoted.

The readers will also notice the shortcomings of my statistical evidence. That a study like this must be based on measurements is something a critical reader will expect and a cursory one must forgive. But as this book is not a piece of original research, its statistics have all been borrowed from other studies. They therefore vary in precision and reliability and frequently also differ in assumptions and methods of computation. Where the series happen to be greatly at variance, I have tried to reconcile them, or else have drawn the attention of the reader to the disparities. When I have failed to do so, I have tried to make sure that the lack of concordance would not affect the conclusions.

More serious, and, in the eyes of some, more venal is my reliance on time series and on aggregate measurements – those of Gross National or Domestic Products, average productivities, national and supra-national rates of growth, saving ratios, rates of investment – and, above all, my readiness to single out individual variables of the 'production function' – labour, capital, technology – and to treat each of them apart from its other co-variables.

The statistical pitfalls of aggregates and time series are well known. Changes over long periods in the composition of inputs and outputs, in the quality of products, or in the relative valuations of commodities are known to impair the usefulness of all long-term series of indices. By integrating our measurements we cannot help obliterating concrete and specific features of reality – be they those of labour or machines, of firms or localities – and replace them by largely fictitious, 'macro-economic', abstractions. No wonder historians fight shy of these as of all other aggregates; their professional preferences are for the concrete, the individual and the unique. And the readers of this book will soon discover that my own inclination is also to disaggregate macro-economic entities, such as national economies, sectors, or industries, and to reduce them to the individual firms and to individual men at their head. Nevertheless, I found I could not eschew macro-economic measurements altogether. Without them the history of Europe as a whole could not be written, and the individual, the 'micro-economic', phenomena themselves could not be fitted into any significant universe of discourse.

Fortunately in this job of fitting the specific into the general, statistical distortions of our aggregates need not be as lethal as they may at first sight appear. They do not make historical conclusions impossible provided the conclusions are not out of scale with the margins of error. Nor need the statistical pitfalls of overlong time-series be too great an impediment, provided the time-span of the study is not excessive – and the 20 years between 1945 and 1965 is almost too short a span to be considered truly historical. In short, the reader must take most of my statistics with a grain of salt, but take them he must.

Elsewhere in this book I shall have to explain why an economic historian must also brave these dangers of the 'production function'. The underlying assumption that individual factors of production – labour, capital, or technology – are entities, which the entrepreneur can combine and substitute at will and the economist can analyse and measure separately, is a much idealized, and to that extent, a distorting abstraction. But can changes in the performance of a national economy or a firm be understood or expounded without some such abstraction? In Samuelson's words, 'a many-sectoral, neoclassical model with heterogenous capital goods and somewhat limited factor substitution can fail to have some of the simple properties of the "idealised models". But recognizing these complications does not justify nihilism.'

Here again the reader will notice that in discussing the course of investment and technological progress in postwar Europe I found it impossible to account for it by relative costs of factors and by the consequent substitutions of capital for labour. But my account itself – indeed the very scaling down of relative-factor-costs as an explanation – would have been impossible without assuming that capital, labour, technology and entrepreneurial decision-making had to be combined if any output was to take place; that the proportions in which they were brought together were not wholly fortuitous; and that the reason why the proportions differed will explain some – even if it cannot account for all – the decisions to invest or to innovate.

Not being based on much original research of my own, this book relies heavily on the work of others; and the appropriate citations will be found in the footnotes. I must, however, acknowledge my special indebtedness to the great corpus of Samuel Kuznets's pioneering studies, Mr Angus Maddison's book on the economic growth in the West which he kindly made available to me in draft, to Mr Andrew Shonfield's book on modern capitalism, Mr Willey's unpublished thesis on the economic development of the United Kingdom and Germany, and above all to the anonymous authors of the standard compendia of the Economic Section of U.N.O. and of the O.E.C.D. In addition I have had the rare, if not wholly legitimate, privilege of reading the draft of Professor Denison's monumental study of 'inputs' in post-war economies. As, at the time of reading, Denison's study was still unpublished, while the present book was already well advanced, the reader will not find in it any direct mention of Mr Denison's conclusions. I hope to repair the omission if and when another occasion presents itself.

Greater even than my debt to other people's books is that to my friends' and colleagues' personal aid. My colleagues in Cambridge, C. Feinstein and K. Berrill read and criticized an early draft; and Mr Feinstein has also generously placed at my disposal some of the statistical studies on which he was engaged. Simon Kuznets was helpful with acute as well as kindly criticisms, especially over my appendix on shares of income. David Landes of Harvard read and commented on an earlier draft of the first six chapters. My colleagues of M.I.T., Robert Solow, Charles Kindleberger, Paul Samuelson, Edwin Kuh, Morris Adelman, Karl Schell, Paul Rodan-

Rosenstein, Peter Temin, have with the utmost generosity allowed me to impose myself on their time and patience. In doing so I took every care not to involve them into the discussion of this book's substance; they therefore bear no responsibility for its conclusions or arguments. But I sought and received from them much help over the worst technical fences. If now and again I have failed to take them in proper style, this is due not to any lack of instruction but to my own inability to profit from it.

ABBREVIATIONS

Most commonly used abbreviations in footnotes and text

C.S.O.	H.M.G's Central Statistical Office, London
D.A.E.	Department of Applied Economics, Cambridge
E.C.E.	United Nations, Economic Commission for Europe, Geneva
F.A.O.	United Nations, Food and Agriculture Organization, Rome
G.D.P.	Gross Domestic Product
G.N.P.	Gross National Product
I.C.O.R.	Incremental Capital Output Ratio
N.I.E.S.R.	National Institute of Economic and Social Research, London
N.B.E.R.	National Bureau of Economic Research, New York
O.E.C.D.	Organization for Economic Co-operation and Development, Paris
O.E.E.C.	Organization for European Economic Co-operation, Paris
Some Factors . . .	*Some Factors in Economic Growth in Europe during the 1950's*, being Part 2 of *Economic Survey of Europe in 1961*, United Nations, Economic Commission for Europe, Geneva, 1964

PART 1

Growth

CHAPTER 1

High and Smooth

To the historian as well as to the ordinary observer the unique feature of the post-war economy in the West is its growth. It reveals itself in various signs of ever-mounting affluence, as well as in more sophisticated statistical and economic measurements. The world as a whole got richer. Its measured and measurable income, or, more precisely, what statisticians call the aggregate Gross Product, increased by well over 85 per cent between 1938 and 1964. Its industrial ouput alone was more than two and a half times greater in 1964 than in 1938: the index number of its industrial production (with 1958 as 100) stood at about 125 in 1963 compared with 44 in 1938, or 62 in 1948. But even though some non-European countries progressed faster than the European ones, economic expansion in Western Europe more than kept pace with the world as a whole. The aggregate Gross National Product of Western Europe, measured at constant prices, was also more than two and a half times higher in 1963 than it had been on the eve of the war; its industrial output (with 1958 as 100) rose from about 50 in 1938 to about 130 in 1963.

Looked at more closely this growth, constant and cumulative as it was, may turn out to have been not quite as uneventful as the average figures may suggest. It went through several, perhaps as many as four, distinct phases, each marked by a clear turning-point. The first two or three years following the capitulation of Germany were obviously the time of demobilization in the simplest sense of the term. Some neutral countries such as Sweden, little touched by the war, were able on the morrow of VE Day to continue their wartime progress without a break: in the first year of peace Sweden's G.N.P. stood at 136 per cent of its 1938 level and went on mounting thereafter. Even the United Kingdom, in spite of the thoroughness – or as Churchill called it, the reckless abandon – of its wartime

B

mobilization, was not so impoverished or disorganized by the war as not to be able to reach its pre-war level of income and output in 1946, the first year of peace, and to exceed it by some 8 per cent in 1947.[1]

Table 1 *Gross Domestic Product 1948–63*

Compound Annual Rates of Growth (%) [2]	
Austria	5·8
Belgium	3·2
Denmark	3·6
France	4·6
Germany	7·6
Italy	6·0
Netherlands	4·7
Norway	3·5
Sweden	3·4
Switzerland	5·1
United Kingdom	2·5

Most other Western European countries had to start from lower depths. Lowest of all were, of course, the depths of Germany's decline. Physical destruction, the paralysis of the transport system, the partition of the country into occupied zones, the atrophy of government, the ruin of the currency and a galloping price rise, all combined to bring German national income and output in 1946 to under one-third, probably to as low as 29 per cent, of that of

[1] These and the subsequent figures for national outputs at different phases have been derived from various sources, but mainly from the annual *Economic Surveys* of Europe produced by E.C.E. in Geneva and the consecutive *Economic Surveys* for individual countries produced by O.E.E.C. and O.E.C.D. in Paris.

[2] Gross Domestic Product at 1954 factor-cost prices (1953 prices for Netherlands). The Table deals with the *domestic* product, and not with the *national* product, in order to eliminate the effects of income from abroad. The figures are based on those for 1949–59 in *Some Factors*, Ch. II, Tables 1 and 2, supplemented for 1948 and 1960–3 mainly from figures in the consecutive *Economic Surveys* of individual countries produced by O.E.E.C. and O.E.C.D. in Paris. Figures for Norway cover the period 1949–59, those for Switzerland the period 1950–60. The series for Germany has been supplemented and corrected by figures for 1948 and 1949, since the figures in *Some Factors* commence in 1950. These German corrections have been based on figures in W. G. Hoffmann and J. H. Müller, *Das deutsche Volkseinkommen, 1851–1957*, Tübingen, 1959.

1938. It was still no higher than 40 per cent in 1947, and stood between 66 per cent and 70 per cent in 1948. The other countries directly affected by the war fared somewhat, but only somewhat, better. France's G.D.P. in 1946 was little under 50 per cent of pre-war and was still 5 per cent below it the following year (1947). Italy's stood at 61 per cent of pre-war in 1946 and at 81 per cent in 1947, the Netherlands' at 74 per cent and 94 per cent. It was not until 1948, or the third full year of peace, that most of the Western countries were able to approach closely or even to exceed the pre-war levels of output and income.

In fact, the end of that year marked the beginning of the second phase – that of recovery proper – the time when economic transition from war to peace was completed, and when most of the war-afflicted countries were able to adopt the remedies without which the smooth progress of their economy would have been impossible. Of these measures the most spectacular and the most immediately effective was the German currency reform of June of 1948. The currency was devalued and stabilized at one-tenth of its inflated level, and devaluation was accompanied by other measures designed to anchor the value of the new currency to the new price level. As a result, on the morrow of the reform, money ceased to chase non-existent goods, long-hoarded commodities suddenly appeared in the shops and on markets, raw materials and semi-finished products began to flow to factories producing consumption goods, and the German economy entered upon that ascending path which it continued to tread with hardly a deviation in the subsequent fifteen years.

In France, where inflation and financial instability were destined to last for many more years, conditions also improved in the course of 1948. The Government took several steps – effective, even if the effects were not very long-lasting – to curb the rise of prices and costs, especially a successful long-term stabilization loan. The good harvest of 1948/9 also helped to hold down prices for a time. When the country appeared to finish the year with its national income well recovered – about 8 per cent above 1938 – it looked as if its prospects of development were set fair. As it turned out, France was as yet by no means out of the woods, but her output and her national income, having begun to expand, were to continue to do so throughout the subsequent period. The other Western countries did equally well and promised to do even better. In the United Kingdom the national product by the end of the year was 21 per cent above pre-war, in Sweden 43 per cent, in Denmark 30 per cent. Belgium, the Netherlands and Norway appeared to be slightly, but only slightly, more laggard.

In the late forties, events outside Europe, and especially in the U.S.A., also worked in Europe's favour. By far the most dramatic, as well as the most effective, contribution to recovery was the announcement in the summer of 1947 and the passing by the American Congress in March 1948 of the so-called 'Marshall Plan' for foreign assistance by which the U.S.A. undertook to provide economic aid to European countries, and thus underwrote the costs of their economic reconstruction for many years to come. On their part most European countries carried out in 1949 a round of currency devaluations which reduced for a time the effects of internal inflation and alleviated the payment difficulties which were besetting the economies of the United Kingdom and France.

There was thus little to impede and much to stimulate the progress of national incomes and outputs, which, in fact, continued uninterrupted until 1952/3. The outbreak of the Korean War in 1950 had an unsettling effect on international trade and world prices, but it also stimulated economic activity in the U.S.A. and elsewhere. The Korean 'boom' lasted until 1952, and during this period the European economy expanded at the annual rate of well above 4 per cent. The national products of France, the Netherlands, and Norway grew at about the same rate, Austria's annual increment approached 6 per cent, Italy's exceeded 6 per cent, while West Germany's economic development went ahead fastest, at the annual rate of growth of 8·7 per cent.

The third phase commenced in, or just before, 1953 and lasted until about 1957. The boom and higher prices for raw materials caused by the Korean War were followed by a slight recession in 1952. But this, in its turn, was followed by what was perhaps the most robust period of European development. Not only was the average rate of economic growth in these years somewhat higher than in the preceding ones, but the countries which had grown fastest also continued to forge ahead. Germany's G.N.P.

grew at the annual rate of 7·7 per cent, France and Italy at 5·5 per cent. What, however, marked this phase from the preceding one were the signs of internal strength and growing economic independence. Continued progress may still have hinged on American aid and expenditure, but not to the same extent as before.

The way to the fourth phase, like that to the third, lay across a trough. At the turn of 1957 and 1958 economic growth appeared to slow down and eventually went into a recession – the first all-European recession since the war. In the preceding period a number of countries and more especially the United Kingdom, France, Denmark and Belgium had suffered more persistently than heretofore from unfavourable balances of payments and from consequent pressures against their currencies. The remedial measures, all restrictive in their effect, put temporary brakes on the national economies and for a time succeeded in slowing down the annual rates of growth. But except for the United Kingdom and perhaps Belgium, the slowdown proved no more than temporary. It was only towards the very end of the period, i.e. by 1963, in Italy and to a smaller extent France and elsewhere, that inflation became serious enough to raise a real threat to continued growth of the economy.

Thus, when followed step by step the upward movement of the European economy may well appear less smooth than it was. Yet for all its variations in pace, the ascent of the European economy after 1945 was both steeper and smoother than at any other period of modern history. It would appear high no matter how measured. The measurements so far applied here have been those of aggregate products, and it is possible to take exception to them on the ground that they do not make allowances for increases in population and do not therefore truly measure productivity, i.e. in output per head.

As we shall see further, the total 'labour input' somewhat increased in most countries. The growth of output or income per person employed as well as per head of population was, therefore, bound to lag, however little, behind the movement of G.N.P. Yet even then, the productivity rates, i.e. outputs per person employed or per head of population, still compared very favourably with similar figures for nearly all the other periods of European history for which evidence is available. As far as our data allows us to judge, the economic product per man-year or per head of population in the heroic decades of the English industrial revolution at the end of the eighteenth century may have increased at a rate comparable to that of post-war Europe. The same is probably true of the rate at which productivity grew in Germany during her most rapid advances in the last quarter of the nineteenth century. But between 1870 and 1913 German output per head increased at a rate well below 2 per cent, probably at 1·8 per cent per annum. In the inter-war years Germany's material progress was rudely disturbed by the two depressions – that of the twenties and that of the early thirties – though both in the mid-twenties and immediately before the outbreak of the second great war the growth of industrial productivity speeded up. Over the inter-war period as a whole, productivity in Western Europe increased at an annual rate of about 1·7 per cent per annum. The comparable rate between 1948 and 1963, however, was at least twice as high – somewhere near 3·5 per cent per annum. It was twice as high even in the United Kingdom, whose aggregate national product was relatively laggard. As population and the labour force in the United Kingdom after the war grew more slowly than between the wars, the smaller-than-elsewhere increases in the national product were partly compensated by some expansion of output per man.[1]

What is more, post-war growth was not only faster but smoother than heretofore, less broken by recurrent crises. Alternation between boom and depression had been the constant and seemingly inescapable feature of European economies ever since the dawn of the modern industrial order in the early nineteenth century. Fluctuations of this kind, their regularity and their length, have been a subject of debate among economists. Some have gone so far as to consider them an essential condition of sustained economic development. Marx and the Marxists have always argued that economic crises belonged to the very nature of the capitalist system and were destined to bring about its eventual collapse. Their entire eschatology, their very vision of the socialist revolution, depended on the diagnosis of crises as an incurable disease of the capital system. And indeed the experience of the inter-war era seemed to

[1] *Vide* Appendix, Note 1, p. 361 below.

bear out the diagnosis. Crises of growing severity succeeded each other with great regularity, and the great depression of 1929–33 surpassed all previous depressions in depth and duration and appeared to condemn the economic and social order that permitted it.

Table 2 *Rates of Growth of Productivity*[1]

	Rates of Growth of Output per Head of Population	
	(a) 1870–1913	(b) 1948–1962
Belgium	1·8	2·2
Denmark	2·1	2·8
France	1·4	3·4
Germany	1·8	6·8
Italy	0·7	5·6
Norway	1·4	2·9
Sweden	2·3	2·6
United Kingdom	1·3	2·4

Both the diagnosis and the prognosis were belied by post-war-experience. As we have seen, some fluctuations there were, but they all were very mild. None of them interrupted for long the continued ascent of production and productivity; and certainly none of them caused that upsurge of unemployment or paralysis of business which had characterized the great depressions of pre-war years. The dip in the growth curve which occurred in 1948–9 was shorter and less widespread than any of the pre-war depressions: some countries were hardly affected by it. The dip of 1951–2

[1] The figures for 1870–1913 are based on Angus Maddison, *Economic Growth in the West*, London 1964, Tables 1, 3, and 7. Those for 1948–63 have been derived mainly from *Some Factors*, Ch. II, Table IV, and from sources listed in footnotes to Table 1 above. The figures in these sources for the United Kingdom have been adjusted to the slightly lower figures in C. H. Feinstein, 'Production and Productivity in the United Kingdom 1920–1962', *The London and Cambridge Economic Bulletin*, December 1963. Maddison's productivity figures are computed per head of population and per man-hour and are not therefore strictly identical with the figures in *Some Factors* and in C. H. Feinstein which are computed per man-year. For the purposes of this study Feinstein's figures have been re-computed on the per-head basis. Cf. also figures in D. G. Paige, F. I. Blackaby, and S. Freund, 'Economic Growth in the Last Hundred Years', *National Institute Economic Review*, July 1961.

affected nearly all the European countries, especially the United Kingdom and Belgium, and perhaps lasted longer than that of 1848, but nowhere did it pull down national production or productivity appreciably below their pre-recession height. The third recession, that of 1958, was again both mild and more local in its incidence. Even in the United Kingdom, where it lasted longer than elsewhere, it did little more than arrest the growth of output.

How mild all the post-war recessions were is shown by the measurements of fluctuations estimated by Mr Angus Maddison of O.E.C.D. According to these measurements, the pre-1913 drops in German national product from peaks to the lowest points in recessions could be as great as 4 per cent of the national product; between the wars the product fell from its peak in the late twenties to the bottom of the depression in the early thirties by more than 16 per cent. But after 1945 German national product never descended below the level it had previously reached; and what characterized German recessions was not falling output but merely slower rates of growth. The same is true of most other countries. In Italian depressions, both before 1913 and between the two wars, national product descended on the average by about 5 per cent below the output at peak; it was 12 per cent below peak in the great depression of the thirties. The G.N.P. was 19 per cent below peak in the great inter-war slump in France, and 13 per cent in Sweden. By contrast, after the war, in none of these countries, with the possible exception of the United Kingdom, Sweden, and Belgium, did national output in any year descend significantly below its previous highest. Only in Belgium, in the general recession of the fifties, did the G.N.P. for a short time fall 1·5–1·8 per cent below the previous peak. In the United Kingdom the worst declines in output experienced before 1965 did not bring the G.N.P. more than 0·5 per cent below preceding high points compared with 4 per cent, by which, on the average, the national output fell below peak in the depressions of the period 1890–1913.[1]

In other words, the European post-war economy was all-but depression-free. Such unevennesses and recessions as there were,

[1] A. Maddison, 'Growth and Fluctuation in the World Economy 1870–1960', *Banca Nazionale del Lavoro Quarterly Review*, January 1962; idem, *Economic Growth in the West*, 46–9.

differed from the pre-war ones not only in amplitude but also in origin and significance. The typical pre-war crises were those of under-consumption and over-production, or else were due to sharp drops in investment. Hardly any of the post-war recessions could be confused with these classical types of cyclical depressions. As we shall see presently the main difficulty of post-war economies was not slack demand, relative over-production, or insufficient investment, but an ungovernable tendency of demand to outrun the economy's capacity to meet it without inflation and price rise.

On the other hand, the advance, though remarkably smooth, was not equally rapid in all countries. Throughout the period the rate of growth was very uneven as between country and country, some advancing faster, others slower, than the average, some slowing down in the course of years, others accelerating.

In this respect the post-war era passed through several distinct re-alignments roughly, but not altogether, corresponding to the phases of alternate retardation and acceleration which the European economy as a whole went through. In the first phase, that of recovery proper, the erstwhile neutral countries and the United Kingdom were in the lead. This initial alignment did not, however, last long: not longer than the four or five years separating the end of the war from the first clear signs of recovery from the effects of war destruction and post-war unsettlement of finance, currency and trade. In this period the United Kingdom and Sweden forged ahead fastest. It was only after the United Kingdom had run into her first payments crisis in 1948–9 that the causes which were to keep her behind most other European nations came to the surface.

The second re-alignment came at the turn of the decade. By the early fifties the countries which had suffered most in the war, West Germany, Italy, and France, and whose road to full recovery was longest, grew fastest and with least interruption, while in the United Kingdom and Belgium and, for a time, in Denmark, economic expansion proceeded at a much slower rate. Between 1954 and 1961, when the distinction between the two groups became most marked, the German Gross Domestic Product grew at the average rate of nearly 6·6 per cent per annum, France's by nearly 4·2 per cent, Italy's by 5·7 per cent, Switzerland's by 4·6 per cent per annum. By contrast, the average rate of growth of the G.D.P. in the United Kingdom was about 2·3 per cent per annum, and in Belgium about 2·5 per cent per annum. In the other countries of Western Europe, i.e. Sweden, Norway, and the Netherlands, the rate of growth was on the whole intermediate between those of the leaders and the laggards.

This relative ranking of European nations in the growth order showed signs of changing again in the sixties and more especially after 1962. In several countries, and in the first place in Italy and France, the mounting dangers of inflation compelled the governments to put the brakes on domestic consumption and on investment, and as a result the rate of economic expansion slowed down. In Italy it fell from the average of 7·5 per cent between 1959 and 1961, to 6·2 per cent in 1962, to 4·8 per cent in 1963, and 2·6 per cent in 1964. In France the G.D.P. in 1964 stayed, almost without moving, at a level little above that in the last quarter of 1963.[1] In Germany the initial impetus of her remarkable expansion showed signs of petering out even earlier. Between 1961 and 1964 her G.D.P. grew at the average annual rate of 4·5 per cent, compared with 9·5 per cent between 1950 and 1955, and 6·3 per cent between 1955 and 1960. On the other hand, Switzerland, whose G.D.P. in the fifties had grown at the average rate of about 5 per cent, accelerated her growth to some 5·7 per cent per annum between 1960 and 1963, and to 6 per cent in 1964, when her rate of growth was actually the highest in Europe. The national product of the Netherlands also showed signs of rapid expansion after 1963. But the most remarkable of all was the change in Belgium. Whereas in the fifties that country had shared with the United Kingdom the bottom rank in the growth order, with her annual rates of growth hovering between 2·8 and 3·1, in 1962 her G.D.P. increased by 4·3 per cent, in 1963 by 3·9 per cent, and in 1964 by 5·5 per cent. In that year she ranked with three or four fastest-growing countries. By that time the top rank was also joined by Sweden, whose G.D.P., having grown by about 3·4 per cent per annum in the fifties and only by 2·9 per cent in 1962, forged ahead by 4·9 per cent in 1963

---

[1] However, measured by annual averages the G.N.P. in 1964 as a whole was still 5·7 per cent higher than in 1963 as a whole: O.E.C.D., *Economic Survey of France for 1964*, Paris, 1965, p. 5.

and 6 per cent in 1964. Only little less marked was the acceleration in Norway and Denmark. Least changed were the positions of the United Kingdom at the bottom and of Austria among the nations at the top.[1]

Yet even then the economic performance of the more laggard countries, that of Belgium before 1962, or that of the United Kingdom after 1948, is not to be disparaged. British growth appears slow only when set against that of some other European countries; it compares very favourably with the United Kingdom's own record in the late nineteenth and early twentieth centuries. Comparisons of gross national products over periods as long as these would be perhaps more than usually misleading, but if our imperfect measurements are to be trusted, the Gross Domestic Product grew in the United Kingdom between 1870 and 1913 at the average annual rate of 1·7 per cent per annum. The corresponding rate in the inter-war period (1924–37) was probably about 2·25 per cent. Between 1948 and 1962 the national product grew at the average annual rate of about 2·5 per cent per annum. The same is even truer of Belgium, or of the relatively slowly growing economies of Denmark and Norway. In other words, for all the variations from country to country, the record of post-war growth for Western Europe as a whole, when viewed historically, may well appear unprecedented.[2]

---

[1] O.E.C.D., *Economic Surveys of: Sweden for 1962 and 1963; Switzerland for 1963, 1964; Belgium–Luxembourg Economic Union for 1962, 1963, and 1964; Austria for 1963 and 1964; Denmark for 1963; Italy for 1963 and 1964; Germany for 1962 and 1964; France for 1964.* The dates of publication are as a rule a year later than the period covered by the surveys.

[2] Footnote 2, p. 12 above. For the United Kingdom, see also J. B. Jefferys and D. Walters, 'National Income and Expenditure of the U.K. 1870–1952', *Income and Wealth*, Series V, London, 1955. These figures are for G.N.P. and therefore include income from overseas, but even if recomputed for the domestic product, they are somewhat higher than Feinstein's figures used here. The difference, however, is not such as to affect the comparisons in the text.

CHAPTER 2
Growthmanship

In their satisfied contemplation of the post-war record, political and economic commentators have made free use of the adjective 'miraculous'. This compliment has been most frequently paid to West Germany in acknowledgement of the speed and thoroughness of her recovery. This and other terms of praise and self-congratulation are not undeserved; yet they may have been somewhat misplaced. The most unprecedented phenomenon in post-war Europe was not so much the purely material record of her economy as the spirit which moved it. What was really remarkable (and to some historians and social scientists unexpected) was that economic growth was so powerfully propelled by public sentiments and policies.

By comparison, the purely material achievements of the age are easier to explain. Of the various features of the post-war economic history the one which deserves the title of miracle least is the act which bears it most conspicuously, i.e. that of initial recovery from the effects of war, more especially the act of German recovery. The man in the street who witnessed or even read about the dislocation of economic life caused by the war, the destruction wrought by bombing, by the passage of troops, and, in the case of Germany, by post-war dismantling of industry, could not help being impressed by the recovery in the first few years after the war. Yet a closer look at what occurred in German and British economies during and immediately after the war might dim somewhat the wonder of the miracle.

Contrary to commonly held views, the war years both in the United Kingdom and in Germany were not wholly years of economic waste but a time when productive potential expanded. It is now generally admitted that the economic potential of warring nations benefited from the engineering and scientific advances in munition industries. As a result of the war, the United Kingdom, the U.S.S.R., the U.S.A., and Germany acquired new technologies, leadership and cadres in a number of industries with great potentialities for future growth.

More significant, though less understood, are the great additions which both the United Kingdom and Germany made to their productive capital during the years of rearmament and war. In conventional discussions of war economies the tragic years of 1939–45 are commonly referred to as years of 'disinvestment': a period when nations allowed their productive capital to run down. In actual fact, these were years of steadily growing capacity. In Britain government investment in fixed capital of industries serving the production of munitions probably approached £1,030 millions between 1936 and 1945, some 80 per cent of which was invested after 1938. In addition, at least £500 and possibly as much as £800 million may have been invested by private firms into munition factories, and both by the Government and private firms into equipment serving civilian as well as military needs. The combined net investment – probably in excess of £1,500 millions – was more than the nation had added to the capital of its industries and utilities in comparable periods before 1935.[1]

The accretions were even greater and more remarkable in Germany. According to the researches of Dr Krengel's team in the Institut für Wirtschaftsforschung, Germany was adding to its productive resources between 1940 and the first half of 1945 at the annual rate of 3·36 thousand million DM at 1950 prices, compared with the annual rate of 0·89 thousand million DM between 1935 and 1939, and 1·86 thousand million DM between 1924 and 1929. As a result of this continuous process of capital formation, Germany had by the end of the war actually increased her capital. Much of the new productive capacity was destroyed by bombing and some was removed by the allies in the process of post-war dismantling. But the effects of bombing and dismantling were not so great as wholly to nullify the additional productive equipment created during and

---

[1] The figure of £1,500 million is based on M. Postan, *British War Production* (History of the Second World War), H.M.S.O., 1952, p. 448; William Hornby, *Factories and Plant* (History of the Second World War), H.M.S.O., 1958, pp. 378–81.

immediately before the war. Dr Krengel and his team of researchers have suggested that although the effects of bombing came to about 13,800 million DM or 28 per cent of capacity in 1936, and dismantling came to 2,800 million DM or 5·7 per cent of 1936 capacity, fixed assets in Germany's industry in 1946 still stood nearly 7,000 million DM higher than in 1936 and were about equal to the value of fixed equipment in 1939.[1]

True enough, some of this productive capital was in the form of highly specialized munitions plants unsuited to peacetime employment. Yet the extent to which wartime machinery and plant were usable in peace is too easy to underestimate. Both in Germany and in the United Kingdom most of the factories built during the war for munitions, their sites, their services and lines of communications were eventually employed in peace. The same is true even of much of the machinery and machine-tools.

Furthermore, war damage through bombing and military operations was far greater in its immediate effects on output than when measured by permanent effect on the equipment itself. Most of the industrial hardware – buildings, plant, and machinery – were easy enough to put out of action, but difficult to destroy altogether. And both the English and German experience in the war and immediately after showed that by a relatively small expenditure on repairs it was possible to bring back into operation a great deal of productive capital – a fact which largely explains how Germany was able to raise so steeply her industrial output in the immediate post-war years.

Indeed, much of the early achievement in economic recovery in most countries after 1948 can largely be accounted for by the fact of the recovery itself. Shortages of goods had been accumulating for years, the needs of reconstruction were great and urgent, the reserves of unemployed resources were immense. Is it to be wondered that the initial momentum of economic growth should have been so strong?

However, the growth was destined to outlast the impetus of

---

[1] Rolf Krengel, 'Some Reasons for the Rapid Economic Growth of the German Federal Republic', *Banca Nazionale del Lavoro Quarterly Review*, No. 64, 1963; idem, 'Anlagevermögen, Produktion und Beschäftigung der Industrie von 1924 bis 1956', *Deutscher Institut für Wirtschaftsforschung*, Special Issue. N.S. No. 42.

recovery. That it could be sustained until the middle sixties and possibly beyond was due to factors other than the stimulus of the recovery itself. These factors are easy enough to list: they were all of the kind which historians and economists normally expect to influence economic activity. First of all, there was the buoyancy of demand and employment. The flow of investment was also abundant and was accompanied by unprecedented technological advances. Similarly, foreign trade expanded throughout the period. European countries were able to remove by degrees the worst obstacles to international trade and payments which had in the past caused recurrent crises of confidence and held back economic activity.

Whenever all or any of these favourable conditions had been present in the past they as a rule helped to revive business and to raise national incomes. It was the great fortune of the post-war world that these conditions combined and remained combined for nearly a generation. The combination may to some extent have been due to such fortuitous circumstances as the growth of population or the progress of applied science or the exigencies of the cold war. Yet to present the post-war growth as one of history's unpremeditated happenings would be most unhistorical. For what distinguishes the post-war era from most other periods of economic history is not only its growth but the extent to which this growth was 'contrived': generated and sustained by governments and the public. In all European countries economic growth became a universal creed and a common expectation to which governments were expected to conform. To this extent economic growth was the product of economic growthmanship.

Needless to say, the policies of growth were overlaid, and at times overborne, by other economic considerations. Post-war governments could no more be expected to suit all their actions to the needs of economic expansion than to serve any other exclusive object of economic policy. Even if they had possessed the gift of consistency – and few of them did – the problems facing them would have prevented them from concentrating on growth as their sole aim. Apart from a number of other and smaller economic objectives, at least one other major issue repeatedly forced itself upon their attention: that of inflation, with its attendant problems of prices, balance of payments, and stability of currencies. They were frequently called upon to defend price levels or balances of payments and, at times, to choose between the dangers of inflation and the prospects of faster growth.

These decisions so often became a matter of choice because, as I shall have to stress again later, the two objectives – the stability of prices and continued economic expansion – repeatedly presented themselves as alternatives. It is therefore all the more remarkable that economic growth should have figured so prominently as a guiding principle of state policy. That it was the business of governments to defend their currencies and their balances of payments was, after all, a universally accepted proposition, as old as the mercantilism of the sixteenth and seventeenth centuries. It was, moreover, uppermost in the minds of the state bankers and the officials of the ministries of finance who had the ears of governments in these matters. That, in spite of these predispositions, both politicians and bureaucrats should have accepted the necessity of using the powers of state to foster growth was a wholly new phenomenon and the hallmark of a new era.

It had certainly not been much in evidence before the war, even though its intellectual or theoretical foundations were laid at that time. In England in 1925 it was possible for Churchill to revalue the pound and to invite the worst penalties of chronic unemployment for the sake of monetary orthodoxy. When in 1931 the National Government in Great Britain introduced economy measures, it also sacrificed – and sacrificed for an indefinitely long future – national output and employment in the interests of solvency and stability. Similar indifference to the volume of economic activity was shown by the German Government at the onset of the great depression in the thirties and, to a smaller extent, by the governments of France, Belgium, and the Low Countries at the same time. They were all unwilling or unable to deal with the crisis except by deflationary measures which merely sped up the 'rundown' of the economy.

By the late nineteen-thirties, however, the lesson had been well learned. The German example demonstrated the political and social dangers of protracted depression and mass unemployment. By that time economists were also able to fashion the intellectual justification and the appropriate tools for the policy of full employment. Keynes's General Theory of Employment which appeared in 1936 may or may not be the epoch-making intellectual discovery most economists believe it to have been. There is, however, no doubt that arriving at the time it did it offered to public opinion in Western countries the assurance that unemployment was curable and the recipe for curing it. All that was necessary was that enough of the national product should be laid out again in consumption and in investment, to maintain the aggregate demand for goods and services at a level at which resources would be fully employed. And all this – so the recipe ran – governments had in their power to do by various measures, and in the first place by varying taxation and their own expenditure.

The prescription was backed by a large volume of expert opinion, and by the end of the war it had been accepted by political parties and governments in nearly all the Western countries. The Beveridge report on social services published in the course of the war and adopted by English political parties as a blueprint of social policy rested on Keynesian assumptions; and since the end of the war both political parties in England, the governments of Scandinavian countries, the Netherlands, France, and Italy all accepted it to be their duty to maintain effective demand at the height necessary to secure full employment. If the governments of Belgium and Switzerland or Western Germany either failed to declare their full adherence to the Keynesian doctrine, or did this half-heartedly and belatedly, this did not prevent them from following its precepts in practice and from using taxation and public expenditure as means for regulating aggregate demand and employment.

Moreover, full employment eventually developed into a policy and economic philosophy much wider in its implications. Since the early post-war years, when it was officially adopted by governments, it rapidly developed into a policy of economic growth. In theory full employment, once attained, need not by itself result in continuous growth of national income. Technological progress or increases in population could be relied upon under conditions of full employment to raise and go on raising the aggregate product of nations and their income, however modestly; and this is what in fact happened in post-war Belgium and the United Kingdom. But

c

modest increases of this order were well below what post-war opinion deemed sufficient. To the post-war public, growth meant growth faster than ever before.

This determination to grow fast was born of the psychological and political compulsions of the time. As prosperity rose and continued to rise in the post-war years all classes of society gradually came to expect continued – indeed perpetual – rises in the material standards of life. The expectations were nurtured by optimistic forecasts of the economists and politicians (*vide* Mr Butler's famous prophecy of doubling the standard of life in twenty-five years) and underlay the constant demands of trade unions for wage increases. But independently of electoral policies and popular pressures rapid growth became for all European nations an inescapable necessity. Military budgets were high and rising, the cost of social services, especially of old age pensions and education, imposed upon governments automatically growing commitments for the future. These calls on national incomes could not be met unless national incomes themselves grew at a pace sufficient not only to satisfy the popular demands for ever-higher standards of life but also to pay for the inexorably mounting costs of governmental functions.

Thus, almost imperceptibly, the official espousal of full employment combined with an espousal of economic growth. Most governments were by the end of the fifties pledged to the policy of maintaining the rate of economic expansion higher than the rate at which economies had expanded in any past period of European economic history. Their policies and plans came to be geared to certain irreducible *minima* of growth. An anonymous and authoritative German article on the Belgian economy written in 1964, in commenting on that country's slow economic expansion, referred to a 3 per cent coefficient growth as being 'the lowest possible rate of satisfactory progress'. (*Mindeszatz eines befriedingenden Fortschrittes*). The agreed 'lowest possible rates' were to be 3–4 per cent for England, and even higher than that for Germany, France and Italy. In this way fast growth, rather than just growth, became the principle of state policy.[1]

[1] *Wochenberichte* of the Deutsches Institut für Wirtschaftsforschung, no. 16,

Nothing illustrates better the conversion of governments to the doctrine of fast growth than its espousal by the international bodies set up in the fifties to co-ordinate the economic interests and policies of individual European governments. Economic growth had by 1960 become the ostensible object of the Common Market policies. Growth also became one of the principal aims of the O.E.C.D. and was enshrined in the very name of the re-formed and enlarged organization. What had hitherto functioned under the name of the Organization for European Economic Co-operation now became the Organization for Economic Co-operation and Development. The word was soon to be followed by the deed. In November 1961, within a few months of the act which transformed the O.E.E.C. into the O.E.C.D., the Ministerial Council of the latter set a collective target for all member countries of 50 per cent growth in Gross National Product in the decade 1960–70.[1]

Even more fundamental were the legislative and institutional innovations introduced by individual governments in their pursuit of economic development. Until 1962 none of the European countries with the exception of France assembled these piecemeal measures into a consistent system or established an administrative machinery capable of formulating and enforcing unified plans for economic development. But, in the words of an O.E.C.D. report commenting upon the resolution of the Ministerial Council, that resolution was not only 'a striking manifestation on the international plane of the fact that economic growth has become one of the main aims of national policies' but also reflected the new attitude to economic growth, i.e. the belief 'that economic progress is not an autonomous historical process that happens accidentally but an evolution which can be promoted by deliberate action and planning'. This belief made new converts at the end of our period. If immediately after the war France was almost alone in trying to

---

1964. A general survey of the evolution of policies of a number of countries will be found in *Growth in the British Economy*, P.E.P., London, 1960. For a corresponding movement of opinion among British business leaders, see letter to *The Times* on 9 January 1961 by Hugh Weeks, Chairman of the Economic Policy Committee of the Federation of British Industries.

[1] O.E.C.D., *Science, Economic Growth, and Government Policy*, Paris, 1963, p. 9; also *Growth and Economic Policy*: a preliminary report to the Economic Policy Committee of O.E.C.D., Paris 1964, p. 1.

work out and to enforce a central 'Plan', eventually most governments equipped themselves with machinery and policies for the concerted planning of economic growth.[1]

By the early sixties these planning machineries and policies had developed to such an extent, and had become so characteristic of the prevailing attitudes, that they deserve a somewhat more detailed account, even at the cost of a slight digression. What may make the account appear digressionary is that not all the planning activities of governments in our period were consciously oriented towards economic growth. In current economic discussion the word 'plans' was used imprecisely (though not unwisely) to denote all purposeful activities of governments designed to correct, to supplement or to guide the action of economic forces. Some of these activities, as those of French governments, served the economic growth of the economy openly and directly; others, as those of the Netherlands or Scandinavian countries, had for their ostensible object the management of incomes or prices. These two sets of planning objectives were not, however, as wide apart as they might at first sight appear. We shall see further that in the course of our period rising incomes and costs proved to be one of the main obstacles to continuous growth of economies. The control of incomes and costs had therefore come to be considered a precondition and safeguard of economic expansion; and, to this extent, it does not fall wholly outside our story of planning for growth.

The one national plan most obviously designed as an instrument of economic growth was that of France. Yet even in France this preoccupation came some time after the earliest plans had been conceived. The intellectual roots of the French Plan went back to the pre-war vogue for state planning. At that time planning was thought of solely as an instrument for securing the economy against depressions and unemployment, but on the morrow of liberation, with the French economy in half-ruined condition and with the intellectual attraction of planning undimmed, the thoughts of politicians and economists turned readily to it as a means of organizing recovery.

[1] O.E.C.D., *Science, Economic Growth, and Government Policy*, Paris, 1963, p. 9; loc. cit.; 'Long-term planning in Western Europe.' *Economic Bulletin for Europe*, vol. 14, no. 2.

The requisite machinery established by the decree of 3 January 1946 comprised a planning commissariat (Commissariat Général au Plan) whose business it was to draw up the plans and to supervise their execution. For detailed consultations the decree of 1946 established a number of 'vertical' committees (Commissions de Modernisation) on which representatives of the different interests negotiated, industry by industry, the forecasts of their investment, output, and employment. To these committees was added a 'horizontal' organization for reconciling the plans of individual industries and sectors with 'macro-economic' expectations, i.e. with the forecasts of the manpower and finances available for the economy as a whole. The edifice was crowned by the Conseil Supérieur du Plan and, after 1949, by the Conseil Economique et Social, both of them co-ordinating and consultative bodies concerned with the general principles of economic policy.[1]

This elaborate machinery gave birth to four successive plans. The principles animating the early plans were the same as those which underlay the post-war programme of modernization commonly associated with the name of Jean Monnet. Under that programme agriculture and industry were to be brought up to date and provided with a modern base of heavy industries and energy supplies; and as the economy was modernizing it was also expected to expand its output and productivity. But in the later plans, the third and the fourth, designed to span the period between 1958 and 1965, the first and foremost object was to promote economic growth and to concert it in the main sectors of economy. The shifting emphasis and the expanding ambitions of the Plan were reflected in its very titles. What in 1948 was named the Plan for Modernization and Equipment became by 1960 the Plan for Economic and Social Development.

As we shall see presently, only a few of the objectives and figures in the plans could be presented as mandatory directives to be enforced à la Russe. Nevertheless, to insist, as some historians of the Plan have done, that it did nothing more than to follow at some distance the course of economic development, or to repeat with

---

[1] J. and A. M. Hackett, *Economic Planning in France*, London, 1963; *Economic Planning in France*, P.E.P., London, 1961; M. Maclennon, *French Planning: Some lessons for Britain*, P.E.P., London, 1963.

Professor Perroux that the rates of growth laid down in the Plan were 'no more than a hope', is to err on the side of excessive modesty.[1] In retrospect French plans, for all their ambitions and achievements, appear to have been too limited to be spoken of in the same breath as the planning activities of the Communist states. They nevertheless had a more powerful effect on the course of French economic development than comparable policies of other Western governments had or could have had on their respective economies. The French plans were more comprehensive than corresponding policies abroad: to a far greater extent concerned with concrete problems of investment, technology, and management, and more discriminating between individual sectors, industries, and even firms.[2]

That French plans should have been cast on this scale and in this shape, administered as successfully as they were, and so willingly accepted by business, may well be no more than a fortunate by-product of France's historical tradition. It can be argued that her prevailing economic attitudes were *étatiste* throughout her history. Her governments were always prepared to initiate and to finance economic developments they regarded as desirable; her bureaucracy was never afraid of intervening in the conduct of private business; her businessmen were always willing to accept state *largesse* and control. It is, however, doubtful whether French *étatiste* tradition would have asserted itself so powerfully and so successfully had the post-war composition of the higher ranks of French bureaucracy, both in government and in industry, not been particularly fitted to planning activities so conceived.

Considering the competitive character of French educational careers and promotions, the high intellectual standards of the 'top men' could be taken for granted. What is not commonly taken for granted is the extent to which the curricula of their education fitted

[1] F. Perroux. 'Le quatrième Plan français', *Economie Appliquée*, 1962, pp. 5–65.

[2] For the problems and achievements of the French Plan, see also: Pierre Massé, *Histoire, Méthode et Doctrine de la Planification Française*, La Documentation Française, 1962; Jean Chardonnet, 'La Politique de Planification en France', *Rivista di Politica e Economica*, 1962; Bernard Cazes, *La Planification en France et le IVᵉ plan*, Paris, 1964; P. L. Blanchard, *La Mystique du Plan*, Paris, 1963; F. Bloch-Laîné, 'Economie concerté et planification démocratique', *Cahiers de la République*, July 1962; 'Colloque sur la planification démocratique', ibid., June 1962.

them for the task they were called upon to perform. Many of them were products of the École Polytechnique, where they acquired the intellectual equipment and the outlook of modern mathematics and engineering. Paradoxically enough, the very paucity of professional economists among them may have proved less of a disability than it might have done if planning had been differently conceived. Before the war the underdeveloped condition of French academic economics may have affected adversely the quality of counsel available to French governments. But for the business of plan-making as practised after the war, a technological outlook and a practical approach to economic problems were important qualifications. They largely account for the specific, or to use the current jargon, micro-economic, conception of French plans.

Needless to say, the general objectives of the plans had to be expressed in global 'macro-economic' figures – those of national product, aggregate investment, total employment, average productivity. But what in practice occupied most of the planners' time and attention was output, employment, and above all, investment, considered sector by sector and industry by industry. These detailed and practical objectives had to be negotiated between officials and representatives of industry, and required the understanding of commercial and technical circumstances of individual sectors and enterprises, which proficiency in economics could not by itself provide.

The peculiar conception of French plans and the manner in which they had to be administered largely explain why the various components of the plan differed so greatly in effectiveness. Whereas some of them were 'indicative' or 'predictive', were commonly described as forecasts and were sometimes no more than statistical guesses, others were laid down as targets, i.e. as prescriptions for action. Thus the figures relating to public expenditure could be conceived as targets, those relating to foreign trade balances or to personal incomes could be no more than forecasts, while those relating to outputs and investments were a mixture of forecast and target. In general, the forecasts and targets were at their most precise and realistic when dealing with goods and services, and most speculative in all matters pertaining to incomes.

Yet even in their handling of facts which they could not possibly control and could not even anticipate with any precision, the plans were of great aid to policy-makers. They reduced the range of uncertainty facing them, or in the words of Monsieur Massé, Director General of the Plan, made it easier to 'recognize facts without being fatalistic about them'. Above all, the planners tried, on the whole successfully, to co-ordinate hitherto disjointed policies and expectations. One of the virtues of plans negotiated industry by industry and then brought together in a single centralized plan is that the estimates and targets for different sectors and factors could be made mutually consistent (by 1960 'coherence' became the pass-word of the planners), and that the French economic system could be conceived as a cohort wherein the different sectors and factors marched in step.

The aspect of the French economy which responded most successfully to the planners' striving after coherence and to their industry-by-industry approaches, was that of investment. For one of the great achievements of the Plan – perhaps its greatest achievement – is that it was able to assign capital available for investment to uses in which they could be relied upon to produce the highest return. This detailed and coherent allocation of capital enabled France to achieve a high rate of industrial growth with a rather modest annual growth of fixed capital. In the words of Pierre Massé himself the plans succeeded in reducing the overlap in spare capacity and thus enabled the country to reach the same growth target with a lower rate of investment.

Needless to say, the political, administrative, and intellectual qualities of the planners would by themselves not have secured for the Plan the degree of compliance, and hence also the degree of success, it was able to command. The planners derived much of their power and success from various instruments of persuasion and correction at their disposal. Some of the instruments were of the intangible psycho-political order, products of French post-war mood and of the social changes in the upper ranks of the business community. In replies to an inquiry by the Institut National de la Statistique into the motives behind the investment decisions of French industrial firms a number of industrial and commercial managers declared themselves to be actuated by nothing other than a desire to contribute to the general advance of French economy and to fulfil their part in the national economic plan.[1] These avowals may not have been as hypocritical as they at first sight appear, since they were to some extent corroborated by what other sources have told us about the behaviour of the higher ranks of French large-scale industry. Several historians of post-war Europe have noted the new spirit animating the post-war leaders of big business in France. The younger business leaders showed themselves not only more rational and more enterprising than the *patrons* old-style, but also better able to accommodate themselves to the purposes and procedures of the successive plans. They owed this ability not only to the high patriotic motives they claimed, but also to the links of education and outlook which bound them to the officials of the Plan. And so readily did officials and business leaders agree on main principles, that at least one recent commentator was able to describe the French plans as acts of 'voluntary collusion between senior Civil Servants and senior managers of big business'.

Yet it can well be doubted whether patriotism and community of outlook would alone have sufficed to procure from private interests their full compliance with the plans, had not the planners also been able to operate with a number of tangible, or even coercive, instruments. Some of the instruments were of the conventional fiscal type. For directing investment into uses and locations favoured by the plans there were tax concessions and privileges more varied and on occasions more drastic than in other European countries. But the most important of all the planning tools was the central supervision of national investments as a whole and of the investments of individual industries in particular. The State, the local authorities and the nationalized industries between them accounted for nearly half of total new investment; and their requirements and use of capital were easily controllable. But the State also possessed certain powers of controlling private investment – powers which were perhaps seldom used, but were always in the background. They derived partly from the public ownership of the principal financial institutions through which flowed the bulk of private or 'household' savings, above all, the Caisse des Dépôts et Consignations. It has been estimated that in the early sixties the funds

---

[1] B. R. Williams, *International Report on Factors in Investment Behaviour*, O.E.C.D., 1962.

administered by these financial bodies and other publicly controlled funds accounted for about one-half of the annual flow of investable savings. Nor did the other 50 per cent of national savings remain wholly undirected. Planning authorities were able to pilot private investments to desired destinations by means of subventions, fiscal incentives, and licences. This system of incentives and permits was administered mainly by the Crédit National, which was the main channel for commercial bills, by the Fonds de Développement Economique et Sociale, controlling much of industrial investment, more especially investment into regional development, and in the final resort, by the Banque Nationale and the Treasury division of the Ministry of Finance.[1]

Thus armed, the planners were able both to instigate the growth of French economy and to watch over its progress. By comparison, economic planning in other countries, except in the U.K. after 1963, was much more rudimentary and different in scope, even where it developed farthest. In the Netherlands it operated mainly in the field which the French Plan hardly touched, that of wages. In that country the Economic and Social Council, set up soon after the war to represent various economic interests, made pronouncements on economic issues, mostly relating to incomes, which had great influence on government policy and on the course of negotiated wages. Wage contracts for individual industries were agreed on a national scale in the Foundation of Labour and were subject to approval by a Government Board of Mediators. This machinery was never able, and indeed never intended, to 'freeze' wages and other incomes, but until 1962 it may have helped to hold back rises in negotiated wages and in labour costs, and to this extent was better tailored to the needs of economic growth than the economic policies of most other European nations.

However, by 1962 the entire system of wage controls ran into an *impasse* and was to a large extent dismantled. So rapid had become the 'wage drift,' i.e. the rise in what the Dutch themselves describe as 'black wages' paid over and above negotiated rates, that the

---

[1] J. S. G. Wilson and R. S. Sayers (eds.), *Banking in Western Europe*, Cambridge, 1962; A. Shonfield, *Modern Capitalism*, London, 1965, pp. 11, 129, 165–70; cf. also authorities in footnote 2 above, p. 32.

[*Vide* Appendix, Note 2, p. 361 below.]

system of uniform and centralized wage settlements became largely irrelevant. From that time onwards wage increases came to be linked to the productivities in individual industries and to be negotiated directly between the respective Trade Unions and employers. In the event wages rose very steeply, while labour costs rose even higher, since the working week was shortened at the same time. The Dutch government may have, however, compensated somewhat for the dissolution of its wage-controls by equipping itself with a Central Planning Committee served by a Central Planning Bureau. The new organization was expected to formulate estimates and projections for the economy as a whole and for its individual sectors. By 1964, however, it had barely eighteen months in which to prove itself, and its effects on the Dutch economic development still remained to be seen.[1]

In the fifties the Scandinavian governments also gradually improved their machinery for forecasting, and thus indirectly also for guiding, the course of the economy. In Sweden, where it had developed furthest, three successive five-year forecasts ('plans') had by 1962 been prepared by the so-called Planning Commission. The plans, however, were not cast into a mandatory form. In fact, the key forecasts in the first two 'plans' were frequently offered in alternative versions to fit a wide choice of alternatives. Purposeful interventions on the part of the Government were largely confined to monetary controls, to anti-cyclical uses of company investments, or else to incomes and wages. The latter proved quite successful, but its success could not be wholly put down to government action. The highly centralized and intelligently conducted organizations of trade unions and employers made it possible for them to negotiate changes in wage rates on a national scale. The actual increases were by no means small; in the early sixties they were higher than in the United Kingdom. But the remarkable increases in productivity absorbed the higher wages without unduly swelling the costs of production. On its part the official Labour Board was able to organize an efficient

---

[1] O.E.C.D., *Policies for Price Stability*, Paris, 1962; idem, *Policies for Prices, Profits and other Non-Wage Incomes*, Paris, 1964; idem, *Economic Surveys for Netherlands for 1962, 1963, and 1964*, Paris, 1963, 1964 and 1965; *Scope and Method of Central Planning Bureau*, The Hague, 1956, p. 215; P. de Wolff, 'Les techniques de la planification néerlandaise', *Les Problèmes de la Planification*, Publications of L'Institut de Sociologie, Brussels, 1960.

system of employment exchanges and vocational training for adults and did much to facilitate the transfer of labour to new occupations. But here again the official bodies were assisted by the enlightened attitude of trade unions to redundancies and labour transfers.

Marked advances in central planning did not come until the sixties. Towards the end of 1962 the Swedish government, like so many other European governments, appeared to require forecasts more definite and mandatory than they had been in the past, and the latest 'Economic Plan' in fact provided a single set of estimates instead of a series of alternatives as heretofore. In addition, the Government set up in 1962 a Council for Economic Planning. The Council's initial terms of reference were also limited to long-term estimates, and the estimates continued, as heretofore, to be confined to the conventional economic measurements, fought shy of technological and commercial specifications and implied no intervention with the policies of industries and firms or with the operations of markets. Nevertheless, the more exalted status of the new body and its representative character could perhaps be taken as a sign that greater importance was now attached to long-term projections, and that the Government and the main economic interests were expected to conform to them in shaping their fiscal, industrial, and commercial policies.[1]

In the early sixties the circle of governments converted to central planning was also joined by that of the United Kingdom. In launching the recovery from the recession of 1962 the Conservative Government of the day followed up its earlier declaration of allegiance to the principle of economic growth by setting up a bifurcated machinery of economic planning: the National Economic Development Council ('Neddy') and the National Incomes Council ('Nicky'). The two bodies were designed for the same range of problems as that covered by the French and Dutch planning

---

[1] The fullest account of Swedish 'plans' will be found in Holger Heide *Die Langfristige Wirtschaftsplannung in Schweden*, Kieler Studien, No. 73, Tübingen, 1965. O.E.C.D., *Growth and Economic Policy* (as in footnote 1, p. 29), sections on Sweden and Norway; *idem, Economic Surveys of Sweden for 1963 and 1964*, Paris, 1964 and 1965; *idem, Economic Surveys for Norway*, Paris, 1964 and 1965; P. J. Bjerve, *Planning in Norway 1947–1956*, Amsterdam 1959; Per Kleppe, *Main Aspects of Economic Policy in Norway since the War*, Oslo, 1960; J. Cooper, *Industrial Relations: Sweden Shows the Way*, Fabian Research Bureau, London, 1963.

organizations. To Neddy was assigned the duty of planning future output, investment, employment, and productivity; its territory was thus co-extensive with that of the French Plan. Nicky was designed to handle changes in incomes; its territory thus corresponded to that of the Dutch and Scandinavian machinery for the control of wages. But while similar to their foreign prototypes in range of interest they were not as yet equal to them in power and potential competence.

It was obvious from the outset that Nicky would not be in a position to do more than pass unenforceable verdicts on wage claims. The power and idiosyncrasies of the British trade-union movement made it impossible for Nicky to lay claim to the same degree of control over wages as that enjoyed by the Netherlands before 1963 or even the degree of orderliness in wage negotiation which the organizations of employers and employed were able to secure for Sweden. The potential effectiveness of Neddy was not much greater. It was expected and, in the event, proved able to formulate well-considered forecasts for the main sectors of the economy and for the national economy as a whole. But it could not turn its forecasts into directives, or in a more general way watch over the realization of its plans to the extent to which this was done in France. It was not instructed to carry its forecasts into effect, and could not have done so even if instructed. For one thing, it possessed hardly any instruments of coercion or persuasion. It had no powers of control over the sources of savings or their disposition in investment; it had no share in the administration of existing inducements for the location of industry in development areas, or authority in matters pertaining to mobility of labour, immigration, training or redundancies. In its original conception it was outside the main structure of British government. Although the main economic departments of state were represented on it, it was not by itself a department of state and not even an organic part of one.

Yet even if Neddy had been closely woven into the machinery of government its ability to use that machinery in the service of plans might not thereby have been greatly enhanced. For one thing, the human agency on which the duty of administering the plans would in that case have fallen, the British bureaucracy, was ill-fitted for the job. The enforcement plans, even in the uneven way in which they were enforced in France, required some discriminatory interference with competing interests; whereas impartiality between interests was a hallowed part of British Civil Service tradition. The current administration of plans might also have required some specialized competence in the commercial and technological problems of industry and trade; whereas the professional skill of the Civil Service lay in its quality of undifferentiated competence, a kind of proud 'laymanship' nurtured by the prevailing methods of recruitment, promotion and transfers. It can even be argued that the outside assistance available to the departments of state was inadequate for the business of planning. Except for some peripheral departments in charge of scientific research, the services of technicians and business managers were as a rule drawn upon by means of the slow and intermittent machinery of departmental enquiries and royal commissions. Even the advice of the economists was not available except in the form least useful for the administration of economic plans. It was largely confined to macroeconomic generalities for which the intellectual traditions and the training of British economists fitted them best. And finally, overriding the limit set to Neddy in its terms of reference and overshadowing the shortcomings of the government machinery and personnel at its disposal, there were the obstacles built into the contemporary political and social setting. The interested parties and the effective public opinion would not at that time have allowed the planning authorities the powers of interference and discrimination needed for the effective enforcement of national economic plans.[1]

The strength, the inertia, and the inhibiting effect of these various impediments to planning were very great, and explain why in the first two years of its life British planning organization produced little visible effect on the economy. Yet their permanence, the depth

---

[1] J. C. R. Dow, *The Management of the British Economy, 1945–1960*, N.I.E.S.R., London, 1964; *Growth in the British Economy*, P.E.P., London, 1960; O.E.C.D., *Economic Surveys of the United Kingdom*, Paris, 1965, 1964, and 1963. With the arrival of the Labour Government in 1964 the two planning bodies were, under a somewhat different name, absorbed into the new Department of Economic Affairs. Greater authority and urgency may thereby have been imparted to their activities, but their functions were not materially altered. The re-organized Department of Economic Affairs was, however, able to enlist the services of some distinguished Industrialists.

of their historical roots and their hold upon the future could be exaggerated. The British attitude to the relation between the State and private interest may go far back into history – perhaps as far back as Sir Edward Coke and the seventeenth-century struggle against monopolies – but it did not prevent the British Government from interfering with the conduct of industry and from overriding private interests of every kind in times of war and national emergency. In the two great wars the British Civil Service exercised controls over raw materials, investments, and employment, more far-reaching than any controls originating in the French post-war plans. It was able to enlist recruits from business, universities and professions, and to employ them in their technical and managerial capacities. Even in times of peace and of 'business as usual' departments of state, above all the defence departments, got involved in the planning or even in current supervision of such industries as aircraft, railways, electronics, generation of electricity, gas, and munitions in general. If the ability and will to be so involved were not shown in the making of economic plans, this was not due solely to ancient restraints and inhibitions of British society and state. What was lacking – and the lack was wholly excusable – was the conviction that a country victorious in war and basking in the heat of post-war prosperity was, in fact, face to face with a national emergency. What was also lacking, and was perhaps less excusable, was the appreciation of the relations which in fact existed in times of peace and prosperity between the Government and a large sector of industry engaged in the making of munitions or in other outputs with which the Government found itself involved.

Towards the very end of our period the incoming Labour Government took steps to make the planning of the economy and of incomes more effective. These changes took place too late in the day to be described and evaluated in this story; but not so late as to be wholly irrelevant to the moral we have so far drawn. The measures which the new Government announced and the reaction to them on the part of the public and the Civil Service suggest that the impediments to a more purposeful planning policy were not so deeply ingrown as to be wholly irremovable. Their power to impede depended not only on the strength of the inherited predispositions of officials, businessmen, and trade unionists but also on the

strength of pressures, economic and political, in favour of fully
planned economic growth.[1]

Even more significant, as a sign of the times, were the corresponding pressures and responses in Germany and Belgium. That a
British Tory Government should have accepted the necessity of
planning for economic growth is revealing but not perhaps surprising. It is in the nature of British politics to be undoctrinal; and
for its part, the Conservative Party had assumed its *laissez-faire*
garb very recently and wore it very lightly. Besides, was not Britain
the first Western country to become a 'welfare state' and to accept
most of the latter's economic and political consequences? By
comparison, Germany, Belgium, and Switzerland remained the
citadels of non-interventionist policies. The steps they took in the
sixties towards a more purposeful control of economic growth was
therefore all the more symptomatic.

Throughout the fifties the prevailing belief in Germany was that
their 'miracle' was brought about by the untrammelled play of
economic forces, and public opinion was inimical to interferences
with the workings of a market economy. This philosophy did not
prevent the Germans from using the financial budget in a vaguely
Keynesian fashion to advance or to hold back economic activity;
nor did it prevent the Government from using company taxation as
an instrument for stimulating investment. Moreover, in the sectors
in which the Government was financially involved, e.g. transport,
agriculture, and energy, it provided itself with the entire para-
phernalia of long-term projections and targets. But this is as far as it
permitted itself to go. In its relations with economic interests, both
employers and labour, it relied on exhortations and appeals to
patriotism, or on what the German publicists have come to designate as a 'massage of consciences' (*Seelenmassage*).

The attitude appeared to change in 1962. The scaling down of
economic growth to about half of its earlier rate, increasing labour
shortages and reduced rates of industrial investment appeared to
require a readjustment of expectations and policies. Hence the

---

[1] Nothing illustrates better the ability of British Governments to override in
time of emergency the reputedly inbred resistance to incomes policy, than the
'freeze' on wages, profits, and prices imposed in July 1966. These measures went
much farther than any wage policies previously considered.

Government's decision to equip itself with forecasts and projections covering the foreseeable (medium-term) future. There also grew up a general agreement about the need to plan public expenditure, and above all public investment, over periods at least as long as five years. And it was also possible to detect a readiness to use anticyclical financial measures as an instrument of economic policy beyond the most immediate future for which they were originally designed. Every care was, of course, taken not to give the impression of a wholly new economic philosophy. In June 1963 Dr Erhard, then still the Finance Minister, while presenting to the Bundestag his proposals for regular forecasts of German economic development, made full use of the semantic facilities of the German language in order to draw distinctions between forecast (*Voraus-schau*) and prediction (*Voraussage*). He nevertheless proposed to set up a Council of Economic Experts to 'pass periodically an opinion on overall economic trends'. Whether the opinions were to be acted upon and what form the action would take was left uncertain. But in spite of the uncertainty, and in spite of all the endeavours to reconcile the new machinery with the prevailing economic ideology, the new body and its terms of reference clearly reflected a change of economic climate and the willingness of the Government to concern itself with the long-term prospect of the economy.[1]

The change was more marked and certainly more concrete in Belgium. From the moment of the liberation until the very end of the fifties Belgian governments refrained from any forceful inter-ventions with the national economy. Monetary and fiscal instru-ments were not spurned, even if since the 'Gutt' devaluation immediately after the war even these orthodox tools of economic policy were used very sparingly. The critics could allege that this non-feasance on the part of the Government was in part responsible for the slow growth of the Belgian economy – the slowest on the con-tinent of Europe – for the accumulated signs of backwardness in a number of key industries and for higher rates of unemployment than in most other European countries. But the defenders of the policy could claim that Belgian prices and wages were on the whole more stable than elsewhere.

---

[1] *Growth and Economic Policy* (op. cit., p. 29, footnote 1), Section on Germany; also O.E.C.D., *Economic Surveys of Germany*, Paris, 1963, 1964, and 1965.

D

By the end of the fifties, however, the dissatisfaction with the sluggish progress of the economy and the mounting feeling that the country was falling behind the other European nations in technology and productivity came to the surface and proved strong enough to produce a crop of measures for the expansion and modernization of industry and for centralized planning of economic development. The clearest break with non-interventionist traditions was perhaps the government-enforced reduction of capacity and nationalization of the antiquated coal industry and also the stringent controls of prices imposed in 1963. But the conversion to the doctrine of planned economic growth revealed itself clearest in a series of administrative contrivances for central planning. At the end of 1959 the National Council of Economic and Scientific Policy was founded. In 1962 came the Société National du Crédit Industriel and the Société National d'Investissement established in order to facilitate productive investment and to provide funds for small firms. Specialized institutions were also established for the purposes of regional investment. But in principle the most far-reaching of all the administrative innovations was the setting up in 1960 of the office for economic programming which proceeded to draw a five-year programme for 1961–5 based on the annual rate of growth of 4 per cent. That the term 'programme', not 'plan', was used may mean that all suggestion of planned economy was to be avoided. Yet a national programme with targets for individual sectors of the economy was in itself a long step towards planned intervention by the State. And as far as it is possible to gather, the key figures in the programmes were, in fact, treated by the Government and the public as set targets.

We have seen that in the sixties Belgian economic national product began to mount very steeply, and that in 1964 it was 5·5 per cent higher than in 1963, and that by that year Belgium could claim a place among two or three fastest-growing countries in Europe. Industrial production increased by 7 per cent in 1964 and 7·5 per cent in 1963. Productivity increased by about 4 per cent. The remarkable up-swing may have owed much to a bumper horticultural harvest; but it is difficult to escape the conclusion that the soaring indices marked a new phase in Belgian economic history. The rate of investment increased, unemployment declined, industrial innovations were apparently more widespread; and, to point a moral, inflation and price rises were higher than heretofore. To what extent the 'programmes' contributed to the rising output and to what extent the absence of an 'incomes policy' was responsible for inflation, is, from the point of view of this chapter, immaterial. What is material is that Belgium should have joined the circle of countries with economic policies consciously directed towards economic growth, and should, for the time being, have been pre- pared to pay for it in higher prices and in greater interference with free markets and with private enterprise.[1]

The history of national plans has been treated here as evidence of the growing preoccupation of post-war governments with economic growth. The preoccupation, however, also revealed itself in a variety of piecemeal measures, such as the fiscal stimuli to company investment in Germany, the Swedish and Norwegian systems of tax-free investment reserves (these were, however, conceived mainly as anticyclic devices), the several layers of British investment allowances, the Italian measures to foster the indigenous steel and petroleum industries, the Danish policies of accelerated industrialization, the government-induced investments in communications and energy in Norway, the Swedish concern with the mobility of labour, the endeavours to improve technical education in most European countries, the much enlarged govern- ment expenditures on research and development and fiscal induce- ments for privately sponsored research. These and many other *ad hoc* measures had come to be employed in the service of economic expansion even where this did not happen to be their original purpose and where they did not form part of a concerted economic plan. The same is also true of the many and various policies to secure full employment or to eliminate cyclical fluctuations. In achieving either or both of these objects these policies also kept up the forward momentum of the national economies.[2]

---

[1] *Wochenberichte* of the Deutsches Institut für Wirtschaftsforschung, 31, no. 16, 1964; O.E.C.D., *Economic Surveys of Belgium–Luxembourg Economic Union for 1962, 1963, and 1964*, Paris, 1963, 1964, and 1965. From the purely administra- tive point of view the Belgian machinery for the control of prices was not an inno- vation of 1960s. A decree of 1945 introduced a system of maximum prices, and in 1951 a Prices Commission was set up. But until 1963 the actual control of prices did not appear to have been very stringent.

[2] A concentrated analytical summary of the effects of government measures, other than planning, on economic growth will be found in Angus Maddison,

So much for growth-oriented policies of governments. However, not all the policies from which European economic expansion derived its strength emanate from European governments. Economic growth in Europe was also sustained by – indeed, required for its sustenance – corresponding government support from abroad. It was very fortunate for Europe that the entire world after 1945 dedicated itself to this object. In communist countries economic expansion (as a rule wholly identified with industrialization) had become not only the aim but also the very justification of communist planning, their main article of pride. It was also their most commendable feature in the eyes of 'underdeveloped' nations. In the eyes of the latter, even more than in the eyes of the Western nations, economic growth (here also identified with industrialization) figured as by far the most important, sometimes even the sole, object of government policy. This dedication of the underdeveloped countries to growth was easy to account for; it had every ethical and economic justification and it was bound to command the support of Western nations. For selfish as well as humanitarian reasons the older nations of the West, ex-colonial powers like Britain, France, or Belgium, as well as the U.S.A., had to take a hand in fostering the economic development of newer countries.

This combination of selfish and unselfish motives explains why most European countries found it necessary to contribute to the economic development of underdeveloped nations. Between 1950 and 1963 the fifteen industrialized countries of O.E.C.D. contributed to the less developed countries, as gifts and loans, more than $50,000 million. Their annual contributions grew from about $1,900 million between 1950 and 1955 to about $16,000 million in the early sixties. In this respect, the French example, being extreme, is also most characteristic. France's contribution to the economic development of her former colonial territories, especially since 1956, was greater relative to her G.N.P. than that of any other country, not excluding the U.S.A. In 1962 she spent on aid nearly N.F., 7,000 million, which was 2 per cent of her G.N.P. compared with

---

Economic Growth in the West, Ch. IV. See also the literature listed, ibid., p. 112, fn. 1. For fiscal incentives to investment and growth, cf. UNO, *Economic Survey of Europe in 1959*, Ch. VI, and *idem*, 1960, Ch. I; *Taxation in Western Europe*, Federation of British Industries, June 1962; G. Terborgh, 'The Tax Depreciation Problem', *Capital Goods Review*, no. 34, 1958.

Britain's 1 per cent, and America's 1¼ per cent. Of this sum, nearly N.F. 5,000 million came from the State, N.F. 4,000 million took the form of outright gifts, only N.F. 1,000 million took the form of credits: mostly long-term loans at an extremely low rate of interest (1½ per cent). Moreover, most of the aid went not into business enterprises or factories or other industrial installations but, to the extent of 60 per cent or more, into educational, medical, and similar services, and into what economists describe as economic infrastructure, i.e. roads, communications, housing, or municipal services.[1]

To repeat, the French case was an extreme one. British involvement was smaller (some $775 million in 1963), came to the extent of 40–50 per cent from private commercial sources and was not so predominantly committed to 'non-remunerative' objects.[2] But the difference was merely one of degree. In the United Kingdom, as in all other Western countries, the benefits accruing from foreign aid were only in part economic. But needless to say, some material advantages were derived from foreign aid. It helped to sustain the world demand for steel-making equipment, electric and hydro-electric installations, the manufacture of chemical and metallurgical plant – all of them fields in which it suited European countries to specialize. But at least as important, though less tangible, was the contribution which the development of underdeveloped territories added to the economic climate of the age. Behind much of the public support of foreign aid was the general belief that in the long run European countries and the Western world as a whole stood to benefit from the growing prosperity of nations now poor. This belief in its turn had helped to sustain the

[1] Wolfgang C. Friedmann, George Kaufmanoff, and Robert F. Meagher, *International Financial Aid*, N.Y., 1966, Chs. II and III; *The Flow of Financial Resources to Less Developed Countries, 1956–1963*, O.E.C.D., Paris, 1964; 'Aperçu général de l'aide française en 1963', *Statistiques et Etudes Financières*, no. 190, Ministère des Finances, Paris, 1964. Cf. also previous reports in the same publication, e.g. '*Statistiques, etc.*', no. 173, Paris, 1963.

[2] The figures for 1963 do not include the values of technical assistance, which, in the case of the United Kingdom, increased from year to year and was more than 25 per cent higher in 1965 than in each of the two previous years. Flow of private resources stood at $360 million in 1963, but had been considerably higher in some earlier years: *The Flow of Financial Resources to Less Developed Countries, 1956–1963*, O.E.C.D., Paris, 1964; *The Times*, 26 May, 1966. German official aid was lower than either the French or the British (*ibid*).

hopeful view of the ever-expanding universe which throughout the post-war period inspired the activities of the more forward-looking members of Europe's business community.

However, none of these external contributions to the doctrine or to the actual process of European growth were nearly as decisive as the contributions made by the U.S.A. After a brief period when it engaged in some hard-headed bargaining with European nations over the ending of wartime Lease-Lend and the repayment of other war loans, American government boldly swung over to the policy of heavy and continuous aid to nations of the world, and, in the first place, to the nations of Western Europe. Within a couple of years after the end of the war the Marshall Plan, with its offer of economic aid to all countries which needed it, released a flow of capital assistance schemes and loans which was to sustain economic development in Europe at a time when shortage of capital and more especially shortage of dollars still impeded economic development. Other American disbursements had the same effects. Military aid and military expenses of American forces and bases helped to buttress up European economies at some of their weakest points. And it was very largely due to American assistance as well as to her urgings that Europe was able to provide herself with machinery for a free or near-free flow of international trade and payments.

The importance of these urgings and encouragements must not be under-estimated. Throughout the post-war period the U.S.A. administrations used their influence to foster all actions and attitudes serving the purposes of European economic expansion. This they did not necessarily do because they happened to share the prevailing doctrinal beliefs in economic growth. At home the successive American administrations before 1961 were by no means wholeheartedly committed to full employment or to high rates of economic growth. They frequently hesitated to use the fiscal or the regulatory measures which such a policy might have required; and in any case, their political system would at that time have prevented them from adopting these measures even if the wish to adopt them had been there. But in dealing with Europe, struggling to overcome the effects of the war and political division, American governments consistently and openly revealed their wish to see European economies grow and their approval of those nations which succeeded in growing faster and better than others.

This concern in the growth of friendly nations had obvious political inspirations. Successive American administrations were preoccupied with communist dangers and came to regard Europe, economically strong and unified, as a guarantee of world stability and as the best possible barrier to communist advance from across the Iron Curtain. In aiding Italian, German, or French growth, America was securing them from communist revolution and defending its own flanks against Russia. A secondary, though by no means an unimportant, part was played by the American belief in the free play of economic forces, unhampered trade and competition. Their influence behind various schemes to liberalize European trade and to set up a freely functioning system of international payments obviously reflected the *laissez-faire* philosophy of American governments and business community.

Transatlantic inspiration to European policies of growth were not, however, confined to overt acts or pronouncements of U.S.A. governments. It came not only from what the U.S.A. gave or preached but also from what the U.S.A. was. America's economic strength, her output and productivity, her technological achievements and ever-mounting prosperity provided Europeans with an object of emulation. Both openly and discreetly the wish to catch up with the U.S.A. became the ambition of governments and the public. European productivities were judged and found wanting by American standards, European investment and provision of capital were measured up against the fixed capital at the disposal of American workers, European technological progress and expenditure on design and development were compared with American achievements and outlays in the same field. Above all, American affluence and American levels of consumption – motor-cars, domestic gadgets, and all – were held up as promise of rewards to come. In short, America's very presence provided an impulse to European growth and a measure of its achievements.

In this way a confluence of tributaries – the policy of high aggregate demand and full employment, the welfare state, the defence of the West, obligations to underdeveloped countries and American pressures and influences created a powerful current of opinion with which every European government had to swim. This current and the government policies it carried were a powerful prime-mover behind the forward march of European economies. Nothing demonstrates better their propellent action than the pauses – 'stops' – in economic expansion which occurred during our period every time governments chose to suspend their growth-promoting policies. But it goes without saying that public moods and state policies would not by themselves account for Europe's economic advance and still less for the remarkable variation in its pace from period to period and from country to country. That the objective circumstances of post-war Europe were also propitious to economic growth, and yet not equally propitious at all times and places, is an obvious truism. Some of the circumstances, especially the military and political ones, influenced economic development in a manner so immediate that their effects could be directly observed and displayed in the behaviour of national economies. But most of the objective circumstances, like most of the acts of governments, influenced the course of economic development more selectively and indirectly through supplies of labour, through savings and investment, technological progress, behaviour of managers, and the course of foreign trade. It will accordingly be the main business of the next four or five chapters to show how these factors, separately and in combination, changed during our period and how their changes affected the behaviour of European economies after the war.

In doing so, I shall try and resist the temptation of invoking the aid of generalized history every time concrete and specific historical explanations have failed me. Above all, I shall try not to impute all the credit and all the blame for economic performances of Western Europe as a whole and of individual countries within it to the stages of historical development in which they happened to find themselves. Generalized theories of historical development, more particularly the various schemes of historical stages, have their uses. Rostow's theory of economic stages has provided historians with a highly effective instrument for classifying national economies. Its usefulness as a semantic device is well proved by the extent to which the Rostow labels – 'take off', 'maturity', and the rest – have passed into the common parlance of economists and historians. Both historians and economists have also derived great profit from Gerschenkron's discussion of backward and advanced economies, and from his convincing display of the ways in which relative backwardness could facilitate economic development. And nothing demonstrates better the aptness of the Gerschenkron concepts than the ease with which some economists have recently misused them to account for laggard development of certain 'mature' countries in the West.

In fact, these and other similar devices of generalized history can be easily abused. However serviceable they may be in helping the historian to group and to classify his scattered evidence and hypotheses, they will not by themselves supply him with either new evidence or new hypotheses. While dealing with the special problems of the United Kingdom I shall briefly review some recent attempts to explain the events of the 1960s by the general character of the economy, and more especially, by the stage of historical development in which Britain found itself at that time. In doing so, I shall have to specify some of the hidden pitfalls in such explanations, and shall myself forswear all recourse to summary classifications of national economies. In obedience to this self-denying ordinance, I shall tell the story of European growth sector by sector and factor by factor, so as to show how the economic fortunes of European countries responded to each new circumstance, and above all, to the changing volumes and qualities of principal 'inputs'. And I shall begin the story by discussing the part which labour input or the changes in the supply of manpower played in the economic fortunes of postwar Europe.

CHAPTER 3

Employment and Inflation

In most West European countries additions to the labour force came from several sources – from demographic increases of indigenous population and from immigration of foreign labour as well as from changing 'activity' rates, i.e. the number of persons in employable age groups who in fact offered themselves for employment and the hours they worked while employed.

Some national demographic increases took place during our period in all Western countries, but on the balance their effects were relatively small. Thanks to the continued fall in mortality and to higher birth rates, total indigenous population grew throughout the period, especially between 1953 and 1958. In some countries, e.g. in France, it grew faster than at any time since the turn of the twentieth century. Yet the corresponding labour inputs did not expand strictly in proportion to the increasing population. To begin with, the numbers of men and women of working age increased more slowly than total population. At least 95 per cent of persons gainfully employed were in the ages between 15 and 64; and before the war in most European countries the relative numbers in these age groups were increasing owing to falling mortalities and rising expectations of life. After the war, however, the tendency was reversed. In most Western countries birth rates increased to such an extent that a larger proportion of population than before was to be found in the age group below 15; at the same time the expectations of life through declining mortality lengthened to such an extent that the proportion of persons of over 64 also increased. As a result the numbers of men and women of working age grew rather slowly: more slowly than the rest of the population.[1]

---

[1] The statistical data of population movements comes mainly from O.E.C.D., *Manpower Statistics, 1950–60* (Paris, 1963), supplemented for later years from other sources, mainly the annual economic surveys of O.E.C.D. for individual

The increases in labour supplies resulting from changing 'activity rates' were somewhat greater, though in fact they differed a great deal from country to country. The years which children were expected to spend at school, or what is called in England the 'school-leaving age', was the main factor determining the ratio of younger people available for employment; the willingness and the ability of women, especially of married women, to hire themselves for wages influenced the ratio of employable adults actually employed; and both these ratios altered somewhat during and after the war in most European countries. Between 1913 and 1939 the general tendency was for activity rates to fall owing to the extension of school education and gradual rise in the school-leaving age. In some countries, e.g. Norway and Belgium, the relative numbers of women offering themselves for employment also declined. But since 1948 the tendency was reversed in a number of countries, especially in Italy, Germany, and the United Kingdom, as steeply rising wage rates tempted larger numbers of women into offices and factories.[1]

In most countries, however, increased labour inputs were sustained not so much by demographic increases and changing activity rates as by immigration. In the United Kingdom the numbers of immigrants were far greater than at any time since 1914. In absolute numbers 'gross' immigration, i.e. not reduced by the numbers of emigrants, was greater than gross immigration to any other European country except Germany and France, and additions to the labour force through 'net immigration' were quite considerable. There were Poles and other 'displaced persons' immediately after the war, a regular stream of Irish labour – some 25,000 per annum – throughout the period, and a flow of immigrants from the West Indies, Pakistan, and Africa in the late fifties and sixties which has been estimated to have injected nearly a million into the population

countries, and also from *Some Factors*, Ch. IV 1–7. The actual demographic situation continued to differ greatly from country to country. Thus infant mortality in Italy in the period was 75 per cent higher than in the United Kingdom and nearly four times higher than in Sweden.

[1] *Some Factors*, loc. cit., for the United Kingdom; cf. R. C. O. Matthews, 'Some aspects of Post-War Growth in the British Economy in relation to Historical Experience', *Manchester Statistical Society*, 1964, f. 5–6. On some general problems of participation rate, cf. Clarence D. Long, *The Labour Force under Changing Income and Employment*, esp. p. 29. According to Professor Long the rate did not change much in the U.S.A.

of the United Kingdom. And although emigration from the United Kingdom resumed after the war, the influx of immigrants was sufficient to leave an appreciable 'net' accretion to labour force. In the early sixties annual 'net' immigration, i.e. excess of immigrants over emigrants, fluctuated round the 70,000 mark and was, relative to the total labour force, also higher than in some other European countries.

Table 3 *Population and Labour Input*[1] *1950–1962*

	Population aged 15–64 as percentage of Total Population		Labour Force as percentage of Population aged 15–64	
	1950	1962	1950	1962
Belgium	68·1	64·4	60·3	61·3
France	65·8	62·0	73·5	74·0
Germany	67·2	67·6	68·9	71·6
Italy	65·5	66·2	63·8	67·6
Netherlands	63·0	61·0	61·2	62·1
Norway	66·0	63·0	64·2	62·6
Sweden	66·3	65·6	66·5	66·3
Switzerland	66·8	66·2	68·4	70·2
United Kingdom	66·9	65·0	70·0	72·3

It was much higher in France, where the cumulative total of immigrants reached some 2¼ million by 1963. It attained its highest point immediately after the end of the war in Algeria, when a flood of expatriates, about a million strong, entered France, adding about 300,000 to its labour force. But the flow of foreign labour – Italian, Spanish, and North African – had been very high even before then: as high as 140,000 in 1957. Italians and Spaniards and other foreign labourers supplied most of Swiss needs of additional labour, and it was reckoned that by 1963 one-third of employed manual labour in that country – over 600,000 – were foreign immigrants. Largest of all was, of course, the accretion to the labour force in Germany. Expatriates from the zones occupied by Poland and the U.S.S.R. and from East Germany numbered about 2½ million by

[1] The table is based on the sources listed in footnote 1, p. 52 above, and A. Maddison, *Economic Growth in the West*, Tables 1–4.

1950 and about 4 million by 1954. The flow subsided after that date, but did not cease altogether until 1961. By that time foreign immigrants from Southern Europe, Greece, and Turkey began to come in large numbers. The net total of immigrants between 1950 and 1962 has been estimated at about 3·6 millions.[1]

What with the increase in the supplies of native labour, however slight, and with continuous drafts of immigrant labour, economists cannot be blamed for concluding that higher labour input was one of the prime causes of economic growth in Western Europe. It is, in fact, possible to establish a slight statistical correlation between the faster-than-average rate of economic growth in countries like Germany, the Netherlands, Austria, and Switzerland (though not France or the Scandinavian countries) and the higher-than-average increases in their labour forces; and conversely the correlation of low rates of growth in the United Kingdom and Belgium with the relatively small increases in their labour forces.

This particular correlation has been greatly emphasized in some authoritative studies; it may nevertheless turn out to be not as obvious, and certainly not as simple, as it at first sight appears.[2] In considering this and all the subsequent statistical arguments in this study it should be borne in mind that all a statistical correlation can do is to suggest that a pair of variables moving in constant agreement with each other might in some way be linked. But the link need not necessarily be one of mutual causation; it may also be one of common dependence on a third factor not present in the correlation. And even if other evidence and common sense make a causal connexion appear very likely, the likelihood is not by itself sufficient to identify which of the correlatives is *the* cause. Some

---

[1] O.E.C.D., *Manpower Statistics 1950–1962*, Paris, 1963; and O.E.C.D. annual economic surveys for individual countries; 'Die Beschäftigung ausländischer Arbeiterkräfte in Deutschland, 1882 bis 1963', *Wirtschaft und Statistik*, February 1963.

[2] A recent though moderate assertion of the role of labour inputs in growth will be found in UNO, *Economic Survey of Europe in 1961*, N.Y. 1962, Ch. II. The authors rely on a slight correlation between productivities in European countries and their labour inputs indicated by regression analysis of the figures: ibid., 30. For a point of view nearer to that represented in the present study cf. *Some Factors*, Ch. II, 13–14, and C. Kindleberger, *Economic Growth in France and Britain, 1851–1950*, Cambridge (Mass.), 1964, Ch. 4. The same author's forthcoming study of labour inputs may, however, assign greater importance to labour supplies, and more especially to immigration.

correlations reflect a connexion so mutual and continuous as to make the juxtaposition of cause and effect impossible or meaningless. Other correlations leave the whole problem open and must be considered in the full setting of the available evidence to establish the probable order of cause and effect.

Table 4 *Output, Labour Force, and Productivity 1948–63*[1]

	Compound Annual Rates of Growth (%)			
	a. G.D.P.[a]	*b.* Active Labour Force	G.D.P. per Head of Population [a]	
			c.	*d.*
	1949–59	1949–59	1949–59	1959–63
Austria	5·7[b]	1·1	5·6	5·2
Belgium	3·1	0·3	2·4	3·3
Denmark	3·5	1·0[c]	2·6	—
France	4·5	0·1	3·6	5·1
Germany	7·4[b]	1·6	6·3	5·6
Italy	6·1	1·1[b]	5·5	6·1
Netherlands	4·5	1·2	3·3	3·7
Norway	3·5	0·3	3·3	—
Sweden	3·4	0·5[d]	2·8	2·6
Switzerland	5·0[c]	1·5[c]	3·8	—
United Kingdom	2·5	0·6	2·1	1·7

[a] At constant prices. [b] 1950–59. [c] 1950–60. [d] 1950–62.

The particular correlation with which we are here concerned is as indeterminate as a correlation can be, and will not disclose the probable connexion between labour supply and the behaviour of the economy unless considered in conjunction with what we already happen to know and think likely. Thus considered, the correlation

[1] Figures in column (*a*) are derived from *Some Factors*, Ch. II, Table 1; those in column (*b*) from *ibid.*, Ch. II, Table 4; those in column (*c*) have been recomputed from the data in A. Maddison, *Economic Growth in the West*, Tables 1–3 and Appendices A and B; those in column (*d*) have been computed from various sources, mainly from the O.E.C.D. annual economic surveys of individual countries. No attempt has been made to reconcile the differences between the figures in the main sources; figures in columns (*a*) and (*b*) are not therefore wholly compatible with those in columns (*c*) and (*d*).

supports the view that labour inputs could by their very size affect national products; but it will not justify the conclusion that national outputs invariably responded to changes in labour inputs and that national outputs of Western countries considered in the aggregate benefited immediately, directly, and commensurately from abundant supplies of labour. In less fortunate parts of the world teeming with population, increasing numbers of imperfectly employed men and women were an impediment to economic growth. Thus in several countries on the fringes of Western Europe, such as Turkey, Spain, Greece, and even Italy, whose economies advanced rapidly during our period, the advances occurred in spite, or perhaps even because, some of their surplus labour was being drawn off by emigration. But in the industrialized countries of Western Europe, with which we are concerned here, demographic accretions to native populations and the flow of immigrants must have done much to facilitate the upward surge of aggregate output. As long as nations pursued policies of full employment, each pair of additional hands could be relied upon to raise their aggregate output and each additional mouth could be relied upon to raise their total demand. There is thus no denying that the remarkable increases in the German national product in the fifties owed much to the millions of additional hands and mouths of its refugees and immigrants, and that the slower rise of aggregate product in the United Kingdom reflected smaller increases in its population.

Yet even this, on the whole incontestable, correlation between labour supplies and aggregate products must not be construed into a simple causal explanation. It will not by itself tell us what initiated the economic upsurge or why it differed from country to country. In considering the initial impetus to economic expansion in Western Europe as a whole, or the local and chronological variations in its tempo, it might be better history and even better sense to consider larger labour supplies not only as the 'cause' of expanding output but also as one of its consequences.

There are several logical and historical reasons why, in discussing labour inputs, the conventional order of cause and effect should be sometimes inverted. We have seen that supplies of additional labour differed from nation to nation not only because their natural demographic trends, i.e. birth rates, death rates and age structure, were different, but also because labour moved across frontiers. It has not, however, been suggested that migrations necessarily preceded and prepared the way for outbursts of economic activity. East Germans may have come to Germany before the German economic 'miracle' had time to reveal itself; but in later years Turks and Greeks came to Germany because labour-hungry Germany needed them. Similarly, it cannot be said that Italians, Spaniards, and Greeks came to Switzerland for the sake of the scenery and stayed to work. They came because the expanding Swiss economy was crying out for labour.

The same conclusion is suggested by those features of labour supply which were not directly related either to natural demographic factors or to immigration. In manufacturing industries where, as we shall see further, both productivity and labour supplies rose highest, much additional labour came from other occupations (mainly from agriculture), or was drawn from elements in the population not previously employed in paid occupations, mainly married women. And the reason why agricultural labour – or married women – were enticed into factories is that expanding economies stood in great need of labour and could offer high and rising wages.

We shall not, therefore, sin much against either common sense or history if we conclude that even in considering aggregate outputs it would be wrong to treat abundant labour as their universal prerequisite. It was certainly not the inescapable prerequisite of high and increasing output in Germany. Between 1958 and 1964 shortage of labour as measured by the average unemployment rate was greater in Germany, with unemployment standing well below 1 per cent, than in the United Kingdom. Yet in Germany the G.N.P. continued to grow at twice the British rate.

Abundant labour supplies were even less essential as a prerequisite of higher productivities. We have seen that after the war aggregate outputs grew faster than populations and faster than the numbers of employed labour, so that productivity per head as well as aggregate products were on the rise. And when it comes to the question why output rose faster than the numbers in employment, the larger numbers will not by themselves provide a sufficient answer. It is a well-known assumption of economic theory that productivity of labour is more likely to be enhanced by its scarcity than by its abundance. As long as capital and labour are complementary, i.e. capable of being substituted for each other, dearth of labour could act as a stimulus to investment in replacement of manpower and thus lead to increased provision of capital per person employed, to lower marginal productivity of capital and higher marginal productivity of labour.[1]

Against these time-honoured propositions of economic theory some students of the modern economy have recently advanced a number of empirical – in fact, sociological – arguments why plentiful supplies of labour should have promoted higher outputs per head and should have done this more in some countries than in others. Of these arguments the one with most evidence to support is that alleging that tight supplies of labour encourage attitudes inimical to high productivity. Post-war experience in the United Kingdom can be cited to show how, in times when employment was over-full, managerial authority was more easily flouted, labour leaders became more militant, and the general deportment on the shop-floor slackened. These morbid symptoms of labour shortage are reputed to have all but vanished every time a recession reduced the demand for labour. So presumably they would also be relieved by augmenting the supplies of manpower.

Such cogency as this argument may possess – and it is by no means incontestable – will not extend to the other sociological demonstrations of the connexion between higher productivity and greater labour inputs. Least of all will it extend to the frequently heard argument concerning the contribution of 'new' labour, mostly that of immigrants from abroad or from the countryside. It has been said – though not proved – that in Germany immigration from Eastern regions brought with it large drafts of skilled manpower. We are also told that in that country immigrants, whether East German or wholly foreign, worked harder and were more

---

[1] This connexion between abundance or scarcity of labour and capital investment is an important Ricardian assumption and underlies Marx's arguments about the oscillating ratios of fixed and circulating capital. For a recent application of the theory to the economic history of Britain and the U.S.A., see H. J. Habakkuk, *American and British Technology in the Nineteenth Century*, Cambridge, 1962, e.g. pp. 11–63. But cf. Preface to this book and the chapters 5 and 6, esp. pp. 163–8.

[*Vide* Appendix Note 8, p. 364 below.]

E

frugal than local labourers. Above all they were easier to move to places and occupations in which the needs of labour were greatest. They also made the labour force more mobile by displacing, and thereby helping to move and to promote, local workers hitherto employed in unskilled occupations. From this enhanced mobility 'new' and progressive industries and firms are supposed to have benefited most. With immigrants and other 'new' labour freely available, progressive industries in Germany or Switzerland, unlike similar industries in the United Kingdom or Sweden, could expand unimpeded by the difficulty of enticing men and women from other industrial employments.

Very few of these claims have so far been backed by actual investigations and are as a rule accepted on trust; and trust alone cannot dissipate certain doubts about them. Labourers of immigrant origin employed in unskilled jobs, mostly out of doors, in Germany and Switzerland may have proved more mobile than the average native working man, but it is by no means certain that they were any more mobile than the other types of 'navvy' labour, whatever its origin. In fact, some categories of unskilled or semi-skilled labour, whether native or foreign, could sometimes be excessively mobile. Under conditions of full employment national economies could suffer not only from lack of mobility among some categories of labour but equally from excessive mobility – or 'labour turnover', as it is sometimes described – among its other categories, especially among building workers or those in domestic service and hotel work.[1]

Equally uncertain were the alleged benefits derived from 'new' labour by the progressive industries. Had the benefits been as real and as large as they are sometimes represented to be, the labour force in these industries would have contained higher-than-average proportions of juveniles, foreigners, or natives displaced from un-

---

[1] The behaviour of 'green' rural labour in industrial employment has been a favourite theme of industrial sociology. The earliest collection of relevant information will be found in the pre-1913 publications of the German *Verein für Sozialwissenschaft und Politik*. The most recent summary of evidence and opinions have been assembled in the report of an international seminar held in Gröningen in September 1960, under the auspices of the European Productivity Agency of O.E.E.C: *Rural Manpower and Industrial Development*, report by H. Krier, Paris, 1961.
[*Vide* Appendix Note 3, p. 362 below.]

skilled occupations. These expectations are not, however, borne out by the little we know of the make-up of industrial employment; and there is very little reason why these expectations should have been borne out. As far as we can judge from the recurrent complaints of labour shortages, the shortages from which 'progressive' industries and firms suffered most were those of skilled operatives, especially of men and women with up-to-date technical qualifications. And these were precisely the categories of labour least likely to be found among the fresh arrivals from abroad or from the countryside, or among unskilled native workers displaced by immigrants.

Mobility of industrial labour in the semi-skilled and skilled ranks was, of course, an essential condition of economic growth, of technological progress, or of smooth and rapid deployment of new industries. But by themselves large inflows of labour from abroad or from the countryside need not have brought about a higher mobility between industrial occupations, just as a slowly-growing labour force need not always have stayed immobile. In the United Kingdom the inflow of labour from abroad was by no means negligible: gross immigration was higher than in any country except Germany, Switzerland or France. Yet the habits of labour-hoarding rooted in a number of industries and the resistance to transfers to new occupations on the part of workers were not visibly affected by the inflow of West Africans or Irishmen.[1] On the other hand, Sweden, in spite of her largely stationary labour supplies and a very low rate of immigration, was able to secure a movement of labour from less productive to more productive occupations throughout our period.

So much for the role played by labour supplies in post-war growth of outputs and productivities. Much more potent than the supplies of labour was its utilization. One of the reasons why national products since the war rose so high above their pre-war levels is that such labour as was available was more fully employed. It is now the consensus of opinion among economic commentators

---

[1] Comparative net figures of annual net immigration between 1958 and 1962 are summarized. O.E.C.D., *Observer*, No. 13, December 1964.
[*Vide* Appendix Note 4, p. 362 below.]

that the most important factor of growth in post-war Europe was the consistently buoyant demand and full employment resulting from it.

Uninterrupted full employment, was, however, a purely post-war phenomenon; between the wars, unemployment in Western Europe as a whole was an endemic disease, periodically broken by outbursts of epidemic mass unemployment. At the height of the great depression of the early thirties the numbers of unemployed rose to over a quarter of the labour force, and were even higher than that in the early thirties in Germany. After 1946, however, unemployment in Europe as a whole seldom rose over 2·5 per cent.

In a few countries labouring under special handicaps post-war unemployment remained above this figure. It was still relatively high in Italy – somewhat above 7 per cent over the period from 1948 to 1961, but then Italy suffered from the chronic difficulty of transferring and absorbing the unemployed population of her southern provinces. Until the end of the fifties it was also relatively high in Belgium (a little above 5 per cent) and in Denmark (about 4 per cent) mainly because the main export trades of these two countries happened to be depressed. Owing to the influx of immigrants from behind the Iron Curtain, unemployment in Germany remained until 1957 somewhat higher than in most other European countries (rather above 4 per cent), but it fell sharply in 1958 and stayed well below 2 per cent in the subsequent five or six years.

In the other European countries taken together unemployment during the fifteen years between 1948 and 1963 averaged about 1·9 per cent. It stood even below that level in countries like Sweden, Switzerland or Germany in the early sixties. And what makes the high level of employment all the more remarkable is that, as I have just pointed out, nearly all the countries of Western Europe, with the exception of Italy and to a smaller extent the Scandinavian countries, imported foreigners to relieve the growing shortage of labour.[1]

At the beginning, this high employment was wholly spontaneous

---

[1] I.L.O., *Yearbooks of Labour Statistics for 1945–6 and 1961*, Geneva, 1946 and 1962; O.E.C.D., *Manpower Statistics 1950–1960*, Paris, 1961; *Wirtschaft und Statistik*, September 1961; A. Maddison, *Economic Growth in the West*, 44 and 220; W. Galenson and A. Zellner, 'International Comparisons of Unemployment Rates', *Measurement and Balancing of Unemployment*, N.B.E.R., Princeton, 1957.

and even accidental, and was due to the circumstances in which Europe found herself rather than to the deliberate policy of governments. The need to assuage the shortage of consumption goods, to replenish the exhausted inventories, to rebuild stocks, to start factories, to restore transport, to repair and rebuild houses generated high demands for labour in most ex-belligerent and occupied countries. In Germany and the Netherlands, the influences of this pent-up demand probably continued to be felt until the early fifties.

Now and again, in later years, certain other events, mostly political and military, helped to stimulate demand and maintain high employment. One such event was American military expenditure during the Korean War 1950 with its inflationary effect on world prices and on economic activity in most countries of the Western world. More enduring were the effects of rearmament resulting from the Cold War and from the formation of NATO. In Western Europe as a whole the proportion of national income devoted to defence and rearmament may not have been as high as it had been in Italy and Germany under Mussolini and Hitler, or in France and the United Kingdom in the three years immediately preceding the war. Yet in most countries, except Germany and Italy, it formed a large proportion of government expenditure and helped to swell the aggregate demand for goods and services.

Military expenditure was, of course, merely part of government expenditure and not even its greater part. In 1962 it formed about 4·5 per cent of the combined G.N.P. of the Western European nations compared with 9·5 per cent of the G.N.P. which governments spent on goods and services for civil use. However, direct public expenditure on goods and services, whether military or civil, itself formed only part of current outlays of governments. The latter also paid interest on national debts, subsidized agriculture and some industries and met claims under various social services, such as old age pensions, family allowances and unemployment benefits. These various public disbursements grew all through our period, and in Western Europe as a whole by 1963 came to exceed one-third of the combined European G.N.P.

With most European budgets in balance (in the late fifties and the sixties most of them were showing current surpluses) public expenditure was all covered by taxes, rates and compulsory contributions to social services; and these amounted in 1962 to 34·2 per cent of the G.N.P. in the United Kingdom, 41 per cent of the G.N.P. in Germany, and 41·1 per cent in France.[1] As it was thus covered, government expenditure, whether on goods and services or on internal payments or on social service benefits, need not necessarily have swollen the aggregate volume of demand and thereby added to total employment. They were mostly what economists call transfer payments, i.e. payment to some people of sums or services drawn from other people by means of taxes. Even when public authorities bought goods and services, they were expending what private individuals might have spent on their own account had they not been taxed. There is, however, no knowing how much of the income appropriated by the state would have been spent, i.e. not saved, had it remained in the hands of individuals. It is also probable that the expenditure of governments was more constant, less prone to oscillate than the expenditure of individuals might have been. So even if government expenditure added relatively little to aggregate demand, it probably helped to make this demand more steady, i.e. less liable to fluctuations; and, as we shall see presently, freedom from violent fluctuations was in itself a circumstance highly propitious to economic growth.

Indeed, so consistently high was aggregate demand and so buoyant was employment that quite early in the post-war period the recurrent trouble in nearly all European countries was the very reverse of the pre-war one; not insufficient demand, but excessive demand leading to inflation. The most conspicuous symptom of inflation, and one of which the public was most aware was the rise in prices, *la vie chère*. In the United Kingdom the retail price index rose by about 82 per cent between 1948 and 1961; the rises in some other countries were even higher.

These rises were not always due to, or were not always signs of, excessive demand. In the United Kingdom or in Germany, they may have been due not only to the excess of purchasing power,

[1] C. H. Feinstein, *National Income and Expenditure, 1870–1963*, University of Cambridge Department of Applied Economics, Reprint 225, 1964, Table IV; S. Andric and J. Veverka, 'The Growth of Expenditure in Germany', *Finanzarchiv*, N.F. 23, Heft 2, 1964.

'too much money chasing too few goods', but to rising costs and more especially labour costs. But even where and when the price rises were apparently due to inflation of demand, they did not always interfere with the continued expansion of the economy. It was the experience of the post-war economy that under conditions of full employment some excessive demand must occur and could not be wholly eliminated. It has even been argued on largely

Table 5 *Consumer Price Indices in 1948 and 1961*[1] (1948 = 100)

Belgium	125
Denmark	144
France	200
Germany	126
Italy	147
Netherlands	130
Norway	168
Sweden	165
Switzerland	118
United Kingdom	161

theoretical grounds that, wherever and whenever economic growth was brought about and kept up by appropriate government policies, it was bound to lead to inflation, however moderate. And whatever may be thought of the argument in this particular form, its obverse variant has much to be said for it. As long as inflation stayed moderate, it was, as a rule, conducive to economic growth. Rising prices promised high and rising profits, and expectations of high profits encouraged entrepreneurs to invest more and to plan for larger output than they would have done if prices had been stable or falling.[2]

Where inflation interfered with the economic progress of Western

[1] U.N., *Statistical Yearbook, 1963*; cf. A. Maddison, *Economic Growth in the West*, 45, Table II, 2. According to *British Economy: Key Statistics 1900–1964*, prices in the United Kingdom rose by 64 per cent between 1948 and 1961, and by a further 10 per cent by 1964.

[2] For brief statements of contrary arguments, cf. Thomas Wilson, 'Inflation and Growth', *The Three Banks Review*, 1961, No. 51; and Ollo Eckstein, 'Inflation, the Wage-Price Spiral and Economic Growth', *The Relationship of Prices to Economic Stability and Growth*, U.S. Gov., Washington, 1958. Markos Marmalakis, 'Growth as a Cause of Inflation', *Journal of Economic Studies*, Vol. I, No. 1, 1965, summarizes the recent arguments that inflationary pressures must follow government-directed growth because of the role which inflationary credit as a rule plays

economies was on occasions in which the excess of demand was so
great and prices rose so rapidly as to create serious distortions in the
economy and to upset the balance of trade and payments. This in
its turn forced governments to try and curb demand and employment and thereby to check the expansion of the economy. These
penalties of excessive demand and of the measures to combat it
afflicted the United Kingdom earlier and worse than any other
country. Indeed, so painful were their effects on British economic
development and so heavily were they charged with ominous
portent for the future of other European economies, that we must
make use of this occasion to deal with them at some detail.

We have seen that in the first few years following the conclusion
of peace the United Kingdom's output and national income rose at
a rate which compared very favourably not only with her own
performances before the war but also with what were to become the
high peaks of achievement in the post-war world. Her G.N.P. grew
between 1947 and 1950 at 3·5 per cent per annum (it grew even
faster between 1946 and 1949). It was at this point that the first (or
the second if the brief payments crisis of 1947 were included) of her
several payment crises occurred. In each of these crises internal
demand had soared so high that stresses developed at several points
in the economy – in the supplies of steel, building materials, and
some categories of labour. But the point at which the strains were
felt most was the balance of payments.

The crises, in fact, recurred several times: in 1949, 1951, 1955,
1957, 1961, 1964. The first of these crises, with its conspicuous
foreign speculation against the pound and flight of foreign 'short-
term' funds, was thought to be mainly a crisis of the currency
itself. The pound was believed to be over-valued and thus made
English exports too dear and foreign imports too cheap. The
obvious remedy against this particular complaint was to devalue the
currency; and the value of the pound was drastically reduced in
1949. This devaluation was followed by devaluations in other

---

in such growth. But in some other theories (Wicksell's) even spontaneous, i.e.
market-stimulated, growth must frequently lead to inflationary pressures by
disturbing the equilibrium of the economy.

countries; it nevertheless acted as a temporary stimulus for exports and as a deterrent to imports. As a result, the trade balance improved for a couple of years, and the country entered on another phase of expansion. But the inflation of prices resulting from devaluation and the impetus it gave to exports spent themselves before long. By 1955 the same symptoms recurred again, as they were also to recur in 1957 and in 1961.[1]

The recurrent symptoms were diagnosed not as indispositions of the pound but as imbalances of the domestic economy due to inflation, and were accordingly treated by doses of deflation. How effective the deflationary measures in fact were is still subject to dispute, but that in combination they succeeded every time in holding back the growth of the economy is only too evident. Immediately after each recourse to deflationary remedies the annual rate of growth was reduced to below 2 per cent, and in the penultimate bout of deflating policies, those of 1961, the United Kingdom, for the first time since the end of the war and almost alone of all European countries, succeeded in keeping her economy from growing at all.

The crises in the British balance of payments and the consequent fluctuations in the economy recurred so frequently and proved so difficult to overcome that in the end they came to be regarded not only as a painful affliction but also as a symptom of an organic malaise of the British body economic. An affliction it was, and its debilitating effects on the confidence of business leaders and investors, on the flow of foreign funds and on the attitudes of policymakers at every level of authority were unmistakable. Yet its causes were not so deeply seated as to justify the laments at the decline of the British economy and at its irretrievable inferiority to that of other Western nations. In actual fact the British economy performed in international markets better than at most times since the middle of the nineteenth century; and the margin by which its performances, and still more its abilities to perform, fell short of those of other nations was not as great as the public has been led to believe.

---

[1] A chronological account of contraction and expansion in the United Kingdom will be found in O.E.C.D., *Economic Survey for the United Kingdom 1962*, Paris, 1963, 6–10; cf. idem, *Economic Survey for the United Kingdom for 1961*, Paris, 1962.

If the indispositions of Britain's foreign balances proved so stubbornly resistant to remedial measures this was not because she was sick beyond all hope of curing but because the morbid causes were in large measure non-economic and therefore not responsive to purely economic cures.

The diagnosis of Britain's recurrent crises can be summarized briefly, if somewhat tautologically, as a tendency of her outlays abroad to outrun the yield of her foreign earnings. Throughout her post-war period the United Kingdom carried burdens of foreign payments and obligations heavier relative to its national income than those borne by any other European country. Most of these burdens originated in the international role Britain preserved or assumed (the precise verb is a matter of choice) after the war. Some of them, above all, the upkeep of the Army of Occupation in Germany (its cost exceeded £80 million in 1964), fell upon Britain as a victor in the war; others arose from lingering imperial commitments. Although during this period Britain liquidated the bulk of her dependent empire, she still preserved some vestiges of her colonial past in the Eastern Mediterranean, in the Middle East and in South-East Asia, which entailed expenditure on bases and troops, subsidies to local rulers and a succession of colonial or post-colonial wars in Palestine, Malaya and Cyprus, Suez and Aden. The fact that some of these obligations appeared inescapable and helped to preserve whole parts of the world from lapsing into chaos or from being taken over by the Communist powers did not make them any less burdensome. The net annual burdens on Britain's foreign exchange represented by military outlays abroad was on the average not much above £100 million in the early fifties, but it grew from year to year, and rose between 1959 and 1964 from about £135 million to very nearly £300 million.[1]

Another high and rising liability was payments abroad for interest on foreign loans. This approached £500 millions by 1958, or eight to ten times as much as before the war. Some of these payments went to the U.S.A. and Canada for loans advanced during and since the war, but some of the increase was due to the interest payable on balances kept in the United Kingdom by nations belonging to the sterling area.

[1] Cf. below, p. 69, footnote 1, p. 70, footnote 1, and Table 6.

The sterling area was yet another liability – perhaps inescapable, perhaps economically valuable, but nevertheless quite burdensome. In essence this 'area' was a combination of trading nations in which the pound sterling served as a monetary medium of international payments and as a security for local currencies. From the international point of view the existence of the area was highly beneficial. It provided a large number of countries with means for settling their mutual accounts without the impediments and restrictions besetting the international payments of other countries. But from the British point of view the sterling balances held in London, of which three-quarters to four-fifths belonged to other countries in the sterling area, represented a large volume of foreign debt (between £3,000 and £4,000 millions in 1960s) and an obligation to defend a medium of payment for a volume of transactions greatly in excess of Britain's own foreign trade, her own receipts from abroad, and of her gold reserves.[1]

Both during and immediately after the war (and again towards the end of 1963), this sterling obligation was relatively easy to discharge. In those years most of the territories in the sterling area had a consistently favourable balance of trade with the rest of the world and were accumulating large sterling credits in London, and were in fact helping to carry Britain's own payments deficits. Moreover, the low Bank Rate which prevailed in the three years immediately following the end of the war made the annual cost of servicing the sterling balances relatively low: on the average between £30 and £40 million per annum. But when, in order to defend the balance of payments, the British bank rate had to be repeatedly lifted to a high level and on occasions rose to as much as 7 per cent, the cost of servicing the sterling balances could exceed £100 million. And in so far as these charges had to be remitted abroad they aggravated the very payments difficulties which the high interest rates were meant to alleviate. The fact that the composition of the sterling debt had also changed in the meantime, and that the proportion of the debt held by individuals somewhat increased, and that held by the governments declined, made the position less stable and more at the mercy of private fears and fancies.

[1] For the break-down of sterling balances, see R. Bailey 'Sterling Balances', *Midland Bank Review*, May 1964; *Colonial Development*, Overseas Development Institute, London, 1964.

Table 6 *The United Kingdom Balance of Payments on Current Account*[1]

	Million pounds of current prices			
	Visible Trade	Invisible (net) Government Payments	Other Payments	Balance
1938	−302	−13	+245	−70
1946	−103	−323	+196	−230
1951	−689	−150	+474	−365
1958	+41	−224	+528	+345
1959	−102	−233	+488	+153
1960	−386	−286	+414	−258
1961	−127	−335	+461	−1
1962	−72	−363	+550	+115
1963	−48	−387	+549	+114

A further charge on the balance of payments came from the movement of private investments. Before the war British investments abroad were very high, but this burden was amply compensated by the current of annual income from abroad which they generated. Since the war the foreign, especially American, investment in the United Kingdom became sufficiently great (its post-war aggregate probably reached $1200 million by 1962) to produce an outgoing flow of profits and interest payments which in some years was more than half as great as the United Kingdom's income from its own investments abroad. At the same time the balance of payments continued to bear the weight of resumed transfers of British capital abroad for investment. In some years, more particularly in 1958, 1959, 1960, and 1963 the outflow of funds on this account outpaced by a large margin the inflow of foreign investment into the United Kingdom; and by all appearances Britain was fast resuming her pre-war role of an international lender and exporter of capital.

This role fitted well the 'built-in' propensities of London's

[1] The figures in this table and in Table 7 are derived from *British Economy: Key Statistics, 1900–1964*, London and Cambridge Economic Service, 1965, Tables F and G.

financial market with its large international clientele and its well-developed network of merchant banks specializing in foreign issues. It was also closely bound up with the interests of some of Britain's greatest firms in mining and oil whose foreign business grew without a halt. Throughout the period this role was willingly assumed. Foreign investment was viewed by economists and businessmen alike as a source of great economic benefits – a stimulus to exports of capital goods, a feeder for the flow of income from abroad, and a prerequisite of the more abundant and cheaper supplies of imported foodstuffs and raw materials. To these traditional commendations advocates of foreign investment could also add the argument that private investment had to play an important part in assisting underdeveloped countries. But plausible as all these arguments may have been in theory, and beneficial as capital exports might in fact have turned out to be in the long run, their immediate effect was to swell the weight of the United Kingdom outlays abroad.

Table 7 *The United Kingdom Balance of Payments on Long-Term Capital Account 1958–1962*[1]

| | ($£$ million) | | | | | |
	1958	1959	1960	1961	1962	1963
Private Investment						
Inflow	165	176	228	416	250	259
Outflow	−307	−311	−314	−321	−253	−309
Total						
Private Investment	−142	−135	−86	95	−3	−50
Public Funds[a]	−50	−124	−102	−35	−104	−105
Balance	−192	−259	−188	60	−107	−155

[a] Balance of intergovernmental loans, the United Kingdom subscriptions to international funds, etc.

The mounting weight of outlays could have been borne only if British receipts from foreign trade had grown at least in the same measure: and this they sometimes failed to do. The failure does not, however, signify that the United Kingdom economy suddenly lost its capacity to compete on foreign markets, and that, as a result, her exports were declining or were lower than before the war. On the

[1] Above, p. 70, footnote 1.

contrary, judged by ordinary standards, i.e. by those of the United Kingdom's performances in earlier periods or the size of the British economy, the United Kingdom's receipts from foreign trade were very high and rising. Even if the United Kingdom's share in world trade had fallen, its exports measured in values, volumes, or proportions of the national product, rose during our period and stood at the end very much higher than the most optimistic of forecasters on the morrow of the war had thought possible.

Mr A. R. Conan reminded us recently that when in 1945 it was authoritatively estimated that in order to maintain her solvency Britain would by the middle fifties have to increase her exports by 75 per cent, economists unanimously predicted that an increase of this magnitude would be historically unprecedented and exceedingly difficult to achieve. Yet the target was exceeded by a large margin and continued to be exceeded through the subsequent decade. In 1964, the year when the United Kingdom payments deficit reached its highest post-war point, the United Kingdom exports, at £4,254 million at current prices, were more than nine times higher than their average value in the eight years between 1930 and 1938, and nearly six times higher than their very high level in the twenties. Expressed in real terms, i.e. in wholesale prices of 1938, the values of British exports in 1964 were three times as high as in 1938; and two and a half times as high as in 1946 at prices of that year. Measured by volume, British exports in 1963 were twice as high as those of 1938 and two and a half times as high as those of 1946. As the aggregate domestic product had since 1938 and 1946 increased by about 70 per cent, exports formed a larger proportion of the Gross Domestic Product in the sixties than before or immediately after the war. In 1963 (admittedly a good year) British exports equalled about 22·5 per cent of G.D.P. as against about 11 per cent in the pre-war decade. This compares with 19·4 per cent for Germany, 17·8 per cent for Italy, 14·5 per cent for France. Even in some later years, as in 1964, when the British performance on foreign markets was least brilliant, its share of the G.N.P. was nevertheless higher than in any other major industrial country, with the occasional exception of Germany.[1]

What is more, British exports were highest and grew fastest in

[1] A. R. Conan, *The Problem of Sterling*, London, 1966, pp. 31–2.

those branches of production in which the exports of other nations were also at their most buoyant. The exports of chemicals in 1964 were, at current prices, worth nearly four times more than in 1948, and nearly twelve times more than in the thirties; the value of exports of metal manufactures grew almost equally steeply. Chemicals, vehicles, and machinery formed about 60 per cent of total exports at the turn of the fifties and sixties: about the same as in Germany and considerably more than in any other European country, including Sweden and Switzerland. Moreover, compared to pre-war, the share of these exports in total exports grew faster in Britain than even in Germany. It more than doubled between 1937 and 1963, whereas in Germany it increased by 50 per cent. Taken by themselves British exports of engineering products, including cars, aircraft and ships in the fifties and early sixties, averaged 30 per cent of total output; and this again was a performance not matched by any other European country except Germany.[1]

Invisible earnings did not do quite so well, but not as badly as is often assumed. Income from 'portfolio' investments i.e. those in foreign securities, declined. In real terms, the aggregate volume of such investments was lower than in 1913, and lower even than in 1938. Net income from shipping also declined compared with 1913 or 1938. But some other sources yielded relatively more than before the war. Profits of direct investments of British firms, especially those of oil companies and mining companies, agency, commission and premium earnings of the City of London, gross yields of the tourist trade, authors' royalties and performing rights (the Beatles!), kept up well. As a result invisible earnings continued to make a sizeable contribution to the balance of payments. They may have been somewhat lower than pre-war in real terms, but were nevertheless high and rising. In 1962–1963 they stood at about £550 million at current prices. In current prices they were lower than in 1938 in

[1] *British Economy: Key Statistics*, as footnote 1, p. 70 above; W. A. P. Manser, 'U.K. Balance of Payments – the Weak Spot', *Westminster Bank Review*, May 1965; cf. A. R. Conan, ibid., February 1961; also S. Paul Chambers, Inaugural Address, *Royal Statistical Society*, Series (A), vol. 128, part 1, 196, 1965. The combined exports of vehicles, machinery, and chemicals, as percentage of total exports were by 1959 as high in the United Kingdom as in Germany, but had grown somewhat faster compared to 1937, and only a little slower compared to 1950: O.E.C.D., *Science, Economic Growth, and Government Policy*, Paris, 1963, Appendix B, Table 8.

only one post-war year – 1946. In some years – 1951, 1958, 1962, 1963 – they were more than twice as high. Altogether the invisible items equalled 23·5 per cent of total current payments abroad, both visible and invisible, compared with the average of 14·5 per cent in the last five years before the war.[1]

This increased yield of exports and of invisible earnings did not, of course, result in commensurate increases in credit balances on Britain's current payments account, for in the meantime imports also increased. In 1964 – a year of specially high imports – they stood at 24 per cent of G.N.P., compared with 18 per cent per annum between 1934 and 1938. Yet, as these figures show, the cost of imports increased less than the combined yields of exports and invisible earnings, and left considerable positive balances in payments accounts in most post-war years except 1946, 1951, and 1964, despite the rising volume of overseas payments on government account and capital transfers.[2]

This performance is all the more creditable for the measures the United Kingdom governments took to deal with the recurrent payments crises. So inhibiting were the effects of periodic restrictions on the economy as a whole, and more particularly on its ability to embark on cost-reducing investments in export industries, that a student of recent European history may be surprised to find how well the economy bore the financial burdens of post-war policies at home and abroad.[3]

---

[1] *British Economy: Key Statistics*, ibid. It is interesting that measured by nights spent in the country the flow of tourists to the United Kingdom was in some years, e.g. 1962, even higher than in France, though in most years the flow to France, and tourist expenditure per night were somewhat higher than in the United Kingdom.

[2] Same sources as above, p. 70, footnote 1 and p. 71, footnote 1; cf. also *The Times* for 25 January 1966.

[3] Year-to-year statistical measurements may not reveal a significant correlation between the government-induced 'stops' and the movements of private investment. These 'short-term' correlations are, however, somewhat irrelevant. In view of the long gestation period of industrial investment, and the importance of long-term expectations, the relevant evidence should be sought not in annual figures but in the trends of investment, coupled if possible, with the concrete evidence of experiences of individual firms. For shortages of components and sub-assemblies in times of boom due to insufficient capacity in the country, cf. annual reports for 1964 of Aveling Barford, Ruston and Hornsby, Leyland, and every major shipbuilding company. For the effects of British 'stop-and-go' policies on some investment decisions, cf. *The Growth of the British Economy*, N.E.D.C., March 1964, para. 269; and with special reference to the chemical industry, cf. A. Shonfield, *Modern Capitalism*, p. 134, fn. 16.

To have borne them well does not, of course, mean that it could not have borne them still better. Its ability to compete in foreign markets and to export its produce abroad was higher than before the war and higher than that of many other industrialized nations; but it did not rise sufficiently fast to match the post-war liabilities and to remove altogether the threat of worse things to come.

The relative insufficiencies of the United Kingdom economy showed themselves in several ways. Its share of world exports was declining. In 1948 British exports of manufactured goods formed 29·3 per cent of the aggregate export of these goods by the eleven top industrial nations; this proportion fell to 20 per cent by 1954 and to 13·7 per cent by 1964. In 1964 the United Kingdom proportion of world exports of manufactured goods was still higher than that of any other European country with the sole exception of Germany; but it had been steadily contracting. On the morrow of the war it formed nearly 25 per cent of the world's export of manufactures, and it gradually came down to 15 per cent by 1962 and perhaps only 13 per cent by 1964.

Needless to say, judged by these figures Britain's performance on the world markets appears much worse than it was. We have seen that the actual volume of British exports was growing fast, but in a world in which total foreign trade was expanding much faster still and in which the circle of countries capable of generating large exports of manufactures was ever widening, a decline in the share of old-established exporters, such as the United Kingdom, was to be expected. The British share had in fact begun to contract long before 1945: it had fallen from 32 per cent in 1899 to 22 per cent in 1937. After the war the share of the U.S.A. also fell from 27 per cent in 1951 to 20 per cent in 1962: and that in spite of the powerful stimuli for exports provided by the American foreign aid. The only European nation whose share of exports outstripped that of the United Kingdom and was growing all the time was Germany. That country's proportion of manufactured exports was only half Britain's in 1950, but caught up with it by 1957 and overtook it in the early sixties. By 1962 it had come up to 20 per cent of the world total and stood 5 per cent above the British share. Nevertheless, even this high rate of growth did little more than bring the German share

F

of the world trade to about the level which it had reached in 1937.[1]

Excessive disparagement of Britain's trading performance commonly goes together with wrong assignments of blame. If the British share of the world trade in manufactures declined, this was not solely or even mainly because Britain's costs of production were getting so high as to price her out of the world markets. Throughout the greater part of the period United Kingdom prices of manufactured goods did not move out of step with international prices. Otherwise how could Britain have continued to sell such a high proportion of her output as she did? Most of the time British wholesale prices were apparently lower than the German ones. By the end of the fifties British prices for many manufactured goods may have caught up with the German ones and in some cases even have exceeded them; but in so far as our imperfect data enables us to judge, German labour costs and export prices in general as well as domestic prices for capital goods were rising in the late fifties and the early sixties faster than the British ones. If the growth of British exports at that time was more laggard than the growth of German or for that matter also Japanese or Italian exports, the blame attaches as much to failures of design or to weak salesmanship or to delays in deliveries as to uncompetitive prices.[2]

The same argument also applies to the inclination to blame the

---

[1] 'Trends of United Kingdom and World Exports of Manufactures in 1964', *Board of Trade Journal*, 189, 3 December, 1965; *National Institute Economic Review*, 1963, No. 23, Table 23, and 1964, No. 29, Table 23; S. J. Wells, *British Export Performance, A Comparative Study*, Cambridge, 1964, *passim*, and pp. 14 *seq.*; H. D. Willey, as in Appendix Note 1, p. 362 below. Ch. V; H. Tyczynski, 'World Trade in Manufactured Commodities, 1899–1950', *Manchester School*, *XIX*, 1951, pp. 272 *seq.*

[2] M. Gilbert and others, *Comparative National Products and Price Levels, A Study of Western Europe and the United States*, O.E.C.D., Paris, 1958; J. Knapp and K. Lomax, 'Britain's Growth Performance: The Enigma of the 1950's', *Lloyds Bank Review*, 74, October 1964, pp. 20 *seq.*; H. D. Willey, as in footnote 1 above, pp. 145 and 169 *seq.*, and Tables 31 and 32; H. B. Junz and R. R. Rhomberg, 'Prices and Export Performances of Industrial Countries, 1953–1963', as quoted by H. D. Willey, *loc. cit.* Between 1951 and 1962 hourly wages rose at the annual rate of 6·6 per cent in the United Kingdom and 8·9 per cent in Germany. Labour costs per unit of output over the period as a whole rose somewhat more slowly in Germany than in the United Kingdom, but the rise in German wage rates accelerated between 1959 and 1963, and in the end German labour costs per unit of output rose at nearly twice the British rate. H. D. Willey, as above, pp. 145 and 169 *seq.*, and Table 32.

declining competitiveness of British products on the domestic market for the tendency of manufactured imports to soar with every upturn of domestic demand. This blame may also have perhaps been pitched too high. What, in the eyes of some commentators, was the worst British failing was the large and rising proportions of total imports represented by manufactured and semi-manufactured goods, most of which, in the opinion of a 1965 report of the Department of Economic Affairs, could have been produced at home. These proportions, however, do not necessarily justify the moral that, taken as a whole, products of British manufacture failed to compete with the products of other countries; and they certainly do not provide a true measure of this failing. Contrary to prevailing notions British imports of manufactured goods throughout our period – in its second half no less than in its first half – formed a smaller proportion of total imports than in any other industrial country. This proportion grew, but no higher and no faster than in other industrial countries. As we shall see again later, the share of manufactured goods in world imports rose steeply between 1954 and 1964; and this is commonly and rightly regarded as a benign symptom of higher prosperity, more rapid industrialization and freer trade in the post-war period.[1]

How closely did the British record in this respect agree with that of other comparable countries and how low imports of manufactures nevertheless were, will be seen from the table below.

Table 8 *Imports of Manufactured Goods as Percentage of Total Imports*

	U.K.	Germany	France	Italy	Sweden	U.S.A.
1957	16·1	20·6	22·4	23·5	48·5	27·8
1963	27·7	38·3	43·3	44·0	62·7	40·7

In the special case of machinery and engineering products, popular lamentations fail to take account of certain special circumstances. The twofold rise in the imports of machinery and engineering components between 1963 and 1964 did not signify that in

[1] Cf. above, pp. 94–5, and p. 94, footnote 3.

these two years the quality and cost of British engineering production fell back that much or at all. Whereas some engineering products were imported because their price was lower or their design more appropriate (and how would British manufactured exports or world trade in general have fared if products of some countries had not been cheaper or better than corresponding products of other countries), their increased importation in these years of boom was to some extent the result of the preceding recessions. In times of boom several branches of the engineering and metallurgical industry proved unable (as they were also to prove unable in Germany in 1964) to meet the rapidly expanded domestic demand, especially the industrial demand for components and sub-assemblies. And this inability was as often as not a by-product of previous slumps with their damped-down expectations and reduced investments.[1]

However, these and other comforting arguments should not be taken to mean that all was well with British trade and British economy. In general, it remains true that the United Kingdom's trade reflected the comparatively laggard record of British post-war economy as a whole: its slower rate of growth, its smaller increases in investment and productivity. In all these respects the failure was also purely relative: relative not to British achievements in the past but to the achievements of some other countries or to political and financial commitment abroad or to rising expectations of good life at home. Moreover, the failure was to some extent due to the government-made, even if inescapable, fluctuations and to the consequent lack of business confidence and the instability and insufficiency of investment. But some residuary blame must also attach to the manner in which the domestic economy conducted itself during the period.

Obviously, something was wrong, and what it was may not be easy to identify. But before we try to do so we must take care not to assume that everything was wrong, or to put it in other words, that

---

[1] Cf. above, p. 74, footnote 3. For pent-up shortages of components in German engineering industries and their endeavours to import them from the United Kingdom, see *The Times*, 8 July 1966.

the fault lay with the economy in the aggregate, with the general direction in which it moved or the stage of historical development in which it found itself. Elsewhere in this study I have mentioned some of the uses and abuses of the summary formulae employed by historians to classify national economies. The particular abuse we must guard ourselves against in discussing the United Kingdom's post-war economy is that of assuming that its shortcomings were deduceable from the position historians have assigned to it in their tables of relative maturities.

The concept of 'maturity' is not, of course, always or wholly irrelevant, but its relevance depends on the sense in which it is employed. Used in the humdrum sense of 'old age' the concept very pertinently draws attention to certain antiquated, and to that extent inhibiting, elements in the economy. Thus in dealing with capital and investment I hope to be able to demonstrate how, because of its early start, British economy found itself saddled with much under-employed capital in older industries. Presently I shall also try to show how traditional patterns of managerial behaviour and in-herited attitudes of organized labour may have slowed down the march of innovation. What I may not have another occasion for pointing out is that the 'older' economies – and that of the United Kingdom more than others – could boast of some compensating advantages: abundant flow of savings, accumulated stocks of in-dustrial skills, dense network of public utilities (or, to put it in more technical terms, large overhead social capital), large conglomera-tions of enterprises capable of supplying major industries with sub-contractors, to say nothing of well-functioning machineries of government.

These advantages and disadvantages of 'old age' may be difficult to balance, but taken individually they are very pertinent and can be usefully discussed. The concepts of 'old age' or maturity are, how-ever, much less relevant in the more precise and technical sense in which they have recently been used by some economists. They are least relevant when used to designate the condition of fully in-dustrialized economies in which primary occupations, and in the first place agriculture, no longer harbour any sizeable reservoir of manpower. For it is difficult to see any theoretical reasons or find any empirical evidence why 'maturity' should have slowed down the economic growth of the United Kingdom compared to other European countries.

To begin with, there are no theoretical reasons why the growth potential of an economy should be judged solely by the size of its reservoir of transferable labour and not by its ability to substitute labour with capital or to improve its performance by innovation or greater efficiency. But even if it were so judged, there would still be no valid theoretical reason why increases in national product and productivity should have depended on the continued ability of industry to draw on the manpower of agriculture and not on the ability of the more productive industries to draw upon the manpower of the less productive ones. If so, how could an economy, like the British, with its large supplies of capital and its easy access to new technologies, be said to suffer from over-all shortage of man-power, as distinct from short-term and local shortages of skilled labour or from high wages ? There may, in fact, be a good theoretical reason for arguing that, if after the war the United Kingdom harbour-ed a large component of old industries with relatively low product-ivity per man and also suffered from over-manning, from a rela-tively (i.e. relative to the U.S.A.) low provision of capital per worker and from relatively sluggish progress of innovation, its potentialities for growth should have been all the higher for that. These very shortcomings should have provided possibilities for economic growth through higher investment, greater technological progress and freer transfers of labour.

So much for theory. But empirical, i.e. historical, evidence for imputing Britain's post-war problems to her 'maturity' is equally doubtful. If increasing maturity could account for the ability of an economy to grow, why should the United Kingdom's growth after 1945 – slow as it was – have been so much faster than at the turn of the century when the economy was more than half a century younger, and had a considerably larger proportion of its population in primary occupations? And why should Germany, whose relative size of industrial employment in the late fifties and sixties was about equal to Britain's, have grown so much faster? And why should Belgium's growth have been so sluggish in the fifties and so rapid in the sixties? In fact, why should post-war Europe as a whole, with its much reduced agricultural sector and enlarged industrial sector, have grown so much more robustly than it had done in its less mature nineteenth-century past?

Obviously, the United Kingdom's 'maturity' will not account for the shortfall of British economic record after the war. The shortfall was very small, but such as there was can be more usefully related to individual features of British economy, and above all to certain failings of its government, its workers, and its employers.

The part government policies played in retarding the growth of the economy has already been mentioned. Restrictions on consumption and output in the successive 'stop' phases were dictated by the need to defend Sterling and were to that extent inescapable consequences of Sterling's role as an international currency. But whether inescapable or not, the measures not only kept the output well below the level it would have otherwise attained but also discouraged long-term investment in the private sector. For assurance of continued and uninterrupted expansion was essential for high and continued investment by private firms.[1]

The failings of labour are well known, or at least have been well publicized. It was not perhaps solely the fault of organized labour that workers did not readily move from backward or over-manned sectors of the economy to the growing ones, and that the economy suffered from every apparent symptom of grave labour shortages at a time when large potential reserves of labour continued to be locked up in coal-mining, railways, steel, or aircraft production. For this labour-hoarding the economic policy and the behaviour of employers were partly to blame. But the most obvious defects in the utilization of labour were clearly due to the attitude of the workers or their unions. Memories of unemployment and fears of redundancy often led the unions to insist on the over-manning of production lines and prevented firms from reaping the full advantages of new labour-saving equipment. The survival and the multiplicity of craft unions and the strength of traditional customs tended to protect antiquated labour practices, inhibited recruitment and promotion into skilled grades, favoured demarcation disputes, and

[1] Cf. above, p. 78, footnote 1.

made it difficult to deploy labour with maximum efficiency. In industries in which piece-rates prevailed, the egalitarian bias of British trade-union traditions could sometimes hold back the output of abler and better workers. Moreover, in most industries the basic rates got overladen with bonuses, incentive awards, and payments for overtime which frequently had the effect opposite to the one intended and acted as brakes on productivity. For so important had overtime and bonuses become as a source of earnings, that workers could often be suspected of reducing the output on basic shifts or at basic rates so as to make sure of overtime and bonuses. And in nearly all industries demands for a shorter week built up simply because under full employment a shorter basic week automatically raised the hours of overtime.

Compared to these disabilities, the actual strikes and demands for higher wages were relatively less important. It is generally and rightly assumed that the *ethos* of the British trade-union movement and the internal politics of individual unions made it difficult for them to agree on a wage policy capable of maintaining a proper relation between wage rates on the one hand and the productivity of labour on the other. But it is doubtful whether costs would have remained stable or grown much more slowly even had the unions been won over to a rational system of fixing wage rates. Much of the post-war rise in wages in all European countries came not through higher rates agreed with unions but through 'wage drift', i.e. payments over and above the standard rates. And wage drift, where it occurred, owed more to the prevailing economic conditions than to unreasonable demands of Trade Unions. Full employment created wage drifts even in countries like Sweden or the Netherlands where the Unions were as reasonable as Unions could be.

In actual fact labour costs per unit of output rose more slowly in the United Kingdom than in most countries, including Germany, especially in the late fifties and sixties. The specific British weakness revealed itself not so much in rising labour costs as in the inability of industries to compensate for them by higher productivity. The gap was not equally wide in all industries, but it may have made some British products – certain types of ships, certain engineering exports, and a wide range of consumer durables – somewhat costlier than comparable products of German, Italian, or Swedish industries. To this extent British entrepreneurs must take much of the blame. In general, the managers of progressive firms in newer industries showed up better than the leaders of some other firms in older industries; but in the latter the inadequacies were sufficiently great to earn a bad name for the British entrepreneurship as a whole. It revealed itself in certain weaknesses of salesmanship abroad, about which so much has been heard; in inadequacies of design, but above all, in the failure to invest and to innovate on the same scale and with the same success as in comparable firms abroad. More about these failures will be said later.

Britain's payments difficulties have been treated here at some length since she was the first and the worst sufferer from the complaint. But few of the other European countries were free from inflation; and towards the end of our period it cast its shadow over almost every country in Europe. Next to Britain, France was perhaps the country most exposed to the penalties of overexpanded demand. The price inflation from which the French economy suffered was, if anything, greater than in any other European country. It was the product of disordered state finance and currency and of inflationary government spending which had reached its climax between 1956 and 1958. It was forced upon the successive governments by the rising cost of social services, by the political difficulties of resisting wage demands in public services and nationalized industries and by the vast expansion of investment, both private and public, in the mid-fifties. And it was much aggravated by military expenditure, for no sooner were the costly operations in Indo-China over than the war in Algeria began.

While the inflationary situation lasted, the balance-of-payments difficulties were grave and continuous. They at one time all but wiped out the reserves; and in spite of massive American aid (some $6·5 billion), they left France with a very large foreign debt. Some attempts, temporarily successful, to stop the rot were made in 1952, but it was not until 1958 that the Pinay–de Gaulle measures (these had been mapped out before de Gaulle had come to power) brought in a radical financial reform designed to halt the piling up of excessive demand and the march of inflation. The tax system and, above all, its collection were made more efficient; the price rise, though not altogether halted, was for a time slowed down, and so were the other overt signs of inflation, such as uncontrollable rises in wages. The devaluation of the franc in that year – following a previous devaluation in 1957 – also prevented the balance of payments difficulties from getting worse. Towards the middle of 1962, however, prices and wages again began to show signs of stress, and by the middle of 1963, inflation again became serious enough to threaten anew the French policy of growth and to compel the Government to take some disinflationary measures and thereby to curb somewhat the prospects of further growth.

That in spite of various anti-inflationary measures the economy continued to expand, and that it in fact reached its apex in 1960 and the following two years, was due partly to the inefficiency of some of the deflationary measures, partly to a certain organic potency of the French post-war economy and partly to fortunate circumstances. The French economy always possessed large un-tapped reserves of productive capacity; the flow of labour from agriculture – at the rate of c. 90,000 per annum – and an even greater flow of immigrant labour from abroad and from Algeria prevented the appearance of labour shortages. If imports increased, as they did markedly in the sixties, this was due as much to lower tariffs (especially on imports from other countries in the Common Market) as to inflation. Nevertheless, the reserves of gold and foreign currency continued to accumulate throughout the late fifties and early sixties. Her greater self-sufficiency in foodstuffs and increasing exports of agricultural produce in the sixties coupled with the discovery of oil and gas within her territory, helped to prevent the negative trade balances from getting out of hand. But some of her manufacturing industries also exported more than in previous years. This, as well as the general buoyancy of the economy, some economists ascribe to two successive devaluations of the franc. The French financial authorities claim most of the credit for themselves; above all, for the vigour with which they applied anti-inflationary policies, restrictions of credit, wage freeze and price controls in the inflationary bouts of 1958 and 1963. Other commentators assign the main credit to the successful working of the plans, especially to the part which the plans played in rational allocation and utilization of investments.[1]

Until 1963 Germany was even more successful than France in avoiding most of the penalties of over-full demand and in maintaining her high rate of growth almost unhampered by excessive inflation. Price rises there were, but for a long time they were smaller than in most other countries; and other signs of inflation were also less conspicuous. American help in the initial phases of German expansion did much to relieve the potential inflationary pressure of her early investment programme. Until 1961 labour supplies were eased by a flow of labour from agriculture (it rose from about 100,000 per annum in the 1950s to over 200,000 in 1960 and 1961), by heavy immigration from across the Iron Curtain and, after 1961, by wholesale importation of foreign labour.

Germany also derived some economic advantages from having been defeated in the war. For many years her military expenditure remained low, her disbursements abroad on troops or on defence of overseas possessions were, to begin with, nil, and later grew very slowly; and when they rose in the late fifties they nevertheless remained lower than those of England or France. Her payments towards the cost of upkeep of the allied armies of occupation at no time equalled the economic burdens of armies and military obligations abroad borne by the United Kingdom, France, or even Belgium and the Netherlands; and, such as they were, they did not entail heavy disbursements abroad. For a number of years Germany also carried a much lighter load of contribution to underdeveloped countries. Her economy also benefited from the ever-green – or rather ever-blue – memories of pre-war inflation and the consequent readiness of organized labour (at least before 1963) to hold back their wage demands sufficiently to prevent too great an inflation of costs. Her managerial cadres also appeared to act under an

[1] O.E.C.D., *Economic Surveys of France for 1961 and 1962*, Paris, 1962 and 1963; R. Aron, *France Steadfast and Changing*, 1960, 64–8. Deficits built up again in payment accounts after 1965.

inner compulsion to work hard and well. In addition, before 1963 investment rate was so high and capacity was utilized so fully that productivity kept pace with wages better than, say, in the United Kingdom. For all these reasons German export industries became and stayed highly competitive, and exports were sufficiently high to remove all danger of payments difficulties.

If considerations of international payments entered at all into the making of Germany's economic policy, they did so in a way contrary to that of England or France. Before 1964 deficits on the payments account were incurred on at least three occasions, but on the whole the deficits were relatively small. The performances of German export industries were so successful that in the course of the fifties Germany was able to build up favourable balances of payments: over $7 billion between 1948 and 1962. In the end they had grown so high as to threaten the functioning of the international financial system. To remedy the situation, Germany (together with the Netherlands which at that time found itself in a similar position) revalued her currency downwards (i.e. raised its value in terms of other currencies) in March 1961, thus making her exports somewhat dearer to foreigners and her imports from abroad correspondingly cheaper to themselves. Partly as a result of this revaluation and partly as a result of gathering inflation, deficits appeared in the German payment accounts in 1961 and 1962. By the end of 1963 a recovery of exports and high imports of capital from abroad restored the favourable balance of payments, though for a while another deficit showed signs of building up towards the end of 1964.

In general, however, in spite of the remarkable buoyancy of her export industries and of her payments balances, Germany's economy did not advance in the sixties quite as miraculously as before 1961. The annual rate of increase of G.N.P. slowed down from 9·5 between 1950 and 1955, to 6·3 between 1955 and 1960, and to about 4·5 between 1961 and 1964. Productivity, i.e. output per person employed, increased at 6·5 per cent per annum in the early fifties, but only by 3·6 per cent in the sixties. Additions to her fixed capital ('gross fixed asset formation') gradually fell from their exceptionally high level of 11·5 per cent in 1960 to 1·7 per cent in 1963, though they recovered again in 1964. In general, inflationary pressures had become strong enough to lift appreciably the costs of production. Labour costs per unit of gross domestic output went up by 4 per cent in 1960, 6 per cent in 1961, and by a still higher margin after 1963. Profit margins declined accordingly and stood lower in 1964 than in the late fifties. And although most of the economic omens were somewhat more favourable in 1965 than in the preceding two years, the inflationary pressures persisted, and the economy had not yet recovered, or seemed likely to recover, the full forward impetus of the 1950s. As we have seen, but for a steep rise in the import of foreign capital, unfavourable balances of payments may have spilled into 1963 – as they were to do towards the end of 1964.[1]

France apart, other European countries did not share either the German or the British experiences in full. The Belgian record before 1963 came nearest to that of the United Kingdom. Of the various belligerent or occupied countries on the Continent, Belgium was the first to carry out a drastic revaluation. The Gutt reforms of 1945–6, which by a single stroke wiped out the wartime accumulation of devalued currency, succeeded not only in stabilizing prices but also in holding back for a couple of years the forces of expansion. But although thereafter Belgian economic growth continued to be held back, her price level remained relatively stationary and her balance of payments relatively healthy, mainly because her miscellaneous exports and receipts of invisible payments were sufficient to pay for her high and rising imports. In the early sixties both output and prices rose, but by 1965 the output showed signs of slipping back, while prices continued to rise. In Switzerland, the heavy inflow of foreign capital neutralized the ill-effects of inflationary tendencies, such as very high imports or investment in excess of domestic savings. In Sweden, rising prices and effects of overfull demand were kept down not only by high exports and by a system of national wage settlement but also by the steady rising productivity in some of her 'key' industries. For a time the same effect was achieved in the Netherlands by a national incomes policy which

[1] O.E.C.D., *Economic Survey of Germany for 1961, 1962, 1963, and 1964*, Paris, 1962, 1963, 1964, and 1965.

linked earnings to the national productivity and kept labour costs low. But even there, by 1962, wage-drift, higher level of agreed wages and a shortening of hours overwhelmed the anti-inflationary defences. In Italy the large surpluses of agricultural labour and a great expansion of exports between 1955 and 1962 also held the worst dangers of inflation at bay. But by 1963 the inflationary forces had gathered speed, wages had broken through the anti-inflationary barriers, prices had risen to dangerous heights and payments difficulties loomed black on the horizon. If towards the end of 1964 the country appeared to be successfully emerging from her inflationary tribulations, the success was still uncertain and possibly impermanent.[1]

It is indeed possible that this will also be the historian's verdict on other countries of Western Europe and that he will have to treat the later sixties and the seventies as a time when Europe as a whole found it impossible to hold domestic demand in check and was confronted with the choice, hitherto purely English: the choice between economic growth and uncontrolled inflation.

So much for the penalties of high demand and full employment. These penalties must not, however, allow us to lose sight of the benign effects: their propellent power in economic growth, to say nothing of the difference they made to the well-being of millions who had suffered from unemployment in the past and might have been suffering from it now.

The propellent power of full employment policies proved so great not merely because full employment meant high employment but also because it meant demand and employment uninterrupted by crises and bouts of economic depression. Freedom from business crises and depressions instilled into European economies the confidence without which few of the firms would have been prepared to plan for expansion and undertake heavy commitments for the future. The psychological reactions, being psychological, have left behind them very little tangible, quantifiable historical evidence. But in general they were well borne out by contrasts with the course

---

[1] The evidence for countries other than France and Germany has also been mainly derived from the consecutive annual economic surveys of O.E.C.D.

of American and English business in the fifties and above all by the dampening effect of stop-and-go *à l'anglaise* on business undertakings most exposed to fluctuations.

Other post-war developments may also have contributed to this entrepreneurial euphoria and thereby assisted the economic expansion. One of them was the flourishing condition in international trade; the other, the success with which the difficulties of international payments were gradually reduced and in some fields wholly eliminated. These benign changes in the international setting will form the subject of the next section.

CHAPTER 4

Trade

How much the foreign trade of European nations grew during the period is shown by the tables below.

Table 9 *European Exports*[1]

	Values: £1,000 million Index (*1958 = 100*)	
1948	16·24	40
1953	26·67	70
1956	35·93	92
1959	42·14	111
1962	54·22	138

Countries as in Table 10 below.

The figures make it clear that the trade grew very fast; what they do not at first sight reveal is that not only the actual quantities (values and volume) of exports and imports grew, but that they represented an ever-growing proportion both of the national products and of the foreign trade of the world as a whole. In general, the foreign trade of European nations after the war grew faster than their G.N.P. Between 1948 and 1962 exports and imports of European countries grew at the annual average rate of about 7 per cent, whereas the Gross National Products grew at the annual average rate of about 4 per cent.

It goes without saying that an increase so high must have exceeded the pace at which foreign trade had grown in the past. Between the wars it had grown hardly at all. The most favourable estimates put the rate of growth during that period at barely above

[1] UNO, *Economic Bulletin for Europe*, vol. 15, no. 1, 1963; also UNO, *Statistical Yearbook, 1963.*

zero; in all probability foreign trade may have slightly declined. What is, however, much more significant is that in the golden age of European economic history, from 1870 to 1913, the foreign trade of the leading continental nations had grown more slowly than it was to grow after 1946. The contrast is even more striking in the case of countries which were to lead in the post-war expansion of exports.

Table 10 *European Exports 1948–1962* [1]

Average Annual Percentage of Increase	
Austria	—
Belgium	7·0
Denmark	6·0
France	7·6
Germany	16·2
Italy	12·1
Netherlands	10·2
Norway	12·0
Sweden	6·0
Switzerland	8·2
United Kingdom	1·8

Of all the European countries the United Kingdom alone failed to expand its exports after the war at a rate faster than before 1914. Yet even British exports rose since 1948 more steeply than between the wars.

Table 11 *Exports: Annual Rates of Growth (per cent)* [2]

	Germany	Italy	Netherlands	United Kingdom
1890–1913	5·1	—	4·6	2·1
1913–48	2·8	1·4 (1913–50)	1·0	0·2
1948–60	16·2	11·8 (1951–60)	10·2	1·8

Moreover, European trade expanded faster than that of the world as a whole. The index of exports of European countries by volume (with those of 1958 as 100) rose from 40 in 1948 to 138 in 1962, or

[1] UNO, *Economic Bulletin for Europe*, vol. 15, no. 1, 1963; also UNO, *Statistical Yearbook, 1963*.　　　　　　　　　　　　[2] *Ibid.*

G

by some 275 per cent, whereas the volume of exports in the world as a whole rose from 57 in 1948 to 131 in 1962 or by some 230 per cent.[1] Measured by value world exports in the same period rose from $57,500 million to $149,000 million or by some 150 per cent, whereas the value of European exports rose from some $16,500 million to $54,200 million or by some 200 per cent.

This faster-than-ever advance in international trade and the higher-than-average proportions of national incomes drawn into it belie a number of earlier prophecies. If historical development had followed the course mapped out for it by the most widely held theory of international trade, that of Heckscher-Ohlin, the share of national products entering international trade should have been declining. That theory assumes that what compelled and enabled nations and regions to exchange their produce was their unequal endowment in factors of production. As some countries abounded in land or labour while others abounded in capital and entrepreneurial personnel, each country tended to specialize in commodities best suited to its own particular combination of factors. In the course of economic development, however, labour and capital moved across frontiers, so that national and regional differences in factor endowment tended to level out; and, as a result, the proportions of national outputs entering international trade tended to decline even if their absolute volume remained high or rose with increasing national product.

We know now that the economic development of Western Europe after the war did not follow this course. The figures we have quoted here are sufficient to show that the foreign trade of European nations grew very much faster than their G.N.P. This propensity of post-war trade to grow at a rate outstripping that of national products can be put down to a number of causes. Some economists have plausibly argued that after the war foreign trade grew so fast because it was making up for the 'unnaturally' low levels to which it had been reduced before the war by quotas, tariffs, and payment difficulties. To this extent its post-war growth was due to liberaliza-

---

[1] *Ibid.* For the rate of increase of exports in Sweden, Belgium and Switzerland in the sixties, cf. O.E.C.D. annual economic surveys for these countries in 1962, 1963, and 1964.

tion of trade and payments about which more will be said later. Other economists have argued that increased trade was a by-product of economic growth itself, and more especially of the underlying increases in the scale of output. These arguments are all highly plausible and will be brought up again later. But, whatever its explanation, the fact remains that the behaviour of foreign trade in our period did not strictly follow the path mapped out for it in the Heckscher-Ohlin theory.

Another widely shared anticipation was that European trade would suffer from worsening terms of trade, i.e. from unfavourable changes in the relative prices of manufactured goods Europe exported and of primary products it imported. These anticipations sprang, however, from two sets of contrary assumptions giving rise to two wholly disparate fears. The earlier and the more widely shared fear had been given its best-known expression by Keynes in the twenties and thirties. Keynes prophesied that the progressive industrialization of countries exporting primary products would make those products relatively scarce and dear and manufactured goods relatively more abundant and cheap. Europe's imports would therefore cost more in terms of goods it could offer in exchange; it would either have to part with a larger share of its output to procure the same volume of imports and its real incomes would suffer; or else it would have to reduce its imports, and its trade would either decline or fail to grow as fast as it might otherwise have done. Soon after the war this prophecy was reasserted by the newly set up European Economic Commission. In some of its earliest reports surveying the economic prospects of post-war Europe, it, by implication, revived Keynes' prophecy and brought it forward.[1]

In the event, the terms moved quite differently. Except for the interval of the Korean War prices of primary products remained low relative to those of manufactured goods, and showed little sign of rising. The terms of trade of O.E.C.D. countries taken together, i.e. the index of their exports divided by the index of their imports (with that of 1953 as 100), rose from 97 in 1950 to 109 in

[1] *A Survey of the Economic Situation and Prospects of Europe,* U.N.O., E.C.E., Geneva, 1948, pp. XIII seq., and 38 seq.; *Economic Survey of Europe in 1949,* E.C.E., Geneva, 1950, pp. 91 seq.

1963. The terms of trade of the United Kingdom rose from 88 in 1951 to 116 in 1963. Between 1955 and 1965 the terms of trade of developing countries – all of them exporters of primary produce – deteriorated by about 16 per cent; and the terms of trade of industrialized countries improved accordingly.[1]

No sooner, however, did this trend reveal itself than it gave rise to a wholly contrary, but equally pessimistic, anticipation. Writing in the fifties some economists predicted that, should the terms of trade continue to move against primary producers, the latters' ability to buy manufactured imports would decline and the trade of industrialized countries would accordingly suffer.[2] This fear was also to prove groundless. At the time when it was first voiced economists could not perhaps foresee that foreign aid would to some extent relieve the lowering effect of terms of trade on the ability of primary producers to import. Even more difficult to foresee were the post-war changes in the roles of different foreign markets. Considered as customers for manufactured imports, countries exporting primary products were ceasing to be as important as of old. It was not that they were less willing to buy, less able to pay, or in fact imported less than hitherto, but that Western countries themselves were now absorbing an ever-increasing share of the world's trade in manufactures. In the fifties and sixties the ability of Western countries to take in each others' outputs rose very steeply, with the result that most of them had come to depend more and more on the markets within Europe itself and in the U.S.A. Between 1950 and 1963 the value of exports of Western European countries (O.E.C.D. Europe) to each other increased more than threefold (from the monthly average of $1,587 million to that of $4,976 million), whereas the exports to non-O.E.C.D. countries in the same period increased little more than twice (from $694 million to $1,466 million), and the total world exports increased only by 80 per cent.[3]

---

[1] UNO *Monthly Bulletin of Statistics*, November 1966.

[2] Some such anticipation is also implied in one of the two hypotheses explored by Professor Arthur Lewis in his 'World Production Prices and Trade, 1870–1960', *The Manchester School*, vol. XX, 1952, p. 105: that of relatively slower growth in the prices of food and raw materials and slower expansion in their trade. The argument is based on a number of assumptions not borne out by later experience such as the assumption that the share of manufactures in world trade would be the same in 1960 as in 1950.

[3] O.E.C.D., *General Statistics*, July 1964, p. 54; Alfred Maizels, *Industrial*

No record of unrealized expectations would be complete without some mention of the assumed historical tendency of 'import substitution'. The underlying argument is a generalized variant of the earlier theories of worsening terms of trade. It was in the nature of industrial progress to reduce the 'import content' of national products. As investment, domestic markets and scales of output of individual countries grew, so the range of commodities they were capable of producing widened and their dependence on foreign supplies lessened. In this process of import substitution technological progress was supposed to play a powerful part. We are told that what in the past enabled nations like Britain to build up their exceptionally high proportion of national products going into exports was 'slow transmission of technology'. After the war, however, the transmission of technological ideas became both easier and quicker, so that the advanced nations could no longer count on the technological advantages Britain enjoyed in the nineteenth century.[1]

The effects of technological progress on international trade have already been mentioned and will be discussed again in greater detail elsewhere. Here it will suffice to record that after the war technological progress kindled new opportunities for foreign trade far greater than those it extinguished. One of the most striking economic effects of recent technological innovations was to confer on some innovating firms and countries competitive advantages capable of generating and sustaining for long periods new currents of trade. In fact, some of the most active branches of post-war exports would be found in 'novelties' created by recent industrial research and development. Moreover, technological progress not

---

Growth and World Trade, N.I.E.S.R., London, 1963, pp. 384–5, 395, 415–16; Hollis B. Chenery 'Patterns of Industrial Growth', *The American Economic Review*, September 1960. Generally speaking the exports of industrialized countries were both very much – about four times – higher in value that the exports of developing countries, and were rising much faster, and never faster than at the very end of our period: UNO, *Monthly Bulletin of Statistics*, November 1966.

[1] O.E.C.D., *ibid.*, pp. 38–43; E. A. G. Robinson in 'Re-thinking Foreign Trade Policy', *Three Banks Review*, 1963, no. 60, p. 21: 'In the nineteenth century with relatively slow transmission of technology we built up exceptionally high ratios of exports to national incomes. In the mid-twentieth century the differences of comparable advantage are becoming narrower and shorter lived . . .'.

only created new and ever-shifting patterns of competitive advantages and thereby created new opportunities for national and regional specialization, but also helped to diversify consumers' demand for manufactured commodities. It is, therefore, no wonder that the most active current of international trade should have been in manufactured commodities made in the advanced industrial countries: currents which flowed faster than corresponding outputs. We have seen that between 1950 and 1959 trade in manufactures in important industrialized nations, i.e. those of Western Europe and North America, grew at the annual rate of more than 9 per cent. But their output of manufactures rose only at the annual rate of 5 per cent.[1]

To sum up: such tendency for import substitution as there may have been was overshadowed by the contrary tendency of fully industrialized countries to absorb increasing proportions of the world's manufactured exports. This trend was part and parcel of something economists have of late come to regard as one of the characteristic disparities in the economic record of the post-war world. In the course of the post-war development the richer countries were not only becoming richer but were also expanding their trade more quickly. The exports of most underdeveloped countries were still largely made up of primary products and of a relatively small trickle of manufactured consumption goods. They were inevitably held back by the sluggish disposition of the world demand for foodstuffs and raw materials. On the other hand, manufactured exports of richer nations forged ahead in response to the ever-growing quality and variety of goods in national shopping baskets, and to the rapid march of technological progress.

These and other benign factors of economic growth and improving technology were sufficient to remove the threat of declining foreign trade. They might not, however, by themselves have brought about increases in that trade so much higher than the

---

[1] Above, pp. 91–2 and below, pp. 111–12. A. Maizels, *op. cit.*, pp. 415–16, arrives at the conclusion that the increase in imports of manufactures into industrialized countries, from 1·5 per cent to 4·4 per cent in 1959, was due to the extent of one-half to increased demand and one-half to the liberalization of trade.

underlying rate of economic growth itself. The most reasonable assumption, therefore, is that economic growth accounted for much, but could not account for the whole, of the post-war increases in European trade. Other factors, and, above all, more liberal commercial policies must also have made their contribution. How great the contribution was we may never know for certain. But it was sufficiently great to be worth describing and assessing in some detail.[1]

The progressive liberalization of international trade during our period appears all the more remarkable for its most unpromising prospects on the morrow of the peace. The commercial régime which Europe inherited from the past was anything but liberal. In the inter-war period, and more especially in its concluding decade, commercial policies of European nations were becoming more and more restrictive. Tariffs were going up everywhere. American tariff walls were raised to their highest ever level by the Hawley–Smoot tariff of 1924; French and German tariffs had been high since the last decades of the nineteenth century; the United Kingdom, the erstwhile bastion of free trade, formally went over to protection after the Conservative victory of 1924 and gradually became one of the most highly protectionist countries in the world.

It was not, however, the tariffs which interfered worst with the flow of international trade. One of the most enduring aftermaths of the First Great War and of the two great depressions of the inter-war period was the chronic shortage of international payment media, above all of dollars, and the disturbances in the international balances of payments. What with high and rising tariffs, the dollar shortages, and the additional strains imposed by the post-1935 rearmament programme, most European nations repeatedly found themselves unable to import freely and to pay for what they imported. A remedy was found in what is now euphemistically described as physical controls of international trade, i.e. in import quotas and attempts to balance trade by means of bilateral exchanges. It was in Germany in the thirties under Dr Schacht's financial management that the system with its various devices developed earliest and farthest, but by 1937 all European nations had adopted it more

---

[1] A succinct account of the liberalization of trade after the war will be found in A. Maddison, *Economic Growth in the West*.

or less in full. By that time 'physical controls' and not the spontaneous interplay of economic advantages ('comparative costs') had come to determine what and how much was to be imported and exported, where the imports were to come from, where the exports were to go, and how both imports and exports were to be paid for.

In the thirties this system may have made it possible to maintain a current of imports and exports which might otherwise have petered out altogether. But whether helpful or not, the system was inimical to the very essence of free international exchange. The return of peace in 1945 did nothing to encourage any hopes that free exchanges might be re-established soon, or at all. On the contrary, the pent-up demand for goods was so high and the European reserves of foreign currency, especially of dollars, so low, that governments were compelled to continue rationing their payments abroad and regulating their imports by rigid quotas. The fact that in 1947 the United Kingdom tried (as it turned out, prematurely) to restore some convertibility to its currency, and failed in the process, merely strengthened the case for continuing the régime of physical controls of imports and of international payments. The only development of these years which may have commended itself to the advocates of freer trade was the gradual consolidation of the sterling and franc areas. Thereby within two large groups of countries trade was enabled to circulate more freely, and national autarchies were prevented from establishing themselves.

For the earliest breaches in this system of quotas and quantitative restrictions American influence and pressures must take the main credit. The first determined assault on the European commercial régime came with the Marshall aid of 1947. Under the Marshall Plan the American Government provided finance for increased imports on the condition that bilateral agreements were removed. The Organization for European Economic Co-operation was then established, with rules and targets for the gradual freeing of international trade from quotas and similar discriminatory impediments.

From 1956 onwards these anti-discrimination policies within Europe were further reinforced by the Treaty of Rome of 1956 establishing the European Common Market and by the formation in 1959 of the parallel European Free Trade Association. More will be said about these two groupings presently; what is worth noting at this point is that opposition to quotas and to similar discriminating devices was the guiding principle of the treaties establishing the two groups and also came to govern the relations of the groups with each other.

This reaction to trade discrimination was not altogether an act of spontaneous or unaided conversion. But for the U.S.A. it might have come much later and more slowly, if at all. It was made possible by American behaviour which – given the political and economic objectives of American post-war policy – must be recognized as long-sighted and forbearing. Until 1956 the lifting of inter-European barriers was not accompanied by a corresponding freeing of American imports into Europe. As long as the dollar shortage persisted, European countries continued to discriminate against certain non-European territories and especially against the U.S.A. Yet so strong was the American concern in the economic strength of Europe, that while they encouraged the European movement of liberalization they were prepared to tolerate the continued restrictions against themselves. Under the cover of this policy, more or less liberal within its own borders, but discriminating against the rest of the world, Europe accumulated reserves of gold and foreign currency which were to enable it to proceed to the second stage of liberalization.

That second stage came after 1956. Between 1956 and 1962 European countries gradually eliminated their quantitative discrimination against dollar imports. In general, by 1962, quotas and other quantitative restrictions were lifted from all commodities whatever their country of origin, except from agricultural produce, oil and coal, and cheap textiles from the East. In 1957–8, while in the throes of her last payments crisis, France imposed some quantitative restrictions on foreign trade, but these restrictions were soon removed and until 1963 were not to be imposed again.

Trade was not made thereby wholly free, for tariffs still remained; but the general tendency was for tariff barriers also to be reduced and in some instances to be removed altogether. Within Europe itself the reduction of tariffs was so closely linked up with the history of the Common Market and with the reactions of other European countries to the Common Market policies, that it behoves us to inspect somewhat more closely the history of the Common Market and its working.[1]

The Common Market, or to give it its official name, the European Economic Community, owed its birth and its progress to the same combination of sentiments and pressures which underlie much of European economic policy and achievement since the war. The war and German occupation left behind it a sense of common destinies and also a yearning after a larger European entity. The inspiration came not only from the reaction against the menace of Stalin's Russia but also from the wish to match the overwhelming influence of the U.S.A. The inspiration was thus by no means wholly economic; but economic unification held out better hopes of early success than political unification. Economic links between European countries, both regional and functional, were accordingly the first to be forged. Projects for the economic co-ordination of Scandinavian countries had been in the air since the economic crisis of the nineteen-thirties, but it was the economic integration of the Low Countries – Belgium, the Netherlands, and Luxembourg – that matured first and led to the formation of Benelux. And no sooner was Benelux formed than it was drawn into the wider meshes which were at the same time being spun across its southern and eastern frontiers.

The conspicuous initiative in this web-spinning operation belongs to a group of French statesmen. Jean Monnet devoted himself from the earliest days of peace to the twofold object of French economic reconstruction and the unification of Europe. The part which his efforts and ideas for reconstruction of France (the Monnet Plan) played in French economic policy has already been described. Similarly, his activities on behalf of European integration contributed much to the process by which, through a number of successive steps, the European Economic Community came into being. Some of the steps are associated with the name of another French statesman, Robert Schumann, the spokesman of a group who soon after the end of the war set out to put an end to the Franco-German fissure

[1] M. Camps, *Britain and the European Community, 1955–1963*, Princeton, 1964; U. W. Kitzinger, *The Politics and Economics of European Integration*, new edn, N.Y., 1963; R. Mayne, 'Economic Integration in new Europe', *Daedalus*, 1964.

and to establish permanent economic links preliminary to the formal unification of European economic policies.

The easiest to commence with, and consequently the first to be achieved was the integration of the heavy industries: iron, steel, and coal. These industries had even before the war been linked by commercial agreements and ties of co-ownership across the frontiers dividing France, Germany, and Belgium. The European Coal, Iron and Steel Community establishing a common market in these products and a common programme of expansion took shape in the mid-fifties. It provided itself with an elaborate and deliberately high-sounding supranational machinery – the executive body of the High Authority, the supervisory bodies of the Council of Ministers, the Common Assembly and the Court of Justice.

By that time, however, preparations for a much more comprehensive combination were under way. At a meeting of representatives of a number of European countries in Messina in May 1955 it was agreed to form the European Economic Community. The documents establishing the Community and defining its constitution and programme were ready within a year and a half of the Messina meeting; and in March 1957 the Treaty of Rome was ready for signature.

The Treaty of Rome established a customs union, i.e. a combination of countries (Germany, France, Italy, the Netherlands, Belgium, and Luxembourg) pledged to reduce and eventually (i.e. by the end of 1969) to abolish altogether all tariffs on their mutual trade. In addition, the treaty laid down rules and principles to safeguard trade from discriminatory policies, to ensure free competition in the mutual trade between member countries, to prevent the recurrence of disequilibria in the balances of payments, to work out a common transport policy, to prescribe uniform principles for municipal policy and for social benefits, to set up a common investment bank and to provide for the association of overseas territories – mostly ex-colonies of contracting powers.

In the subsequent six years the Economic Community, directed from Brussels by a very able and devoted *congerie* of officials, progressed fast and far. By July 1963, in accordance with the treaty, quantitative restrictions of trade between member countries had been abolished, and customs had been cut to 60 per cent below their 1957 level. In two successive steps, that of December 1960 and that of July 1963, the external tariffs, i.e. those on trade with countries outside the community, were lowered and then brought much closer to their eventual merging into a common external tariff.[1]

Slower, yet by no means inconsiderable, progress had also been achieved in freeing the movements of capital and labour. Movement of funds for direct investment within the Community were set almost wholly free; the movement of labour was made easier by arrangements for minimizing losses of social benefits resulting from migration. The Investment Bank on its part had by 1963 provided loans in excess of $230 million and is claimed to have thereby made possible new investment totalling $1,200 million. Some agreement had by that time also been reached about trade in a number of agricultural commodities, though, as we shall see further, in this field a common policy proved more difficult to achieve.

By these means six countries representing about two-thirds of Western Europe's resources formed a single trading area, within which the movement of goods and of factors of production was wholly free from restrictions, and tariffs were reduced sufficiently to stimulate the flow of trade. By the end of 1963 the final abolition of all internal tariffs in the Community was well within sight. With regard to the rest of Europe, however, the liberal intentions of the E.E.C. were more uncertain and certainly more hesitant. The underlying philosophy of the Common Market was that of a *Zollverein*: a customs union protected by some tariff walls against the rest of the world. Some advocates of the Common Market, including its chief inspirers, Monsieur Monnet and Monsieur Schumann, and some of the officials who ran it from Brussels, envisaged that in the end, perhaps in the long end, these walls would be reduced to a very low level. The total abolition was not, however, promised or agreed on.

For a time, in 1961 and 1962, it appeared as if in Western Europe,

---

[1] In 1965 the time-table of E.E.C. appeared to be endangered by French policies, which were directed mainly at the political aims of the European Community, but were also accompanied by non-co-operative actions in the economic field; but the negotiation in July 1966 ended, or at least moderated, the French opposition to the future economic (as distinct to political) integration of the Common Market, reaffirmed the time-table for the complete abolition of internal tariffs on manufactured products and arrived at a compromise over common agricultural policies.

at least, tariff barriers would eventually fall as a result of a Common Market embracing all the Western European countries. Largely in response to the formation of the Common Market, the United Kingdom, having failed to turn E.E.C. into a West European free-trade area for industrial products, took a lead in 1959 in forming the European Free Trade Association (EFTA) of the seven European countries outside the Common Market (the United Kingdom, the Scandinavian countries, Switzerland, Austria, and Portugal). The original intention was to provide these countries with a temporary alternative to the Common Market: temporary because it was expected that in the end the two organizations would merge, or be replaced by some other West European or Atlantic union of freely trading nations.

In the course of 1961 these tactical measures failed to produce the expected results; and with the success of the Common Market becoming more apparent, opinion in British government circles moved in favour of joining the Market. The negotiations between the latter and Britain did not, however, succeed. British negotiators endeavoured to reconcile the entry of the country into the European Economic Community with British agricultural policy, with Britain's ties with the Commonwealth and with her obligations to EFTA. Negotiations therefore dragged on, and as they were nearing their apparently successful end, France in the person of de Gaulle revealed itself as opposed in principle to British entry at that particular moment in European and world history.

As a result, Europe acquired two free-trading areas. The commercial policy of EFTA for industrial products was conceived in the same image as that of the Common Market, so that tariff dues within it were to be gradually reduced on the same time-table as those of the Common Market. As for the relations between the two areas and with countries outside the area, all that could be hoped for was a mutual agreement to lower the tariff walls.

Thus, as the mid-sixties approached, the two halves of Western Europe enjoyed within their limits freer, if not wholly free, trade. The initiative to extend the freedom to the world at large came again from the U.S.A. In spite of its implied intention to remain protected by tariffs against countries outside the Market, the Treaty of Rome and the European Economic Community received from the very outset the whole-hearted support of successive American governments. The latter saw in the Market yet another means of increasing the strength of Europe, but they also hoped that the liberalization of trade within Europe would be followed by its liberalization beyond. Whether because these hopes were being delayed or because America herself was beginning to feel the pinch of unbalanced international payments, the sixties were marked by a series of determined efforts by American governments to force upon hesitating Europeans a more liberal commercial policy towards other parts of the world. The co-called Dillon round of negotiations of 1962 resulted in agreed reductions of industrial tariffs by 20 per cent. The U.S.A. Trade Expansion Act of the same year gave the President powers to cut tariffs by one-half or to eliminate them altogether on commodities on which the U.S.A. and its negotiating partners had more than 80 per cent of the world trade. The immediate effect of this particular measure was to promote the protracted but promising talks about the so-called 'Kennedy Round' of tariff cuts: cuts which would match lower American duties with freer imports of American and other agricultural produce into Europe and elsewhere.

In relation to international payments progress was equally great and American policy was equally purposeful. The breakdown of the international financial system in the inter-war period had been if anything even more thorough than the breakdown of international trade. The system was greatly disturbed quite early in the twenties by the weight and uncertainty of German reparation payments. Capital moving across frontiers, which was mostly privately owned and was frequently lent or deposited for the short term, also developed its malaise quite early. In the best of times private capital currents have a 'jittery' disposition; this disposition grew worse as the boom of the late twenties was nearing its end. With the fears of a recession and the threat of exchange controls gathering on the horizon, American capital began to withdraw fast, especially from Germany, where it had been invested in large quantities. The ensuing crises resulted in a breakdown of credit which spread all over Europe. The run on the pound led to the devaluation of sterling in 1931; in the wake of this crisis the United Kingdom set up thoroughgoing exchange controls and suspended all the borrowing facilities which had previously made London the financial centre of the world. An American devaluation followed suit, and so did devaluations in other countries. Yet by themselves the devaluations proved unable to restore the full flow of payments. On the contrary, the imbalances grew worse, and by 1935 international payments were everywhere subjected to a highly restrictive régime of controls and prohibitions. Each country equipped itself with tier upon tier of special currencies and accounts, each distinguished by a different degree of convertibility, but mostly not convertible at all ('blocked'). From now on international trade had to subsist on a meagre diet of quotas of foreign currency doled out for private commercial transactions.

When Europe emerged from the war, its network of quotas and special accounts and bilateral treaties regulating them still enmeshed its foreign trade and financial relations across frontiers. The sterling area and the emerging franc area were the only fields within which funds still moved with relative freedom. This constriction of payments was too incapacitating a malady to be left untreated; and remedial measures began to be thought of while the war was still on. The Bretton Woods Conference of 1944 tried to forestall the impending payment difficulties by establishing the International Monetary Fund of $7 billion upon which member nations could draw when in need. The existing Bank for International Settlements was given a new lease of life. However, in the first ten or twelve years of its existence the Fund failed to play the part it was designed for. It was not sufficiently large for the demands that could have been made upon it; above all it was made up of contributions of member nations and therefore largely consisted of 'soft' currencies.

The first really effective contribution to freer movement of funds in Europe came with the Marshall Plan and with the European Payments Union of 1950 which provided European nations with a 'clearing house' for settling mutual financial claims arising out of their current trade. An added convenience offered by the Union was that in the process of settlements it automatically created a certain amount of short-term credit for member nations. By these clearing and credit arrangements trade between European nations was freed from the worst of the formalities, restrictions, and shortages which had impeded the settlements of commercial claims before the war.

However, little as yet could be done to free the movement of capital. Nations were still very much afraid of allowing the free export of capital, sometimes even of its untrammelled import. The 'transitional' restrictions on capital movements laid down in the statutes of the International Monetary Fund were to remain almost in full force until 1958, and in some countries, e.g. the United Kingdom, even after that date. The liberalization of capital movements finally came not because of a newer and more perfect international machinery (though, as we shall see, this played its part), but because world reserves of gold and hard currency had, for a time, come to be better distributed.

The redistribution was brought about by the actual flow of funds, mostly from the U.S.A. to Europe. The flow began and was constantly fed by American payments under the Marshall Plan, by American military disbursements of every kind, and by American private investment in Europe. Between 1945 and 1958 American loans and aid to Europe probably totalled at least $25 billion. The net inflow of private American funds during the same period, allowing for a contrary movement of European funds to the U.S.A., may not have exceeded $200–400 million; but a net inflow there nevertheless was.

Over the period as a whole the payments and loans made by the American Government, as well as the balances accruing to Europe from its foreign trade, were gradually making it possible for most European countries to build up their reserves of dollars and gold. The reserves, which probably amounted to about $10 billion in 1950, were doubled by 1958 and increased by another $8 or $9 billion by 1963. Even at their 1958 level they appeared high enough to justify the first major de-restrictions of capital movements: the convertibility of sterling held by non-residents. The following years saw some relaxations in the exchange controls for residents as well; and as a result, by 1962 Europe could boast of having established an even greater freedom of international payment than that envisaged when the International Monetary Fund was set up. The freedom was by then almost complete in the countries which accumulated the largest balances, e.g. Germany, or in those which quite early established fully convertible currencies, e.g. Switzerland. It became all but free in capital transactions between the countries in the Common Market and between the countries in the Sterling Area.

By then the financial strength of Europe taken as a whole and of some nations within it were sufficiently well established to lay the ghost of the dollar shortage which had haunted European economies for nearly half a century. Some commentators writing in the sixties even began to speak of 'the end of the dollar era'. What justified this terminology is that by 1963 the movement of American public funds in the form of loans, grants, and military disbursements to European countries had very greatly diminished. Their place was in part, but only in small part, taken by private American investments. The winter of 1960–1 witnessed a large-scale outflow of short-term funds from the U.S.A., whereupon the American Government in its anxiety to buttress up its own balance of payments began to discourage further outflows of this nature. Partly as a result of these measures and partly as a result of the expanding foreign investment of European firms, the flow of European private funds into the U.S.A. had by the end of 1963 exceeded the volume of American private investment in Europe.[1] The new relations between the U.S.A. and Europe and the healing of Europe's financial ailments found a fitting symbol in 1963 when the U.S.A.'s financial authorities received a 'stand-by' loan from the International Monetary Fund in support of their balance of payments; and indeed on other occasions in that year when European banks extended to the Federal Reserve Bank that informal assistance which they had previously given to each other, mostly by refraining from converting their dollars into gold or other currencies.

This story of 'liberty through strength' will not, however, be complete without making it clear that some credit for both the liberty and the strength belongs to the international and inter-European machinery of international payments. Between 1956 and 1963 that machinery was much improved. In 1958 and again in 1962 the International Monetary Fund took steps to increase its

---

[1] According to a 1964 survey by the U.S.A. Department of Commerce, European investment in the U.S.A. had in the eight years between 1955 and 1963 risen by some $7 billion to $16·2 billion, whereas U.S.A. investment in Europe in 1963 stood at $10·3 billion.

H

efficiency. Its new role was perhaps heralded by the very large loan, the first of its kind, it gave to France and England in 1956 to enable them to overcome the financial aftermath of Suez. But its greater influence in later years was due partly to increases in its total holdings in 1958 and again in 1963, and partly to the fact that in the meantime the financial strength of European countries had grown to such an extent that the Fund's holdings in members' currencies were now as 'hard' as the dollar itself. Within Europe the end of the European Payments Union in 1958 was followed by the European Monetary Agreement which provided guarantees of exchange rates for credits opened by one member state to another; and it greatly facilitated mutual lending and borrowing between European countries. The enlarged Organization for European Economic Co-operation (the O.E.E.C., was now joined by the U.S.A. and Canada and rechristened O.E.C.D.) also developed into an important meeting-point of European and Atlantic nations where the settlement of outstanding financial problems could be discussed and prepared. Finally, the central banks, in co-operation with the Bank of International Settlements in Basle, entered in the spring of 1961 into an agreement for mutual assistance which took the form of an undertaking to hold unconverted the currency of a country in need while that need lasted.

How did this liberalizing process contribute to Europe's economic expansion? With bilateral treaties and quotas removed, tariffs lowered, and international payments eased, foreign trade should have been able to flow with greater ease and grow at greater speed. In its turn, unimpeded and expanding trade was bound to make its contribution to the economic growth of Europe as a whole and of certain countries in particular. It promoted the flow of resources to the exporting industries – more particularly the engineering, chemical, and electronic industries, all of which expanded faster than others and in doing so raised the general tempo of economic expansion. It helped to keep up personal incomes and the level of economic activity, especially in countries like Belgium and Germany or Switzerland, where domestic demand alone might in some years have been insufficient to sustain full employment. Above all, in countries like Germany, Belgium, Sweden, ever-buoyant exports made it possible to avoid some of the worst penalties of much expanded domestic consumption. They supplied the wherewithal to pay for increases in imports resulting from higher demand and thus made it possible to expand the latter without jeopardizing national payments balances and national currencies.

Some of the beneficial effects of expanding trade may have gone even deeper, and conferred on the national economies the far-reaching benefits with which foreign trade is credited in classical theory. What these benefits should be is well known to students of economic theory. Freely flowing foreign trade, like all free and unimpeded economic processes, is supposed to make competition more effective and to help economic development by eliminating inefficient firms and industries. Above all, foreign trade is supposed to make it easier for countries to specialize, i.e. to concentrate on economic activities and products best suited to their physical endowment, to their acquired skills and to the composition of their productive resources: the qualities, abundances, and scarcities of their labour, capital, and land. Production thus specialized also stood to benefit from the 'economies of scale', or in other words, could afford industrial and commercial establishments of a size necessary to reduce the costs of production to their minimum.

This is the theory. Its relevance to modern Europe has of late been questioned by some economists and politicians. It can be argued, and was in fact argued during the debate over Britain's proposed entry into the Common Market, that the advantages of regional specialization and the economies of scale expected of the large free-trade areas in Europe were not as great as the classical theory of foreign trade would make them out to be. According to this argument Western Europe of the 1960s was a homogeneous region. Its physical endowment was fairly uniform; within it, factors of production and acquired skills were distributed in roughly the same proportions everywhere. Its three major countries, France, Germany, and the United Kingdom were at approximately the same stage of economic development and differed little in their assortments of industries, even if in each of them agriculture was differently organized and differently treated. For all these reasons the scope for specialization within Western Europe was very restricted. Moreover, the principal European countries were large enough and possessed internal markets sufficiently wide to enable firms and factories to operate very near their optimum size, i.e. the size at which they could realize the fullest economies of scale.[1]

However, in the light of the most recent historical experience, some of these arguments against applying to Europe the old-fashioned theories of foreign trade may themselves turn out to be somewhat out of date. In some of the most advanced and modern industries – chemical, petrochemical, electro-metallurgical, electronic, aircraft, and motor-car – scales of production increased much faster than the size of domestic markets. In the chemical industry this trend was widespread. The first nylon polymer plant of I.C.I. built soon after the war was at that time considered to be as large as economics of production required, but it had an output seven or eight times smaller than the polymer plant which succeeded it in the fifties. The planned scale of the latest, the third generation, of polymer plant was to be twice as large again. The same is true of the most recent and the most economical I.C.I. plant for some other chemicals, such as polythene, or its main component, ethylene. For a plant of this size British domestic markets were not large enough, and this perhaps explains why the British chemical industry was so favourable to entry into the Common Market and to world-wide tariff cuts.[2]

The disadvantages of producing for too restricted a market and the consequent difficulties of competing against American manufactures in part account for the tribulations of the European computer industry. Since the war the civil aircraft industry became more dependent on exports than almost any other national industry in either France or the United Kingdom. By the early sixties manufacture of motor-cars had already reached a stage in which domestic markets were beginning to prove insufficient to allow for the most economic production. At that time not only were the smaller car-makers in all European countries being absorbed by larger firms but the latter themselves were establishing links of

[1] In his *Economic Theory and West European Integration*, London, 1958, T. Scitovsky supplies, without fully endorsing, the most recent as well as the most moderate formulation of this view.
[2] See below, p. 113.

co-ownership and co-production running across the Franco-Italian frontiers. If public pronouncements are to be trusted, two of the largest producers in continental Europe – Renault and Fiat – began in 1962 to press for an even closer integration of the European motor-car industry to enable it to compete on costs in domestic and neutral markets against the American mass producers. But long before then the manufacture of some of the principal components of motor-cars – carburettors, sparking plugs, steering mechanisms – had been organized on an international, or rather Pan-European, scale and came to be oriented towards international markets.

Post-war technologies also created international links and dependencies. The pursuit of new processes and products often required projects for research and development on a scale beyond the means of even the largest firms working in isolation. By 1960 the design and development of new types of aircraft – whether supersonic or very large subsonic – was proving beyond the means of the British or any other European aircraft industry: hence the international effort behind the Concord project for supersonic aircraft, large cargo planes or most types of vertical-lift aircraft. The development of new aircraft engines had by that time also become too costly for the major aircraft firms. The same is true of new and advanced types of computers, new types of atomic generators or even of some of the industrial researches in the chemical and pharmaceutical industries. Projects as costly and as adventurous as these could not be undertaken except by co-operative efforts of firms in more than one country, or else in the expectation that, if successful, they would have international markets at their disposal.

What was even more important is that advances in industrial technology often conferred on individual countries and on firms within them economic advantages capable of stimulating commercial exchanges across frontiers and indeed responsible for a great deal of post-war trade. The whole nature of international specialization was slowly changing and was to an ever greater extent becoming dependent on the competitive powers, however temporary, which new products and processes gave the countries or the firms which pioneered them. Such benefits as British foreign trade in the fifties derived from its exports of radar equipment, jet engines, or nuclear power plants, were due to early British technological leadership in these fields. The same is true of many engineering, electronic, petrochemical and pharmaceutical goods entering foreign trade in the fifties and early sixties. Indeed, the main reason why firms in new and science-oriented industries were throughout our period in the forefront of expanding foreign trade is that their progress in new technologies gave them a lead in international markets with which their would-be foreign competitors could not quickly catch up. This is one of the main reasons why the so-called 'growth industries', i.e. those which led in the advance of national outputs and showed the greatest capacity for innovation, also happened to be the exporting industries *par excellence*. They sent abroad a larger proportion of their products than other industries and depended more for their growth on the products thus sent out. So great was the part they played in the expanding foreign trade that some economists could justifiably argue that the ability of those industries to export was one of the main reasons why they expanded, and *ergo* one of the main reasons why national economies in which they were embedded also grew very fast.[1]

These latter-day glosses on the classical theory of international trade should be borne in mind in assessing the effects which expanding foreign trade had, or should have had, on European economic development. The might-have-beens of history are not a profitable subject of discussion; we cannot say with any certainty what would have been the technical and economic progress of the continental iron and steel industry or of the petrochemical industries of Italy and the Netherlands or of the motor-car industry of Germany, but for the facilities opened to them by the wider markets and great resources of E.E.C. Nor can we say how much in economic development the United Kingdom suffered from Britain's non-participation in the Common Market, and how much would her industries have benefited from her adhesion to E.E.C. But some indirect indication of what the advantages of the larger

---

[1] O.E.C.D., *Science, Economic Growth, and Government Policy*, 26–29, 36, and Appendix B, Tables 7 and 8. It appears that between 1937 and 1959 in the 12 principal industrialized countries the exports of industries in Group A, defined by the high rate of technological change, grew from 34·4 to 51·5 per cent of the total exports, whereas the share of traditional industries (Group B) fell from 65·7 per cent to 48·5 per cent.

European market were or would have been, had the United Kingdom been able to join them, can be found in the behaviour of many British firms. Almost immediately after the Brussels negotiations for British entry into E.E.C. had collapsed, a large number of British firms in almost every modern industry took steps to acquire production facilities within the Common Market. That firms exporting to Europe should have thereby tried to 'jump' the customs barriers of E.E.C. is only too natural and requires no comment. It is, however, important to note that but for the collapse of the Brussels negotiations most of these firms would have continued to produce in the United Kingdom and exported their products; the advantages of specialization and the economies of scale within a larger market would have justified their doing so.

The *raison d'être* for I.C.I.'s new plant in Rozenburg near Amsterdam is a case in point. The decision to construct the plant followed directly upon the failure of the Brussels talks; had the United Kingdom entered the Common Market I.C.I. might not have found it necessary to duplicate the facilities of Wilton and Billingham by a separate integrated works in Holland. This and other similar examples clearly suggest that in estimating how economic development benefited from expanding free-trading areas, we must not dismiss the benefits accruing from easier and more highly developed regional specialization and from the resulting economies of scale.

The history of foreign trade and payments in our period, reveals the existence of yet another link between international trade and payments on the one hand and the expanding economies on the other. The link, like so many others I have discussed here, concerns the stability of the economy and the psychological effect which that stability had on the entrepreneurs and managers. In the past history of the European economy, foreign trade and foreign payments as a rule played an unsettling part. Even where and when slumps in exports or failures in international payments did not themselves cause economic depressions, commercial and financial transactions across frontiers helped to transmit depressions from countries in which they originated to the rest of the world. This was certainly true of the major depressions between the wars: that of the twenties, which originated in the U.S.A., and that of the early thirties which originated in Germany, was amplified in the American crises of 1929–30, and travelled from there to other countries.

It is highly significant of the changed economic climate since 1946 that trade, even trade with the United States, did not play an important part in originating or aggravating such recessions as there were. In general, the export trade, especially the exports of European countries, acted as a stabilizing agent, for it continued on a high level at times when other economic indicators presaged depressions. The effects of imports were somewhat more uncertain. American imports of foreign goods, which had fluctuated so much before the war, were remarkably stable after 1946. But in the United Kingdom, on at least three occasions during our period, and also in France and Italy in the early fifties and again in 1963–4, economic expansion was threatened by excessive imports which created an imbalance in foreign trade and made restrictions on economic growth necessary. On none of these occasions, however, was it the slump in foreign trade itself, i.e. the failure of demand abroad and the inability to dispose of exports, that had caused the crisis. Demand for European imports within Europe and outside it remained high throughout the period. Towards its very end pessimists detected in the current statistics of foreign trade signs of a slowing down in the expansion of international commerce; but it was as yet early to say how real or enduring was the deceleration going to prove.

The buoyancy of foreign trade, and still more the removal of the fears and uncertainties besetting international payments, must have had the same effect on the behaviour of managers and entrepreneurs as the crisis-free record of domestic economies. It made it possible for them to plan and to invest for the future with the confidence which Western business required for its smooth and continuous expansion. In various less obvious ways the growth of international trade and its freedom from violent crises may also have encouraged the forward policies of governments and a sense of security among workers. Indirect and intangible as all these influences were, they all contributed to Europe's 'fair weather'.

CHAPTER 5
Investment

The story of post-war growth cannot be told and its 'miracle' cannot be accounted for as if it were mainly the product of business confidence generated by high and steady demand and by the smooth expansion of international trade. In the eyes of most economists and historians who have so far written about this period the most important factor, and certainly the most tangible and easiest to measure, was the high volume of investment.

How high that flow was is shown by the table below.

Table 12 *Rate of Growth of Output and Relationship[1] between Investment and Output 1949–62*

	1 Annual rate of growth in real Gross *Domestic* Product (% per annum)	2 Gross *domestic* fixed capital formation[a] (% of Gross Domestic Product)	3 Incremental capital-output ratios
Austria	5·8	23·3	3·9
Belgium	3·0	16·9	5·6
Denmark	3·8	17·5	5·5
France	4·8	20·6	4·6
Italy	6·0	22·0	3·7
Netherlands	5·0	25·0	5·2
Norway	3·5	32·6	9·5
Sweden	3·5	21·4	6·3
Switzerland	5·0	23·6	4·5
United Kingdom	2·5	16·1	6·7
Germany	6·8	24·3	3·3

[a] At constant prices, the period covered for most countries is 1949–59 inclusive.
[1] The table is based on the figures in UNO, *Economic Survey of Europe 1961*, part 2, Geneva, 1964, Ch. II, Table 6, supplemented by figures for 1960–2 derived mainly from O.E.C.D. annual surveys of individual countries, and adjusted

At no other period of European history, for which the proportions of national income devoted to investment could be reliably estimated, were they so high as after the war. In most European countries they were even higher than the exceptionally high investment in the decade immediately following the First World War. According to some recent computations the annual rates of growth of capital investment in the United Kingdom between 1948 and 1962 were 2·7 per cent, compared with 1·3 per cent between 1856 and 1898, 1·8 per cent between 1899 and 1913, and 2·3 per cent between 1924 and 1927. Strictly comparable figures are not available for other European countries, but such figures as we possess make it clear that in most countries, and especially in Norway, Austria, Switzerland, Italy and Germany, the contrast between post-war rates for capital formation and the pre-war ones was even greater than in the United Kingdom. Moreover, investment rose progressively throughout our period. The estimates of new investment year by year would show that in most European countries the rate of investment was higher between 1955 and 1959 than in the previous five years and, in some countries, higher still between 1960 and 1963.[1]

This unprecedented flow of investments was obviously a powerful force behind the expanding outputs and the rising productivities of labour. Its effects on aggregate output are almost too obvious to be worth expounding; and its effects on productivity would appear to be only little less clear. In theory a high rate of investment could enhance productivity in several ways, but mainly by increasing the amount of capital per worker and by speeding up the march of innovations. This multiple role of investment is well understood and is fully emphasized, perhaps even over-emphasized, in the writings of economists and in the pronouncements and plans of politicians receptive to the teachings of economics. In this they appear to be

---

for the United Kingdom on the basis of the figures in the paper by R. C. O. Matthews, as below, p. 118, footnote 1.

[1] The alternative United Kingdom estimates are those of capital stock. They will be found in E. H. Phelps Brown and B. Weber, 'Accumulation, Productivity and Distribution in the British Economy, 1870–1938', *Economic Journal*, LXIII, June 1953, and H. D. Willey, as in Note 1, p. 129 below, and do not include buildings. The post-war figures in H. D. Willey's thesis are confined to manufacturing. Both sets are subject to all the doubt which attaches to all current estimates of capital stock. They are, however, fully consistent with the estimates of investment during the period.

well supported by evidence. Post-war statistics have been repeatedly quoted to show that, as a rule, the countries and industries in which investment rose fastest were also those in which total output and output per man increased most. An historian may therefore be strongly tempted to present the history of post-war growth as a simple consequence of high input of capital. This temptation must be resisted. At a closer inspection neither history nor theory will allow us to treat investment as the 'first cause' and the all-determining factor of higher outputs and productivities and to tell the story of post-war economy as a latter-day version of the book of Genesis – first came investment and then came growth.[1]

Such a story would not survive more sophisticated statistical tests. Econometricians have in recent years tried to estimate how much higher output and productivities owed to 'material inputs', i.e. additional labour and capital, and how much to 'residual' causes (the latter an omnibus term covering the entire gamut of social and institutional factors, mainly the efficiency of management and the quality of labour, and technological improvements). Most of these estimates suffer from some obvious statistical and logical limitations. In actual life the various 'inputs' were too closely interrelated to be statistically separable. More particularly, new investment as a rule carried with it changes in most other factors; and considered apart from the new techniques or changes of scale or managerial methods it embodied it could be no more than an abstraction, or in J. R. Hicks' words, a metaphysical concept. It is nevertheless significant that all the recent attempts to measure the effects of different 'inputs' should have all brought out the relatively small part which additional investment played in bringing about higher outputs and productivities. According to computations recently carried out by Professor R. C. O. Matthews and his Cambridge colleagues, the contribution of capital to the United

---

[1] The most recent statement of the case for investment as the overriding factor of economic growth will be found in A. Maddison, *Economic Growth in the West*, *passim*. The contrary view is however much better represented in current economic discussion. The theoretical case for regarding a high rate of investment as a consequence of economic growth was recently presented by N. Kaldor in 'Capital Accumulation and Economic Growth' in *Theory of Capital*, International Economic Association 1961, and is implied in the Harrod–Domar theory of capital formation (below, pp. 125–6).
[*Vide* Appendix Note 5, pp. 362–3 below.]

Kingdom's growth was relatively small. While productivity in the post-war period increased at the rate of 1·9 per cent per annum, the increment attributable to material inputs, and mainly to capital was not greater than 0·6 per cent, or one-third of the total, whereas the increment attributable to the 'residual' factors was 1·3 per cent or two-thirds of the total. According to the same calculations residual factors were also responsible for most of the increases in productivity in the second half of the nineteenth and the early part of the twentieth centuries. Investment may have made a somewhat larger contribution to productivity after the war than before 1938 (about one-third compared with less than one-fifth), but then post-war investment was also much higher than before the war.

Table 13 *Annual Percentage Rates of Growth of Output and Capital Input in the United Kingdom*[1]

	Capital	G.D.P. per Man-year	Growth due to:	
			Residual	Change in Capital per Man
1856–99	1·3	1·1	0·9	0·2
1899–1913	1·8	0·1	−0·2	0·3
1924–37	1·7	1·1	0·9	0·2
1948–62	2·7	1·9	1·3	0·6

These numerical coefficients can be paralleled by a historical argument. The argument cannot match the statistics in the table with a direct estimate of capital's contribution to growth, but it can offer some historical reasons for scaling that estimate down. Of these reasons, two deserve special attention. One is the 'derived' nature of investment itself. The rate of investment varied widely between countries, industries and firms, and most of the variations could best be accounted for by the local and historical characteristics of economic growth itself. In the second place, equal doses of invest-

[1] The table is derived from R. C. O. Matthews 'Some Aspects of Post-War Growth in the British Economy in Relation to Historical Experience', *Manchester Statistical Society*, 1964, and the unpublished paper to an economics seminar in Cambridge kindly placed at my disposal by the writer.

ment appeared to have had different effects on outputs in different countries, industries, and firms. At least two historical circumstances must therefore be considered. First, why should Western Europe as a whole, and some countries within it, have been able or willing to invest on a larger scale than heretofore? Secondly, why should some countries and some firms have been able to turn their investments to better account than others?

Let us begin with the ability and willingness to invest. This has always been an important, though little studied, problem. Writing recently about demand for capital, an economist lamented the lack of appropriate theory; he could with equal reason have lamented the lack of appropriate history. Yet the key to the part investment played in the post-war era, why it was greater at that time than at other times, and why some countries invested more than others, is more likely to be found in the changing demand for capital than in its supply.[1]

To stress the importance of demand for capital is not to disparage the importance of its supply. Capital has always been and cannot but be a scarce resource – or, as economists would put it, it is not a 'free good'. To this extent it has always and everywhere been in limited supply and has had to be paid for. Nations and individuals, be they never so rich and profligate, have always been compelled to adjust themselves to this scarcity. In Western societies the scarcity enters into the planning of capital expenditure so automatically and discreetly that projects of investment patently out of scale with society's financial resources are hardly ever launched. In an economic environment so conditioned, capital will always be short and therefore command a price, and its shortage and its price could be (and in our period, in fact, were) greater in some countries and in some years than in others. Capital was relatively short and interest high in most continental countries in the years of reconstruction immediately after the war. Again at the very end of our period, in 1964 and 1965, the demand for capital rose so high that its price, i.e. its average rate of interest, steadily mounted. Shortage of capital in this sense of the term was throughout our period greater in Germany than in most

[1] Trygve Haavelmo. *A Study in the Theory of Investment*, Chicago, 1960, p. v.

other European countries, mainly because throughout our period, with the possible exception of some periods in the mid-sixties, investment stood at exceptionally high levels.

Shortage of capital was not, of course, the sole cause of high interest rates. In some European countries rates of interest happened to be high because it suited the governments to keep them high in order to hold inflation in check, or because lenders went in fear of inflation (in France until 1953 and perhaps even until 1958). Elsewhere rates on private industrial borrowing were relatively high because most private, as distinct from institutional, lenders took a pessimistic view of industrial investment.

Supplies of funds could also be short and interest high in certain specialized fields of industry and commerce. Interest rates on French industrial bonds were high because this kind of industrial borrowing was preferred by French businessmen to all other types, with the result that demand invariably ran ahead of supply: so far ahead sometimes that authorities had to ration the available funds among the competing applicants.[1] It is also possible that in most European countries small private businesses were charged higher-than-average rates of interest on the rare occasions when they sought outside capital.

These local shortages, however, were not as important as they are sometimes said to have been. Even where and when higher interest rates were due to high demand for funds and to their relative shortage, they did not greatly slow down either the general flow of investment or the average rate of economic growth. The profitability of housing and public utilities was perhaps sufficiently closely dependent on capital charges to be influenced by them. On the other hand, in most industrial and commercial enterprises the profitability of new investments was judged by a whole combination of *pros* and *cons* in which the cost of money was by no means overwhelmingly important. The anticipated rate of obsolescence, future movements of prices and the probable structure of costs – each of these considerations weighed at least as much as, if not more than, the

---

[1] The writer in *U.N.O. Economic Survey for Europe in 1957*, E.C.E., Geneva, 1958, also argues that high rates of interest in industrial and commercial investment in Germany were due not to shortage of savings but to deficiencies of the capital market. See also below, p. 241, footnote 1. For industrial financing in France, see below, p. 242.

rate of interest.[1] And this is why very few large or medium-sized undertakings with free access to the capital market (as distinct from small firms to whom this access was denied) were deterred by the dearth of investable funds from proceeding with their projects of investment or unduly tempted by the plethora and cheapness of money. A few marginal projects on the very limits of profitability may have been thus frustrated or stimulated; but the great majority of investment decisions were not apparently among them.[2]

This view of investment is borne out by some recent data. In a series of inquiries into industrial investment which was carried out in the late fifties by statistical institutes in various European countries, a large number of firms were asked why and how they arrived at their investment decisions. In their replies a few firms – some 17 per cent of the sample in Germany, 20 per cent in France, 6 per cent in the Netherlands, and almost none in the United Kingdom – complained of difficulties of financing their investments. But even those which blamed their failure to invest on difficulties of finance complained not of the shortage of outside funds but of the insufficiency of their own accumulated reserves. They were almost invariably small family firms. Larger firms responsible for the bulk of the total output in the various national samples did not allege any lack of funds. On the contrary, some of the larger German firms, whose internal savings had by the late fifties become sufficiently large to make them independent of outside sources of finance, found themselves exposed to selling pressures from banks anxious to lend.[3]

It may well be that financial institutions, including banks, were

---

[1] The record of investment decisions of great industrial firms will bear out the irrelevance of interest rates. In analysing their record of past investments the Board of the British Cocoa and Chocolate Corporation state that all calculations were based on a variety of factors such as sales estimates, and that 'the uncertainty surrounding the estimates is increased when plant has to be ordered two or three years in advance of sales'. No wonder that 'neither the amount of capital, nor the rate of interest, are the main determining factors' of the firm's investment record, and that in the preceding eighteen years only once, during the credit squeeze of 1956, did this have an effect on the decisions of the firm; *Industrial Challenge: The Experience of Cadburys of Bournville*, Birmingham 1964, pp. 78–80.

[2] See below, p. 123.

[3] B. R. Williams, *International Report on Investment Behaviour*, O.E.C.D., Paris, 1962.

not equally forthcoming in their dealings with smaller firms. In the United Kingdom before the war it was believed that smaller firms were badly served by the money market (the so-called 'Macmillan Gap'); and a number of replies to the inquiries I have just referred to also alleged that banks were reluctant to lend to small firms. But at least some of these allegations were probably little more than excuses for not investing. On the firms' own showing the fault lay most often not with the financial market as a whole but with their own attitude to investment and expansion. So anxious were they not to get into 'the hands of the banks' or not to admit outside shareholders that they almost invariably cut their investment plans to suit their own accumulated savings.

In any case, in several countries facilities for smaller firms were in recent years not so deficient as they had been before the war, and were improving in the late fifties and early sixties. In the United Kingdom smaller enterprises wishing to borrow for expansion or renovation had access to the Industrial and Commercial Finance Corporation established in 1946 with the object of filling the Macmillan Gap. It is also more than probable that the attitude of the commercial money market also changed in the United Kingdom after the war. Except in intervals of government-ordained restrictions on credits, clearing banks were more willing than before the war to lend 'long', and to allow their loans to be used for financing buildings, machinery, and plant. In addition, investment trusts had of late years made it their business to forage for clients in the lowlier ranks of industry and trade. Facilities also improved in some of the continental countries. In Germany, since the late fifties, a wholly new race of financial intermediaries, operating with revolving credits from insurance companies and pension funds, did something to provide funds for firms who would otherwise have found it difficult to raise them on the market. In Belgium it fell to the Government to provide for smaller firms through the Société nationale d'investissement established in the early sixties. In France the same purpose was, since the early fifties, served by a variety of government-sponsored institutions and devices, and further measures to facilitate investment in small enterprises were being launched in the early sixties.

These being the attitudes and the influences behind investment decisions of firms, it is not surprising that there should have been so little concordance between rates of investment in different countries and in different phases of post-war history on the one hand and the supplies of capital as reflected in its price on the others. Germany, with its higher-than-average price of industrial loans, invested more than most other countries. The rise in rate of interest at the turn of 1964 and 1965 did not prevent the revival of German investment after a year of relative stagnation. Similarly, plentiful supplies of investable funds, such as characterized the Belgian capital market throughout the fifties and the early sixties, or that of the Netherlands after 1961, or that of the United Kingdom in the later fifties, did not provoke a correspondingly higher rate of investment. Broadly speaking, in Western Europe as a whole, and in each individual country taken separately investment was very seldom held back by shortages of capital or unduly stimulated by its plethora.

If this view is not always held by economists and historians writing on the subject, their lack of agreement can be blamed on differences of contexts and definitions. In current discussion the problem is most often formulated in terms of savings, and when it comes to savings their sufficiency can be judged directly and indirectly. The direct way of judging it is to measure and to collate – in practice, this means to guess – the volumes of current savings and investments. Indirect judgments are usually derived from two types of evidence – the presence or absence of inflationary symptoms or the current rates of interest.

These two indirect indications are those most commonly consulted, but they are not strictly relevant to the phenomena which concern us here. The first indicator – inflationary symptom – is less relevant to the problem of capital supplies, as it figures at this stage of our discussion, than it may be to some other aspects of capital formation and investment. In theory nations could finance investment by overspending incomes and by incurring debt of every kind. Investment thus financed would set up or intensify inflationary pressures in the economy and be, as a rule, reflected in rising prices, in excessive imports, and in negative foreign balances of payments. That since the war some European nations in fact suffered from recurrent negative balances in their foreign payments and that inflationary pressures were present almost everywhere, is taken by

I

some economists as proof that European countries in fact 'over-spent' – over-consumed and over-invested – or that to this extent their supply of savings was insufficient for the investments they indulged in.

This diagnosis, for all its plausibility, has not been fully borne out by European experience after the war. Of the various morbid causes of post-war inflation in Europe investment in excess of savings was probably the least virulent. European inflations after the war were to some extent the product of rising costs, mostly wages, which only partly and indirectly reflected excesses in demand and spending power. Where and when inflation could be ascribed mainly to ex-cessive demand, the demand which weighed most, was that of private consumers or of governments spending on their current accounts. By comparison, additional demand represented by higher rates of industrial investment was relatively small. It is largely for this reason that the European countries which suffered most from inflation or its repercussions were not those which invested most. Germany before 1964 and Sweden before 1963 invested more than most European countries through our period; yet they suffered least from inflation or from payment deficits. On the other hand, France before 1958 and the United Kingdom throughout the period, with their lower than average rates of investment, were also the worst sufferers from inflation or from imbalances of payments accounts or from both.

However, even if it were to be proved that inflation resulted from investment in excess of savings, the argument would still be some-what irrelevant to our problem. What concerns us at this stage of our story is not whether supplies of savings were large enough to keep inflation at bay, but whether the actual funds available for investment were sufficient to meet the demand for them. Were industrialists prevented by shortage of actual finance from carrying out their in-vestment plans? If investments were lower in some countries and industries than in others, was this because investable funds at their disposal were smaller or dearer than those available in other in-dustries and other countries?

To all these questions I have already returned a negative answer. Indeed, a negative answer follows from the questions with a neces-sity which is almost tautological. For, considered in matter-of-fact financial terms the flow of investable funds and their investment must synchronize. But economists reared on the orthodoxies of their subject might insist on judging supplies of capital by the other indirect indicator, i.e. by that of the rates of interest. They would in that case point to the high charges for industrial loans in countries like Germany or France – though not Switzerland, Belgium, or, in most years, the Netherlands and the United Kingdom – as proof that although the supply of investable funds and their use in investment balanced, the point at which they balanced was sometimes lower than it would have been, had the rate of savings been higher. This diagnosis also appears to be unduly sombre. We have seen that the supply of investable funds and the demand for them synchronized at a point at which the price of capital was not so high as to hold back industrial projects or to prevent aggregate investment from rising to its unprecedentedly high post-war levels. And this justifies the guess that not only the flow of investable funds but also real savings as well were flowing at a rate which could not have greatly lagged behind the rising trends of the economy and the underlying needs of new capital. The guess is supported by much of the direct evidence now available, as well as by the logic of economic probabilities. Savings kept, in fact, high and mounted, and it was in the nature of things that they should have done so.

The high and mounting record of savings should not be difficult to account for. According to at least one widely held view an increasingly abundant flow of savings was inherent in the very process of economic growth. The increasing product resulted in higher personal incomes and company profits, and *ergo* in greater savings. The latter, when invested, helped in their turn to increase the national products.[1]

Needless to say, the underlying theoretical presumptions, like all such theoretical presumptions, will not fit the historical record except very loosely. They assume that higher incomes always generated higher savings, that all such savings were invested, that all such investments produced commensurate increases in national

[1] E. Domar, 'Capital Expansion. Rates of Growth and Employment', *Econometrica*, 1946; R. Harrod, 'Essay in Dynamic Economics', *Economic Journal*, 1939. However, S. Kuznets, 'Quantitative Aspects of Economic Growth', *Economic Development and Cultural Change*, ix. pt. 2, July 1961, pp. 55–6, casts doubt on the validity of the long-term correlation between economic growth and savings.

incomes: and none of these assumptions fully accord with historical facts. But in the historical experience of post-war Europe some such chain reaction, however loose, was obviously at work. As the Report of the Economic Division of UNO for 1959 pointed out, post-war experience bore out the presumption that a growing national product, higher rates of saving, and increasing investment were all linked in a sort of chain reaction. The two principal streams of private saving – the so-called 'personal' or 'household' savings and the savings of enterprises – flowed abundantly during the post-war period in almost every European country. They not only stimulated the general expansion of European economies but were themselves stimulated by it.[1]

Moreover, in those countries where the flow of private savings appeared insufficient to support the current investment pro-grammes – in Norway or in the early phases of the German 'miracle', or in France, where for a long time private savings and private domestic investment were held back by the lack of confidence in the political system and in the franc – the state took upon itself to bridge the gap between private savings and investment. Funds also came from abroad: from the U.S.A. (mainly to Germany and Italy), from Switzerland after the middle fifties, from Holland after 1961; and a trickle came even from the United Kingdom, especially after the collapse of the negotiations for the British entry into the Common Market.[2]

With private savings growing as incomes expanded, and with public and foreign funds available to supplement savings from private and domestic sources, it is not surprising that the total flow of savings should have proved quite adequate. If its flow could be statistically matched against the effective demand of firms and governments, the match would probably turn out to have been quite close. And the sufficiency of savings – or rather the probability

[1] A recent demonstration of total supply of savings increasing relatively to G.N.P. and of the connexion between increasing rate of savings and growing *per capita* disposable income, will be found in UNO, *World Economic Survey 1960*, pp. 9–10, also ibid., pp. 33–7.

[2] According to some estimates, public authorities in Germany in the fifties supplied one-half of net savings and one-third of gross savings for capital forma-tion: K. W. Roskamp, *Capital Formation in West Germany*, Detroit, 1965, p. 162. However, even according to these computations a relatively small proportion of these savings went into manufacturing investment.

that their insufficiency was never great – may help to explain why the suppliers of actual finance – of investable funds – should never have fallen so greatly behind the mounting demand for capital as to impede economic development or to produce painful distortions in national economics.

If this argument about the supply of capital holds good, our first conundrum – why countries, industries, and firms in post-war Europe differed as they did in their rates of investment – could be best understood, if not altogether resolved, by looking at the underlying differences in the willingness and ability to invest. And once the existence of these differences is recognized, the reasons for them are not far to seek.

The region where most economists have sought them is that which treatises nowadays designate as 'relative factor costs'. When labour happened to be scarce while capital was relatively abundant, so that wages stood high in terms of product, while the rate of interest was relatively low, business enterprises were induced to replace labour with machines and to this extent to increase their investment in fixed capital. In its more up-to-date version the theory assumes that the cost of capital exercised its influence on investment not through the rate of interest but through the prices of capital goods. In this version the theory has also been drawn upon to provide the rationale of investment in innovation and thus to account for technological change.[1]

Whatever we may think of the theory – and it is outside our scope and competence to do so – it apparently makes some sense in its historical contexts, that of post-war investment and that of technological progress. Yet even in its historical context it cannot provide the sole, or the most relevant, explanation. Had relative factor costs been the main cause of higher rates of investments and of speedier technological progress, both the former and the latter would have varied from country to country and from industry to industry in a manner different from that in which they actually distributed themselves in the post-war world. This lack of clear correlation between investment, technology and changing factor

[1] See below, pp. 163–6.

costs will have to be discussed in greater detail in the section concerned with innovation. But at the cost of anticipating the subject matter of later chapters, the links between investment and technology will also have to be dealt with here, if only because they may help us to identify some of the 'other' factors behind the high rate of post-war investment.[1]

What these factors were and how they were linked with technological change is suggested by the very order in which industries arrangèd themselves for their demand for new capital. In almost every European country the industries heading the list, i.e. those with the largest infusion of capital, were the 'modern' or the modernized industries. The chemical and petroleum industries, with their joint offspring in petrochemicals, plastics, and man-made fibres, developed a voracious appetite for new capital as they grew and renewed their equipment. Equally voracious for capital were the engineering and metal-working industries, especially their newer branches, such as electro-mechanical, electronic, and motor-car. On the other hand, new investment was low relatively to output, and also grew rather slowly, in such industries as cotton and wool, coal-mining (except where they were in the process of wholesale modernization as in the United Kingdom), wood-working, or in such older branches of the engineering and metal-working industry as manufacture of railway equipment and milling machinery.

Thus in Germany, where annual investment in all manufacturing industries stood in 1961 at nearly DM 9,000 million, it was at that date some 260 per cent higher than in 1950. Investment into mechanical engineering (a mixture of new and old) rose in the same period at approximately the same rate. But the annual investment into electrical engineering and electronic industry increased by at least 300 per cent and, in round figures, stood in 1961 at nearly DM 1,200,000 million compared with some DM 300 million in 1952. The combined annual investment of the various branches of the chemical industry stood in 1961 at nearly DM 2,300 million and was about six times higher than in the early nineteen-fifties. On the other hand, annual investment into mining over the same period increased by little over 100 per cent (from DM 800 million to DM 1,700 million at 1954 prices) while annual investment into textiles

[1] See below, pp. 163–6.

increased even less. In Sweden annual investment in all industries except transport increased between 1954 and 1961 by about 75 per cent (from 1,778 to 3,104 million Crowns). In much of its modern or modernized mechanical engineering it increased by a little under 85 per cent, in electrical engineering by 120–140 per cent. On the other hand, in shipbuilding it increased by only about 40 per cent. In the Netherlands all industrial investment except transport amounted in 1961 to 2,770 million Guilders and was some 60 per cent higher than in 1950, but in mechanical and electrical engineering (also a relatively new industry in that country) annual investment in 1960 was nearly four times as high as in the early 1950s. Investment in textiles, however, increased very slowly, and annual investment in shipbuilding actually declined between 1955 and 1961. In the United Kingdom annual investment in manufacturing industries grew between 1948 and 1962 at the annual rate of 4 per cent compared with 1·1 per cent between 1924 and 1937, but the rate differed greatly from sector to sector. It was 6·5 per cent in chemicals, 4·6 per cent in iron and steel, 4 per cent in engineering, and 5·4 per cent in bricks, pottery, and glass (the latter reflecting exceptionally high investment in construction). By contrast, investment into mining, paper and printing, timber and furniture, grew at much less than 3 per cent per annum, while investment into textiles actually decelerated at the rate of about 3 per cent per annum.[1]

There is thus a strong presumption – a presumption bordering on the obvious – that in our period demand for capital was linked with

[1] On the average share of individual sectors in investment in 1954–8 and 1959–61 in Germany, the United Kingdom, France, and the Netherlands, see UNO, *Economic Survey of Europe 1962*, N.Y., 1963; cf. also *Some Factors*, Ch. III, p. 16, Table 12. The United Kingdom figures have been tabulated and analysed in R. C. O. Matthews, 'Some Aspects of Post-war Growth', p. 20, Table VI. The high figures for steel industry in the table reflect the expansion and renovation of the industry in the fifties and early sixties. The high figures for construction reflect much higher rate of building and road building. On the other hand, the deceleration of investment in textile industries before 1963 would have stood out even clearer had it been possible to separate the data of older textiles from that of man-made fibres. Investment in the latter apparently grew at a rate comparable with that of chemical industry. A somewhat differently computed United Kingdom series of additions to gross capital stock between 1951 and 1962, estimates annual increases at 6·9 per cent for chemicals and petroleum compared to 1·9 per cent for textiles; H. D. Willey, *Growth of British and German Manufacturing* (Ph.D. thesis, University of Columbia), pp. 55–6, Table 6.

technological innovations and the proneness of industries to innovate. In theory, technological advances could be both the cause and the consequence of investment; they could prompt it and be prompted by it. That the introduction of new products and of improved ways of making old products should have required additional investment is self-evident. In theory innovations could be not only labour-saving but also capital-saving, i.e. reduce the amount of capital required for the same volume of output. But in actual practice most of the twentieth-century innovations were labour-saving and required a higher investment of capital per worker, and often also required larger investment per unit of output. A major post-war innovation capable of conspicuous savings of capital were computers employed in controlling the flow of materials and components. They may have helped to reduce the vast capital resources tied up in stocks. But the great majority of other new equipment had a contrary effect, and contributed to the general 'intensification' or 'deepening' of industrial equipment and to higher demand for capital.

Somewhat, but only somewhat less evident is the reciprocal connexion, that between new capital and innovations resulting from it. Economists have for some time held the view, popularized by Keynes, that 'all new equipment was better equipment', or that, in other words, additions to fixed capital, whether for wholly new lines of production or in the replacement of older equipment, brought with them technological improvements in machines and methods. Viewed in a longer historical prospective this generalization may not turn out to be universally true. In the somewhat more distant past it was always possible for an industry to add its capacity by setting up additional units equipped and operating in exactly the same manner as its units already in existence. This is precisely what happened in the British steel industry between 1896 and 1913, to the British coal and cotton industries during their great expansion at the turn of the nineteenth and twentieth centuries, or to the textile industries in France, Belgium, and Germany at the beginning of the twentieth century. But if facts visible to the observer's naked eye are to be trusted, Keynes's generalization must hold good for the experience of more recent years. In the course of the last generation the quality of machines, plant, and methods of production progressed so continuously and so fast that most new investments and most additions to the fixed capital of industries embodied technological innovations.

This particular link between expansion and innovation is directly relevant to the history of technological progress and will be recapitulated at greater length in that connexion. The sole reason why it is brought into the story of investment is that modern and innovating industries expanded and, therefore, invested in expansion more readily than the old and traditional ones. It is because in modern and innovating industries innovation and growth went together, that their demand for capital was so heavy and that countries such as Germany, blessed with a high proportion of 'modern' or 'modernized' industries, invested more than countries like the United Kingdom or Belgium in which this proportion was lower.[1]

This proneness of new and innovating industries to invest need not, however, be taken as anything more than an observed fact of economic history. As we have already seen, it followed from the labour-saving purposes of investment and from technological improvements frequently embodied in new investment. But we have also seen that in the not-too-distant historical past fixed capital of industries could expand without bringing about any significant innovations; and some students of individual industries have argued that even in the most recent times the introduction and diffusion of inventions seemed 'merely to accompany but not to cause the waves of investment'.[2] The truth of the matter is that the connexion between expanding investment and innovation need not be, and did not always happen to be, economic in the narrow sense of the word. The two frequently went together for reasons which were social, institutional, and even personal.

[1] The interrelation between higher propensity to invest, the more pronounced rate of technological progress and high rates of growth underlie Professor Perroux's definition of 'les industries motrices' in his model. The relative weights of these industries in the make-up of national economy accounts for existing differences in rates of growth. F. Perroux, 'Les industries motrices et la croissance d'une économie nationale', *Economie Appliquée*, 1963, pp. 198–9; *idem*, 'L'investissement d'innovation par un modèle à deux secteurs, etc.', *ibid.*, 1963, pp. 555–8.

[2] *Cf.* the discussion and the authorities cited in Robert E. Johnston, 'Technical Progress and Innovation', *Oxford Economic Papers* (New Series), Vol. 18, No. 2, July 1966, p. 172.

If these reasons – and more particularly the personal ones – are frequently neglected in economic and historical literature (as they have so far been here) it is because economists and economic historians are inclined to discuss the problems and the history of investment in the aggregate; and social and personal factors do not clearly emerge from the stories of economic development of nations and industries in their entirety. The history of investment, as the history of other aspects of the economy, must not, however, be confined to national economies or even to industries considered as wholes, since demand for capital varied not only from industry to industry but also between firms within the same industries. Variations like these could best be accounted for by the features differentiating one firm from another, and of these features one of the most important was the presence in firms of men willing and able to innovate and to expand.[1]

New and innovating firms were as a rule led by men of enterprising and rational type. Business leaders who refused to be satisfied with existing methods of production or with the established products were also likely to be men who would not remain satisfied for long with the scale of their firms' operations, with the volume of their output, or their share of the market. As long as active and adventurous conduct of business entailed both innovation and expansion, the new and innovating industries owed their urge to expand not only to the 'objective' advantages of being new or to the close technical links between expansion and renewal, but also to managerial leaders anxious both to expand and to innovate.

So much for the first 'rider' to our 'growth-by-investment' formula. The high rate of investment since the war, its height and the variations from country to country and from industry to industry, can best be understood if considered not only as the independent factor of economic growth but also as one of its symptoms. For it derived from the same historical and social causes – the expansive tendencies of demand and output, technological progress, and improvements in industrial leadership and attitudes – which

---

[1] *Pari passu* the same argument applies to the so-called 'Verdoorn law'. [*Vide* Appendix Note 7, p. 364 below.]

underlay the general process of European expansion since the war. Similar conclusions are suggested by our second 'rider', i.e. the differences in the productivity of new investment in different countries and industries.

Differences in the productivity of capital are as a rule represented statistically as differences in 'capital-output ratios', and more especially by the incremental capital-output ratios (I.C.O.R.s), i.e. ratios between increments in the national product and those in investment, measuring the actual spurts of output in response to successive injections of capital. As Table 12 shows, these ratios differed greatly after the war, and their differences corresponded well to the different rates of growth in individual countries.[1] They were very low in Germany and Italy, high in the United Kingdom, Belgium, and the Scandinavian countries. A more detailed analysis of these figures would reveal that the capital-output ratios could differ within each country from industry to industry, and also from firm to firm in the same industry. They also changed from time to time. Even in countries such as Germany, where the connexion between investment and output appeared to be closest, capital-output ratios were not the same throughout the post-war period; and in most other countries they were also, as a rule, higher in the late fifties and the early sixties than in the ten years immediately after the war. Some factors, which differed from place to place and from time to time must have been at work. What were they?[2]

An obvious, though clearly incomplete, answer to this question will be found in the material, indeed geographical, circumstances of certain countries. Sweden, and more especially Norway, had to spend a very large proportion of their investment on transport, the generation of energy, and housing, with the result that their investment into manufacturing industry was relatively smaller than the figures of their gross investments might suggest. Dutch investment may have been swollen by large amounts drawn during the earlier

---

[1] Above, p. 115.
[2] For a summary of the data on variations of I.C.O.R.s between sectors and industries, see UNO, *Economic Survey of Europe*, N.Y., 1961, part 2, Ch. III; also UNO, *World Economic Survey*, N.Y., 1959, Ch. I.

period into large land reclamation schemes. In the United Kingdom a high proportion was devoted to capital-intensive uses – coal-mining, railways, electricity, and atomic power.

Another factor more frequently invoked is that of the 'age' of a nation's capital equipment. We are often told that the reason why older industrial countries required higher gross investment to increase their outputs is that a much larger proportion of that investment was required to maintain their ageing capital equipment. Of each pound or franc they invested a much smaller proportion was 'net', i.e. left to pay for additions to the existing machinery and plant. Their 'incremental capital-output ratios' were correspondingly higher: the dose of gross investment they needed to obtain the same amount of additional productive capacity was larger than in countries with younger industries.[1]

This argument is true only in part, and in very small part at that. It assumes that the main cost of replacement arose from the physical wear-and-tear of ageing plant, whereas in post-war industry the main compulsion to replace came from technological obsolescence. And technological obsolescence in older industries was not higher than in modern ones: on the contrary, equipment got out of date most quickly and had for this reason to be replaced most frequently in modern, science-oriented industries, and the cost of replacement was highest for the most recent generation of machines and plant. Mr Shonfield has recently quoted some striking evidence of the obsolescence allowances of I.C.I., where renewals used to be planned before the war on the assumption of twenty years' life of installed equipment, compared with its planned life of seven or even

---

[1] A. Maddison, *Economic Growth*, I, *passim*. In economic discussion as well as in historical experience old age of capital may reflect the survival of ancient and presumably antiquated technologies or greater physical endurance ('longevity') of the equipment. In the latter case the cost of replacement would be lower than that of more recently installed but less 'enduring' installations: cf. Evsey D. Domar, 'Depreciation, Replacement, and Growth', *Economic Journal*, Vol. 163, March 1953. This argument takes into account the possibility that this more-enduring equipment might cost more to make and to install, but, like Maddison's argument, it assumes that the charges for replacement are mainly determined by the physical wear and tear: an assumption far removed from reality. For a recent discussion of the contrast between 'physical' production of capital and its 'value productivity', and of irrelevance of mere age and longevity of capital, cf. S. K. Bhattacharyya, 'Capital Longevity and Economic Growth', *Review of Economic Studies*, Vol. XXXII (1), No. 89, 1965, pp. 43–4.

five years in more recent times. The shorter life and higher costs of replacements of fixed capital in new industries is reflected in much of other post-war evidence. In spite of its statistical shortcomings, this evidence would not allow us to put the main blame for high capital-output ratios on the heavier cost of repairs and renewal of old equipment.[1]

If the 'age' of an industry had any influence on its capital output ratios and on the productivity of its capital equipment in general, this was not because older industries were burdened with heavier maintenance costs but for other, more fundamental, reasons. Of these reasons, none were more fundamental than the social and human factors which determined the manner – or would the 'spirit' be the better word? – in which industries and individual firms within them were conducted; and more will be said about these factors presently. But some of the reasons were of a more material and tangible kind and have of late figured prominently in the discussion of the advantages and disadvantages of 'early' and 'late' start of industrialization.

One of the disabilities of countries which started early, and of older industries within them, was the prevalence of obsolescent equipment. Most of it would have proved unremunerative had it not been so well written down for depreciation as to be from the accounting point of view still commercially viable. For this reason, and also because most older industries built themselves up when the markets for their products were larger and more expansive than in the post-war world, they also carried much surplus capital equipment and suffered from chronic unemployment of capacity.

This unemployed capacity and changes in the degree of its utilization may help to explain some of the post-war differences in the outputs which individual European countries were able to obtain

---

[1] A. Shonfield, *Modern Capitalism*, p. 42, fn. 6. Cf. the report on the experience of the firm of Birfield in *The Financial Times*, 22 November 1965. The report also mentions the contrasting evidence of very low replacement rate in older textile enterprises taken over by Viyella. The evidence of the high proportion of 'young' capital equipment in German industry produced by Krengel and others is not by itself evidence of low allocation for replacements and of high ratio of 'net' investments. Replacements can have as rejuvenating an effect as 'net' investment. R. Krengel, 'Anlagevermogen, Produktion und Beschäftigung der Industrie im Gebiet der Bundesrepublik von 1924 bis 1956', *Sonderhefte* of the *Deutsches Institut für Wirtschaftsforschung*, N.S., 42, pp. 52 seq.

from their capital. It will not, however, explain all of them.[1] The existence of large unemployed capacity and the ease with which it could be brought into employment may account for much of Germany's, or Austria's, spectacular expansion in the late forties and may also account for some of the French achievements after 1958. Yet it will leave much of the British and even some of the German, French, or Scandinavian, experience unaccounted for. The utilization of reserve capacity was so important yet so contradictory a feature of the post-war progress that it will bear looking into more closely.

Full capacity and coefficients of its utilization are, of course, imperfect statistical entities, as difficult to define as they are to measure. However, the estimates made by the Deutsches Institut für Wirtschaftsforschung in Germany, the Institut National de la Statistique Economique in France, and the National Institute of Economic and Social Research in the United Kingdom, probably have a bearing on the underlying realities and can serve as a rough guide to the real differences in the utilization of capital equipment in these countries during our period. They suggest that in the years immediately following the war and the currency reform of 1948 German industry was able to draw on large reserves built up since 1934 but put out of employment by wartime bombing and post-war dislocation. This capacity could be brought into use with very small expenditure of capital: no more than was necessary to repair or to reorganize factories damaged or otherwise immobilized in the concluding phase of the war; and the capital-output ratios in that period were correspondingly low. They rose somewhat between 1950 and 1955 as wholly new capital was brought in to pay for the erection of new factories and for additions to the 'economic infra-structure', such as roads or energy. But the rise was not very great. For in the meantime the utilization of capacity had also increased from about 63 per cent in 1949 to 82 per cent in 1954. It continued to increase thereafter, and may have risen by another 5 or 6 per cent towards the end of 1962. But as the remaining reserves of unemployed

[1] Readers new to the subject may find the following eight paragraphs dealing with the connexion between unutilized capacity and capital-output ratios somewhat difficult to follow. They will be advised to omit the section and to resume their reading with para. 2 on p. 140, beginning with the words 'Utilization of capacity could not . . .'.

capacity were being used up, the additional output was coming to depend more and more on new investment, and incremental capital-output ratios were rising accordingly. In fact, they rose from 1·2 in the early post-war years to 1·9 in 1959, and to possibly more than 2·0 in the early sixties.[1] Even at that time they were still much lower in the United Kingdom, Belgium, or the Scandinavian countries, but they were nearly twice as high as in the late forties and early fifties.

The Austrian experience was somewhat similar. The country came out of the war with large reserves of capacity, and its initial progress largely depended upon fuller utilization of its equipment, with the result that its incremental capital-output ratios were comparatively low. France had also accumulated much under-utilized capacity in the late fifties, mostly because investment had been high during the years of the Korean War of 1950–1 and had left behind it a large reserve of machinery and plant. This reserve was taken up in the subsequent years, and the capital-output ratios were accordingly low.

Different, and at first sight more difficult to account for, were the experiences in the United Kingdom. The trend there appears to have moved in the opposite direction to the German. The proportion of capacity in use rapidly increased immediately after the war and reached a high point in 1951. The recession of 1952 reduced it,

[1] On concept and measurement of capacity utilization, cf. *Some Factors*, Ch. IV, 18–19. The relevant statistical evidence in historical perspective is summarized in S. Kuznets, 'Quantitative Aspects of Economic Growth', *Economic Development and Cultural Change*, IX, pt. 2, July 1961, where utilization of capacity is demonstrated as the principal factor of growth of G.D.P. and of differences in capital-output ratios in fully developed countries. On utilization of capacity in Germany, see R. Krengel, 'Produktionskapazitäten, Kapitalintensität und Kapazitätausnützung der Westdeutschen Industrie', *Vierteljahrshefte zur Wirtschaftsforschung*, ft. 1, 1962: *idem* 'Some Reasons for the Rapid Economic Growth of the German Federal Republic', *Quarterly Review of Banca Nazionale del Lavoro*, no. 64, 1963; D. Mertens, 'Die Kurzfristige Kapazitätausnützungs rechnung der DIW', *Vierteljahrshefte zur Wirtschaftsforschung*, Hft. 1, 1961. However the survey in the *Wochenbericht* of the *Deutsches Institut für Wirtschaftsforschung*, 1964, no. 17, points out that although in the past capital-output ratios depended mainly on utilization of capacity, their increase in the sixties was to some extent due to growing tendency to increase investment in substitution for labour. For Austrian inquiries, cf. F. Nemschak, 'Aspekte der Österreichischen Konjunkturpolitik im Herbst 1960', *Österreichisches Institut für Wirtschaftsforschung*. For other countries, cf. Max Balbenspenger, 'Die Arbeitsproduktivität in der Schweizerschen Volkswirtschaft', *Zeits. für Volkswirtschaft*, March 1963.

which entered the post-war period over-provided with fixed capital but it rose soon after, and by 1955, though still not full, it stood at the highest point it was ever to reach. It fell thereafter, and stayed low until the sixties. According to the estimates of the National Institute of Economic and Social Research, the level at which output stood at the beginning of 1959 would have had to be raised by as much as 30 per cent to bring the capital-output ratios down again to the levels of 1950-1 or 1955.[1]

The under-employment in the United Kingdom was to some extent 'chronic' and 'structural', or, in other words, related to the proportions of different industries in the make-up of the economy. Industries differed in the rate at which their outputs and productivities grew and in the speed with which that growth responded to additional investment. To take one example, the United Kingdom output per man after the war grew at a higher pace in services than in manufacturing industry. Yet capital increased more slowly and eventually stood at a lower level in the former than in the latter. In 1948 both industries and services disposed of the same amount of capital per worker (£2,300), but by 1963 capital per worker in industry rose to some £3,450 or by about 50 per cent, whereas in services it rose to only £2,850 or by about 23 per cent.[2]

These particular responses to additional investment may be quite easy to account for. Some services – banking, finance, and possibly certain branches of distribution – were in the process of being mechanized, and, like most trades in the initial phases of their mechanizations, they were able to show dramatic rises in productivity and to affect the national capital-output ratios accordingly. Other 'structural' differences could also have affected capital-output ratios, but the differences of 'structure' which concern us at this point in our story are those of employed capacity. The United Kingdom had the misfortune of harbouring a high proportion of industries

---

[1] *National Institute Economic Review*, no. 17, N.I.E.S.R., 1959. The high figures of utilization in the United Kingdom cited in F. W. Paish, 'Economic Position of the U.K.', *Westminster Bank Review*, August 1962, are irrelevant, since in the author's usage 'capacity' mainly refers to the employment of labour.

[2] R. C. O. Matthews, the unpublished paper and 'Some Aspects of Post-war Growth', as cited above, p. 118, footnote 1, Table V and pp. 14–16. However, it must be borne in mind that measurements of productivity in services must be very imperfect and are to a large extent based on earnings.

and thus unable to employ it fully. In the British cotton industry output had been declining since the early twenties, and, after a short post-war spurt, continued to decline during most of our period. It is not therefore surprising that throughout the post-war years the industry should have been saddled with much idle plant and machinery. Its unemployed capacity was at one time estimated to be as high as 40 or 50 per cent. Under these conditions the most effective way of raising the productivity of capital and the one which the Government adopted was to induce the industry to scrap redundant spindles and looms. This particular transformation was still far from complete in 1962, and the proportion of capacity in employment was at that date still lower than in most other industries.

The story of the British coal industry, British shipbuilding and railways and of certain branches of engineering differed from that of cotton only in degree. Some industries, such as the branches of the steel industry specializing in the making of heavy products, were bound to carry excessive capacity in order to provide for the wide fluctuations of demand for their products. Their experience was shared by steel industries in other European countries. Industries such as coal and railways were also saddled with excess capacity merely because the demand for their products had been declining for a long time and was now well below its peak. The plight of the British railways was to be matched by all European railways, barring those of Switzerland and Holland, and the plight of the British coal industry was if anything less parlous than that of the French, German, or Belgian. But the unfortunate fact that these industries, all characterized by much under-utilized capacity, formed a relatively large component of British economic structure, helps to explain why *average* capital-output ratios were so high and why, relative to the size of its installed capital capacity, British national product was not higher than we have seen it to have been.[1]

What it does not explain is why additional outputs from successive

---

[1] Hence some of the advantages – high initial rates of growth and low capital-output ratios of newly industrialized countries: A. Gerschenkron, 'Economic Backwardness in Historical Perspective' in B. Hoselitz (ed.), *The Progress of Underdeveloped Areas*, 1952; also M. Frankel, 'Obsolescence and Technical Change in Mature Economy', *American Economic Review*, 1955.

Vide Appendix Note 7, p. 364 below.

K

injections of new investment – or in more technical language, the 'incremental' capital-output ratios (I.C.O.R.s) as distinct from the average ones – should also have been high. The relations between average and incremental ratios are by no means simple, and there are some cogent, though well hidden, reasons why in certain circumstances they should have moved together. But the most obvious and the best-known relation between them should be a reciprocal one. Whenever and wherever average or aggregate capital-output ratios happened to be high because capacity was not fully employed, the existence of unemployed capacity (especially if it was not confined to a few sectors of industry) should have made it possible for the country to obtain high additional output from relatively little additional investment and thus to chalk up low incremental ratios. If this *a priori* reasoning holds good, the United Kingdom's unemployed capacity, always high and growing after 1955, should have led to higher outputs from post-1955 investment than those which Germany, whose equipment was fully utilized, was obtaining from her additional investment at the same time. But we have seen that this is not what, in fact, happened. The United Kingdom's incremental capital-output ratios stood higher relatively to Germany's and to those of most other European countries, and were rising throughout the times of high unemployment of capacity after 1955.[1]

Utilization of capacity could not therefore have been as omnipotent a factor behind national differences in capital-output ratios as the German experiences might at first sight suggest; and the reasons for that are not far to seek. For what makes the current notion of capital utilization insufficient as a tool of analysis is that it confines itself to the quantitative aspects of utilization – tells us how much of the existing equipment was in operation – and disregards its qualitative aspects, i.e. how well was the employed capacity employed. And one need not be an economist or even an historian to realize that the same amount of capital would have

---

[1] Where the average capital-output ratios are high because the industrial equipment is old and obsolescent, a more rapid improvement in its I.C.O.R. and in that of the national economy as a whole could be expected from technological innovation. The latter is likely to result in relatively 'greater improvement in the average quality of a country's capital stock if the previously existing stock was relatively old and out of date', *Some Factors*, Ch. V, p. 3.
Vide Appendix Note 8, pp. 364–5 below.

yielded higher output to countries, industries, and firms whose products were more novel, whose technologies were more advanced, production lines better laid out, labour relations smoother, marketing more effective. Assessed by these criteria, the new or modern industries may be found to owe their low post-war I.C.O.R.s not to the fact that they were more fully employed (this should have had the opposite effect) or less capital-intensive (the chemical and petroleum industries happened to be highly capitalized) but to the fortunate circumstance that firms in most modern industries were comparatively well-managed and employed their capital not only fully but also better than firms predominating in older industries.

These last-mentioned differences, those between firm and firm, were perhaps the most significant ones. Indeed, so significant were they that the most reasonable way of presenting and explaining the international and inter-industrial variations in productivity of capital is by showing how in some industries and some countries firms with favourable, i.e. low, capital-output ratios were more fully represented than in others. And – to repeat – differences which mark off one firm from another in the same country and the same industry – especially as between firms of roughly equal size and age – must be in one way or another related to differences in the quality of management, which, as we said, must also have accounted for some of the most significant variations in the demand for capital.[1]

These converging references to management bring to its close the story of investment as part of the general history of economic growth. The moral of the story is not that growth was not greatly dependent on the rate of new investment but that the dependence was neither simple nor immediate. A host of other factors interposed themselves between the flow of capital available for investment and the expanding output. Some firms, some industries, and some countries asked for more capital than others; some obtained higher outputs from the capital they received. And behind these higher and

[1] 'In the final resort the successful firms performed a given function with fewer fixed assets', B. R. Williams, *International Report on Investment Behaviour*, O.E.C.D., Paris, the United Kingdom section. For the clearest exposition of this view see Tibor Barna, *Investment and Growth Policies of British Industrial Firms*, N.I.E.S.R., 1952, pp. 36–8, Ch. V.

lower outputs were the various historical differences between countries, industries, and firms. For various reasons industrial equipment was more fully employed in some countries than in others; new industries were more fully represented in some countries; some countries were better provided with efficient managers and with a well-trained and amenable labour force. None of these conditions might have been sufficient to promote high rates of economic growth without constant injections of new capital. But the effects of the injections were amplified as in Germany, or muffled as in the United Kingdom, by the action of these 'other' factors.

CHAPTER 6

Innovation

The story of post-war investment has thus run into that of technological progress and the behaviour of entrepreneurs. As we shall presently see, the two strands – advancing technology and evolving attitudes of business leaders – were so closely interwoven as to be almost inseparable. I propose, however, to treat them here as independent themes, if only because to the naked eye technological advances since 1945 are clearer than the related changes in the behaviour of entrepreneurs.

It is now generally agreed that after 1946 the world witnessed a technical advance more widespread and rapid than at any time in the past. The most conspicuous manifestations of the advance were the new products which have since the war entered into everyday use. The modern aircraft industry and air transport were to all intents and purposes a post-war development. So was the electronic industry – the making not only of television and radio equipment but of various electronic devices for measurement, signals, and telecommunications, as well as of computers and transfer devices on which the modern automation and cybernetic techniques are based. In this very new industry the coming of the transistor in the fifties ushered in a wholly new generation of devices still in their infancy in the early sixties. Modern plastics, synthetic resins and man-made fibres were nearly all post-war commodities and were, with a few exceptions, products of the new hydrocarbon chemistry and of the petrochemical industry based on it. Of the new metals, aluminium and most of the alloy steels had, of course, been well known and much used before the war, but their growth into a major industry and their widespread use was also a post-1939 phenomenon. Even more 'post-war' was the large-scale use and the production of titanium. The civilian use of atomic power for the generation of electricity may still have been in its infancy, but by the late fifties it already represented a considerable volume of investment in the United Kingdom and France, and by 1964 also in Belgium, Italy, and Germany. And as the sixties were drawing towards their middle year, the laser promised to open new possibilities to technologists and manufacturers.

These are, of course, all highly conspicuous examples of new products known to the man in the street; but a proper technological history of the modern world will also include many hundreds of less obvious and less known objects, from various water-repelling substances, leather substitutes, antibiotics, and antihistamines to new engineering and electronic components based on recent and, in most cases, revolutionary departures in applied science and technology.

He would, however, be a superficial economist and historian who would confine his account of post-war technology to its products. From the point of view of the modern economy, more important than the new products were the new processes, e.g. the new ways of making old products. They affected most industries, including some of the older ones. Steel technology, which had also been dormant for several generations, was transformed by new processes. Several varieties of the oxygen process were introduced after the war with all-but revolutionary effects at the smelting stage, and by 1964 they were themselves threatened by more modern methods, including those of making steel directly from ore. In other stages of steel-making those of refining, fabricating, and annealing, the electric furnaces for special steels, continuous rolling of sheet, continuous casting – some of them processes and devices of pre-war origin – were being universally adopted or came to the point of being so adopted in the post-war period with a revolutionary effect on productivity and costs. Similarly, the cotton industry, whose technology had changed little since the end of the nineteenth century, found itself on the verge of general transformation by means of automatic production lines. The glass industry, one of the oldest manufacturing industries in Europe, was during our period in the process of being modernized out of all recognition, especially in the making of containers, and more recently also of plate glass. Ship-building was deeply affected by welding and prefabrication, by improved designs of hulls and engines and by scientific planning of output. Even the building industry, the most conservative of all industrial occupations, was lifted into a new technological phase by the wider use of new earth-moving and lifting equipment, by new materials, by prefabrication and 'phased' planning. At a still lower level, piecemeal introduction of new methods and new types of equipment was effecting profound changes in most branches of production.[1]

How is an historian to account for this outburst of technological innovation? Was it one of those spontaneous mutations of European culture and society, self-generated and inexplicable, or was it rooted in ascertainable historical circumstances?

Undoubtedly, the range of new technological possibilities was wider, or to put it in terms more akin to current economic vocabulary, the supply of new technologies was more abundant after the war than in any other period of European history. One of the causes of this upsurge will be found in the war itself, since a great deal of modern technology originated in the war or was part and parcel of the cold-war weaponry. Post-war aircraft stood in direct line of succession from wartime aircraft. The development of its prime mover, the gas turbine, had simmered in the late thirties in Germany, Britain and elsewhere; but had it not been for the war neither Whittle's pioneering engine nor its highly developed successors in Germany and Britain would have seen the light of day. Most of the radar and radio development of post-war years derived from the apparatus conceived and developed in the Telecommunications Research Establishment in Malvern during the war years and from the electronic devices developed in the later stages of the war by firms in the U.S.A. Wartime weapons also accounted for the vast development of electronic instrumentation and computer techniques. The modern petrochemical industry owed its development to the technology of high octane fuels required for the last generation of reciprocating aircraft engines as well as to the German and American wartime search for synthetic rubbers and synthetic petrols. And

---

[1] Schumpeter's thesis on the connexion between expansion and innovations cannot be countered, as in *Some Factors*, Ch. V, p. 2, by the contention that new products would not themselves provide a convincing explanation of observed differences in growth rates. This contribution does not take into account the very important part of innovation in the making of old products.

there is no need to remind the modern reader of the connexion between nuclear technology and 'the bomb'.[1]

The link between new technological opportunities and the development of weapons did not get any looser after the war. British, French, German, Swedish, and even Swiss governments continued to sponsor large and costly projects for the design and development of weapons, and much of the effort was bound to overflow into general science and technology.

Some of the overflow was very direct. Airframes and air engines developed for military purposes could without much difficulty be adapted for commercial uses. The debt which electronic instrumentation in industrial use owed to the instruments evolved for and by the military and for various state-sponsored space programmes is equally obvious. So also is the military and 'space' stimulus behind the theory and engineering practice of modern cybernetics.

Military programmes also had some indirect effects. In their definition of military objectives, defence departments in all Western countries, and above all in the U.S.A., were very liberal, and financed a great deal of research only remotely related to defence and much of it serving the interests of pure science. For these and other reasons general technology and science stood to benefit from high and rising expenditures on defence-inspired research. Expenditure under this head was higher in the United Kingdom and France than in any other European country, and their experience is not therefore fully representative. It is nevertheless worth noting that in the United Kingdom the annual expenditure on research and development financed out of the defence budget grew from about £177 million in 1955–6 to over £234 million at the end of the fifties and to some £245 million in 1959–62, even though its share of the total national expenditure on research and development declined from 22 per cent in the mid-fifties to about 15 per cent in the early sixties. In France military expenditure on research and development, though somewhat lower, grew very fast (it had doubled between 1958 and 1962) and exceeded N.F. 1,500 million by 1962. And as in the United Kingdom a large, though unmeasurable, pro-

---

[1] M. Postan, D. Hay, and J. D. Scott, *Design and Development of Weapons*, H.M.S.O., 1964, *passim*.

portion of this expenditure spilled over into objects of civilian import.[1]

Nevertheless, it would not be right to assign all the credit for new technologies – products as well as processes – to military research projects. Since 1945 European nations devoted to all kinds of research larger resources and larger proportions of their national products than at any other period of their history. The world suddenly became research-conscious. In every country statesmen and journalists suddenly woke up to the part which the progress of science and technology and the abundant supply of scientists and technologists could play in enhancing the power of their countries and in raising the efficiency of their economies. On their part, large firms provided themselves with ever-expanding departments for research and development. Most trade associations, i.e. combinations of firms belonging to certain industries, did likewise. A number of individual firms also began dispensing largesse in support of universities and of scientific activity in general on the very creditable theory that it was in their economic interest to further the general advance of science and technology. How great and growing this expenditure became is clearly shown by the figures in Table 14.

Table 14 *Expenditure on Research and Development 1950–62*[2]

	1955		1959		1962	
	Total (mill.)	Per Cent of G.N.P.	Total (mill.)	Per Cent of G.N.P.	Total (mill.)	Per Cent of G.N.P.
United Kingdom	£300 [a]	1·7	£478 [b]	2·3	£634 [c]	3·1
Netherlands	—	—	—	2·0 [d]	—	—
Sweden	—	—	—	1·8	—	—
Germany	—	0·8	—	1·2	—	—
France	—	—	2,230 frs.	1·1 [d]	3,436 frs.	1·6

[a] 1955–6. [b] 1958–9. [c] 1960–2. [d] 1960.

[1] Below, pp. 149–50, *Some Factors*, Ch. V, pp. 4 *seq.*: UNO, *Economic and Social Consequences of Disarmament*, N.Y., 1962. Cf. also *Annual Report of the Advisory Committee on Scientific Policy 1961–62*, Cd. Paper, 1920, H.M.S.O. 1963. For French data, see also *L'Usine nouvelle*, for 18 May 1961.

[2] The table is based on Table 1 in *Some Factors*, Ch. V.

Chart 1[1]

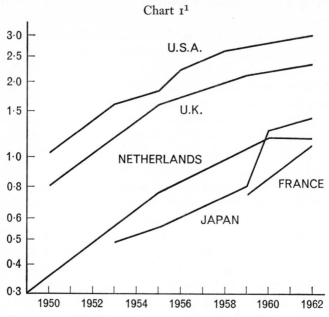

The figures on which this graph is based are not wholly identical with the figures in Table 14, but the differences are not so great as to be statistically significant.

Indeed, so high was the expenditure and so fast did it rise – especially after 1955 – that a correlation between innovation and economic growth on the one hand, and expenditure on research on the other, springs naturally to mind. As this correlation also appears well grounded in common sense it is not surprising that statesmen and their economic and scientific advisers should invariably have accepted higher expenditure on scientific and technological research as an unfailing recipe for technological progress and increasing national wealth.

In the long run and in a purely international setting this correlation, like the recipe based on it, is plausible to the point of truism. There is no need to argue that if somewhere and at some time during our period men had not pursued their researches into the cracking and reformation of the petroleum molecule or into the conductivity of materials, the immensely important technology of petrochemicals and of transistors – to take the two most obvious examples – would never have developed as fast as it did.

The correlation is, however, less obvious when considered in relation to individual Western countries after the war. A close look at our Table 14 and Chart I will show that there was little connexion between the rate at which individual European countries increased their expenditure on design and development and the rate at which they increased their productivities, and, presumably, modernized their economies. The expenditure in the United Kingdom as a proportion of the G.N.P. was higher than in any other European country and was little below that of the U.S.A.; yet the apparent progress of industrial innovation in the United Kingdom was the most laggard in Western Europe. The next largest pro-rata expenditure was that of the Netherlands and Sweden, yet their economic performance, and probably also their rate of industrial innovation, was by no means faster than that of France, Italy, or Germany. On the other hand, Germany whose progress of innovations after 1945 was the envy of other nations and whose rate of economic growth was the fastest, spent (at least before 1961) a smaller proportion of her national income on research and development than any other European country for which the relevant information is available.[1]

In considering these figures, it should, of course, be borne in mind that defence projects absorbed a much larger proportion of research funds in the United Kingdom than in Germany. Yet even if expenditure on civil research alone were counted and no allowance were made for the defence-oriented researches capable of benefiting civil industries, the share of G.N.P. spent on research in the

[1] For a critical summary of the relevant literature and issues, see Robert E. Johnston, 'Technical Progress and Innovation', *Oxford Economic Papers*, Vol. 18, No. 2, July 1966, pp. 165–6, which specifies some of the dangers of using the expenditure on research and development as indices of effective technological inputs, and, above all, the danger of disregarding the differences in the productivity of research and development in different environments. On this, cf. also C. Freeman, 'An Experimental International Comparison of Research Expenditure and Manpower in 1962', O.E.C.D.: SR (65.31), Paris, 1965. A more general discussion of direct effects of expenditure on R. and D. on growth will be found in B. R. Williams, 'Investment and Technology in Growth', *The Manchester School*, 1964, pp. 68 *seq.*; C. F. Carter and B. R. Williams, *Science Industry*, London, 1959; D. L. Burn, 'Investment, Innovation and Planning in the U.K.', *Progress*, September 1962.

United Kingdom would still appear as high as in the U.S.A., and higher than the same share in Germany and France.[1]

The correlation between growth and innovation on the one hand, and expenditure on research on the other, comes out somewhat more clearly in the post-war performances of individual industries. These performances are, of course, exceedingly difficult to measure and even to observe. What economists and historians as a rule record is not technological progress *per se* but superficial impressions of novel products and processes and changes in productivity which can be reasonably attributed to innovations. These impressions indeed show that most of the industries which, judged by these signs, appear to have been in the van of technological progress, devoted large resources to research and development. Thus, in the United Kingdom, the chemical and electrical industries could in the late fifties and early sixties boast of rates of growth, of increases in productivity and of visible technological advances greater than in most other industries; and their expenditure on research and development was also well above the average (11·5 and 24·5 per cent of the total in 1962). On the other hand, the British paper industry, with a rate of growth above the average (4·5 per cent) and an impressive record of productivity and visible technological innovation, appeared to spend on research and development at a rate (0·9 per cent), which was somewhat lower than in industry as a whole. The same is to some extent true of the rubber industry and food and drink. Conversely, energy, transport and general engineering, in spite of their higher-than-average expenditure on research (between 4·4 and 6 per cent), did not appear to achieve commensurate increases in productivity.[2]

If these indirect assessments have any significance at all, they will lend further support to the conclusion we have already derived from the aggregate figures of national expenditures on research and development, i.e. that over a span of years as short as that of the post-

[1] See discussion of figures in Graph I in O.E.C.D., *Science, Economic Growth, and Government Policy*, Paris, 1963, p. 25. In the United Kingdom about one-half of gross national expenditure on research and development was military. The proportion of government-financed research devoted to military objects was two-thirds of total in the United Kingdom, France, and the U.S.A., but only one-third in Germany, *ibid.*, pp. 42–3.

[2] *Some Factors*, Ch. V, p. 9, Table 5; C. Freedman and A. Young, *The Research and Development Efforts*, O.E.C.D., Paris 1965, Table 5.

war period, outlays on research and development and technological progress were but imperfectly correlated. And, once observed, this imperfection is not difficult to account for. In the first place there was no reason why the benefits of advancing science and technology should have been confined to the nations or the firms which did most to advance them. In spite of all the obstacles to international migrations of technology, to which Professor Cairncross has drawn our attention, few countries in our period depended for new technological opportunities solely on their own discoveries. As several writers have recently reminded us, technical progress often consisted not in the discovery of new products and techniques, but in the adoption of existing technology or its imitation.[1]

It is in this way that countries, industries and firms were able to make greater technological advances than their own researches would have supported. Under the existing system of licenses and business links it was possible for nations and firms to acquire designs, equipment and the technical 'know how' from outside. The history of most of the recent processes and products abounds with examples of such acquisitions. The most famous example is, of course, that of the American firm of Du Pont. Throughout our period it continued to rank as the leading firm in an industry more dependent on research than most other industries; and it is known to have devoted immense resources to its own research activities. Yet a recent investigation has revealed that at least three out of every five important new products and processes it introduced in the post-war period were based on ideas and discoveries of other firms. On the international scale the clearest example was that of Japanese industry, where, until the late fifties, technological advances were largely sustained by foreign licenses. A good European example was the progress of German electronic and petro-chemical industries before 1955, which was to a large extent based on processes developed abroad.[2]

A somewhat indirect statistical measurement of the international

---

[1] A. K. Cairncross, 'The Migration of Technology', *Factors in Economic Development*, 1962; C. D. Kindleberger, 'Obsolescence and Technical Change', *Papers of the Oxford Institute of Statistics*, 23, No. 3, 1961, p. 289.

[2] W. Mueller, 'The Origins of the Basic Inventions Underlying Du Pont's Main Product and Process Innovations', *The Rate and Direction of Inventive Activity*, N.B.E.R., N.Y., 1964.

role of imported technologies will be found in the balances of international payments for royalties on new products and processes. The aggregate receipts of American firms for fees and licences of this kind greatly exceeded the sums they themselves had to pay to foreign firms. In 1956 the aggregate American receipts for technological royalties and fees approached $100 million, but American payments abroad on this account were merely $15 million. The American balances on this account rose steeply in the subsequent five years. They averaged $450 million per annum whereas payments to foreign firms ranged between $47 and $60 million per annum. By comparison, France had a steady negative balance. In 1956 French enterprises paid some N.F. 272 million to American firms as fees and royalties but received from the U.S.A. only N.F. 108 million. This negative balance obviously reflected the extent to which French technological progress (in this period it was quite considerable) depended upon American researches. The same is true of Western Europe as a whole. Its balance of technological payments was heavily in the red. In the same five years between 1957 and 1961 European countries paid to the U.S.A. on the average some $175 million per annum, but received from the U.S.A. on the average not more than $41 million per annum.[1] Unfortunately, comparable figures for similar payments within Europe itself are not yet available. But preliminary soundings suggest – not unexpectedly – that European countries took in each others' innovations, and that some countries took in more than they gave out. What this means is that some European countries and firms within them were able to make greater technological advances than their own direct outlays on research and development would have made possible.

Needless to say, technologies purchased from outside were not a true alternative to innovations generated by home-based research and development. Post-war experience showed that the firms which spent most generously on research and development were also the firms most prone to acquire ready-made discoveries from others. In the words of the O.E.C.D. report already cited here, 'it is those who are themselves grappling with research and development problems who are best able to appreciate the advances made else-

---

[1] O.E.C.D., *Science, Economic Growth, and Government Policy*, Appendix B, Tables 9 and 10.

where'.[1] In a more general way large outlays on research and development and the readiness to buy licences and to pay royalties were merely different ways of satisfying the urge to innovate. And as long as both ways were open, the technological progress of firms and nations did not depend entirely on the scale of their own researches and could not be measured solely by their cost.

So much for the first, the so-to-speak exogenous, reason why technological progress and outlays in research and development did not necessarily synchronize. The second reason was endogenous, inherent in the very nature of technological progress. For even where and when innovations followed home-based discoveries, the progress of discovery and the flow of innovations were not always commensurate or concomitant. In this respect post-war experience did not greatly diverge from the historical norm. In the past history of the European economy the connexion between the march of industrial technology and advancing scientific knowledge was seldom very close. I doubt whether we can measure the time-lag between scientific progress and industrial technology as precisely as Professor D. E. Marlow has recently tried to do, and to assert, as he has done, that whereas the earlier technological innovations such as photography followed more than a century behind the underlying scientific discovery, the most recent technological innovations came within a few years of the corresponding discoveries.[2] On the whole, the time-lag between scientific discovery and its industrial application was undoubtedly shorter in the post-war world than it had been a few generations earlier. Yet at all periods, even in most recent ones, industrial technology followed at some distance behind the

[1] *Ibid.*, p. 34; see also statement of the Federation of British Industries in *Industrial Research in Manufacturing Industry*, London, 1961, p. 50.

[2] Cf. also Pierre Lelong, 'L'évolution de la planification de la recherche', *Revue Economique*, 1964, no. 1. There have been several recent attempts to measure and account for the time-lags between discovery and commercial use of innovations in different industries and countries: e.g. J. R. Minasian, 'The Economics of Research and Development', *The Rate and Direction of Inventive Activity*, N.B.E.R., N.Y., 1964; and the numerous articles by E. Mansfield, more especially his 'Industrial Research and Development Expenditures', *Journal of Political Economy*, August 1964, and 'Research and Technological Change', *Industrial Research*, February 1964.

progress of scientific and technical discovery, and sometimes did not follow it at all.

The upsurge of technical innovation in eighteenth- and early nineteenth-century England which bears the name of the Industrial Revolution owed a little, but only a little, to the contemporary scientific discovery. The connexion between the latter and the new machines and processes, especially in textiles where they came first, was very accidental and most remote. It is easy enough to cite cases where an industrialist, a Wilkinson, a Wedgwood, or a Watt, consulted noted scientists about technical problems. But in general it remains true that with a few exceptions, such as the manufacture of certain crude chemicals and some stages in the ceramic technique, technological progress in British industry did not, until the last quarter of the nineteenth century, follow closely in the footsteps of science. It was not until the turn of the century that a regular flow of ideas between laboratories and firms set in, and that in countries, such as Germany, scientific advances in electromagnetic theory and organic chemistry could be put to industrial uses without too much delay, and that the names of such scientists as Faraday, Kelvin, Maxwell, Hertz, and Hopkins became intimately linked with development of industrial technology.[1]

Yet even in countries and in periods in which ideas fully and regularly flowed between scientific laboratories and factory workshops, this flow was not smooth and continuous, but passed through several, at least three, phases. The initial phase, that of new advances in scientific knowledge, had to be followed by the phase in which potentially useful design projects and inventions were conceived; the latter, in its turn, had to go through the process of 'development', i.e. engineering adaptation and testing and that of commercial spread. In history these three ages of technology ranged themselves at some remove from each other, and as I have just suggested, the length of the remove varied with historical circumstances.

[1] Recent studies of the English Industrial Revolution have demonstrated that some of the industrial leaders of the time frequently consulted scientists on technical problems and were themselves educated men interested in scientific problems: A. E. Musson and E. Robinson, 'Science and Industry in the Late Eighteenth Century', *Economic History Review*, Second Series, Vol. XIII, No. 2, 1960. These interesting facts are, however, irrelevant to the problem discussed here, that of, how directly were advances of technology linked to, and how closely did they follow on, the contemporary advances in scientific knowledge.

Thus, the first phase – that of advancing scientific knowledge – did not always and necessarily lead to the second – that of invention and design; and the same is true of the transition from designs and inventions to their commercial application. In addition, even where these links could be and were created, the process of forging them was beset with difficulties and delays. For in recent industrial experience it is 'development' rather than 'design' that proved to be the costliest phase of organized technological progress – costliest in money, in manpower, and in time. In the process of development not all the inventions fulfilled their initial promise; and those which did required time before they could be provided with the appropriate engineering techniques and still more time before they entered into general industrial practice.[1]

However, these endogenous factors of research and development, like the exogenous factor of imported or borrowed innovations, will account for some but not for all the puzzling discordances in technological progress. To account for these discordances we must invoke a range of influences wholly different from those commonly discussed. The progress of pure and applied science, the expenditure on research and development, the purchase and importation of new technologies from outside, gaps between discovery and industrial innovations – all these were 'supply factors'. They all account for the flow of new technical projects, products, and processes. But in the history of innovation, as in the history of investment, the demand for new products and processes was of at least equal importance. If a country or firm within it happened to be technically more advanced than others this was not merely because it was able to create by its own researches, or was offered by others, a more abundant choice of new products and methods, but also because it was 'in the market' for innovations, or in other words, happened to be more receptive than others to the possibilities provided by science and engineering.

[1] C. Freeman has shown that even in an industry as modern and as science-oriented as plastics a gap of twenty-five to thirty-five years could exist between the inception of a research project and the general adoption of its results: 'The Plastics Industry: A Comparative Study of Research and Innovation', *National Institute Economic Review*, May 1962.

L

It is in these differing receptivities of firms, industries and countries that one of the principal problems of technological progress will be found. Why should Germany in the late nineteenth century have been thus more receptive than contemporary England, and even more receptive in the inter-war period than in the late nineteenth century? So important were these local and historical variations that the history of technological change must perforce occupy itself with the changes in the nations' ability to seek new products and processes. A story of post-war technology must accordingly occupy itself with the reasons why the post-war economy, and some post-war countries more than others, became sensitive to the possible benefits of technological change.

In such a story a large variety of influences, social as well as more purely economic, will figure. In recent popular, and more particularly in political, discussion of technological progress and of influences favouring or disfavouring it, most attention has been paid to certain obvious features of the social background, above all, to the qualities of the educational systems and labour attitudes. Of these influences, education stands out as the one best known, most commonly discussed and most frequently reflected in government pronouncements and policies.

Whether economists, or historians should imitate the example of Professor E. Denison and assign to education a precisely calculated share in the past increases in productivity (Denison credits education with about 42 per cent of increases in American real income per person) is perhaps doubtful.[1] But however imprecise and unmeasurable may have been the role of education there are *a priori* grounds as well as good historical reasons for regarding education in general and the supply of university-trained technicians in particular as a *sine qua non* of technological progress and consequently also of economic growth. In a more distant historical perspective superior technological and industrial education may be shown to underlie the ability and the willingness of nations to make

[1] E. Denison, *The Sources of Economic Growth in the U.S.A. and the Alternatives Before Us*, Council for Economic Development, N.Y., 1962, pp. 244–5; also idem in *The Residual Factor and Economic Growth*, O.E.C.D., Paris, 1964, pp. 13–66.

use of new technologies. Historians have taught us to ascribe the technological advances of German industry in the nineteenth and twentieth centuries to the high quality of the educational system and of technical training in that country. They have also demonstrated how much Japan's remarkable industrial and technological progress since the 1880's owed to her equally remarkable achievements in popular education. A similar, though a somewhat more recent, historical lesson, has been provided by Sweden and Switzerland. The high technological standards of their industries – chemical, electrical, and engineering – is reputed to owe a great deal to the excellence of their school systems.

The *a priori* reasons why better education, especially better technical education, favoured technological progress and fostered economic growth are too well known to need expounding in detail. Modern technology required a large and growing flow of university-trained engineers and industrial scientists. But technically trained cadres were also needed in lower ranks of industrial employment. Machines and plant in most modern industries, especially in electrical, engineering and chemical, had to be served by men able to read and follow technical manuals and blueprints and familiar with fundamental principles of engineering, physics and chemistry. Equally important were the diffused effects of better education in industrial society at large: the more frequent recourse to literate and articulate forms of communication, the greater reliance on book-fed rationality, the increasing emphasis on intellectual standards in the selection and promotion of personnel.[1]

So obvious is on *a priori* grounds the bridge between education and economic progress, and so prominently does it stand out in any bird's-eye view of historical past, that no historian or economist would even dare to question its importance. We should not, therefore, be surprised to find it reflected in the evidence of post-war Europe. The most relevant evidence at our disposal is that of the supply of university-trained engineers and of the national expenditure on education. This evidence, summarized in Tables 15 and 16 below, clearly indicates that in Western Europe, taken as a whole, and in most countries within it, the supplies of engineers greatly increased after 1946.

The tables show that in the countries for which the figures for the

---

[1] *Vide* Appendix Note 9, p. 365 below.

Table 15 *Higher Technical Personnel*[1]

Engineers with
University or Similar
Training as Per Cent
of Labour Force

	Year	
Austria	1951	0·38
Belgium	{1947	0·23
	1956	0·28
Denmark	1956	0·35
France	1955	0·47
Germany	1956	0·33
Italy	1951	0·28
Norway	1955	0·60
Sweden	{1950	0·33
	1955	0·38
Switzerland	1950	0·45
United Kingdom	{1958	0·33
	1959	0·37

Table 16 *Public Expenditure on Education 1937–1955*[2]

	1937 [a]	1950 [a]	1955 [b]	1959 [b]
Netherlands	3·9	3·2	4·5	3·7
Sweden	2·7	3·3	4·3	3·6
United Kingdom	2·7	3·7	4·0	3·5
Denmark	2·8	2·9	3·9	3·7
Western Germany	2·8	3·0	3·5	4·1
Norway	3·3	3·3	3·1	3·5

[a] Per cent of G.N.P.   [b] Per cent of National
Income per head

[1] The figures in the table are very similar to those in *Some Factors*, Ch. V, Tables 5–7, but not wholly identical with them. They have been supplemented and earlier years by F. Edding, *Internazionale Tendenzen in der Entwicklung der Ausgaben fur Schulen und Hochschulen*, Kieler Studien of the Institut für Weltwirtschaft, 1958, and are no more than approximate.

[2] The figures for 1937, 1950, and 1955 are based on *Some Factors*, Ch. V, Table 9. Those for 1959 have been derived mainly from the sources used for earlier years by F. Edding, as in footnote 1.

numbers of engineers are available for more than one year, i.e. Belgium, Sweden, and the United Kingdom, they grew relatively to the total labour force as a whole even over periods as short as three years. Other figures at our disposal, not tabulated here, also show that in the short space of four years between 1954 and 1958 the total 'stock' of engineers with first degrees in engineering may have grown by 15 per cent in France, 10 per cent in the United Kingdom, and 8 per cent in Germany. In the period between 1954 and 1963 these numbers in France and the United Kingdom may have grown by nearly 25 per cent. As we shall presently see, European nations devoted ever-greater proportions of their incomes to popular education. On the strength of these figures alone it is difficult not to conclude that the mounting output of European schools and universities must have had something to do with the progress of industrial technology and innovation in general.

This, however, is as far as our evidence will take us. It brings out the connexion between higher technical education and technological progress in Western Europe as a whole and over the period of the last thirty or forty years taken in its entirety, but it does not explain why the pace of technological progress and the march of innovation should have differed from one country to another in the way it did.

Our evidence may, of course, be at fault. The figures of university-trained engineers may not mean the same thing for every country. In the United Kingdom until the end of the fifties universities did not, as they did in the U.S.A., turn out engineers of lower academic rank capable of filling subordinate positions in drawing offices or in the workshops. The output of universities was almost wholly confined to the 'fully qualified' ranks. Similarly, state expenditure on education – a good index of growing educational facilities – cannot help us much in international comparisons since the content and quality of education in individual countries could differ in a variety of ways not reflected in their costs.

These shortcomings of our evidence make it difficult to derive from it any but the most superficial conclusions. But such conclusions as it permits do not accord well with the presumption that technical education could provide an obvious explanation for the relatively great advances in innovation in post-war Germany and the relatively laggard performances of countries like the United Kingdom or Belgium. As I have already suggested, total supplies of engineers grew in most European countries all through our period; but measured as a proportion of the total labour force, the supplies of fully qualified engineers did not differ from country to country in a manner related to their industrial and technological achievements. It was highest in Norway, France and Switzerland, and was somewhat higher in Great Britain than either in Germany or in Sweden. Yet these two countries enjoyed the highest reputation for the technological excellence of their industries and for their innovating propensities. Perhaps there was a higher correlation between innovation and the supply of lower ranks of technical personnel, but our evidence about the latter is too scanty to permit any statistical or historical generalization.

What we have noted about the supply of engineers also applies to expenditures on education. In 1955 expenditure on education, measured both per head of population and as proportion of G.N.P., was somewhat higher in the United Kingdom than in Germany, and the gap apparently widened by 1960. Moreover, since British outlay on education had begun to approach the German early in the thirties, the bulk of industrial labour force in the two countries, i.e. most men and and women under the ages of 45 employed in 1963, should have benefited from approximately equal educational provisions.[1]

Other, less direct, measurements of educational progress since the war tell the same story. In nearly all the countries educational standards rose in response to greater expenditure: more children and young persons went to school, and those who went were better provided for than in previous generations. But although all European countries shared in this progress, its pace was not the same everywhere; and what is more, the differences in pace did not in any obvious way match up with economic performances. On almost every count popular education in the United Kingdom progressed farther and faster since 1945, or indeed since 1920, than elsewhere in Europe. As a result, British educational levels, judged by purely material standards, had by the early sixties risen as high, or

---

[1] *Some Factors*, Ch. V, Table 77; also *U.N.E.S.C.O.: World Handbook o Educational Organisations and Statistics*, Paris (in progress).

even higher, than in almost any other country. On some counts the Belgian record was almost equally good, whereas that of Germany and Sweden – the paragons of economic and educational virtues – stood rather low. Thus the numbers of years of compulsory education increased in the same period from 8 to 9 in Germany, from 7 to 8 in Sweden. The latter was also the 1960 figure for the Netherlands and France. The pupil-teacher ratios in the under-15 age group improved most and was lowest in Belgium, where it declined between 1945 and 1960 from 26 to 20, compared with the decline from 30 to 26 in the United Kingdom, from 34 to 30 in Germany, from 30 to 27 in Sweden. In the 15 to 19 age group the ratios improved most and stood lowest in the sixties in Austria and Denmark. The ratio in the United Kingdom – 13 per teacher – was almost equally low, but that in Germany in the early sixties was 23 and in France 25. The proportions of children and young persons attending school ('enrolment ratios') were equally uneven. In Germany they were 80 per hundred for the lower age group and 18 per hundred for the higher age group compared with 95 and 32 in Belgium. The ratios in the United Kingdom and Scandinavian countries were slightly lower than in Belgium but higher than in Germany.[1]

These figures must not be cited to disparage the role of education in economic progress. At the cost of yet another repetition I must affirm the incontestable historical case for education as a propellant of economic growth. In a broad historical perspective, i.e. in expounding the economic achievement of the nineteenth and twentieth centuries compared with that of the earlier periods, or of Western countries compared to the rest of the world, the contributions of better and more widespread schooling and learning stand out very clearly. It is only when economic performances within Europe itself are compared, and the comparisons do not extend beyond the postwar years, or perhaps even beyond the forty-five years since 1920, that doubts arise about the effect of further improvements in education on economic and technological progress. The probability is that further improvements in education in countries already equipped with modern school systems did not pay, in terms of technological and economic achievements, as handsomely as in more backward

---

[1] *Some Factors*, Ch. V, Table 77; also *U.N.E.S.C.O.: World Handbook of Educational Organisations and Statistics*, Paris (in progress).

countries, or that they required a longer time to 'pay off', than any history of a recent period can span.[1]

So much for education. Another social factor which may have affected the ability of European nations and of individual firms within them to seek out and to make use of opportunities for technological innovations was the quality of labour. The aptitudes and attitudes of labour influenced technology in obvious ways. In countries and periods most afflicted with unemployment, e.g. in the United Kingdom before the war, labour-saving innovations in industry were not welcome to trade unions and provoked open opposition from their rank-and-file. Dislike of time-saving devices of modern production engineering – 'stop-watch' and all that – had come to be built into the trade-union traditions in the United Kingdom, in Germany, and in France, particularly in the engineering industries. For twenty or thirty years before the war the introduction of automatic looms into the British textile industries was impeded by the opposition of textile labour to multiple shift working. In the printing industry of most European countries technical innovations were also held back by the overwatchful attitude of the trade unions. The more rapid advance of labour-saving technology in some countries since the war may, therefore, have in part been due to the more relaxed posture of organized labour no longer obsessed by its old fear of unemployment. This evidence, however, like that of research and education, is difficult to fit into the known pattern of international divergences.

As we shall see presently these divergences agree better with differences in the behaviour of managers. Nevertheless, most economists who have written about technological change have fought shy of explanations invoking such sociological or psychological phenomena as the attitudes of workmen or managers. Most of them prefer to rely on hard and measurable facts of supply and demand, and more especially on relative scarcities, abundances, and changes in

[1] It is one of Denison's predictions (as in footnote 1, p. 156 above) that the contribution of education to economic growth would tend to decline in the future, i.e. after its initial benefits had been realized. See also Bruce W. Wilkinson (as in Appendix Note 9), pp. 25 *seq*. In his section of *The Residual Factor in Economic Growth*, O.E.C.D., Paris, 1964, pp. 46–8. Denison estimates that, as between the United Kingdom and the United States, only 3 points, out of 45 points' difference in real product per head can be ascribed to differences in education.

the prices of main factors of production – capital and labour – in the economy as a whole.

This approach – 'macro-economic' and 'objective' – comes naturally to economists; and it is not surprising that it should have hardened into a veritable intellectual tradition. In its simpler form it inspired T. S. Ashton's well-known argument about the great part which abundance of capital and low rates of interest played in bringing on the English Industrial Revolution of the eighteenth century. Its canons also underlie Habakkuk's elegant demonstration of the manner in which scarcity of labour and high wages accounted for the greater investment in fixed capital and more rapid technological progress in American industry. In its sophisticated form the explanation by factor-costs invokes not changes in average rates of wages and the market rate of interest, but the difference between changes in the cost of labour in a given industry and the changing costs of the capital equipment it employs or could employ if it wished. In consequence of rising productivity in capital-goods industries, the cost of plant and machinery relative to the price of their product did not climb as high or as fast as labour costs in industry in general. This provided firms with the inducement to install machinery and plant in substitution of labour, and thereby to increase their investment in fixed capital. And we have seen that in the recent past additions to fixed capital as a rule embodied technical improvements and to this extent stimulated technological progress in industry.[1]

The underlying theoretical assumption is that of the 'production function' wherein the factors of production are taken to be complementary and substitutable. Not all economists share this assumption or share it in full; but it is not for mere economic historians to question. What they must, however, question is the evidence as far as it is relevant to our problem; and the evidence is, to say the least, ambiguous. American data for 1940–50 reveal a clear gap between

[1] T. S. Ashton. *The Industrial Revolution, 1760–1830*, London, 1948; H. J. Habakkuk, *American and British Technology in the 19th Century*, Cambridge, 1962; W. E. G. Salter, *Productivity and Technical Change*, Cambridge, 1960 (esp. p. 37).

the rapidly rising real wages and the slowly increasing prices of plant and equipment, but European evidence, especially over longer periods, is much less certain. In the United Kingdom both wages and prices of capital goods were all but stationary between 1900 and 1914. After the violent disturbances of the war years both series settled again to a very much similar trend which continued until the outbreak of the Second World War. The index of wages (with those of 1958 at 100) rose in the inter-war years from 32 in 1924 to 34 in 1938, while the price index for capital goods rose from 26 to 28; and both series sagged a little in the middle decade. They rose violently and, on the whole, concomitantly during the second war and the first year of peace. Between 1946 and 1958 both the indices of wages and prices of capital goods rose in roughly the same degree; wages from 55 to 100, prices from 54 to 100, with prices growing somewhat faster before 1953, wages somewhat faster thereafter. It was only between 1958 and 1964 that the two trends parted company; the index of prices of capital goods rose from 100 to 109, while wages rose from 100 to 120. In some European countries, however, e.g. Germany and Sweden, the disparity may have appeared even later – perhaps as late as the 1960s.[1]

The conflict between the American and the United Kingdom evidence may in part explain why investment in innovations was so much higher in the U.S.A. But investment rose also in the United Kingdom, where it was much higher in the inter-war years than before 1914, and higher still in the ten years after 1946, even though throughout this period wages and prices moved in step.[2]

So much for the evidence. Yet even if it were fully borne out by the historical statistical record of prices, the theory accounting for innovation by relative factor costs would still remain somewhat irrelevant to the problem of post-war technological progress. It

---

[1] *The British Economy: Key Statistics, 1900 and 1964, Table C.* The theory of relative factor costs in its sophisticated version does not now command unanimous agreement. Cf. *Some Factors*, Ch. IV, p. 16: 'There is little reason to believe that the relative prices of capital goods exerted a major influence on investment decision.'

[*Vide*, Appendix Note 10, p. 365 below.]

[2] In the following five paragraphs the discussion of relative factor costs may prove too technical and too compressed for readers new to the subject. They could, however, leave out the passage and proceed directly to para. 2 on p. 166, beginning with the words 'The imperfect fit . . .'.

would certainly not be relevant enough to cover some of the most important post-war innovations or to fit into what is known of their geographical and industrial incidence. By definition it would apply only to technological improvement resulting from substitution of factors in established industries and lines of production. But we have already seen that striking advances in post-war technology occurred in new industries based on such wholly new products as plastics, petrochemicals, or electronic instruments, or in such new services as air travel or television. And even within the restricted range of industries and products able to benefit from the substitution of capital for labour, changes in the relative costs of these two factors would not accord with the way in which technological progress actually varied from one country to another, from one period to another, and from one industrial sector to another.[1]

These discordances were very significant and are worth looking into. If technological progress in Western Europe were so greatly dependent on the prevailing rates of interest and wages, we should expect it to manifest itself most in countries like the United Kingdom, Belgium, or Switzerland, where capital was more abundant and interest was on the whole lower than in other European countries, or in France before 1958, or in Sweden in the late fifties and the early sixties where wages were relatively higher or were rising faster than elsewhere in Europe. For the same reason additions to fixed capital in substitution for labour should have been smallest in Germany or Italy, where supplies of capital were short, rates of interest high, and wages – at least before 1956 – rose more gently than elsewhere. We know, however, that this was not what the geographical or chronological incidence of technological innovations in fact turned out to be.

More significant still was the divergence between the incidence of post-war innovations and the logic of the theory in its more sophisticated version. If this variant of the theory held good, and the costs of capital equipment relative to those of labour were the most important influence behind the varying pace of innovation, industries like the older textiles, general engineering, or clothing and boots and shoes should have been the investing and innovating

---

[1] *Vide* Appendix Note 12, pp. 366 below.

ones *par excellence*. In these industries, labour costs formed a
larger proportion of total costs than in most other industries, while
fixed equipment was in the main made up of 'general purpose'
machines or machines which, however specialized, were made in
large quantities and were therefore most likely to benefit – and
apparently benefited – from cost-reducing improvements in their
manufacture. By the same logic, innovation and investment in
innovation should have been relatively laggard in the chemical
and petrochemical industries, in oil refining or in the generation
of electricity. For in these branches of the economy the quotient
of labour costs was very low; and capital equipment consisted
to a very large extent of costly buildings and sites and of 'bespoke'
or 'custom-built' installations supplied by industries least likely
to benefit from rapidly rising productivity of quantity production.
Yet these were precisely the branches of the economy in which
during our period investment in innovation was higher than the
average and in which the visible signs of technological progress
were most conspicuous.

The imperfect fit of the factor-cost theory to recent facts will not
only cast doubt on its relevance to the post-war experience, but may
also help us in our search for a relevant explanation. In this respect
the conflict between the logic of the theory and the actual industrial
incidence of technological progress is most significant, since differences from industry to industry may hold the key to the pattern of
post-war innovation. I have tried to exhibit elsewhere the hierarchical order in which industries ranged themselves in their willingness and ability to invest, and have argued that this was also how
they ranged themselves in their rising scale of productivity. But it
should not be difficult to demonstrate that the same hierarchy of
industries may also represent their relative positions on the rising
scale of technological progress. It is therefore highly significant
that the gaps between industries at the top of our scale and those
at its bottom should so frequently have been wider than those
between country and country. For this may well mean that national
differences in the willingness and ability to innovate were to a
large extent 'structural'; that in other words, the countries which
invested in innovations more than others and made larger technological advances, did so mainly because in them 'modern'

industries, better able to invest in innovation, were more fully represented.[1]

National differences can be broken up still further. For if in the absence of direct measurements of technological progress we look at increases in productivities to reveal the effects of innovation, our proper unit of evidence should be not entire sectors of the economy or industries considered as wholes, but individual firms within them. Certain much-cited statistics of the American iron-and-steel industries between the wars show that productivities differed more widely between the technologically most advanced establishments and the technologically most backward ones, than we know them to have differed between country and country. It would therefore be legitimate to argue that if productivities and rates of innovation were higher in one nation or one industry than in another, this was mainly because in that industry or in that nation, innovating firms had a larger share of output. The inquiry into the reason why some countries and industries innovated, or invested into innovation, more readily and more generously than others must therefore be conducted not on 'macro-economic' but on 'micro-economic' lines and must resolve itself into the why and how of innovating decisions of individual firms.

Innovating decisions of firms have, in fact, drawn the attention of most recent students of technological progress. Not all this attention, however, has been directed to the firm as a complete social entity: a unit of social organization or a network of human relationships. The prevailing tendency among economists has been to confine the discussion to the same 'objective' factors, above all, the same market forces which figure in macro-economic discussions, and to assume that the decisions of individual firms to adopt or not to adopt new products or new techniques were mere responses to the relevant price indicators – mainly those of labour and capital. These indicators form the framework of the very cogent model of technological change recently constructed by Dr Salter. In his model, the decisions of firms to adopt the 'best' technique – the timing of the decision and the choice of the technique deemed 'best' – are in the final resort dependent on the relative cost of capital and labour in terms of prices for its products.[2]

[1] *Vide* Appendix Note 7, p. 364 below.
[2] W. E. G. Salter, as in footnote 1, p. 163 above.

There is no doubt that these three economic variables – cost of capital, cost of labour, and prices of the firm's products – come, or at least should come, into consideration every time a firm decides how much of its technology should be changed or changed at all. Yet it is very doubtful whether on historical evidence or on purely *a priori* grounds, we can take it for granted that a firm inquiring into the *pros* and *cons* of a technological innovation would find the answer to its problems clearly and firmly located at the one point at which the relative costs of its factors and the prices for its products were found in equilibrium. However willing a firm might be to resolve its problems of innovation on these terms it would still be faced not with one, the perfect, solution, but with a vast range of equivalent solutions; not the one and only 'best practice' but an assortment of good practices. At the time when a firm trading in competitive conditions plans an innovation, the costs of labour and the 'notional' rate of interest are the only variables it can take 'as given' and as not influenced by the way its own decision would go. On the other hand, the prices of its products and the scale of its sales and outputs would still lie in the future, would partly depend on the firm's own decisions, and would for this and other reasons remain highly speculative. Similarly, its calculation of capital costs would depend not only on its assumed rates of interest but also on the life of the new equipment, and this, in its turn, would hinge on the planners' anticipation and intentions as to the future rate of technical progress and obsolescence. So wide would therefore be the firm's choice that the decision whether and how much to innovate would in the final resort depend on the predilections, qualities of judgment, and temperament of the men who have to choose, no matter how rational their processes of choice.

Historians must, moreover, go still farther, and refuse to take for granted this rationality of managers and their ability or willingness to base their actions on objective assessments of the possibilities open to them. For the experience of European industry in the nineteenth and twentieth centuries will not permit the historian to assume that decisions to innovate or not to innovate were always taken on what economists or even sociologists would accept as rational grounds. In a recent inquiry into technological progress in British industry Professors Carter and Williams, following the hunches of their historically minded predecessors – Schumpeter, Weber, and Sombart – distinguished between firms rationally conducted and those wedded to their traditional ways. They showed how the ability and willingness of a firm to adopt the best technological practice and re-equip itself for this purpose depended mainly on the degree to which its management was rational. On this showing a firm's technological progress in the past depended much less on the precise reasons for its innovating decisions than on its ability to take any reasoned decision at all.

This historical lesson has recently been reflected in the findings of a British commission inquiring into turnover taxation. The Commission found that most of the firms in their sample, in making their decisions about investment into the new fixed equipment, took no account of tax allowances or burdens. The implied suggestion is that the heads of the firms were unable to understand and to measure the effects of taxes; but their failure to calculate the financial *pros* and *cons* of their new investment also reflected their rule-of-thumb methods of conducting business.[1]

It may well be that this particular failure was more characteristic of British managers than it would be of their contemporaries in other countries; but if true, this makes it all the more necessary to assign to these differences their full weight in a historical discussion. If the British example (and for that matter, similar facts available for French and German industry) has any significance, it clearly indicates that the ability of firms to approach their production methods rationally and the prevalence of such firms in any given industry or country go far to explain that country's or industry's technological record.

Furthermore, within each firm the ability to proceed rationally and to innovate was largely focussed at one of its points: the topmost. Individual enterprises changed in organization, in scale of operations, in ownership and in social relations within them – and all these variations had some influence on their ability or willingness to innovate. But of all the historical changes that came over industrial and commercial enterprises, those which occurred at the very top, among its leaders, mattered most. The changing qualities of

[1] *Report of the Committee on Turnover Taxation, 1964*, H.M.S.O., Cmnd 2300, p. 77.

character and judgment in the higher ranks of managerial personnel imprinted themselves upon the organization and the performances of enterprises whether private or public; and it was through them that some of the impersonal historical factors bore upon the innovating propensities of the economy.

These 'entrepreneurial' aspects of post-war history will be dealt with in greater detail in the section of this study concerned with the changing organization of industry. Here, they are mentioned, as they were in our story of investment, only in order to bring out the crucial part which this particular human factor played among the other 'residual', i.e. non-material determinants of economic growth.

PART 2

The Changing Shape

M

CHAPTER 7
Contracting Agriculture

Economic expansion with its attendant changes in employment, investment, trade, technology and management was bound to affect the proportions of the economy and the composition of society, or what in academic language is usually described as 'economic and social structure'. The importance of individual branches of the economy – their respective contributions to the national product – was bound to alter during the period. The share of agriculture greatly declined; nor did the relative weights of other sectors of the economy remain the same. In addition, in some industries their constituent units, firms or single commercial and industrial establishments, changed in size and organization. The period also witnessed some further mutations in the ownership of industrial and commercial capital and in the make-up of the higher executive ranks of firms. There were also changes in the labour force. Slowly and almost imperceptibly the economy and society of Western Europe, while growing, were also acquiring a new shape unlike the shape they possessed in the nineteenth century.

The relative position of agriculture in the economies of Western European countries has attracted most of the attention of historians mainly because it gave rise to social and economic problems which required and received the attention of politicians and administrators. It is not as if agriculture did not participate in the general upward movement of the economy. The aggregate output grew more slowly in agriculture than in industry and had by 1962 grown in Western Europe as a whole by little more than 30–32 per cent above pre-war. On the other hand, agricultural productivity in most countries was rising in response to the same influences, which

bore upon the industry and rose, if anything, faster than in manufactures.[1]

Agricultural investment in most Western countries was well above
pre-war. In France a very great increase in that investment was an
essential part of the Monnet Plan. In the United Kingdom the
underlying principle of agricultural policies of governments, as first
laid down by the Labour Government in 1947, was to secure for the
farmers an income sufficiently large to enable them to invest in
agricultural machinery and improvements. The annual amounts of
investment which resulted from this policy are difficult to measure
with any accuracy, but all the estimates which so far have been
attempted agree that during our period the total volume of agricultural investment grew both absolutely and relatively, and
amounted to 4–5 per cent of the total annual capital formation in
this period: a ratio about equal to the share of agricultural output in
the gross national product.

If investment in British agriculture drew any critical comment it
was as often as not directed at its 'over-capitalization': the excessive
amount of capital equipment which was not fully worked. Similarly,
in Germany, the Netherlands and the Scandinavian countries
agricultural investment soared well above pre-war; though of these
countries Germany alone allocated to her agriculture a share in total
investment fully corresponding to the share of agriculture in G.N.P.
In Italy where before the war agricultural investment, except on
some major schemes of drainage and reclamation, was exceedingly
low, investment into agriculture increased after the war not only as
a result of higher incomes of agricultural producers in northern
Italy but also as a result of government schemes for the rehabilita-
tion of southern Italy. In Belgium and Switzerland the increases in
agricultural investment were relatively lower, but increases there
nevertheless were.[2]

The most obvious consequence and sign of the higher investment

---

[1] Most of the statistical evidence in this chapter comes from the *Production
Yearbooks* of the Food and Agriculture Organization, more especially Vols. 17–19,
Rome, 1963–66, and from O.E.C.D., *Agriculture and Economic Growth*, Paris,
1965, and *Some Factors*, Ch. III and *passim*.

[2] *Some Factors*, Ch. III, Table 18. For more scientific instances of increases in
capital stock of agriculture by the middle fifties, see A.F.O. *Betriebsorganisation und
Kapitalintensität in der Landwirtschaft*, 1958.

was the progress of mechanization. In this, the United Kingdom perhaps led the way. Even before the war the employment of tractors in the United Kingdom had been higher than in any other European country, and it increased greatly during the war. It is therefore not surprising that the tractor 'population' of the United Kingdom should have grown more slowly after the war than that of Germany or France. In France and Germany, where the numbers of tractors before 1946 had been very small, the increase in their number since 1948 was all the more spectacular.

Table 17 *Number of Tractors in Agriculture* [1]

	1950	1962
Belgium	8,059	57,420
Denmark	17,182	141,000
France	142,000	900,000
Germany	139,493	960,000
Italy	56,941	300,000
Netherlands	17,488	75,000
Norway	11,000	51,000
Sweden	63,750	180,000
Switzerland	13,096	55,000
United Kingdom	325,000	443,000

Tractors symbolized the higher investment in agriculture, but did not fully represent the march of technological progress. Indeed, what probably helped most to raise the yields per acre was not so much the greater mechanization, as the much increased use of fertilizers and, to a somewhat smaller extent, the use of pesticides, insecticides and antibiotics. In the case of fertilizers, Belgium, the Netherlands and Denmark led the way, though the United Kingdom and Germany did not lag far behind. Altogether, the consumption of fertilizers in Western Europe (including all Mediterranean countries) grew by over 85 per cent between pre-war years and 1959, while the average application of fertilizers per hectare of arable land grew from under 35 kilograms (65 kilograms in the Common Market countries) to 75 kilograms (122 kilograms in

[1] *O.E.C.D. Agriculture and Economic Growth* (as in footnote 1, p. 174 above, Appendix, Table 7).

Common Market countries) in the same period. Even in the Netherlands, where the use of fertilizers had already been high before 1938, the total consumption increased from some 412,000 tons in 1948–53 to some 556,000 tons in 1964.[1]

It will take too long to recount and is often impossible to measure the effects of other technological improvements in agriculture during the period, such as the improvements in seed, or the progress in animal breeding, especially in that of pigs, by purposeful selection of types and widespread use of artificial insemination. The improvements in breeding as well as in feeding of cattle raised milk yields in all countries; more rational and improved methods of feeding also enabled farmers to control better the weights of carcases and the qualities of meat. Finally, large investment of capital and the new methods of battery feeding and breeding wholly revolutionized the production of poultry and eggs. And in the early sixties new 'industrialized' methods of feeding and rearing calves and pigs held out the prospect of a similar revolution in the production of meat.

It is therefore not surprising that productivity, when measured per acre and, still more, per person employed, should have been rising fast and stood very high in 1963. Whereas the pre-war yields of cereals (all grains) averaged in Western Europe as a whole (excluding Italy) some 17·5 quintals per hectare, they approached 25 quintals in the early sixties. Milk production per cow which in the Common Market countries stood at about 2,100 kilograms on the eve of the war, approached 2,900 in the early sixties.[2] Output per man, i.e. the productivity of labour, increased at an even higher rate, as the table below clearly demonstrates.

What this table does not reveal is the extent to which the marginal productivity of labour in agriculture in the course of post-war years approached, and in some countries even appeared to overtake, the productivity of labour in manufacturing industry. It has always been an unquestioned assumption of economic theory and policy

[1] F.A.O., *European Agriculture in 1965*, Geneva, 1961, Annex. I, Table 5. For the continued growth in the use of fertilizers after 1959, see F.A.O., *Production Yearbooks*, Vol. 19, Tables 109–11, and F.A.O., *Fertilisers: An Annual Review of World Production, Consumption and Trade*, Rome (in progress).

[2] F.A.O., *European Agriculture in 1965*, Annex. I, Tables; F.A.O., *Production Yearbook*, vol. 19, Tables 37–9, 93–4. Also O.E.E.C., *Statistical Bulletin*, 1959, Table II.

that productivity in the so-called 'primary' occupations, i.e. mainly agriculture, always was and is destined to be lower than productivity in 'secondary' occupations (mainly manufacturing). Hence the generally accepted historical generalization that all past increases in national *per capita* incomes were primarily due to transfers of labour from agriculture to industry, and hence also the equally general prescription of industrialization as the sole recipe for economic development.

Table 18 *Agricultural Productivity in Some European Countries in 1961–62*[1]

	1950–1 = 100	
	Production	Productivity
Germany	135	176
Denmark	130	145
United Kingdom	131	150
Netherlands	148	120
France	133	183
Norway	112	143
Belgium	130	—
Sweden	99	—

We shall see presently that for most European countries the historical generalization and the economic recipe still hold good. Yet so great was the post-war progress in agriculture that in a number of countries the gap between its productivity and that in manufacturing industries was getting narrower from year to year. In two countries – Belgium and Denmark – the marginal productivity of labour in agriculture had by 1962 nearly equalled that in manufacture; and in one country – the United Kingdom – the marginal value of agricultural production per man employed may have exceeded the *per capita* product of industry by 15 per cent.[2]

---

[1] O.E.C.D., *Agriculture and Economic Growth*, Table 3. Productivity is defined as *increases* in G.D.P. per employed person at factor cost and constant price.

[2] With productivity in industry at 100, that in agriculture in 1960 was 91 in Netherlands, 93 in Denmark, 84 in Belgium, and 115 in the United Kingdom: *Some Factors*, Ch. III, pp. 37–6, Table 24. The figures are, of course, based on values of output inclusive of subsidies but as values of non-agricultural output,

In the United Kingdom this progress was achieved largely by reducing employment and by concentrating production on better lands and more efficient farms. As a result, in the United Kingdom as elsewhere in Europe, the increases in productivity were not accompanied by commensurate increase in total output. Had the demand for agricultural produce been as elastic as that of most industrial commodities, the aggregate output of agriculture might have risen much faster and agriculture might have taken its place among Europe's fast-growing industries. But fortunately or unfortunately, Western Europeans had reached standards of both production and nutrition which left little room for expanding agricultural sales much beyond the increases necessary to provide for additional population. In the early sixties European countries (other than the United Kingdom) were capable of meeting out of their own production over 95 per cent of their needs of grain and over 100 per cent of their consumption of potatoes, sugar, vegetables, pig-meat, cheese and butter. Increased prosperity and improved diets during the period held out prospects of increased consumption of meat, fodder grains and horticultural produce, but the consumption of bread grains declined somewhat and was unlikely to expand. The possibilities of expanding agricultural exports beyond Europe or even into such food-importing European countries as the United Kingdom or Germany were no greater. They were limited by the fact that agricultural production was also high and growing in the countries of North and South America and Australasia, better suited than Europe to the production of staple foodstuffs for export. With the possibility of sales outside Europe almost nil and of greater sales in Europe itself narrowly circumscribed, European agriculture, though expanding, could not increase its total output in step with its higher productivity. So, while its productivity was rising fast, the share of agriculture in aggregate national outputs declined.

Therefore the main consequence of increased productivity of labour in agriculture was to release much of the labour force it hitherto employed. The flow of manpower from agriculture to industry or services, which had been a constant feature of the Euro-

especially in the United Kingdom, were also affected by subsidies (e.g. coal and transport) and by tariffs, the figures for both industry and agriculture are probably fairly comparable.

pean scene since the early nineteenth century, was now greatly accelerated. In France the transfers of labour from agriculture to various urban employments averaged about 90,000 per annum. In Germany it steadily rose, as the alternative supplies of industrial recruits from beyond the Iron Curtain dried up. Similarly, the industries in Scandinavian countries were receiving larger drafts of labour from agriculture than before the war. In the Netherlands the movement of labour from agriculture was sufficient not only to supply the expanding industry but also, for a few years at the beginning of our period, to sustain a considerable emigration.

As a result of this movement into other occupations, the labour force in agriculture declined steadily throughout the period; and it is one of the essential assumptions of the agricultural plans of the European Economic Community that the labour force engaged in agriculture would continue to decline at least until 1970. By that time its numbers, in spite of the slightly rising total agricultural output, were expected to fall to about one-third of their pre-war level.

Table 19 *Indices of Agricultural Employment in 1962*[1]

1950=100	
Germany	69
Denmark	78
United Kingdom	78·7
Norway	73
Belgium	65·2

The labour force would probably have fallen even more steeply, and the aggregate output might have declined, instead of slightly increasing, had not the various governments pursued policies designed to maintain domestic agricultural production and to hold

[1] The table is based on O.E.C.D., *Agriculture and Economic Growth*, Appendix I, Table 6; cf. F.A.O., *Production Yearbook*, Vol. 19, Rome, 1966, Table 57; O.E.E.C., *Fifth Report on Agricultural Policies in Europe and North America*, *1961*, Paris, 1961, Table II. The decline had of course, begun much earlier, above all in the United Kingdom. Agricultural employment in the United Kingdom was 10 per cent of total employment in 1891, 8 per cent in 1911, 5 per cent in 1951, and 4 per cent in 1964.

back the flight from the countryside. These policies were actuated by a variety of motives. In most of the European countries the agricultural sector still represented a large slice of the electorate, and the farmers were a political power to reckon with. Their pressure had always been behind agricultural protection and continued to be felt throughout the period. Most European countries therefore pursued agricultural and fiscal policies designed not only to safeguard the farming community against a return of the rural distress of the 1930s but also to secure for farmers and their labourers incomes comparable with those of the non-agricultural population. In some countries this became the avowed objective of new agricultural legislation. In France, as the fifties advanced, the philoagrarian tendencies of official policy received a further boost from mounting peasant unrest and from the Gaullist idea of France, of which peasantry, agriculture and rural culture were essential ingredients. The policy found its full expression in the 'Loi d'orientation' of 1960 designed to establish economic and social parity between agriculture and other sectors.

Pro-peasant policies also prevailed in Germany, partly for sentimental reasons, but mainly in response to pressure from peasant voters. The Agricultural Law of 1955 was drawn up to ensure that agriculture and the men in it should 'participate fully' in the general advance of the economy. The same objectives (in almost identical terms) were avowed in the Austrian Agricultural Law of 1960. In Belgium and the Netherlands legislation was designed to secure fair incomes for farmers and fair wages for hired labour. Denmark's and Holland's concern with the fortunes of their farming communities also reflected the vital part which agricultural production and exports played in their national economies.[1]

In no country could these objectives be pursued regardless of other considerations. In the years of food scarcity immediately following the end of the war most countries were trying to expand output. Throughout the period governments tried to keep down the cost of food to consumers; most of them also tried to reconcile their agricultural policies of economic growth with a desire for more

---

[1] 'Low Incomes in Agriculture', O.E.C.D., *Agricultural Policy Reports*, Paris, 1964, Ch. II, and country chapters for Germany, France, and the United Kingdom.

active foreign trade. Above all, in Italy, with its large and backward rural areas, agriculture had to be considered as the linch-pin of economic growth. It was expected to feed the rising population, to contribute to exports and to provide manpower for other sectors. And most of these objectives were apt to clash with the policy designed solely with a view to maintaining agricultural incomes.

In no other country was the medley of motives more evident than in the United Kingdom. British agrarian policies were to some extent inspired by considerations of national defence and a wish to ward off the threat of wartime starvation through enemy blockade of sea-lanes. It was commonly believed in Britain that between the wars British agricultural production had declined below the limits of national safety; and both during and after the war political parties declared themselves determined not to allow agriculture to sink that low again. This policy of 'never again' eventually got overlaid with a variety of other considerations: the familiar wish to satisfy the agricultural community, the notion that a decline of agricultural production would aggravate Britain's payments problem, as well as a vague but politically important preference of the public for a well-cared-for countryside.

On this miscellany of motives and interests a policy of agricultural defence established itself firmly all over Western Europe. The instruments of the policy and the underlying ambitions may have differed from country to country, but in most countries direct price supports were the chosen instrument. In a number of countries direct payments to farmers and input subsidies were also adopted. The United Kingdom, in continuation of wartime policies of keeping the cost of living stable, employed farming subsidies as the chief instrument of agricultural defence. Some of these were subsidies for fertilizers or hill-farming, but most of them were 'deficiency payments' designed to bridge the difference between the world prices (or rather prices at which agricultural produce was actually saleable in Britain) and the higher costs of domestic production. When Denmark gave up her erstwhile policy of agricultural *laissez-faire* (as she did in 1954), her system of agricultural protection came to be made up of farm subsidies and of price controls differentiating between export prices and domestic ones. In most continental countries agricultural defence also depended on the time-honoured system of tariff walls, but the height of the walls and the national ambitions they sheltered differed from country to country.

The contrast was greatest in the case of France and Germany. France's agricultural production under the impetus of post-war investments and technical changes increased so greatly that by the late fifties she found herself producing cereals in excess of her home demand and potentially capable of producing even greater and more regular surpluses. France's agricultural policy within the Common Market therefore came to be shaped with a view to greater exports of agricultural products, and she became an advocate of moderate agricultural protection. In this context, moderate protection meant protection sufficiently high to shield the French producers from American or Canadian or British imports, yet sufficiently low to prevent high-cost producers in Germany from expanding their output at the expense of potential French imports. This conception of the French role as the future provider of agricultural produce for the whole of continental Europe ran counter to the German desire for tariffs high enough to protect their high-cost peasant farming: a desire which was not unmixed with the reluctance to be cut off altogether from the sources of cheap agricultural produce outside the Common Market.[1]

In relation to animal produce, especially dairy products, the prevailing policies were also protectionist; even if protection was mild in Denmark, where dairying and pig-meat production were relatively efficient. It was also mild in countries like the Netherlands or Belgium, anxious to expand their dairy and horticultural exports.

The effect of these various policies of agricultural protection was to hold back the decline in the aggregate volume of production and to keep it higher than the level it would have reached had it been exposed to the full blast of international competition. As a result, not only was the flight of manpower from agricultural industry slower than it might have otherwise been but also the productivity of labour

---

[1] At the time of writing (July 1966) the long-drawn-out negotiations between the E.E.C. ended in a compromise. The common agricultural policy agreed on was based on a scale of prices (other than those for fruit and horticultural produce) much nearer the high level demanded by the Germans than the French had previously been willing to concede, but in other respects, especially with regard to the use and administration of levies, the compromise came quite near the French *desiderata*.

did not everywhere rise to the full height made possible by new investment and technological progress. In countries like Switzerland, where agricultural progress was most laggard, the productivity of agricultural labour in the early sixties was still little more than half that of industrial labour. We have seen that in some other countries, especially in the United Kingdom, Denmark, and Belgium, productivity in agriculture caught up or nearly caught up with that in industry. But for the protective measures designed to keep up production and employment, it might have caught up in other countries as well.

The objectives of the protective policies were not, however, confined solely to maintaining the aggregate agricultural output and retaining the agricultural manpower, but also included the preserving the social structure of agricultural industry which in 1963 was still largely peasant. The United Kingdom was perhaps the only European country where problems of social structure did not intrude much on agrarian policies. With the exception of certain fringes of the English farming community – mostly in the Celtic uplands where small-scale units possessing some characteristics of peasant farming still prevailed – the bulk of British agricultural production in 1963 as in 1938 was in the hands of commercial farmers, mostly large and medium-sized. It may well be, as agricultural economists persistently argued, that on the average English farms were still too small to derive the full benefit of specialized and mechanized production; but they approached this optimum size in several branches of agriculture, such as cereal and beet farming in the eastern counties, sheep farming, and lately also corn growing in the extreme south-east, or in the newly established commercialized egg-and-poultry farming in various parts of the country. Elsewhere, the survival of smaller units – except in Wales and the Scottish highlands – was due not so much to the social policy of the Government as to the effects of its price policy which made it possible for smaller and less efficient units to continue in operation. It would not be too unhistorical to hazard a guess that, without farming subsidies and with a somewhat reduced aggregate output, the social structure of British farming would have changed and the proportion of large and middle-sized farms would have increased. As it was, in the fifties smaller holdings were dropping out of cultivation (mostly absorbed by larger units) at the annual rate of 2·4 per cent, and the total number of holdings declined by 11 per cent. But by that time small units had become so unimportant that the slow decline in their numbers did not threaten a major transformation of British rural society to be controlled or warded off by legislation.[1]

Not so in most continental countries. There, perhaps for the first time in Western European history, the entire peasant economy faced the prospect of complete erosion. Hitherto, throughout the nineteenth and the early decades of the twentieth centuries, the peasant economy proved itself the most viable form of agricultural enterprise, fully able to hold its own against the competition of large-scale units of production, whether capitalist or traditional. As long as the small farm continued in the main to conform to the ideal type of peasant economy and remained a family unit engaged in subsistence farming, it was less exposed to effects of violent price changes than commercialized farming, both large and small. Its money receipts and its money outlays were relatively low, it was less dependent on cash crops for its real income, and it could draw on the more elastic supplies of labour from its own family. For these and other reasons it weathered the great agricultural depressions of the 1870s, the early 1890s, and the 1920s with fewer scars and relatively fewer losses from its ranks than commercial farming.

Needless to say, for centuries before 1939, peasant agriculture had in most countries been slowly moving away from its ideal type and was thereby losing some of its viability, while at the same time the proportion of its non-economic units, unable to provide their owners with a living, was increasing. Yet in 1939, most European countries, even in such technically advanced countries as Belgium and Holland, the peasant economy still preserved enough of its essential characteristics to remain the most representative form of agricultural enterprise. In the post-war period, however, the characteristic features of the peasant economy weakened to such an extent that for the first time the very existence of peasant agriculture was put into jeopardy. The very mode of life on which it was based was receding very fast. The rising standards of life in society at large

---

[1] For the changes in the numbers and sizes of holdings, see O.E.C.D., *Low Incomes in Agriculture*, Table 2; also F.A.O., *European Agriculture, 1965*, Annex. II, Note 5, ii, and Note 6.

and the new needs and demands which came with it, threatened to whittle away whatever remained of the subsistence element in family farming. Better, or merely more urban, clothing, domestic gadgets and motor-cars required larger cash outlays and generated a demand for larger money incomes. More mechanized methods of cultivation and greater expenditure on chemicals required ever larger money inputs into production. And in an agriculture so cash-prone and commercialized, peasant farming was bound to lose most of its relative advantages.

At the same time, agriculture continued to harbour large numbers of farming units too small to provide their owners with sustenance under the existing economic and technological conditions. A French inquiry in the fifties produced the verdict that nearly 40 per cent of the country's holdings – 900,000 in all – were not viable in the sense of not being able to support their occupants; and it appears from the inquiry that most of the occupiers of these farms had no opportunities for outside earnings. In Germany some 50 per cent of farms of over one-half hectare in size were in 1958 occupied by part-time farmers. Even in the United Kingdom a study made in 1959 indicated that about a third of the total number of holdings in the country could do no more than supplement the occupiers' main sources of income outside agriculture; and that, in addition, a number of somewhat larger holdings were probably also no more than part-time farms. In Italy the proportion of non-viable agricultural units was at about the same time estimated at 64 per cent of the total.[1]

Under these conditions the movement of population away from agriculture meant not merely a reduction in the numbers of agricultural wage-earners or even the withdrawal of under-employed members of peasant families, but a gradual and accelerated liquidation of entire units of husbandry. The agricultural policies of European governments and of the Common Market were accordingly designed with a view to slowing down the social changes in the countryside or at least of reducing their human and political costs.

The problem was tackled most constructively in Sweden. Swedish measures, like those of most other countries, provided some price

[1] O.E.C.D., *Low Incomes in Agriculture*, *passim*, and *The Small Family Farm*, O.E.E.C., project 199/2, p. 21.

support for the main agricultural products and direct financial support to farms which were too small to yield adequate incomes. But the mainstay of the policy was reconstruction, and in the first place the promotion of 'viable' farms of about 25 hectares of arable capable of providing full-time employment to one or two men. This policy of reconstruction was served by a variety of devices: loans and other forms of financial assistance, controls over the land market and active land purchases and sales by a government agency. As a result, the change in the structure of agriculture, the decline in the number of small holdings and the increase in the average size of peasant farms, were greater in Sweden than in almost any other European country. By degrees, similar objectives also entered the agricultural policies of other countries. In Germany 'viable' peasant units were favoured by the measures which restricted fiscal and other financial supports to holdings capable of providing a livelihood for a family. In France the latest measures of peasant protection were also apparently meant to be confined to holdings capable of providing full-time work for two labour units. The latest Italian five-year plan also declared it to be its objective to 'create and establish efficient and well-managed farms'.

These policies were, of course, intended to hold back the decline of peasant agriculture, but not to arrest it altogether. In fact, the sheer numerical decline in agricultural employment and in number of holdings in the sixties was greatest in Sweden, the country in which the defence of peasant farming was most active and purposeful. The object of most of the policies of defending the peasants was to make possible a painless transition to a future equilibrium between agriculture and other occupations when agricultural production would at last become sufficiently efficient and productive to secure for workers within it incomes comparable with those in industrial employments. Whether these policies will, in fact, succeed in preserving all or any of the peasant elements in European economy and society depends not only on the future balance of interests and pressures behind the agrarian policies of European states but also on the future trends of the world economy and the future shape of its agriculture.[1]

[1] O.E.C.D., *Low Incomes in Agriculture*, passim.

CHAPTER 8
Industrial Regrouping

Changes in the structure of industry have not perhaps been as much before the public eye as those in agriculture; they were nevertheless widespread and in some respects more fundamental. There were first of all changes in the relative importance of individual industries, in their share of the aggregate employment and the G.N.P. That the shrinkage of agricultural employment had for its counterpart a corresponding increase in non-agricultural employments, is, of course, a statistical tautology. Almost equally tautological are the implications of what we already know about old and declining industries and new and rising ones. It will, however, be worth noting how continuous were the resulting changes in employment. In the United Kingdom and in Germany during the war workers were transferred by the million to industries directly engaged in munitions production, mostly those classified in the British census as metal-working, chemical, and electrical.[1] Contrary to all expectations, the pre-war balance of employments was not restored after demobilization, but continued to be heavily weighted in favour of the industries stimulated by the war. This was partly because modern weapons continued to be made on a large scale after the war, and partly because the industries engaged on munitions happened to be those which had grown fast in the inter-war period and were destined to grow fastest after the war.

This post-war destiny was shaped by several influences. The one most familiar to economic historians – familiar mainly because of the attention given to it in economic writings – was the growing preponderance of industries turning out capital goods. In Rostow's

---

[1] Cf. *History of the Second World War*; M. M. Postan, *British War Production*, H.M.S.O., London, 1952, pp. 383 *seq.*; William Hornby, *Factories and Plant*, H.M.S.O., 1958, pp. 382 *seq.*; P. Inman, *Labour in the Munitions Industries*, 1957, *passim*.

N

scheme of economic stages this preponderance is typical of economies which had passed the initial phases of their industrialization; similarly, in Chenery's statistical schedules higher proportions of capital goods in the total flow of output characterize the pattern of development in fully industrialized countries. These shifts in favour of capital goods are clearly reflected in the industrial records of most European countries. In Germany the index of production between 1950 and 1963–64 rose from 100 to 249 for investment goods, but only to 178 for consumption goods. For Austria the corresponding figures were 209 and 199, for Sweden 152 and 137, for Belgium 177 (all 'producers goods') and 152, for Italy 243 and 209. Fully comparable data is not available for France, Switzerland, or the United Kingdom, but the statistics of engineering industries in these countries clearly exhibit the forward surge of capital-goods industries. In the United Kingdom the index of home deliveries of engineering goods at 1958 prices rose from 56 in 1946 to 135 in 1964, or two and a half times; and as exports of engineering goods were even more buoyant, their total deliveries must have risen even higher. At the same time the general index of industrial production rose from 65 to just under 128, or less than twice.[1]

The higher-than-average increase in demand for capital goods would not, however, be sufficient to account for all the differences in the growth of individual industries. The post-war shifts in industrial structure also reflected the changing composition of consumption, in which the, so-called, durable consumption goods, especially cars and electrical appliances, claimed an ever-greater share. Finally, there was the phenomenon repeatedly referred to in previous pages, i.e. the higher growth potential of the 'new' technologically advanced and science-oriented industries.

Most of the expanding industries benefited from one or the other of these trends: the most expansive of them – the electronic, the heavy electrical, chemical, petrochemical, and chemical engineering

---

[1] O.E.C.D., *General Statistics*, January 1964, pp. 87, 95, 103, 113. The Belgian figure for 'capital goods' includes all 'producers' goods'. The United Kingdom figures are derived from *The British Economy: Key Statistics 1900–1964*, Tables A and E. Exports, and hence also total orders for engineering goods, increased faster than home deliveries. It is significant to note that the index of deliveries of engineering goods calculated on the same basis increased from 19 in 1900 to 28 in 1934, when it accelerated under the impetus of rearmament to 38. This represented an annual rate of increase about one-half of that after 1946.

– were exposed to all the favourable influences in combination. In addition, nearly all these industries received a further impetus from their high export potential. In this they reaped the benefits of high demand for capital goods in most countries and also profited from the trading advantages conferred on them by their position in the forefront of technological progress. It is therefore not surprising that these industries should have proved to be the chief beneficiaries of the post-war dispensation and that their output and employment should have grown throughout the period at the expense of other, mostly older, industries – cotton, wool, coal, railways, agriculture and potteries.

Needless to say the emphasis on individual industries was not the same in every country. Agricultural occupations declined less in countries like Denmark or Switzerland than elsewhere, and relatively greater increases occurred in machine-building and chemical industries in Germany and Switzerland or of electrical and engineering industries in Sweden, than in France or Italy.

In most European countries the deep-seated trends of the post-war economy revealed themselves even more clearly in the shifts from employment in all manufacturing industries taken together to occupations usually classified as tertiary – services of every kind, such as transport, communications, distribution, banking, finance, as well as professions, including government service. The movement away from industrial employment into services had also begun long before the war, and in some countries may even have been slowed down somewhat in the fifties. Nevertheless, as Table 21 below shows, in most countries (the exceptions were not only Italy, as revealed in the table, but also Austria, Denmark, and, in the early part of the period, Germany) the combined employment in services in transport and commerce increased between 1950 and 1962 faster than in manufacturing industry, even if it had not, as yet, gone to the same length as in the U.S.A., where it grew between 1947 and 1951 from 51 to 57 per cent of total civilian employment.

Fundamental changes were also taking place within each industry and occupation. Here again, certain pre-war trends were merely accelerated after 1946. One of these trends was the progressive

Table 20 Indices of Production in Selected Sectors, 1950 (a) and 1963 (b)[1]

1953 = 100

	Western Europe		Austria		Belgium		France		Germany		Italy		Netherlands		Sweden		U.K.	
	a	b	a	b	a	b	a	b	a	b	a	b	a	b	a	b	a	b
Total industrial production	86	178																
Mining and quarrying	88	114	74	115	92	80	89	146	81	128	69	190	98	121	81	145	96	90
Total manufactures	86	182	87	205	94	167	90	207	71	213	78	246	88	177	97	155	94	138
All metal products	83	196	91	238	92	178	82	233	65	249	78	265	82	203	99	118	91	147
Motor-cars	78	427							77	139	96	140	84	146	102	120	107	92
All textiles	95	128	93	175	108	141	102	132	81	105	101	124	—		110	95	118	73
Cotton fabrics	96	100	91	118	120	125	100	104										
Electric power	80	225	72	210	87	180	81	225	73	233	79	218	77	220	82	180	101	233
Chemical industry	78	260	95	226	83	207	81	288	70	305	66	373	75^c	269	92	145^d	83	172

^{c} Exclusive. ^{d} Extrapolated.

[1] The figures in the table are derived from O.E.C.D., *General Statistics*, as above, pp. 2, 3, 4, 5, 7, 9, 10, 11, and 25; cf. the United Kingdom figures in G. C. Allen, *The Structure of Industry in Britain*, 2nd edn, 1966, pp. 12–15, and Statistical Appendix, Tables IV, VI and VII. The figures in K. S. Lomax, 'Production and Productivity Movements in the United Kingdom since 1900', *Journal of the Royal Statistical Society*, Vol. 122, Pt. 2, 1959, trace the changes in relative outputs of industries during a period of over fifty years.

increase in the size and the corresponding reduction in numbers of enterprises in principal industries. That some such tendency to concentration was inherent in the nature of the modern economy was noted and welcomed in the first half of the nineteenth century by the earliest English writers upon the 'philosophy' of manufacturers: men like Ure or Barbour. But the man who raised this

Table 21 *Civilian Employment by Activities (per cent of total employment)*[1]

	France		Germany		Italy		U.K.	
	1954	1962	1950	1962	1954	1962	1948	1963
Agriculture	28·2	20·7	24·7	13·5	39·9	28·0	50·8	50·6
Industry	37·1	40·1	42·9	49·0	32·8	41·1		
Distribution, Transport and communications Other services	34·7 [a]	39·2 [a]	32·5 [a]	37·5 [a]	27·3 [a]	31·0 [a]	45·2	47·7

[a] Including miscellaneous unspecified occupations

tendency to the dignity of an immutable law and built on it his entire prognosis of the world's destinies was, of course, Karl Marx. He foretold that, as a result of their superior competitive powers, larger establishments would progressively displace the smaller ones until the entire economy would be absorbed into a few mammoth enterprises employing the entire humanity as wage-earners.

The actual economic developments of the late nineteenth and

[1] Figures in the text and in Table 21 are derived mainly from sources cited in footnote 1, p. 191 above. The United Kingdom figures in the text are based on those in B. M. Deakin and K. D. George, 'Productivity Trends in Service Industries', *London-Cambridge Economic Bulletin*, No. 53, 1965, Table I. Comparable U.S.A. figures will be found *ibid.* and in U. R. Fuchs, *Productivity Trends in the Goods and Service Sectors*, N.B.E.R., New York, 1964. The estimate in B. Hoselitz, 'Some Problems in the Quantitative Structure of Industrialisation', *Economic Development and Cultural Change*, IX, No. 3, differ somewhat from those in Table 21, but reveal similar changes of about the same magnitude. The composite nature of the concept of 'tertiary' occupations and the disparate character of tertiary employments mask some of the most significant changes within them. Thus, in the United Kingdom domestic service in the 1960s stood at a level of about 30 per cent of that of 1911, whereas employment in transport, communications, government, education, and the professions increased to a far larger extent than the aggregate figures of tertiary employment.

early twentieth centuries both bore out and belied these prophecies. The prophecies were borne out in the 'capitalist sector' of
the economy narrowly defined: above all, in the relations between
the medium- and the large-scale enterprises. There, slowly but
inexorably, throughout the nineteenth century and the first decade
of the twentieth, large firms and actual manufacturing units grew in
size. In addition, firms, considered as units of management, grew
by multiplying the number of individual factories and shops under
their control, or by buying up other, usually smaller, firms. A number of industries in the United Kingdom, Germany, the Netherlands and Belgium, and to a smaller extent in France, Italy and
Sweden, had come to harbour very large productive units and
mammoth firms.

In so far as this process called into existence monopolistic or
near-monopolistic combines, trusts and cartels, it will be discussed
again later. What is of interest to us at this stage of the story is that
very large establishments and firms continued to grow after 1945.
But at the same time, the small and very small enterprises, compris-
ing the bulk of the artisans and handicraftsmen, betrayed a remarkable capacity for survival. Their survival in France was commonly
credited to the important part played in the French economy by
luxury and artistic goods best suited for small handicraft establishments. Yet diminutive industrial units were no less viable in
Germany and in England where the number of enterprises employing very few wage-earners or none at all was very high in the
1930s and had apparently declined little in the preceding half-
century. Contrary to earlier expectations, some of the new technical inventions (Marx expected the sewing machine to put an end
to artisan tailoring) provided small establishments with new
opportunities as some of the older opportunities dwindled. Thus
the invention and spread of motor-cars and electrical equipment
provided openings for small garages and repair shops. Even in the
engineering industries larger enterprises sometimes found it to their
advantage to sub-contract to smaller specialized workshops the
making of certain components or sub-assemblies. In fact, the proliferation of industrial minnows in the company of whales created
some of those 'external economies' of industrial centres like
Birmingham and Manchester in the United Kingdom or Berlin,

Düsseldorf, and Mannheim in Germany, which made it more economical for great engineering firms to operate in the neighbourhood of those towns than elsewhere.

These two disparate tendencies – the rapid increase in the size and relative importance of the largest enterprises and the continued survival of diminutive ones – continued after the war. Perhaps small undertakings declined somewhat faster in Germany, the United Kingdom, and in the Netherlands than in France or in Switzerland; but these differences were not so marked as to invalidate our main conclusion about the relative stability of the very small establishments.

In Germany the census of undertakings in 1961 revealed that establishments in industry and commerce employing fewer than 5 persons were 81 per cent of the total in 1950 and 76 per cent of the total in 1961. In that year, 97 per cent of undertakings employed fewer than 50 persons, and accounted for over 40 per cent of total non-agricultural employment. In engineering (*Maschinenbau*) some 3,000 out of the total of 5,500, employed fewer than 50; and more than 1,250 employed fewer than 20 workers. In optics and fine mechanics, some 530 out of 1,437 undertakings employed fewer than 10 persons. The corresponding numbers in the manufacture of miscellaneous metal ware were 3,000 out of a total of 6,500 undertakings. All these numbers were apparently not much more than 10 per cent lower than comparable figures before the war.[1]

In the United Kingdom the information of the first two post-war censuses of production – those of 1951 and 1958 – reveal what appears to be some decline in manufacturing establishments employing fewer than 25 persons. Between the two dates their number suffered an apparent drop from about 66,000 to 53,000. Most of the decline, however, appears to have taken place in the numbers of establishments employing between 5 and 10 persons. Judging by various indirect signs there was very little decline in the numbers of establishments employing fewer than 5 persons; while the numbers employing from 11 to 24 persons may have increased; from just under 17,500 in 1951 to nearly 21,000 in 1958. What is more, in the census groupings of 'new' branches of electrical and engineering industries the numbers of small undertakings either declined very little or not at all. In metal-manufacturing (Order V

---

[1] *Wirtschaft und Statistik*, 1965, Heft 4, pp. 223–4.

in the Census) the numbers at the two dates were 555 and 590, in engineering and electrical (Order VI), excluding the small electrical retail shops, the numbers were c. 5,665 and 4,980; in miscellaneous metal and instrument trades the numbers may have risen. In 1958 about one-half of all the firms in manufacturing industries employed 5 persons and less; and the proportion of such firms in all industry including building exceeded 25 per cent of the total. In 1958 some 87,000 out of a total of 95,500 firms in the building industry belonged to this category. The proportions in the distributive trades were of a similar order.[1]

Somewhat more dramatic were the post-war increases in the scale of output and management in the higher ranges of business. Some of the largest firms in Europe controlling exceptionally high proportions of their nations' economies may have reached the upper limit of their expansion some time before 1945. The combine which, after the war, controlled the largest share of a nation's business is probably the Belgian Société Général. It is supposed to have owned in the late fifties over 50 per cent of Belgium's deposit banking, nearly 60 per cent of its insurance business, 70 per cent of its non-ferrous metal trade, over 40 per cent of its iron and steel, 30 per cent of its coal and 25 per cent of its electric power. But its position in the economy had probably been equally great between the wars. The position of Wallenberg interests in Sweden was not equally overwhelming but was nevertheless very great, and had become great long before 1948.[2] In Germany cartelization already

---

[1] Board of Trade: Census of Production for 1951: Summary Tables with comparative figures for 1935, 1948, and 1949, H.M.S.O., 1956, Table 4 (establishments employing more than 10 persons); but cf. figures in Table I, columns 19 and 20, in which firms described as 'small' frequently employed little more than 5 persons on the average: Census of Production for 1954, Reports 2, 3, 4, 5, 6, 10, H.M.S.O., 1957–8, Table 3; also Reports on the Census of Production for 1958, Report on the Census of Distribution and Other Services, 1961, Part 2, H.M.S.O., 1964, Table I; cf. B. Hoselitz, op. cit., Economic Development and Cultural Change, IX, No. 3, 1961. The United Kingdom electronic industry provides an example of high concentration on top combined with a large number of small undertakings. Forty-seven top firms employed 90 per cent of its labour, the remaining 10 per cent were shared by 900 small undertakings: 1965 Pocket Guide to the Electrical and Instruments Industry in the U.K., David Rayner Associates, 1965. According to G. C. Allen's computations (op. cit., p. 51) the number of establishments employing ten or less was approximately the same in 1951 and 1958.

[2] For the Société Général, see Holdings et Démocratie Economique, published by the Belgian Fédération Générale du Travail, Liège, 1956.

far advanced in 1913, was carried still further in the twenties in the course of the so-called 'rationalization' of industry. With the help of American investment numerous mergers and amalgamations took place at that time in coal-mining, iron and steel, the chemical industry, and shipbuilding. In the United Kingdom somewhat similar amalgamations occurred between the wars in the steel industry, in chemicals, in heavy electrical industries and in the manufacture of vegetable fats, and many other amalgamations had also occurred in the early decades of the century.

Table 22 *The Largest Firms in Germany*[1]
Increases in Turnover from 1954 to 1960

(Percentage of total turnover in each industry commanded by the aggregate output of the ten largest firms)

Refining and coal processing	72·6–91·5
Tobacco manufacturing	68·8–84·5
Ship construction	71·5–69
Vehicles	58·6–67
Rubber and asbestos processing	60·7–59·7
Iron and Steel	54·6–57·6
Glass	45·7–51·6
Non-ferrous metals	44 –44·7
Coal mining	34·6–42
Chemicals	37·6–40·6
Electrotechnical industry	37·8–38·4

On the whole great firms and great industrial and commercial establishments continued to increase in size, though not necessarily in the share of markets, after 1945. How fast, or slowly, these increases proceeded in the late fifties is shown by the results of an inquiry into the changes in the turnover of large German firms between 1954 and 1960. In the latter year the hundred largest firms accounted for 40 per cent of industrial output and employed one-third of the industrial labour force. In seven industries (oil-refining and coal processing, tobacco, shipbuilding, motor-cars, rubber and asbestos, iron and steel, and glass) the aggregate output of the ten

[1] Cf. *Berichte über das Ergebnis einer Untersuchung der Konzentration in der Wirtschaft*, Bundestag Publications, IV/2320, 1964.

dominant firms represented more than 50 per cent of their industries' total turnover; and the proportion apparently had increased between 1948 and 1954, though it was not necessarily higher at the later date than before the war.

The corresponding data for the United Kingdom, brought together in successive censuses of production, makes it possible to trace the process of concentration at the three stages corresponding to the census of 1935, 1951, and 1958. A recent analysis of this data by Armstrong and Silberston has shown that in British manufacturing industry, establishments employing 1,500 workers and more accounted for 15·2 per cent of total employment in 1935, for 23·6 per cent in 1951, and 27·4 per cent in 1958.

On the other hand, 'concentration ratio' measured by the combined activity of the three largest enterprises or by their shares of the markets, was less striking.[1] In general, concentration appeared to be faster before 1938 than after 1945, yet even by comparison with the returns for 1931 those of the 1958 Census do not reveal any revolutionary changes. In 1931 firms with 1,000 and more employees accounted for just under 50 per cent of total industrial employment and 55 per cent of total industrial output. In 1958 the corresponding percentages were 45 per cent and just under 50 per cent. In short, concentration of industry went on, but neither its speed nor its extent were such as to bring about dramatic changes in the structure of industry.

The progress of concentration was more marked in some industries than in others, and affected most the industries which grew or innovated most rapidly. In the chemical industry the output of

---

[1] Joe S. Bain, *International Differences in Industrial Structure*, New Haven (U.S.A.), 1956; Alan Armstrong and Aubrey Silberston, 'Size of Enterprise and Concentration in British Manufacturing Industry', 1935–58, *Journ. Roy. Stat. Soc.*, Series A, Vol. 128, Pt. 3, 1965; cf. 'Company Assets, Income and Finance', Board of Trade, 1962; 'Finance and Growth of Companies, 1958–60', *Board of Trade Journal*, 30 November 1962; P. Sargant Florence, *Ownership, Control and Success of Large Companies*, London, 1961; G. C. Allen, *The Structure of Industry in Britain*, pp. 40–6; J. Leak and A. Maizels, 'The Structure of British Industry', *Inst. of Roy. Stat. Soc.*, Vol. 108, Pt. 2, 1945, London, 1945; R. Eveley and I. M. D. Little, *Concentration in British Industry*, N.I.E.S.R., Cambridge, 1960; F. E. Hart and S. D. Prais, 'The Analysis of Business Concentrations', *Journ. Roy. Stat. Soc.*, Vol. 119, Pt. 2 (1950), pp. 173–5. Cf. also M. A. Adelman, 'La firme et son environnement', *Economie Appliquée*, 1965, pp. 204 *seq.*

[*Vide* Appendix Note 11, pp. 365–6 below.]

82 establishments employing 1,000 persons and more – some 2 per cent of the total in 1958 (*c*. £1,050 million) was about £200 million greater than the output of the entire chemical industry in 1950. In the metal industry (mainly steel and non-ferrous metals) the 52 largest firms employing 2,000 persons and more produced as much in 1958 (*c*. £950 million) as the entire industry in 1949. In electrical engineering the 40 establishments employing 1,000 persons and more, out of a total of 781, produced as much in 1958 as the entire electrical engineering industry in 1950. On the other hand, in woodworking, shipbuilding, cotton textiles (before 1962), or building, increases in scale of output were very slow.[1]

In France throughout her recent history scales of output did not grow as far or as fast as in the United Kingdom or Germany; or at least they did not call into being industrial concerns as gigantic as Europe's fifteen or twenty largest firms. In 1963 no French firm could boast of sales over £1,000 million, whereas the sales of at least six British and five German firms exceeded this amount by a large margin. Nevertheless, their concentration had by then become somewhat more pronounced: in that year fifty firms accounted for 65 per cent of the output of the top five hundred firms, which was apparently a larger proportion than they could have claimed in earlier years.[2]

Increases in scale emerge even more clearly from what we know of the history of individual firms than it does from statistical aggregates. From this point of view most characteristic is the history of firms in heavy industries. Immediately after the war the great German combines in the heavy industries were dissolved at the behest of the occupying powers. Subsequently, however, they either reconstituted themselves or had their place taken by newborn colossi. By a series of steps the combine of Friedrich Krupp

[1] *Census of Production for 1951* (as in footnote 1, p. 194 above), Tables 4 and 5; *Census of Production for 1954*, as above.

[2] The French figures are derived from 'Les 500 Premières Sociétés Françaises' in *Entreprise*, No. 316, 1961; from the lists of large firms in *Fortune* magazine; and from the statistical data in *Ministère des Finances: Statistiques et Etudes Financières*, No. 147 (1961). For Italian data, see 'Italy's 200 Largest Companies', *Economic News for Italy*, March 1962, and *Annuario Statistico Italiano 1962*, Rome, 1963. For later data and somewhat different ranking of British and foreign firms, see *300 Leading Companies in Britain & Europe* published by *The Times*.

redeployed itself on a scale if anything greater than that of the mid-thirties. In 1962, with sales well in excess of $1,000 million, it was the largest firm in the heavy industry of Germany, and was harbouring plans for yet further expansion and absorptions. The great coal and steel empire of Baron Thyssen was similarly broken up after the war and similarly reassembled in the fifties and sixties. The process ended in 1963 by the merger of Phoenix-Rheinrohr with August Thyssen Hütten (the principal splinters of the old combine) which created a steel-making firm with an output of over 8 million tons: even larger than that of Krupp and the largest in Western Europe. The period also witnessed the remarkable progress of other mammoth steel-making and engineering combines, such as Mannersmann's Guttenshoffnunghütte, or the Rheinische Stahlwerke. The latter, having acquired in 1962 the great engineering and armament firm of Henschels, lifted its annual turnover to close on $1,000 million and took its place among the three or four largest units in the world's heavy industries. As the sixties drew to their mid-year, further and still more far-reaching mergers were in the course of being formed in the iron and steel industry.

Individual firms in the French heavy industries may have operated on a smaller scale; yet the largest among them, Lorraine-Escaut, Usinor, Sidelor, De Wendel, had greatly grown in size, by mergers and in other ways. By 1964 further, and rather drastic, steps were taken to achieve a concentration of steel output comparable with that in Germany; and links between Usinor and Lorraine-Escaut and similar links between De Wendel and Sidelor were in the process of being forged. In the United Kingdom, where the output of steel nearly doubled, from some 13 million in 1938 to 22½ million tons in 1963, the number of steel-making firms actually declined, with the result that the largest firms (e.g. United Steel, Stewarts and Lloyds, or Richard Thomas and Baldwin), each with capital near or in excess of £150 million, came to operate on a scale several times that of the 1930s, even if it was still smaller than the scale of the largest German firms. The concentration was specially marked in the sheet trade, where 3·5 million tons came from five works in 1963 compared with 1·3 million tons from fifty works in 1937; and in the tinplate trade, where two companies produced 1·2 million tons compared with 0·9 million tons from thirty-four companies in 1937.[1]

The 'top' firms grew even faster in the chemical, petroleum and petrochemical industries. In the United Kingdom the most important single step in this direction was the formation of I.C.I. in the 1920s by the amalgamation of Brunner-Mond, Nobel Industries, and the Dyestuffs Corporation. But the most spectacular expansion in the size of the I.C.I. combine – about threefold – came after the war. By 1963 its turnover reached $1,800 million, its current investment programme was estimated at over $850 million, and its assets at over $2,800 million on a well-written-down basis. Though by no means a monopolist on the British and still less the world market, I.C.I. was very much larger in 1963 than in 1945. By 1963 it in fact ranked among Europe's five or six largest industrial concerns.[2]

On the Continent the chemical industry also harboured large and growing firms, even if no single one attained the size of I.C.I. In Germany the giant I.G. Farben had been split after the war, but the firms which succeeded it, the Farbenfabriken Bayer, the Farbenwerke Hoechst, and Badische Anilin-und-Soda Fabrik, had by 1963 become almost as great as I.G. Farben itself had been in 1938. In France the chemical and electro-metallurgical industries regrouped themselves round a close-knit nucleus of vast and growing combines – Rhône-Poulenc, Péchiney, and St Gobain. In Italy the older chemical combine of Montecatini not only grew itself, but came to be matched by new chemical and petrochemical installations of the Edison company and E.N.I. each of which had by 1963 grown to a size larger than that of the near-monopolist Montecatini in the 1930s. In the course of the following year or two

[1] The information on the steel mergers in Germany and France in the sixties is derived from the current issues of financial and other Press: e.g. the report in *The Times* of 16 February 1965. The information about the French steel and chemical firms is to some extent also based on the annual reports of Usinor and Sidelor for 1963, which together with other information, were made available to me by the courtesy of Messieurs Jean-Claude Casenova and François Hetman of S.E.D.E.I.S., Paris.

[2] Until the projected history of I.C.I. has been written historians must depend for their information on the Company's publicity and annual reports and on occasional articles and notes in the financial press. Of these most directly relevant is P. Coldstream, 'The Chemical Industry's Investment in Size', *Financial Times*, 18 October, 1965.

Montecatini and Edison negotiated a merger resulting in the creation of the largest single private enterprise in Italy and one of the largest chemical combines in the world: with an output about half that of I.C.I. itself.[1]

In the petroleum industry Shell and British Petroleum in the United Kingdom, two or three French, German, and Italian firms, as well as the European branches of great American petroleum combines, immensely increased their capital and turnover. In 1963 the British Shell Transport Company, British Petroleum Co, the French Compagnie Française des Pétroles, and the Italian E.N.I. each sold on their domestic markets more petrol than their countries, taken separately, consumed in the late thirties. In the artificial fibres industry in the United Kingdom, well-concentrated before 1939, great advances occurred in the scale on which leading firms operated, especially after Courtaulds had absorbed the British Celanese Company. Thereafter its turnover and assets continued to grow almost uninterruptedly. The same also applies to the Dutch Algemene Kunstzijde Unie, little inferior to Courtaulds in size, and, to a smaller extent, the German Vereinigte Glanzstoff and the Italian Snia Viscosa.

The post-war record of great firms in other 'modern' industries was no different. While the output of motor vehicles soared, production was in the hands of a few great firms. By 1963 Volkswagen, Fiat, Daimler-Benz, and the British Motor Corporation, measured by their sales, were among Europe's fifteen largest firms, while several motor firms of the second rank in France, the United Kingdom, Germany, and Italy were eliminated or absorbed. In some fields, such as aircraft, combinations were either forced on the industry by nationalization as in France, or were made a precondition of government orders as in the United Kingdom. Moreover, some of the giant firms which had operated in miscellaneous industries before the war grew in size, though not always in their share of the market. The list would include the great combines of the Anglo-Dutch Unilever Group and the Swiss Nestlés and the

[1] The growth of Farbenwerke Hoechst between 1952 and 1960 is briefly summarized in the London Stock Exchange Prospectus of 1961: *The Times Book of Prospectuses*, vol. 129, London, 1961, pp. 183–8. Comparable data for Farbenfabriken Bayer for 1952–9, see *ibid.*, vol. 128, pp. 62–7. For Montecatini, see *ibid.*, vol. 129, pp. 28–35, and pp. 203–4 below.

British Unigate in the food industries, the Dutch firm of Philips Gloeilampenfabrieken in the electrical and electronic industry, and the three or four giant tobacco and cigarette firms in the United Kingdom, Germany, and Netherlands.

Some of the most spectacular increases in the size of large firms occurred in the fifties, but as the sixties were drawing towards their mid-year large firms continued to add to their already immense resources and turnovers. This they were able to do for a variety of reasons, but not necessarily because large manufacturing and trading establishments could produce more economically than smaller ones. Gigantic firms, considered as units of management, were not necessarily made up of manufacturing establishments larger than those run by smaller firms. In fact, many of the firms absorbed by larger ones were themselves large enough to operate units of production of the most economical size. But size of enterprises – as distinct from the scale of individual manufacturing establishments – brought with it some other benefits. As a rule, very large firms had better access to finance and larger resources for research and development. Large and growing firms were also more likely to be better run.

However, even if increases in the size of the greater firms were in the main due to causes other than those sometimes alleged, increases they nevertheless were; and to this extent they may at first sight correspond to late-Marxist description of the recent phase in economic development as that of 'monopoly capitalism'. Does the description fit?

The theoretical reasons why it should fit are very compelling. Firms with a very large share of the market should be in a position to exercise in it the powers of monopoly or oligopoly, i.e. to control or at least strongly to influence the demand for their products and their price, and in doing so to set their own standards of expected returns on capital and, in general, to use their resources in quantities and proportions which are not necessarily those that might have prevailed in markets wholly unaffected by monopolistic influences. There is thus every *a priori* reason to expect that, as large firms were getting larger, their monopoly powers should also have grown and the monopolistic features of the Western economy should have become more pronounced.

These expectations did not appear to have come altogether true. In the first place, the increased size of the great firms did not necessarily confer upon them a correspondingly greater share in a market for individual products. Secondly, even where and when their share of the market, and with it their power to dominate it, greatly increased, they were not always able or willing to exercise that power to the full. Finally, the monopolies we find in fact operating in the post-war world did not always result from concentration of production.

Let us begin with the share of the markets. In considering the connexion between the increasing size of firms and their potential powers as monopolies it is important to distinguish not only between firms as units of management and individual manufacturing establishments but also between firms, establishments and even entire industries, on the one hand, and markets for individual products, on the other. In a number of industries, more especially in certain branches of the chemical industries, leading firms were able to increase their share of total output of individual commodities every time they increased their scale of operations. Such connexion between scales of output and shares of markets were not, however, either inevitable or very widespread. There is no need to labour the obvious point that in certain commodities, such as motor-cars, plastics, or petroleum, aggregate national and world outputs could increase so much that individual firms, however much they expanded, found it difficult to secure for themselves a substantially larger proportion of total sales. Less obvious are some of the other reasons why mammoth firms sometimes failed to increase their share of the markets. This failure as a rule resulted from several characteristically post-war phenomena – from the so-called 'lateral' entry of outside firms, from expanding foreign trade, and from the policy of industrial 'diversification'.[1]

'Lateral' entries of powerful outsiders into markets previously controlled by one or very few producers were to some extent the

[1] Information in this and preceding five paragraphs is partly derived from reports in financial and other Press, and on firms' prospectuses and annual accounts issued to shareholders.

natural consequences of the technological progress and of the post-war expansion in supply and demand. Classical examples of 'lateral' entries were therefore to be found in the technologically most advanced and expansive industries – chemical, petrochemical, man-made fibres, and electronics.

An example of a near-monopoly diluted by lateral entries is provided by the recent history of the chemical industry. In the United Kingdom that industry was never nearer to being dominated by a single large combine than in the inter-war period immediately following the formation of I.C.I. Yet in spite of its immense growth since the war, and its near-monopolistic position in a number of individual chemical products, I.C.I. lost some of its overwhelming predominance in several fields and more especially in some of the most modern carbon compounds. In the first place, the domestic market expanded so greatly as to provide room for other large firms engaged in the manufacture of fertilizers, pesticides or phosphorous compounds. In the second place, so large and so profitable had the British market become that branches of foreign-based (mostly American) firms sought and found secure lodgement in it. But much more important were the consequences of the post-war progress in petrochemicals which provided an entry into the industry to petroleum firms. By the early sixties the Shell Transport Company, the United Kingdom's largest petroleum combine, also emerged as the country's second or third largest chemical manufacturer. The entry into the field of the Distillers' combine was apparently due to other causes, and proved impermanent, but it also helped to prevent other firms from establishing their predominance in a number of commodities.

A similar development also occurred in the chemical industries of most other countries, though not perhaps in that of France. The markets of the E.E.C. were gradually invaded by the powerfully backed subsidiaries of Dupont's, Monsanto, I.C.I., Union Carbide and other foreign firms; and petroleum firms, foreign and domestic, also spread their tentacles over the chemical industry. As a result, the near-monopolistic hold of the older chemical firms slackened in spite of the immense expansion of their output and assets.

This process can be well observed in the case of Italy. Before 1948 the predominance of the Montecatini combine in that country's

o

chemical industry was overwhelming. At that time the bulk of production, apart from dyestuffs and acetate film, was in basic, mostly inorganic, chemicals – pyrites, superphosphates, copper sulphate, sulphuric acid, nitrates, and aluminium. In all these products Montecatini accounted for at least three-quarters of the output. The first breaches in this position occurred in 1949–50 when the great electrical combine of Edison, seeking to reduce its dependence on the Italian electrical industry, started the production of fertilizers on a large scale. By 1954 the field had also been invaded by the state-owned petroleum firm of E.N.I. which established itself powerfully in petrochemicals (especially in synthetic resins) and fertilizers. In the end all these new and growing markets came to be shared by Montecatini, E.N.I., and Edison operating in conjunction with the American firms of Monsanto and Union Carbide. The purchase of Montecatini by the British Shell in the early sixties and the associated changes in the man-made fibre industry completed the dissolution of the Montecatini monopoly; yet in the intervening period the scale of Montecatini's operation had expanded.[1]

The changes in the man-made fibre industry followed a similar course. We have seen that soon after the war the prospects of the artificial fibre industry in the United Kingdom were suddenly transformed by the merger of Courtaulds and British Celanese. Yet the promise, or the threat, of a monopoly never materialized. The development of the new man-made fibres – nylon, Terylene, and others – provided an opening for other great firms: Calico Printers who discovered Terylene, various subsidiaries of American makers of artificial fibres (British Monsanto and others), and above all I.C.I. who made most of the organic compounds required for the manufacture of man-made fibres. The attempts of I.C.I. in 1962 to take over Courtaulds itself failed, but within little more than a year of their failure I.C.I. took over Courtaulds share in Nylon Spinners, and by this and other means established its position as the

---

[1] Cf. Eugenio Sclafari, *Rapporto sul Neocapitalismo in Italia*, Bari, 1961, esp. pp. 19 *seq.*; *The Economist*, 8 January 1966. In 1960 the output of Montecatini accounted for 47 per cent of Italy's output of agricultural chemicals, 62 per cent of her output of aluminium, 57 per cent of resins, and 48 per cent of synthetic dyes and 44 per cent of plastics, but only of 10 per cent of industrial chemicals, 35 per cent of lead, and 25 per cent of zincs: see *London Stock Exchange Prospectus*, as in footnote 1, p. 200 above.

second largest interest in the man-made fibres industry in the United Kingdom. By 1963 the assets and turnover of Courtaulds was very much greater than in 1948, but their share in the total output of man-made fibres other than rayon was not much greater than ten or fifteen years previously.

The inroads of petroleum combines into the chemical industry, and of the chemical combines into artificial fibres had for their counterpart the reciprocal movement of chemical giants into petroleum refining and of the makers of fibres into general chemical manufacture. If E.N.I. invaded the field previously held by Montecatini and the Edison electric company, the latter began to compete with E.N.I. in the search for petrol in Abruzzi and Sicily and in petrochemicals elsewhere. Similarly, in the United Kingdom the overspill of Shell into the chemical industry was matched by the growing involvement of I.C.I. in the refining of petroleum. Having swung away from coal as raw material for its carbon compounds, I.C.I. found itself greatly dependent on petroleum products. No wonder its 1963 plans of expansion envisaged the refining of 5 million tons on Tees-side and a possible doubling of this activity by 1970. Like the great petroleum companies and the Gas Council, it also committed itself to the search for oil and gas in the North Sea; an interest which combined naturally with its discovery of the new process of turning light petroleum distillate into town-gas.

Similar 'lateral' movements of giant firms into markets hitherto outside their interests occurred in many other fields. The Distillers' large-scale involvement with chemicals, Courtaulds newly acquired stake in the highly concentrated paint industry and in the manufacture of wood pulp, the involvement of French chemical combines with glass and aluminium, and of the great German chemical firms with man-made fibres, plastics and metals, are but examples of the post-war tendency to interpenetration of monopoly-prone markets.

The interpretation was often the result of deliberate policy, that of diversification. The policy was well suited to post-war conditions. So rapidly had the flow of new commodities and pastimes grown, so quickly did consumption goods get out of date and consequently so unstable had become consumers' preferences, that it was now more dangerous than ever before for a firm to have all its eggs in one basket. In order to ward off this danger many a large firm tried to expand not by acquiring a larger stake in a single commodity or industry but by spreading into several industries at once. Diversification, rather than monopolistic concentration, was now the guiding light of a number of expanding firms and the main motive behind many of the post-war takeovers and amalgamations. In the United Kingdom some of the firms nearest to the position of full monopoly – Unilever, Distillers, Beecham, Hawker, Vickers, and to some extent such hitherto specialized giants as Shell, Imperial Tobacco, or Courtaulds – branched out into several industrial fields in order to 'diversify'. The same policy was pursued by great French firms, such as Michelin, or the chemical combines. In Italy, Fiat and Olivetti, as well as Edison and E.N.I., showed a similar tendency to diversification. In Germany some of the great steel-making and chemical empires, more especially Krupp, also involved themselves in a wider range of industries and commodities than their counterparts had done before the war; though in general in that country diversification had been fostered long before the war by the bank ownership of industrial capital.[1]

It is for these various reasons that the concentration of production, if measured product by product, appears to have advanced more slowly than industrial concentration measured by the turnover, capital or employment of firms. Analysed by groups of products, the figures of outputs and sales in the United Kingdom Census of Production of 1958 reveal that, of some 125 commodity groups in the census, in only a score or at most in thirty of the 125 commodity groups listed in the census were single firms or a small group of firms responsible for the greater share of the output. In twelve commodity groups the combined output of the three largest enterprises was appreciably higher than half the total sales (oil refining 87·9 per cent, soaps and detergents 71·7 per cent, wires and

---

[1] For one of the best-known, even if impermanent, instances of diversification on a large scale, see *Industrial Activity of the Distillers' Company*, published by the Company in 1961. A very recent instance of diversification is that of the British Cocoa Corporation (Cadbury's): cf. interview with Mr Adrian Cadbury in *Sunday Times*, 14 August 1966. A more general discussion will be found in S. P. Chambers' 'Investment and British Industrial Future', *The Listener*, 24 January 1957.

cables 54·2 per cent, telegraph and telephone apparatus 61·8 per cent, motor-cars 52·6 per cent, cycles and motor-cycles 62·9 per cent, man-made fibres 72·4 per cent, metal-mining 59·9 per cent, abrasives 57·3 per cent, and asbestos 61·4 per cent). In a further seven commodity groups the combined product of the four largest firms overtopped 50 per cent of the market (sugar 86 per cent, margarine 80 per cent, tobacco 94 per cent, dyestuffs 81·8 per cent, fertilisers and pesticides 64·3 per cent, railway carriages 70·5 per cent, and glass 51·8 per cent). But even in these nineteen concentrated industries the average output of the single largest firm appears to have accounted for less than 25 per cent of the total sales, and only in four industries (sugar, margarine, tobacco, and artificial fibres) did it appear to exceed 40 per cent of the sales. Moreover, if similar figures were compiled from the pre-war Census of Production (as they were for 1935 by Messrs Leak and Maizels) they would be found to differ little from those of 1958.[1]

Fully comparable figures are not available for either Germany or France but what is known of individual commodities suggests that the shares of markets falling to mammoth firms in continental countries did not increase to an extent greater than in the United Kingdom, even though it may have been much swollen in a few commodities, e.g. petroleum, man-made fibres, and motor-cars in Italy, chemicals, motor-cars, and steel in France, petroleum and electrotechnical products in the Netherlands.[2]

So much for the effects of concentration on the shares of markets. Yet even if and when a firm happened to command an overwhelming share in any national market for a commodity this did not necessarily confer on it commensurate – or indeed any – power of monopoly. For these powers were also limited by consumers' capacity for

[1] Reports on the Census of Production of 1958 (as in footnote 1, p. 194 above); G. C. Allen, *The Structure of Industry in Britain*, p. 40, and J. Leak and A. Maizels, *The Structure of British Industry* (as in footnote 1, p. 196 above).

[2] In 1960 Farbenwerke Hoechst accounted for 11·9 per cent of the total output of German chemical industry. The output of Farbenfabriken Bayer in 1959 amounted to 11·7 per cent. The combined output of the three 'successor' firms to I.G. Farben in 1910 could not have exceeded 36 per cent of total output of the industry: above, footnote 1, p. 200. Even in the U.S.A. the share of markets controlled by large companies may not have grown. According to M. A. Adelman. 'The Measurement of Industrial Concentration', *Review of Economics and Statistics*, November 1951, the share of the market appropriated by the four or eight largest sellers did not increase in recent times.

substitution and by international trade. And both these limitations became more severe after the war than they had been in pre-war Europe.

It is a commonplace of political economy that substitutes – alternative commodities serving consumer needs – could limit and sometimes reduce to nought a firm's control over its prices and output. To be thus effective there was no need for the substitutes to be actually available. It was sufficient for would-be monopolists to realize that high prices might call forth new products capable of replacing those they produced. Nor need substitution be limited to commodities serving the same uses. Consumers' demands themselves, especially those for non-essentials, could be as interchangeable as the commodities serving them; and there is no reason why consumers should not respond to high prices for a commodity by shifting their demand to other commodities serving different requirements – to clothes and food in lieu of motor-cars or refrigerators.

The consumers' capacity for substitution was by no means a recent phenomenon, but there is every reason why it should have grown in our period. As national and individual incomes increased, the proportions which nations and persons had to devote to necessities, such as essential foods, declined. On the other hand non-essentials, i.e. goods men could more easily dispense with and consequently replace with other goods, formed an ever larger proportion of popular consumption. Moreover, their variety and number, and consequently also the range of consumers' choices, increased as technological progress quickened and the flow of new commodities grew more abundant.

These simple propositions of economic theory and even simpler deductions from recent historical trends are well exemplified in the actual experience of post-war Europe. Although the production of aluminium in Italy, France, Norway, and Sweden, and to a somewhat smaller extent in the United Kingdom and Germany, was very largely in the hands of few potentially monopolistic firms, the existence of substitutes and the international trade in aluminium acted as powerful checks on monopolistic practices and kept national prices near their international price levels. Plastics, one of aluminium's substitutes, was itself subject to the same anti-monopoly deterrents. So were also most man-made fibres. Thus the output of rayon in the United Kingdom or the Netherlands was highly concentrated, yet the competition from other fibres was sufficient to keep the prices low and fully competitive. But the best example of monopoly held in check by substitutes was provided by the history of the fuel industries: coal, oil, gas, electricity and atomic power. Most of these industries were highly concentrated and some operated as nationalized monopolies. Yet such was the deterrent effect of substitution, innovation and foreign trade that prices for the different sources of heat – with the possible exception of state-protected coal prices – were as highly competitive as the state tutelage of coal would permit.

Equally obvious were the effects of international trade. Economists have always known that protection and autarchy bred monopolies and that free trade was inimical to them. To this extent the spread of free trade in post-war Europe, the evolution of the E.E.C. and E.F.T.A. and the lowering of the internal and reciprocal tariff barriers made it more difficult for a large firm in any single country to establish a monopoly in its domestic market. What did it matter that Krupp, Rheinstahl, and August Thyssen Hütten each possessed a very large share of the German steel market? The steel markets of countries belonging to the European Iron and Steel Community were in the process of being merged into a single market wherein the share of Krupps was not a third as in Germany, but nearer one-tenth. If in some years prices for some products, such as petrol, were largely artificial and trade appeared to be held in check, the explanation of this will be found in agreements between petroleum firms – however temporary and informal – rather than in the large share of domestic markets claimed by Shell, B.P., or the Compagnie Française de Pétroles. In this particular case international competition had by 1961 become more aggressive than for a long time past.

Similarly, international competition in tyres, chocolate, many chemicals and heavy electrical machinery, made it difficult to measure the monopolistic potential of firms like Dunlop, Michelin, Pirelli, Nestlé, or Unilevers, by their shares of domestic markets. For many of these giant firms their share of a domestic market or employment had become an altogether meaningless yardstick. Most of them had branches in every important country and had become international concerns whose propensity and ability to act as monopolists had to be measured by international, or indeed, world standards. And thus measured, the figures of their outputs or employments in this or that country would not explain why some of them established themselves as monopolists, while others – the great majority – failed to do so.

For these and other reasons the statistics of industrial concentration must give an exaggerated impression of the monopolistic or oligopolistic potential of firms. They exaggerate even more the extent to which this potential was exploited. For when we come to consider the use which firms made of the monopolistic powers which they in theory possessed we must take account of the various obstacles, economic, psychological, and political, which stood in the way of monopolies after the war.

We do not know to what extent the mood of potential monopolists changed in recent times. If modern corporations had, in fact, become as 'soulful', as imbued with public spirit and a wish to serve society, as some American students of modern economy believe, their soulfulness should have prevented them from exploiting their monopolistic powers as fully as their American predecessors had done at the turn of the century. But even if the average monopolist could be shown not to have changed his spots, other people on whom he depended, certainly did.[1] Throughout their modern history monopolies and monopoly-prone industries drew upon themselves a great deal of public attention, and the attention was as a rule charged with opprobrium. In the minds of post-war observers monopoly stood for restrictions of output, higher prices and inefficiency. The policy of governments was correspondingly anti-monopolist. In no European country were these policies as firmly established or far-reaching as in the U.S.A.; but since the war most European governments enacted measures against monopolies, restrictive practices and the maintenance of retail prices. The measures turned out to be less thorough and much slower in operation than their advocates hoped for; nevertheless, the German Law of 1957 against restraining competition and the Federal Control Office established under

---

[1] Carl Kaysen, 'The Social Significance of Modern Corporation', *American Economic Review*, May, 1957, pp. 313–14.

the law, and the British Anti-Monopoly legislation of 1948, 1956, and 1964, and of Monopolies Commission, as well as the corresponding devices in France, Sweden, the Netherlands, helped to curb the worst excesses of monopolies and restrictive practices and to reduce their sway.[1]

Since the war the scope of monopolies was also reduced by the effects or the threats of nationalization. European governments may not have faithfully followed Lord Beveridge's precept that whenever a monopoly was fostered by economic conditions it must automatically pass into public ownership. But, in fact, in the United Kingdom, France, and Austria, and to a smaller extent elsewhere, most of the 'naturally' monopolistic industries – mainly railways, public utilities, and some of the monopoly-prone heavy industries – passed into public ownership; and the threat of nationalization hung over other industries whose size, markets, or methods of production favoured the creation of monopolies.

The connexion between industrial concentration and the growth of monopoly was thus much looser than is assumed in the current notions of 'monopoly capitalism'. In fact, the connexion was always very loose. Many of the functioning monopolies resulted not from the absorption of other firms and the domination of markets by one or very few over-mighty ones, but were brought about by agreements to share markets and to maintain prices. Since Adam Smith's day economists have discussed the conditions which favoured monopolistic agreements, and are, on the whole, of the opinion that the lure of agreements of this kind and their chances of success depended on conditions of demand and supply, on the relation between costs and output and on the structure of the market. With regard to the latter, economists have also agreed that 'oligopoly' or concentration of

[1] For anti-monopoly measures in the United Kingdom, see Paul H. Guénault and J. M. Jackson. *The Control of Monopoly in the United Kingdom*, London, 1960. The story does not, of course, deal with the 1964 legislation against resale price maintenance. German evidence is well summarized in Fritz Voigt, 'German Experience with Cartels and Control during Pre-War and Post-War Periods' in John Perry Miller (ed.), *Competition, Cartels and their Regulation*, Amsterdam, 1962. Other Essays in the collection, especially William Boswup and Uffe Schlicht-krull, 'Alternative Approaches to the Control of Competition', deal with the experience of other countries. See also, Corwin D. Edwards, *Cartelization in Western Europe*, Bureau of Intelligence and Research, U.S.A., Department of State, 1964, Ch. II.

output in the hands of very few firms made it easier for them to combine. And it is, in fact, undeniable that many of the best-known pre-war cartels were formed by agreements between few oligopolists. Yet even before the war, and still more so after the war, cartels and price-agreements in the United Kingdom in Germany and Belgium (and these happened to be the countries in which restrictive agreements of this kind received the attention of historians) frequently embraced industries containing large numbers of firms of every size.[1]

In general, monopolies by restrictive agreements were not specially characteristic of the post-war era. As far as we know, cartels and the cartel-like price-agreements had their hey-day in Germany in the nineties of the last century and in the first decade of the twentieth century. In the German iron and steel industry concentration had gone much farther in the late thirties than in the fifties or sixties. Whereas before the war eight trusts accounted for 95 per cent of the German crude steel output and 57 per cent of coal output, in 1958 the eight largest trusts produced not more than 76 per cent of steel (perhaps as much as 85 per cent in 1963) and only 30 per cent of coal. The degree of concentration in the German chemical and electrical industries was also greater in 1938 than in 1964. Similarly, in the United Kingdom the time when trusts and combinations became conspicuous was the early twentieth century. If more was heard about them after the war, this was as much a sign of growing awareness on the part of the public and the State as of the wider spread of restrictive agreements themselves.[2]

This does not mean that twentieth-century Europe was little affected by the commercial power of mammoth firms, or that markets functioned as freely and spontaneously as they should have done under conditions of untrammelled competition. In the United

---

[1] R. Liefmann, *Kartelle, Konzerne und Trusts*, 8th edn., Stuttgart, 1930, though not confined to German experience, contains what still is the most convenient historical compendium of German cartels in the late nineteenth and the early twentieth centuries. Cf. also D. Warriner, *Combines and Rationalisation in Germany, 1924–1928*, London, 1931. For most recent United Kingdom facts, see the P.E.P. report on 'Structure of Industry', *Planning*, XIX, and P.E.P. report on *Industrial Trade Associations*, London, 1957, Ch. 5; also Monopolies Commission, *Collective Discrimination*, Cmd. 9504, 1955.
[*Vide* Appendix Note 13, p. 366 below.]
[2] Footnote 1, p. 195 above.

Kingdom even before the war nearly 30 per cent of industrial labour was employed in trades subject to monopolies or international cartels. This proportion may not have increased after the war, but it probably did not decline much either. Moreover, monopolies may have established a stronger hold over popular consumption. The readers of Professor Galbraith's *The Affluent Society* will be familiar with the devices by means of which great firms in the U.S.A. were able to generate and to control the demand for their own products and to shape consumers' preferences at will. This American picture may have been painted in colours too lurid to be wholly life-like, but copies of it, however faint, would be found all over post-war Europe. Durable consumption goods, cosmetics, detergents, soft drinks, cigarettes, patent medicines, and even holidays abroad had come to be demanded and supplied in quantities and sometimes also at prices contrived by the firms which offered them.[1]

These features of the post-war economy were not, however, a direct consequence of the increasing scale of enterprises. They owed as much to the general configuration of modern civilization – its material values, its distribution of income and leisure, and above all, its advertising industry, television, and the Press – as to the concentration of production or the 'economies of scale'. They were more frequent in such unconcentrated industries as durable consumption goods, patent medicines and cosmetics, hair-dressing and entertainments than in fields dominated by near-monopolistic giant firms, such as sugar-refining and cement manufacture in the United Kingdom, petroleum in Italy, rubber tyres in France. If post-war Europe deserves the derogatory title of 'monopolistic' it does so not so much by virtue of its growing concentration of

---

[1] W. A. Lewis, *Monopoly in British Industry*, Fabian Society Research Series No. 91, London, 1945. The more refined comparison of the figures for 1935 and 1951 by R. Eveley and I. M. D. Little suggests that whereas 25 per cent of employment was in outputs serving wholly free markets, 10 per cent was in markets wholly monopolistic, while 65 per cent was in industry and trades to some extent affected by restrictive practices. See footnote 1, p. 196 above. The Report of the 1949 Commission on Retail Price Maintenance (p. 1) put this proportion of domestic consumption in 1938 devoted to commodities with fixed or agreed prices at 30 per cent. On the other hand, Professor B. Yamey in his *Resale Price Maintenance and Shoppers' Choice*, London, 1960, p. 8, Hobart Papers I, put the percentage in 1960 at 25.

production, but by virtue of its rapidly changing scales and methods of mass consumption.

It may well be said that of late even the public and governments had ceased to think of monopolies as inevitable consequences of industrial concentration. Towards the end of the fifties a wholly novel notion had crept into the discussion of economic growth and of policies required to foster it – a notion that increases in the 'scale' of production, i.e. production shared by fewer larger firms, could be a desirable object for the government to foster. In the United Kingdom the attitude of the public and the policy of governments towards the aircraft industry, the cotton industry and shipbuilding, iron and steel, had come to be strongly coloured by the view that these industries suffered from a superfluity of firms, none sufficiently large to derive full benefits from economies of scale. Similarly, in the early sixties the discovery that production was less concentrated in France than in Germany or the United Kingdom did not cause much regret among economists and statesmen in Germany or self-congratulation among their opposite numbers in France. The prevailing theme of French comments was that this was a fault of the French national economy sooner or later to be corrected. This does not mean that monopoly lost its opprobrium; it merely ceased to be indissolubly linked in public discussion with the concentration of production.

CHAPTER 9

Ownership: Democratic and Public

The post-war period witnessed numerous changes in the ownership and control of enterprises, some more conspicuous than others. The two most conspicuous changes were the expanding areas of public ownership and the wider spread, or 'democratization' of company holdings. Of the two, the so-called 'democratization' of ownership was the less significant one; it has, however, received most publicity. Throughout our period writings in praise of the existing economic order invariably made play of the spread of ownership – not only of houses and motor-cars but also of industrial capital – among the broad masses of population. The statistics commonly cited were those of larger numbers of people with investments in shares of companies. Some great companies published analyses of their share-ownership, showing that their capital was to an increasing degree owned by very large numbers of individuals and institutions. In the United Kingdom, Shell, Courtaulds and other great firms repeatedly drew attention to the very large numbers – hundreds of thousands – of their shareholders. A recent survey of eleven major steel companies in 1963, showed that their capital was held by more than 275,000 shareholders; that the average shareholding was £885 a head in nominal value, and that more than 92 per cent of the shareholders held less than 1,000 shares each. Of the remaining 8 per cent the bulk was held not by private persons but by insurance companies, pension funds, unit trusts, and trade unions. These figures could be capped by the published statistics of shareholders in a number of large firms in every European country – Philips Lamps, Royal Dutch, Unilever N.V., and many others.[1]

---

[1] Numbers of shareholders are as a rule published in annual reports of a number of large companies in all countries; but as these figures do not allow for

In most countries the 'democratization' was stimulated by government policies and by certain recent developments of the capital market. In the United Kingdom, and to a smaller extent in Germany and the Netherlands, the proliferation of investment trusts and unit trusts did much to foster the spread of industrial ownership. The same purpose was consciously pursued by certain governments and above all by that of Germany. In denationalizing the state-owned Volkswagen and V.E.B.A. combine the German Government took special measures to spread the ownership of their shares as widely as possible.[1]

These manifestations of 'democratic' ownership, impressive though they may be, must not, however, colour our view of the European economy in its entirety. The United Kingdom statistics of shareholding in individual companies somewhat exaggerate the dispersal of ownership, since they fail to aggregate the holdings of individuals in more than one company. But even if the United Kingdom figures were taken at their face value, it would still remain very doubtful whether the dispersal went far enough to affect by itself the distribution of wealth or to confer on the masses of small owners the direct ownership of great firms. It did not go even that far in other countries, since the proportions of industrial and commercial capital directly held by 'little men' were probably much larger in the United Kingdom than in continental countries, where the habit of direct investment in industry was less widespread and unit trusts were as yet relatively few and small. The true significance of the so-called 'democratization' will probably be found in the contribution it made to the changing composition of new investment and thereby also to the progressive displacement of controlling authority in industry; both of them changes about which more will have to be said presently.

overlapping ownership in more than one company they are of little statistical use. In 1965 the British Market Research Bureau carried out an investigation into shareholding of British Companies on behalf of the Zürich Stock Exchange; and according to its preliminary report out of 2½ million investors in the United Kingdom, 1,800,000 held industrial and commercial shares and 900,000 held shares in units and investment trusts. Most of the shareholders were persons in the middle-class ranges of incomes; yet 11 per cent of shareholders occupied council houses: Gordon Cummings, 'Who Are the Shareholders?' in *Stock Exchange Journal*, April 1966.   [1] See below, p. 222.

The second of the most conspicuous changes – the spread of public ownership – deserves much better the publicity it has received, though whether it deserves it in full and everywhere still remains to be seen. That public ownership expanded in the twentieth century, and especially after the war, is very obvious and requires no stressing. Its expansion since 1914, and still more since 1940, was sufficiently marked to influence current political ideologies. It has generally been interpreted as a concession to the socialist principle and as an instalment of the socialist order. And where the instalment happened to be large, the economy as a whole has been as a rule described and commended as 'mixed', part-capitalist and part-socialist.

In general, after 1945, its publicly owned components grew large enough to earn for Western economy as a whole the reputation of being 'mixed'. The mixture will, however, bear a closer scrutiny. Were the two components of post-war economies, the private and the public, of comparable size? And was their combination nothing more than a mixture of two disparate ingredients, one as wholly private as it had been before it entered the mixture, and the other wholly socialist in inspiration and performance; or was the economy a 'mixed' one because its ingredients, the public and the private, lost (if they ever possessed) the unadulterated purity of conduct unrestrictedly private or ideally public?

There are thus two questions: one concerns the relative size of the public sector, the other concerns its character. The size, in its turn, can be measured by several yardsticks, but mainly by the employment and investment it represented. Judged by pure size public ownership was bound to differ from country to country. There was much of it in the United Kingdom, France, Italy, and Austria: there was almost none in Germany, Belgium, Switzerland, or the Scandinavian countries. Nor were the additions everywhere and always made for the same reasons. In some countries nationalizing governments acted in pursuance of socialist or near-socialist programmes of political parties; in others they found themselves in possession of manufacturing and commercial enterprises by accident or by inheritance; either because they carried over some pre-war engagements, or because they had to take over the properties of defaulting or outlawed owners.

The United Kingdom provides the most obvious example of nationalization in fulfilment of political programmes. In that country some public utilities – telephones and telegraph, the major port authorities, some water supplies, air transport, London transport, broadcasting and some radio communications and most local public utilities – had been in the hands of the state, municipalities or public corporations long before the war. The main accessions, however, came with the victory at the polls in 1945 of the Labour Party pledged to a programme of wide-ranging nationalization. In the first years of its rule the Labour Government established state ownership over the generation and distribution of electricity and gas, cable and wireless communications, railways, the sections of road transport serving long and middle distances, and the coal and steel industries. The Conservative Government on its accession to power in 1951 proceeded to denationalize the steel industry and to reduce the hold of the state corporations over road transport. Their subsequent policy with regard to air transport and television was to facilitate or at least to tolerate the entry of private companies. But with these few exceptions, the areas of public ownership stayed under Conservative rule within the frontiers set by the Labour governments. On their part, the Labour Party in their 1963 programme for the coming general election proposed to do little more than to restore to public ownership the steel industry and road transport denationalized by the Conservatives.[1]

The origin of State ownership in France was somewhat more mixed. State participation in the ownership and control of enterprises was not as inimical to French historical tradition as it was to the English. At all periods of history, from the end of the seventeenth century onwards, the French State could be found owning or at least sponsoring industrial establishments. In the inter-war period the French State owned a large proportion of the railway lines and a number of enterprises deemed essential from the national point of view, such as the Compagnie Française des Pétroles, or the Crédit Nationale. It also established for fiscal purposes a number of State monopolies of which the tobacco monopoly was the most important. By the late thirties there were in France some seventy-five to

---

[1] William Robson, *Nationalised Industry and Public Ownership*, 2nd edn, London, 1962.

eighty enterprises owned wholly or partly by the State, each of which functioned as an independent commercial or industrial undertaking.[1]

State ownership greatly expanded after the war. The railways were now all brought under national ownership. So were also electricity and gas, cables, wireless, and, later, television. We have also seen that the State took over the country's major banking and saving institutions. This was done with the intention of placing the Government in occupation of the 'commanding heights' from which control and the planning of the economy could be effectively directed. The principal companies in the aircraft industry were acquired and reorganized into two great State corporations mainly because in the immediate post-war years the aircraft industry appeared to be of crucial importance to the national economy, defence, and prestige. The same view of public interest led the State to assume the ownership of the Compagnie Française de Raffinage, and the Societé Nationale des Pétroles d'Aquitaine, thus turning the bulk of the indigenous petroleum industry into a state enterprise. On the other hand, in a number of enterprises, of which the Renault motor-car factory was the most important, the State merely replaced the previous owners compromised by their collaboration with the occupying power during the war.

A still larger complex of nationalized industries came into existence in Austria, where on the morrow of the war the State stepped into the possession of the bulk of heavy industry and much of light industry, especially in its engineering and electrical branches. In addition, its ownership of the principal banks gave the State an indirect share in a large number of undertakings in miscellaneous industries. This large and multifarious complex of State-owned establishments was, to begin with, made up largely of German enterprises set up or expanded under the National Socialist armament plans, confiscated by the Russians and transferred to the Austrian Government at the end of Russian occupation. To this extent, the Austrian State can be said to have acquired its nationalized sector by inheritance. But the care which successive governments took to maintain and even to enlarge their inheritance

---

[1] Below, p. 280; also Mario Einaudi, Maurice Byé, and Ernesto Rossi, *Nationalisation in France and Italy*, N.Y., 1955, pp. 67–81.

P

must be put down to the socialist influences in the coalition governments, as well as to the peculiar conditions in which the Austrian
economy found itself immediately after the war – above all an acute
shortage of privately-held investable capital.[1]

Different again were the origins of State ownership in Italy. The
Italian State had been drawn into direct ownership of enterprises
during and in consequence of the great inter-war depression. Before
that time Italy, even more than Germany, suffered from the lack of
private investors willing or able to finance her new industrial
ventures. As in Germany the gap had to be filled by the banks, with
the result that by the late twenties most of the major industrial and
commercial undertakings were owned by the banks or were heavily
in debt to them. A financial structure of this kind, wherein banks
committed to long-term investment funds lent to them on short
term deposits, could function smoothly only as long as the public
confidence in the banks remained unshaken. But when the crisis
came in 1929, the banks, with their assets tied up in industry, found
it difficult to continue shouldering their obligations to their depositors, and the State had to come to their rescue. The I.R.I. (Istituto
de Reconstruzione Industriale) was formed to take over the frozen
assets of the banks, and in this way the fascist State found itself by
1933 holding a large slice of Italian industry and commerce.

The I.R.I. maintained this holding throughout the subsequent
years of uneasy peace and of war, and greatly enlarged it after the
war. By 1963 its six principal 'sectoral' companies controlled
groups of enterprises in every major branch of economic activity.
One holding company, S.T.E.T., owned the telephones; another,
Finsider, owned the greater part of the steel industry; the company
of Finmare controlled such major shipping companies as Lloyd
Triestino and Italia; Fincanteli did the same in shipbuilding, and
controlled, among others, the great enterprises of Ansaldo, C.R.D.A.,
and Naval-meccanica; while the company of Finmeccanica controlled a number of engineering concerns including Alfa Romeo,
Ansaldo San Giorgio and others. One other 'sectoral' company,
Finelectrica, held an important position in the electrical industry,
but was destined to be merged with the E.N.E.I., the independently

[1] K. W. Rothschild, *Oesterreichs Wirtschaftsstruktur*, Berlin, 1962.

functioning electricity corporation in charge of the electrical industry, nationalized in 1962. In the course of the post-war period the I.R.I. also added to its possessions the State air company, Alitalia, the State radio and television and the growing network of toll-paying motorways. At the same time outside the system of 'sectoral' companies there grew up a collection of enterprises under the direct control of the I.R.I. itself, producing a wide assortment of commodities – cellulose, paper, glass, mercury, and textiles. Similarly, outside the 'sectoral' companies were the banks – Banca Commerciale Italiana, Credito Italiano, Banco di Roma, Banco di Santo Spirito, Mediobanca, and Credito Fondiario Sardo. Wholly outside the I.R.I. there grew up since 1945 the great nationalized petroleum enterprise of E.N.I.[1]

In this way an immense State holding in industry and commerce grew up by accretions to pre-war commitments. Some of these accretions, and more especially the growing stake in the steel industry, had an origin almost as adventitious as the I.R.I. itself. In the early post-war years the leaders of privately-owned steel companies took a pessimistic view of the prospects for the large-scale steel industry, so that the main drive behind the ambitious plans of expansion passed to the as-yet small State-owned steel enterprises headed by the dynamic Signor Sinigaglia. It is also impossible to minimize the part which the dynamism of Signor Enrico Mattei played in the expansion of E.N.I. On the other hand, the nationalization of the electrical industry under way in 1963 was obviously a product of deliberate political choice.

No such political choice lay behind State ownership in Germany. Apart from the railway system, nationalized in the late seventies and the eighties of the nineteenth century, and certain industrial properties in the hands of the *Länder* and of municipalities, public ownership in Germany was confined to a few enterprises which had

---

[1] For the early history of I.R.I. and its activities in the fifties, see V. Lutz, *Italy: A Study in Economic Development*, pp. 270–3, and Eugenie Sclafari, *Rapporto sul Neocapitalismo in Italia*, Bari, 1961. The I.R.I.'s own exposition of its origin and of reason for its existence will be found in I.R.I., *Studi i Documenti*, I, pp. 3–17. The Annual Reports (*Esercizii*) of I.R.I. contain a full description of its operations in different fields. For the 'privatistic' principle animating the conduct of nationally owned enterprises, see Einaudi, Byé, and Rossi (as in footnote 1, p. 219 above).

come into the hands of the Federal Government in a wholly un-premeditated way. The largest of them turned out to be the Volkswagen enterprise whose origins went back to Hitler's project of 'people's car', and which was still in operation and owned by the State at the end of the war. The immense success of the car in the post-war markets, both at home and abroad, greatly enhanced the size and the value of this property, but to the Christian-Democratic Government it was something of an embarrassment to be got rid of at the earliest opportunity. By 1963 the greater part of Volks-wagen capital was already in the hands of a large number of private shareholders. The other large State holding was represented by the Vereinigte Elektrizitäts- und Bergwerke A.G. (V.E.B.A.) compris-ing a group of electrical undertakings with appendages in the chemical, mining and metallurgical industries. But the V.E.B.A., like the Volkswagen, was also destined to be transferred to private ownership, and preparations for the transfer were under way by 1963. Equally accidental was the State's participation in one of the sections of the erstwhile Stinnes enterprises resulting from the repatriation of the American holding in a Stinnes succession company.

The involvement of the German State in industry and commerce was thus not only small and unpremeditated but also in the process of being liquidated. The involvement was even smaller in Scandin-avian countries, Belgium and Switzerland, and only little larger in the Netherlands. In the Netherlands the sole important industrial enterprise in the hands of the State was the coal-mines, of which the Government held three-fifths of the capital. This venture into State ownership was part and parcel of the reconstruction of the coal-mining industry conceived and carried out as an act of national policy. But although in more recent years the State mines extended their interests into some adjoining fields (mostly chemicals), their relative weight in the Dutch economy was not to be compared with that of the nationalized enterprises of France, Italy, and Austria or the United Kingdom.

In the United Kingdom, France, Italy, and Austria the purely statistical weight of nationally owned industries was undoubtedly great, but it was also of some importance elsewhere. If we were to aggregate the activities of the State, i.e. not only the nationalized enterprises but also the traditional functions of the State – the army, police, civil bureaucracy, education and social services – the total volume of economic activity they represented would be very large indeed. Thus reckoned the total government employment in most European states would by 1964 exceed 40 per cent and approach (as in Austria) 50 per cent of the employed labour force. Investment absorbed by various State activities – schools and roads as well as factories – would be of the same order and would exhibit the same tendency to grow, as defence commitments, social services and the educational budgets of European governments expanded.

In the United Kingdom, Italy, France, and Austria the volume of state employment and capital would still appear to be very high even if industrial, commercial, and transport undertakings alone were considered, but would not represent an overwhelmingly important share of national economies. In the United Kingdom the size of the nationalized sector of industry and trade, measured by the employment it gave (about 3 million), accounted for about 15 per cent of the total number of wage-earners and salaried employees. This ratio may, moreover, underestimate the full weight of nationalized industries in the economy of the United Kingdom. Considered not in relation to total employment but in relation to the manpower in manufacturing industries, mines, transport and public utilities, the employment in State-owned enterprises probably approached 20 per cent between 1946 and 1952 and was only a little less than that between 1952 and 1962. Measured by the capital it employed the public sector would appear even weightier, since it comprised such capital-intensive industries as coal, railways, electricity, atomic power, and gas.[1] But whatever statistical measurement is adopted the share of State ownership in the national economy would still be below one quarter.

Similarly evaluated the size of the public sectors of the French economy would appear to be of the same order of magnitude as the

---

[1] In the United Kingdom total employment in the public sector in 1963 was estimated at about 5 million or 20 per cent of total employed population: *Growth and Economic Policy*, Report to the Economic Policy Committee of O.E.C.D., 1964, pp. 53 and 123 *seq.*
[*Vide* Appendix Note 14, p. 367 below.]

British. The total employment they gave in 1962 approached 1 million or 14 per cent of the industrial labour force, or nearly 13 per cent of the total number of wage-earners and salaried employees. Their capital was estimated to represent 40 per cent of the total fixed assets of enterprises, and their output roughly equalled 10 per cent of G.N.P. But the State-owned enterprises dominated a number of important sectors of the economy: they accounted for 60 per cent of aircraft production, 30 per cent of motor-car output, 30 per cent of nitrates, the entire railway and maritime transport, 50 per cent of deposit banking, and 40 per cent of insurance business.[1]

In Austria, State-owned industrial, commercial, and banking establishments were responsible for just under a quarter of total non-agricultural output of 1961 and rather more than a quarter of total exports in that year. In Italy direct employment in State-owned enterprises in 1962 was about 375,000, or about 10 per cent of the national industrial employment. But if the employment in firms partly-owned by the State and I.R.I. were to be reckoned, the proportion might exceed 20 per cent. The stake of I.R.I. in national output was at least equally high, and even higher in certain key branches of the economy. In 1963 I.R.I. controlled over one-half of the country's steel production, two-thirds of its passenger shipping tonnage, and more than three-quarters of its shipbuilding capacity. In 1962 the combined investment of I.R.I. and E.N.I. represented about 20 per cent of the capital invested in industry, commerce, and transport, and was responsible for one-half of all new capital issues.[2]

The economic significance of these purely quantitative weights is not to be gainsaid. In some countries the very size of nationalized concerns, their greater financial stability and their easier access to

---

[1] In France total employment by public authorities and nationalized undertakings in 1962 was estimated at 2,200,000 or some 18 per cent of the total number of employees. P. Bauchet, *Propriété publique et planification*, Paris, 1962; A. Chozel and H. Poyet, *L'économie mixte*, Paris, 1963.

[2] Direct employment in I.R.I. enterprises was 288,000: *E.R.I. Esercizio, 1962*, p. 19. Total capital invested in I.R.I. enterprises at the end of 1962 was estimated at 1·740 billion *lire*, of which between two-thirds and three-quarters were represented by privately owned capital; *ibid.*, p. 17; cf. Aldo Frascati, *Scritti e Discorsi*, Milan, 1960, and Vera Lutz, *Italy: A Study in Economic Development*, Royal Inst. of International Affairs, London, 1962.

capital, conferred on them a position in the economy more influential than that of most privately owned enterprises. In Italy, I.R.I. proved less susceptible to the ups and downs of economic fluctuations than wholly private enterprises and could invest and expand at times when the economy was at its least buoyant. For this and other reasons nationalized undertakings were often able to shoulder costly responsibilities which might have deterred wholly private undertakings, such as the atomic generation of electricity in the United Kingdom, Atlantic shipping in France, and steel-making in Austria.

However, the size of the public sector, or of individual enterprises within it, is not the true measure of its role. Its role was, from some points of view considerably greater than its dimensions alone would justify. It was sometimes that of a planning tool. High officials of I.R.I. recently spoke of situations in which the nationalized undertakings would be 'ready to assume whatever function the non-predictable bottle-necks in the development process may have placed upon it'.[1] In accordance with this doctrine, I.R.I. pioneered important industrial projects in southern Italy and took upon itself to build up the Italian road system. But even when they did not assume these ambitious pioneering or first-aid roles, the nationalized sectors could still play a vital part in directing economic life. In countries where they comprised the principal financial institutions – in France, Austria, and Italy – they spread their tentacles to all the important enterprises and transactions. In France public ownership of saving institutions (though not necessarily of banks) provided the State and its planning bodies with a most effective means for directing the distribution of investment. In Austria and to a smaller extent in Italy it also gave the State an indirect hold over the capital of large numbers of firms nominally private. Similarly, public ownership of certain basic industries could carry with it great economic influence, since the pricing policies and outputs of railways and public utilities, or of industries, like coal, petroleum, and steel, affected national development more powerfully than the outputs and prices of consumption goods or intermediate commodities.

[1] Professor Saraceno as cited in *The Times*, 23 April 1966.

At the same time, in a certain very fundamental sense, the part played by nationalized industry fell short of the highest and fondest expectations of its advocates. It was a powerful, but not a predominant, ingredient in the so-called 'mixed' economies. In some of them it was perhaps strong enough to season the mixture to some non-capitalist tastes; yet nowhere was it sufficiently strong, and above all, sufficiently different from other ingredients, to impart its own characteristic flavour to the recipe as a whole. It can be justly argued that what entitled Western economy to the reputation of being 'mixed' was the growing authority of the State in economic matters and its powers over industries and enterprises. What cannot be argued is that that entitlement was wholly derived from national ownership. In discussing the relations of large firms with the State I suggested that the power of the State over them sprang mainly from the new conception of the Government and of its responsibilities, from the popular concern with economic growth and economic security, from the growing dependence of major industries on government purchases, aid and guidance, and from the increasing popularity and refinements of planning techniques. These powers of the State affected all industries and occupations, and if some felt it more than others, they did so not necessarily because they were nationally owned, but because they happened to stand nearer to the main sources of state bounty or to the most sensitive points of national economy. In the United Kingdom privately owned and managed agriculture was more at the mercy of the State than the British Petroleum Company with its 51 per cent of State-owned shares; in France the conduct of private agriculture or the iron-and-steel industry was as much dependent on government policies as the conduct of nationalized deposit banks or of the nationally owned Renault Company. In Italy the wholly nationalized petroleum industry was no less independent of State discretion than the wholly private chemical industry.

The same also applies to influences radiating in the opposite direction: from enterprises to the State. Here again the influence might vary according to the role which an industry or an occupation played in economic life, to its contribution to exports, innovation and employment, to its command over votes, or to its ability to stand on its own feet. We have seen that national ownership played its part, but the part was by no means decisive. The opinions, interests, and pressures of the City, the insurance companies, the banks, the aircraft and electronics industries – all of them privately owned – did not necessarily weigh less with the British government than the interests and opinions of nationally owned electrical or gas industries. In short the interpenetration of national policies and considerations of *raison d'état*, on the one hand, and private interests on the other had gone a long distance in the generation after 1945, but the distance was not always determined by the size of the nationalized sector.

Somewhat less significant (though perhaps more disappointing to the ideologists) was the absence of clear distinctions in the conduct – economic motivation, managerial methods, and human relations – of public and private enterprises. The former failed to develop those very attributes which are commonly supposed to distinguish socialist enterprises from privately owned ones; on their part, privately owned enterprises had in the meantime lost many of the attributes which had in the past been regarded as characteristic of capitalist business.

To begin with, nationalized enterprises did not as a matter of course conduct their business on principles markedly different from those of privately owned enterprises. They frequently tried where they could to maximize their profits and were not always willing or enjoined to disregard the test of profitability and to function as providers of profitless social services. In the nationalized industries in the United Kingdom, in most publicly owned enterprises in Austria, France and Germany, the individual undertakings were expected to 'pay their way' even when, as in the case of British Railways and coalmines, this was patently beyond their power to do. We have seen that the great nationally owned combines, such as I.R.I., were sometimes willing to pursue national and social objectives transcending those of private gain. We shall see later that the centralized financial machinery of the French saving institutions could develop into powerful instruments of State planning. But most state-owned enterprises, taken individually, did not and could not depart from the methods and obligations of other enterprises. The business of the nationally owned Renault factory was actuated by the same incentives and pursued the same commercial ends as the other French motor-car combines. The French deposit banks did not cease to behave 'commercially' after they had been nationalized, and did not become, as the Banque de France and the saving institutions did, mere tools of the State.

In this respect many nationalized undertakings were left with little choice. Not only were they often instructed by governments to pay their way but they had to obey the same incentives and employ the same methods as private enterprises if they were to survive and to grow in the competitive or near-competitive conditions of Western economy. But, in addition, most state-owned undertakings conformed to ordinary business objectives and methods merely because the motivation and behaviour of their personnel, their labour force and their managers, were also the same as in private business.

Labour in state enterprises – its part in the internal government of enterprises, its general attitude to production, wages and profits, and its relations with managers – differed much less from its position in private ones than advocates of public ownership may have hoped. Several countries tried to introduce an element of industrial democracy into the government of industry, mainly in the form of managerial or consultative committees with labour representatives. In the United Kingdom Joint Consultative Committees were written into the constitutions of most nationalized industries. But Germany was perhaps the only Western country where at the end of the war ambitious attempts were made to enhance the role of labour in the government of all industry, both national and private. In accordance with the industrial code of 1946, boards of directors (Aufsichtsräthe) had to contain workers' representatives. In the event, this first instalment of industrial democracy – the German 'co-determination' or the British Consultative Committees – fell far short of its early promise. It may have facilitated the labour-management contacts, but it did not greatly raise the workers' share in the direction of factories or shops. As a result, in Germany as elsewhere in Western Europe, the dichotomy of management and Unions, the workers' influence on the policies of firms and the liability to industrial conflicts were about the same in nationalized undertakings as in private ones.[1]

---

[1] On the causes of ineffectiveness of joint consultation in industry in the United

On their part, most managers of public enterprises also failed to disport themselves differently from their opposite numbers in private firms. In ancient socialist theory they were conceived as a wholly new category of business leaders; new mainly because their ranks would be made up not of 'owners of the means of production' but of functionaries appointed or risen to their positions solely by virtue of their qualifications. But in the course of the twentieth century this also became the image of the managerial *élite* of private industry and commerce. In private firms leadership had as often as not passed into the hands of professional managers and directors, functionaries of their firms, who as a rule did not own any or much of their firm's capital and did not belong to the owners' families. As we shall see later the professional directors and managers had since pre-war days been fast displacing the capitalist owner-managers old-style; and where the displacement was complete, the leading personnel of private and public enterprises had grown to be very similar and, in some cases, interchangeable.

However, this *rapprochement* of managerial *élites* in the private and public sectors, is part and parcel of a much more general and a more deeply rooted change in the control of industry and trade. If, broadly speaking, the economic and social system in countries with a high proportion of state-owned industries did not function much differently from systems in countries whose industries, in the main, remained in private ownership, this was not merely because nationalized industry turned out to be less socialist than its advocates had hoped, but also because capitalist industry had ceased to be as capitalist as some of its detractors had imagined. Since the end of the nineteenth century large sections of 'private' business were themselves moving away from positions in which they could have appeared to stand in clear contrast to nationalized enterprises.

The story of this movement deserves to be told in greater detail and will form the main subject of the next chapters.

Kingdom see *The Framework of Joint Consultation*, Acton Society Trust, 1952, pp. 21–6. An endeavour not only to understand but also to forgive will be found in William Robson, *Nationalised Industries and Public Ownership*, 2nd edn, London, 1962, Ch. XII.

CHAPTER 10

Ownership: Anonymous

Professional directors and managers not dependent for their position on the ownership of their firms' capital arrived on the scene long before 1939 and even before 1900. But it was in the twentieth century, and more especially since the war, that the control of most great firms passed into their hands and that owner-managers ceased to be the representative type of business leadership. This transformation at the top levels of industrial and commercial personnel was not, however, purely administrative, or as some people would call it, 'organizational'. It was deeply rooted in the changes which for some time had been taking place in the very structure of industrial and commercial property. For some decades before the war and also after the war, the *provenance* of capital was in the process of transformation. Some old sources of investable capital were drying up; new ones were flowing in ever-greater abundance. These shifts in the ownership of capital and in the sources of its current flow must be taken into account before the changes in industrial and commercial leadership itself can be understood.

The post-war shifts in the principal sources of new capital are reflected in Table 22 below. The reflection is imperfect as it is not projected against a comparable nineteenth-century background. What is worse, it is of necessity so arranged as to conceal from view the socially significant demarcations between different sources. The conventional manner of classifying and measuring sources of new capital, which is also that adopted in our table, is to distinguish public savings from private ones and to break up the latter into those of private persons or households on the one hand and those of enterprises on the other. Thus arranged the post-war figures, as indeed all figures of savings in the last fifty or seventy-five years, may blur certain important historical changes. Above all, they may create the impression that the mixture was always as before and that the composition of savings did not alter much in the course of its recorded history.

Table 23 *Gross Domestic Savings by Sources: 1950–61*[1]

| | (% of G.N.P.) | | |
| | | Private Savings | |
	Gross Domestic Savings	Household	Enterprise	Public Savings
Austria	20·4	5·8	8·0	6·6
Belgium	17·6	8·6	10·5	−1·5
France	18·4	3·4	11·1	3·9
Germany	26·3	8·1	10·5	7·7
Denmark	18·5	7·0	7·4	4·1
Italy	21·6	19·2		2·4
Netherlands	25·9	4·1	14·8	7·0
Norway	27·3	6·2	14·0	7·1
United Kingdom	16·6	3·3	11·3	2·0
(1961 only)	17·9	7·7	8·5[a]	1·7

[a] Corporation.

Judged by statistical appearances the tables of gross domestic savings by sources for the end of the nineteenth century would not greatly differ from our Table here. Such tables compiled at frequent intervals might record some movements in individual figures, but the movements would reflect irregular fluctuations in economic conditions or changes in government policies rather than the deep-seated historical processes common to the Western world as a whole. It is only when we go behind the blank façade of official statistics and try to uncover the social identity of the actual savers that the underlying historical transformations become discernible.

Treated thus, the most important source of private savings, that

---

[1] The Table is based on figures in U.N.O. *World Economic Survey 1960*, N.Y., 1961, Tables 1–3, p. 19, adjusted to include returns for 1960 and 1961. The latter have been derived from various sources, mostly O.E.C.D. Annual National Surveys, *Wirtschaft und Statistik*, and *Statistisches Jahrbuch* for 1960 and 1961, and *Central Statistical Office: National Income and Expenditure, 1964*, Table 28.

of persons and households, loses much of its apparent sameness. As far as we can gather from the little evidence we have, personal savings in the earlier phases of their nineteenth-century history came mainly from the source deserving best to be described as 'capitalist'. The historical physiognomy of the 'capitalist', still more of the capitalist in his capacity as investor, has never been clearly delineated; his main features, however, are easily recognizable. In the first place the capitalist investor – he might be a 'feudal' aristocrat as well as a middle-class merchant, manufacturer or rentier – was, by definition, a person with an income sufficiently large to leave him with substantial surpluses after all his habitual expenditure had been met. These 'true' surpluses were his investable savings. In the second place he could be expected to invest with a view to further income. As often as not he would derive much or most of his income from his or his progenitors' investments. Finally, whether advised by lawyers and brokers or not, he would be expected to acquire his investments directly and hold them in his own name.

Investors of this type were always to be found in all periods of European history, but they were becoming more prominent as the modern industrial system was reaching maturity. By the second half of the nineteenth century, and especially by its last quarter, 'capitalist' savings and investing became the habit of very large numbers of the well-to-do in the United Kingdom and, in the end, also in other European countries. In Sir J. H. Clapham's well-known phrase, stocks and shares had by the late seventies become an admissible topic of drawing-room conversation. What Sir John Clapham could have added is that the men who discussed shares in drawing-rooms were responsible for a great part of current savings. Most historians also hold them responsible for the rapid spread of joint-stock companies, bourses and stock-exchanges, and indeed for the entire evolution of national capital markets as reservoirs of new capital.

From this position the 'capitalist' savers and investors had begun to recede some time before 1939; they may have all but abandoned it since the war. This does not mean that even in the post-war world men's ability to save did not depend on the size of their incomes or that wealthy men saving and investing on a large scale were not to be found in considerable numbers in all the European countries. It nevertheless remains true that they contributed to the total flow of savings relatively less than in earlier times. The reasons why their contribution declined are well known. Incomes were being redistributed, slowly but surely, to the disadvantage of large incomes. In most countries progressive taxation made it more difficult for men with large incomes to save; death duties, however erratic their incidence, helped to reduce the unearned incomes from inherited wealth. Inflations had the same effects, even if they were mainly felt by persons who were ill-advised to hold their wealth in fixed-interest securities.

The decline in the flow of 'capitalist' savings, though very real, must not, of course, be exaggerated. The main reason why the social composition of personal savings was changing was not that the total flow of 'capitalist' savings ebbed, but that the various streams of small men's contributions were flowing more abundantly. Their savings are sometimes referred to as 'popular'; but as savings of persons in the very lowest income groups, i.e. manual workers in unskilled or semi-skilled occupations, still contributed disproportionally little to the total stream of personal savings, the term 'popular' may be something of a misnomer. 'More popular than before' might be a better, though a much more cumbrous appellation. They could, however, be best described as 'prudential', since their small or individual size was not the only feature distinguishing them from their 'capitalist' counterpart.

In the first place, what a typical prudential saver saved came not out of his 'natural' surpluses comparable to the unspent balances of wealthy men's revenues but out of what he withdrew from consumption under the pressure of various obligations. Some of the obligations were self-imposed, others were contractual and even compulsory. They could arise from superannuation and pension schemes, or follow from contracts for the repayment of mortgages and loans, or be accumulated under life-insurance policies. Where they happened to reflect men's thrifty behaviour, the thrift itself was, as often as not, a prudent reaction to the insecurity of humble existences. Its object was not so much to increase current income as to accumulate capital sums for eventual disbursements, such as house purchase, or for emergencies, such as death, illness, marriage, or unemployment.

In the second place a large, and perhaps a growing proportion of prudential savings was accumulated through financial institutions whose business it was to gather them. To this extent, the economic use to which they were put was not in the saver's own hands. It was almost wholly 'mediatized', or, in other words, left to the decision of institutions which interposed themselves between the saver and the management of his savings.

These general characteristics of 'prudential' savings have been presented here in their purest form. In actual practice they were frequently diluted by ingredients easily recognizable as 'capitalist'; and the strength of the dilution was not the same all through our period and in every European country. Our data will not permit us to follow closely, still less to measure, all these variations, but such figures as we possess are sufficient to demonstrate what happened in most Western countries during our period. In all of them 'prudential' savings grew continually, and in the end came to represent the major bulk of private savings. Most of them were also 'mediatized'.

The evidence is clearest for the United Kingdom, though even for the United Kingdom precise estimates are not easily formed. Taken as a whole, household savings in the United Kingdom grew in the late forties and the early fifties rather slowly, and over the period as a whole formed not more than about a quarter of total gross savings. But in 1952, in 1956, and in 1960, they spurted ahead and in 1961 they stood at £1,680 million and accounted for more than 8 per cent of the G.N.P. and for about 45 per cent of total gross national savings. In this growth prudential savings played a decisive role and formed a very high proportion of total personal savings. Savings of a 'prudential' nature made by insurance payments, superannuations, deposits in Savings Banks, Premium Bonds, Savings Bonds, direct repayments of mortgage loans, deposits in building societies, deposits in clearing banks, and the purchase of shares in investment and unit trusts are difficult to separate from 'capitalist' saving. But the analysis of personal savings in the mid-fifties suggests that about one-third of these savings came from incomes of £2,000 and over, and were therefore in the main classifiable as 'capitalist'. If so, 'prudential' savings accounted for about two-thirds of personal savings. Such indirect evidence as we possess suggests that the ratio of 'prudential' savings to those of the well-to-do remained approximately the same in the late fifties and the early sixties.[1]

A somewhat smaller proportion of these savings flowed through financial institutions than in some other Western countries, but it was nevertheless very large. In the course of the decade just over £3,000 million were invested directly by small savers and in their individual names in various government stocks, mostly in National Savings Certificates and Premium Savings Bonds; an unknown but not large amount not included in our totals of 'prudential' savings were apparently held directly as debentures and shares of commercial companies. The bulk of the 'prudential' funds, however, were channelled through various savings institutions: Trustee Savings Banks, Post Office Savings Banks, Building Societies, Industrial Assurance Companies, Friendly Societies, Trade Unions, authorized Unit Trusts, Superannuation Funds, and, above all, Life Insurance Companies. As I have just said, the amounts accumulated through these institutions grew very much faster than personal savings as a whole. Whereas the latter had grown during the period by 66 per cent, the accumulated premiums of life insurance companies alone grew by 154 per cent and accumulated payments to Building Societies by 152 per cent.[2]

It is possible that in Germany popular savings of the prudential type had begun to expand fast much earlier than in the United Kingdom; at any rate, it was in Germany that their overwhelming

[1] There was some dissaving by recipients of low incomes at the beginning of our period, but by mid-fifties personal savings had begun to mount: F. W. Paish, 'The Economic Position of the United Kingdom', *Westminster Bank Review*, August 1962; M. B. Erritt and F. L. Nicholson, 'The 1955 Savings Survey', *Bulletin of the Oxford Institute of Statistics*, vol. 20, 1958, *passim*, and Tables XXV and XV. According to the latter, £389 millions were saved in 1953/4 out of incomes of £400 and above. Of this, £255 millions came from incomes under £2,000, £161 million out of incomes under £1,000. In the following year incomes under £1,000 accounted for £153 million, out of £318 million saved out of incomes over £400.

[2] Estimates of aggregate premium payments come from annual *Summaries of Statements of Assurance Business*, published by the British Insurance Association. Figures of pensions are based on the *Report on Superannuation* (Cmd 9333) and the figures for repayments on mortgages come from the annual *Reports of the Registrar of Friendly Societies*. The figures have been interpreted and treated as in M. B. Erritt and F. L. Nicholson, *op. cit.*

Q

importance was first noticed and described by historians and economists. This may, in part, have been due to the frugal and thrifty habits of the German working-man, and in part, to the precocious development of credit establishments designed to serve the needs of popular savers. The mounting progress of these funds in Germany was rudely interrupted by the catastrophic inflations and devaluations following the two great wars. Since 1948, however, the trend again asserted itself. It would not be too wild a guess to suggest that by 1961 small savings probably accounted for the bulk, possibly as much as 80 per cent, of personal savings, though what they amounted to in absolute totals can only be guessed at.

Our main excuse for imprecision is that the German figures of household savings like those of most other countries, include the savings of family enterprises, and this makes the share of prudential savings difficult to measure. But as the overwhelming proportion of prudential savings in Germany flowed through savings institutions, their size can approximately be judged from the returns of the various institutional funds. Their main repositories were the various specialized saving offices and banks – Sparkassen, Postsparkassen, Kreditgenossenschaften of several kinds, Zentralkassen, as well as mortgage institutions and commercial banks. The savings accumulating in these institutions grew from little more than DM 5,000 million in 1950 to DM 17,000 million in 1954, and DM 60,000 million by 1961.

To these sums must be added the popular savings through insurance companies. In general, insurance funds did not grow in Germany to the same giddy heights as in the United Kingdom and did not attract the same proportion of small savings. The returns of insurance companies show, however, that the annual premiums of insurance companies (life offices) in 1962 amounted to over DM 4,000 million, compared with DM 1,200 million in 1953, and that the total savings accumulated at this progression rate in the intervening nine years. It also appears that about half of life and annuity insurances outstanding in 1962 were for sums less than DM 5,000, and that more than 75 per cent were for sums less than DM 10,000. So even if we reckoned as 'prudential' no more than one-half of the accumulated insurance funds, accrued small savings under this head would by 1961 appear to have reached not less than

DM 12,000 million. Thus aggregated, the total of prudential savings through institutions listed here would approach very closely to within 80 per cent of total personal savings, i.e. of the recorded volume of household savings minus the presumed allowance for savings of family enterprises.[1]

For France exact computations are even more difficult since a very large proportion of new savings went directly into government funds, and the returns for the latter make it impossible to define the proportion held by small savers. The main stream of popular savings in that country, however, flowed through the Caisses d'Epargne, and the latter's account therefore represents well the general trend of popular savings. The funds of the Caisses, like all French personal savings, grew very slowly in the forties and the early fifties. Inflation and monetary and political instability militated against this and other forms of personal savings, and kept them relatively lower than in most other Western countries. They recovered, however, in the late fifties, and the recovery was led by savings prudential in character. The accrued savings of the Caisses d'Epargne rose to N.F. 15,200 million; and this sum alone probably accounted for more than one-half of all the personal savings (not counting the savings of enterprises). To these sums we must add the accumulated payments to insurance companies. How much of these insurances belonged to small savers and could be classified as prudential is difficult to tell. But whatever their proportion, their total volume must have risen exceptionally fast. The annual value of new business in life endowment and annuity insurance rose from c. N.F. 2,500 million in 1953 to c. N.F. 7,000 million in 1960, and may have risen more than sixfold between 1949 and 1962.

[1] The estimates are based on figures in *Wirtschaft und Statistik*, July 1963, pp. 431 *seq.* (insurance), *Statistisches Jahrbuch*, 1962, Table XVI, 60 (*Sparkassen*, etc.), and a monthly report of *Deutsche Bundesbank*. According to the monthly report, XII, no. 9, savings from 'mass incomes' in proportion to G.N.P. had risen at least twofold in the fifties. An important source of savings was surpluses of social service funds, especially those of unemployment insurance and old age pensions. By 1963 the total accumulated reserves of the social funds exceeded DM 27,000 million. These reserves financed 10 per cent of all bonds issued between 1960 and 1963 and made up a large proportion of loan funds at the disposal of commercial banks. In strict theory, however, these savings should be classified not as personal savings but as public savings since they were fed by compulsory contributions levied by the State.

These figures for the United Kingdom, France, and Germany, however different in detail, represent well the experience of Western Europe as a whole. In some Western countries, e.g. Switzerland, personal savings and prudential savings with them, were relatively lower and rose more slowly than elsewhere; in others, such as the Netherlands, they declined somewhat in 1961. Whatever the local differences, prudential savings everywhere accounted for the lion's share of personal savings, and the share rose much faster than personal savings as a whole.[1]

The changes in the origin and composition of personal savings were thus unmistakable. Did they, it may be asked, have any profound effects on the economy, its character, and its progress? Best known but perhaps also least fundamental were their direct effects, i.e. those reflected in the supply and distribution of investable funds. As prudential savings were replacing the 'capitalist' ones, risk capital was bound to become scarcer. It is in the nature of prudential savings, especially those mediatized by institutions, to seek investment in safe fixed-interest securities and to shun industrial equities. This phenomenon was probably as old as prudential savings themselves and, like these savings, antedated the post-war era by at least two generations. Between the wars it was well observed by German writers, who blamed on it the characteristic distortions of Germany's capital market – the super-abundance of funds for municipal and state projects and the dearth of risk-bearing industrial capital.

This mal-distribution must, however, have become more pronounced after 1945. On the morrow of the peace, and even in the years immediately following the currency reforms of 1948, the German economy found itself depleted of liquid funds, and firms were starved of new capital. The liquidity of firms greatly improved in the next decade, but the rising tide of prudential savings had little to do with this. In 1962 some 75 per cent of Insurance Funds were invested in government securities, mortgages, loans to public authorities, and miscellaneous obligations. Loans to industry

[1] For 'prudential' savings in countries other than the United Kingdom, France, and Germany, see the Annual Surveys of O.E.C.D. A noteworthy change apparently occurred after 1962 in Sweden where the flow of popular savings, hitherto very high, was channelled into the pension funds created under the new social insurance laws, O.E.C.D., *Survey of Sweden, 1961–2*, Paris, 1963.

(some DM 750 million) formed about 20 per cent of the total, but were mainly in the form of short-term credits. Some ingenious intermediaries were able to convert revolving credits from insurance companies into long-term loans, but the aggregate amounts thus converted were small and did not form a significant proportion of insurance funds. The investment of Sparkassen was even more exclusively devoted to bonds (mostly those of public authorities) and mortgages.[1]

Is it to be wondered that in these conditions German industry should have come to depend even more than before the war on its own retained profits and on loans from banks and other financial institutions? The performance of the economy and its ability to grow were not thereby seriously affected, but the financial tribulations of certain great firms in the early sixties (Borgward, the motor manufacturers, the Schlicker shipbuilding concern, and some of the Hugo Stinnes companies) helped to bring home the worst penalties of expanding without sufficient backing of risk capital.

In France personal savings were similarly oriented. The savings in the Caisses d'Epargne, where the bulk of French popular savings went, were invested mainly through the Caisses des Dépôts et Consignations into bonds. The investments of insurance companies were similarly directed into the bond and mortgage market.

By comparison with France and Germany, the swelling volume of prudential savings in the United Kingdom did not create a comparable dearth of risk capital. Insurance companies and pension funds, which drew a larger proportion of popular savings in the United Kingdom than abroad, were more willing and better able to invest into industrial stocks, including equities. The first large entry of insurance companies into the industrial field dates to the early inter-war years. Since then a variety of inducements, but mainly the desire to profit from capital appreciation and thereby to build a defence against inflation, led all insurance companies to put a large part of their funds into industrial stocks, including equities. By 1964 the assets of member offices of the British Insurance Association, representing the bulk of insurance companies operating in the United Kingdom, were held to the extent of 22·5

[1] Cf. *Wirtschaft und Statistik*, July 1963, pp. 431 *seq. Statistisches Jahrbuch*, 1962, Table B1, p. 418.

per cent in ordinary stocks, 21 per cent in industrial debentures, 19 per cent in government stocks, some 17·5 per cent in mortgages and some 10·5 per cent in real property. Ten years earlier, however, in 1954, only 14 per cent of insurance companies' assets had been held in ordinary shares and more than 30 per cent was held in government stocks.[1]

The investments of pension funds were distributed in somewhat similar fashion, except that the proportion of their holdings in ordinary shares had by 1964 risen higher than the corresponding proportion of insurance companies' holdings and approached 45 per cent. In later years, mainly in the early sixties, prudential holdings of industrial stock, mostly equities, were further swollen by popular investments through unit trusts.

The growing volume of institutional investment helped to change the structure of industrial and commercial ownership, and had for one of its corollaries the continued decline of the private or capitalist investor. In a sample of 184 United Kingdom firms, including all the 39 largest, recently studied by the Department of Applied Economics in Cambridge, private persons, their executors and trustees held 65·8 per cent of the quoted industrial shares in 1957. Their holding declined to 54 per cent by 1963, and probably to 50 per cent by 1966. On the other hand, the proportion of institutional holdings rose from 20·6 per cent in 1957 to 30·2 per cent in 1963, and possibly to 34 per cent in 1966. The rest – about 13·6 per cent in 1957 and 15·8 per cent in 1963 – was accounted for by foreigners and unspecified shareholders, and both categories probably contained a large proportion of institutional investors, more especially, non-financial companies with headquarters abroad.[2]

---

[1] Comprehensive evidence of institutional investments has been available only since 1962, when it began to be collected and published in accordance with the recommendations of the Radcliffe Committee of 1959. For an analysis, cf. J. G. Blease in *District Bank Review*, 1965. According to Mr Blease's computations total assets of insurance companies at the end of 1963 stood at just under £8,400 million, of which just under 21 per cent were held in equities and about the same proportion in industrial debentures. Ten years earlier investment in government stock represented 30·6 per cent of their assets, while ordinary stock only 14·1 per cent: *The Times, Financial and Commercial Review*, 4 October 1965.

[2] Jack Revell and John Moyle, *The Owners of Quoted Ordinary Shares: A Survey for 1963*, London, 1966: the novelty and chief interest of this study is that it attempts to go behind the nominee and trustee shareholders to the true or 'beneficial' ownership of shares. The results of a survey of an earlier date (1957)

In this, however, the United Kingdom, was somewhat exceptional. In most other countries, including Austria, Norway, and Sweden, insurance companies and savings institutions largely confined themselves to government stocks and bonds even where they were not required by law to do so. So in general it would be right to conclude that, taking Western Europe as a whole, the high and rising flow of prudential savings was bound to keep down the movement of funds into risk stocks.[1]

If, in spite of this reduction and of the complaints it generated, industrial development did not appear to suffer, but on the contrary proceeded at the double, the presumption is that for all the tribulations of some over-expanded firms, and for all the potential dangers of a topsy-turvy capital structure, industry and trade as a whole were not seriously held back by a shortage of capital. The shortage did not become serious because companies learned to do without much 'risk' capital. Whether by preference or by necessity they relied very little on public issues of stock and least of all on issues of ordinary shares. They raised most of their capital in a variety of ways – by relying more than ever before on bonds as in France; by drawing heavily on bank loans *modo Germanico*; by borrowing from insurance companies for a term of years as in the British real-estate business; or by invoking State aid, as in all the enterprises in nearly every European country in which risks appeared specially great and national interest could be claimed. But most enterprises depended to a large and increasing extent on their own savings; and 'most' in this case includes the great industrial and

---

were published by C. H. Feinstein and Jack Revell in *The Times* of June 23, 1960.

[1] In all continental countries ordinary stock formed a much smaller proportion of outstanding securities and of the current flow of investment. In Germany the total nominal value of commercial and industrial securities (*Festverzinsliche Wertpapieren und Aktien*) issued between 1941 and 1951 stood at about DM 30,000 million, of which little more than DM 6,500 million was in ordinary stock. The corresponding figures for 1961 were *c.* DM 12,000 million and *c.* DM 3,650 million: *Statistisches Jahrbuch*, 1962, Table XVI, 9*a*. The low proportion of securities representing risk capital have always been blamed on the imperfections of the German capital market. But as a whole they represented the traditional preference of German private investors and institutions for fixed-interest securities and more especially for municipal and government stock. For the similar position in France, see footnote 1, p. 243 below. In the Netherlands the preference of institutional investors for fixed-interest stock was largely due to fiscal causes: B. R. Williams, as in footnote 3, p. 121 above.

commercial companies in the van of economic growth and technological progress.

The immense increase in company savings was the other salient feature of capital formation in the post-war world. How great they were, and how vital was the part they played can be gleaned from our Table 22. In almost every country they provided the finance for some of the most spectacular post-war increases in the productive capacity of great industries and enterprises. In the United Kingdom the near-doubling of the productive capacity of the iron-and-steel industry was financed by the accumulated reserves of steel companies to the approximate extent of about 45 per cent; and of the remainder a large proportion was raised from the banks or the Finance Corporation for Industry in the hope that the loans would eventually be repaid out of profits. To an even greater extent accumulated reserves were called upon to pay for the vastly increased capacity and turnover in the petroleum, man-made fibre, chemical, cement, chocolate and glass industries.[1]

In post-war France, more than in the United Kingdom, the main access to the nation's savings no longer, as before 1914, lay through the Bourse. Except where and when new capital was procured from the Government agencies or met by the issue of bonds it was as a rule financed by drawing on firms' own resources. Corporation savings formed about 4·9 per cent of G.N.P. in the mid-fifties compared with 2·5-3·3 per cent in the inter-war period, and showed a tendency to rise in years of high profits between 1958 and 1961. It has been estimated that in all French enterprises, whether

[1] Between 1953 and 1963 internal savings of companies operating in the United Kingdom (gross trading profits *plus* all non-trading income less taxes and dividends) fluctuated round 60 per cent of their total gross income, *Central Statistical Office: National Income and Expenditure*, 1964, Table 28. Of the £683 million which the British steel industry invested into new fixed equipment between 1961 and 1965, £316 million or 46·4 per cent came from internal resources: *The Steel Industry*, Report of the Development Co-ordinating Committee of the British Iron and Steel Federation, 1966, pp. 136–7, and Appendix 18. The corresponding contribution of depreciation and retained profits to the investment of Cadbury Brothers was 77 per cent: *Industrial Challenge: the Experience of Cadbury's of Bournville*, Birmingham, 1964, p. 77.

corporate or not, retained profits in 1959 (their highest point) may have exceeded 80 per cent of total profits.[1] In Germany company reserves may not have counted for much in the capital hungry years immediately following the end of the war. But they rapidly soared to about one-quarter of total savings after the currency reform of 1948 and kept pace with total savings thereafter. They apparently stood at DM 1,470 million in 1950, rose to DM 5,910 million by 1960, continued to rise till 1962, and slumped somewhat in the subsequent two or three years, partly as a result of a change in the fiscal policy of the State and partly through a fall in company profits in 1963 and 1964. By that time, however, most of the well-established companies – some few notorious exceptions apart – found themselves largely independent of outside sources of finance, perhaps even more so than before the war. According to a recent estimate corporate savings paid for as much as 90 per cent of new fixed capital of companies in the fifties.[2]

Corporate savings played a part equally important in other countries. Even in Sweden, the Netherlands and Switzerland, countries with well-ordered financial markets and with well-established firms deserving the full confidence of the investing public, self-financing was the prevailing method of providing industry with additional capital, and the prevalence if anything grew during the period. In Sweden, after 1963, aggregate savings of large firms nearly equalled their gross investment.

In British trade and industry as a whole undistributed profits

---

[1] In the fifties 'external' finance, i.e. shares, bonds, long-term bank loans, and (especially in France) government loans, formed 60 per cent of total corporate investment in France, 59 per cent in Germany, 49·1 per cent in the United Kingdom. The rest came from internal resources: UNO, *World Economic Survey*, 1960, p. 52. 'Internal' financing played an even greater part in the investments of private, i.e. non-corporate, firms. In France self-financing of all enterprises, whether corporate or not, was estimated at 83 per cent of the total investment in 1959 (its highest point), but apparently descended to 60 per cent by 1964 in consequence of falling profits, O.E.C.D., *Surveys for France*, esp. that for 1961.

[2] K. V. Roskamp (as in footnote 2, p. 126 above), p. 120. In the fifties, corporate savings in most countries, though rising in absolute volume, remained stable in relation to G.N.P. This relation became less stable in the sixties, partly as a result of changes in taxation in Germany and industrial recession in France and Italy; cf. UNO, *World Economic Survey*, 1960, pp. 38–9.

[*Vide* Appendix Note 15, p. 367 below.]

grew uninterruptedly for at least half a century. An official inquiry in the inter-war years (the Colwyn Committee of 1927) estimated that whereas in 1912 the allocations to reserves may have been as low as 33 per cent of total profits, they rose to 47 per cent in 1922. The rise continued beyond that date. According to the computations of the Institute for Economic and Social Research, undistributed profits formed 44 per cent of total profits in 1948 and fluctuated between 67 and 70 per cent between that date and 1956. The average for the whole post-war period was probably in the neighbourhood of 60 per cent.[1]

Self-financing was not, of course, a new phenomenon. There was hardly a time in European history when business undertakings did not supply their requirements of capital by ploughing back profits. It is even probable that before the modern capital market emerged in the late eighteenth and early nineteenth centuries, the bulk of industrial and commercial capital was thus formed. In the commercial revolution of the sixteenth and seventeenth centuries and in the industrial revolutions of the eighteenth and nineteenth centuries most of the leading enterprises financed their growth largely out of their own savings.

What is new in the self-financing of more recent times is the overwhelming part played in it by the savings of corporations or joint-stock companies. It is not that the savings of privately owned businesses ceased to be of any importance. As I have already indicated most family firms continued to depend on their own savings for their additional capital. But as we have seen, from the end of the nineteenth century onwards, an ever larger proportion of savings came from retained profits of companies, and ever larger proportions of these profits were ploughed back.

Corporation savings grew not only because corporate ownership became more widespread but also because large and progressive firms – and corporations were very often larger and, in general, more progressive than the family firms they supplanted – were apt

---

[1] *The Report of the Committee on National Debt and Taxation, 1937* (H.M.S.O., Cmd. 2800), Par. 48; P. Sargant Florence, *The Ownership, Control and Success of Large Companies*, London, 1961, pp. 52 *seq.* W.I.E.S. *Company Income and Finance, 1949–53*, London, 1956. B. Tew and R. F. Henderson. *Studies in Company Finance'*, Cambridge, 1959; S. J. Prais 'The Financial Experience of Giant Companies', *Economic Journal*, June 1957.

to provide for replacements, for expansion and for innovation more liberally than small or private or conservative firms. It is very largely for these reasons that in the United Kingdom a larger proportion of profits was retained in some industries than in others. According to Sargant Florence in 1951 about 42 per cent of company profits was retained in distributive trades and in brewing, but more than 58 per cent in engineering.[1]

This growing propensity of companies, and especially of the large and progressive ones, for financial self-sufficiency may at first sight appear surprising. If small, and above all private, firms carried their self-financing practices over into the post-war world, this can be put down to the idiosyncrasies of family ownership. But it certainly is not in the nature of joint-stock ownership to go in fear of outside capital. The official philosophy, the economic *raison d'être* and the historical origins of joint-stock companies should have made them more, not less, inclined to seek their capital from shareholders. Were not the early joint-stock companies called into existence in the sixteenth and seventeenth centuries in order to enlist outside funds for enterprises too large for single individuals? And was not limited liability advocated and finally accepted in law during the second half of the nineteenth century in the belief that limited responsibility of shareholders for company debts would make it easier to attract outside investors? Yet since the closing years of the nineteenth century limited liability companies while spreading their tentacles over European economies, also did their best to finance their expansion out of their own undistributed profits; and apparently did so to an increasing extent in the inter-war and post-war periods.

The reasons for this vast amount of self-financing were many and various. One reason was that very often, especially in countries like Germany and Italy, the true alternative to self-financing was not public issues of shares, but loans from banks or financial groups; such loans could threaten the entrenched positions of directors or of established shareholders. Some companies found it convenient to finance their additional capital out of their reserves merely because they were thereby spared the necessity of disclosing their costs, their profits, or their future prospects. In these respects,

[1] P. Sargant Florence, *op. cit.*, Ch. VI.

they were not unlike family firms. They were also like family firms in that they acted on the assumption that they could judge their needs and their possibilities better than the market. The boards of certain firms in the United Kingdom and the Netherlands were sometimes criticized for retaining in their own businesses capital capable of earning higher return if lent out. To this they might have replied that investment, like charity, began at home, for the simple reason that profitable openings like compassionate needs were best appreciated at close quarters.[1]

In general, however, most companies ploughed back their savings merely because savings happened to be available. Firms with large liquid resources financed themselves more readily than firms in less liquid condition; and in the history of individual countries the periods when liquidity of firms was higher than usual were also the periods when their self-financing was greater than average. The liquidity of companies, i.e. their accumulations of uninvested funds, depended partly on government taxation and partly on the proportions in which companies chose to allocate their profits between reserves and shareholders; but the most important influence was obviously the level of profits themselves. Before 1963 business prospered more then ever, its turnover grew almost uninterruptedly, and its profit margins were wide. Business prospering in this manner brought high profits, high profits swelled the reserves, and swollen reserves meant an increased capacity for self-financing. No wonder corporation savings played a powerful part in capital formation, and with it, in the economic development of post-war Europe.

A part so powerful must have impressed itself on the post-war scene as a whole. The impression was not, however, at its deepest on the side of European economy most directly exposed to it, i.e. the allocation of capital among its possible users. Devotees of the untrammelled price-mechanism are apt to represent corporation

[1] A different and more sweeping statement of the creed will be found in the definition of the 'American business system' by an American company – the Standard Steel Corporation – as 'a system which permits management to assure progress for itself, its employees and its stockholders by ploughing back earnings into the business'. Quoted in Francis X. Sutton, Seymour E. Harris, Carl Kaysen, and James Tobin, *The American Business Creed*, Cambridge (Mass.), 1956, pp. 85 *seq.*

savings and self-financing of companies as yet another distortion of the economy. Self-financing is often said to have aggravated the maldistribution of capital by reserving an unduly large slice of a nation's savings to the well-established firms fortunate enough to have made large profits in the recent past, and denying it to the new and pioneering enterprises whose profitability still lay in the future. This maldistribution may have been as real as the critics believe; our evidence will not permit anything in the nature of an assessment. But the maldistribution, like that caused by mediatized prudential savings, could not have been so debilitating as to hold back economic growth. The European economy grew while and although corporation savings and self-financing were rampant. In winding up my discussion of rising prudential savings I suggested that their main effects were probably not the direct ones, i.e. not those felt within the capital market itself. I must repeat the same suggestion in winding up the subject of corporation savings. Their main effect must be sought not solely in the provenance and allocation of new capital, but also in the deeper and wider ranges of economic experience, in the working of the economic system as a whole, and more particularly in the ownership and control of industry and trade. To these more general and indirect effects we must now pass.

Shifts in the sources of capital could affect the structure of the European economy in many different ways, but their most important effect was to disassociate the control of enterprises from the ownership of their assets. The classical conception of nineteenth-century business combined in the same image of the business entrepreneur the person who directed the business and the person who owned it. An indissoluble link between the ownership of 'means of production' and the power to manage them is also at the root of the Marxian concept of capitalism. These theoretical constructions, though much idealized, had an obvious historical justification, since in the large majority of nineteenth-century businesses their 'bosses' were at once their owners and their top managers.

The only type of nineteenth-century enterprise where ownership and control was not always in the same hands was partnerships, and more particularly sleeping partnerships in which some partners did not participate in the daily conduct of affairs. In the last thirty or forty years of the nineteenth century the arrival of the joint-stock company with limited liability – in itself an extended form of sleeping partnership – carried this disassociation a step farther; the subsequent developments of company organization – above all, the use of various kinds of non-voting and non-participating stocks – carried it further still. In the late nineteenth and the early twentieth centuries, as company ownership spread from firm to firm and from industry to industry, an ever larger number of enterprises came to be effectively controlled by people who did not own a significant part of their capital.

Needless to say, the process had not yet gone all the way by 1964. It had not gone far enough to remove single owners, or family combinations, or small groups of shareholders from owning large proportions of some firms' share capital and from using that ownership to control the firms' affairs. In the United Kingdom, the voting capital of the second and third largest retail businesses in the country (Marks and Spencer and Great Universal Stores), one of the largest catering firms (J. Lyons and Co.), the largest chocolate firm (the British Cocoa and Chocolate Corporation), one of the largest pharmaceutical company (Boots Pure Drug Company), the largest or second largest glass firm (Pilkingtons), and most of the great brewing firms were privately controlled. Some of them were, to use a recently coined term, 'close' firms. They were controlled by single persons or families or groups of closely bound associates who owned the whole or the most of the capital.[1]

---

[1] In addition to evidence from authorities cited in subsequent footnotes the evidence in this and the following six paragraphs comes from a great variety of miscellaneous sources: from financial and general periodicals; but also from compendia of companies and company ownership, such as *Kompass Comprehensive Register of Industry and Trade*, vol. 3, London, 1964; O. Roskill (ed.), *Who Owns Whom*, O. W. Roskill & Co. (Reports), 9th edn., London, 1966; *Wer Gehört zu Wem*, 1959; *Leitende Männer der Wirtschaft*. Darmstadt, 1961. The ranking of firms by size is derived from the annual Stock Exchange Lists of the 100 largest companies; 'The 200 Largest Foreign Industrial Companies' in *Fortune*, August 1964; *300 Leading Companies in Britain and Europe*, published by *The Times*; from annual lists in the *Enterprise* journal; and from interviews with individuals. Some of the information comes from semi-popular works like those of Eugenio Sclafari (as in footnote 1, p. 204 above) or M. Drancourt, *Les Clés du Pouvoir*, Paris, 1964.

In France, Michelin, the largest firm of tyre manufacturers, was family-owned and itself owned some 55 per cent of the capital of Citroën, the second largest car firm. Peugeot, the third largest car firm, was also privately owned. About 62 per cent of the capital of the second largest steel firm, De Wendels, was in the hands of the Petits-Fils de François de Wendel. And all these are merely the best-known examples of French firms privately owned or controlled. How many of the 'top 500' French firms were similarly owned is difficult to say with any assurance; but though not in the majority, they were certainly quite numerous in the early sixties.

Their numbers may have been even larger in Germany. The rising wave of German growth since 1948 swept to great heights a number of wholly new enterprises. Numerous large firms had sprung from humble beginnings since the war, and a larger proportion of German industrial and commercial enterprises operating in the sixties was still in the hands of their founders than in the United Kingdom or France. The same is apparently true of Italy, where the rise of the Zanussi electrical enterprise from a small workshop in Pordenone, or the spectacular growth of the privately owned Olivetti concern, fully matched the post-war career of such German firms as Grundig or the numerous British firms in the building and real-estate business reared in the building-and-land boom of the late fifties.

New and surviving family enterprises and 'close' firms of every kind were not, of course, the only vehicles whereby owners of capital could control great industrial and commercial enterprises. Holding companies, investment banks and credit institutions continued to serve as instruments of private ownership and private control in industry and trade. By their means persons and families of great fortune were able to combine their interests into veritable constellations of firms.[1]

The best examples of such interests in the United Kingdom were

---

[1] This is what G. C. Allen presumably has in mind in drawing our attention to the surviving powers of large shareholders in numerous companies, *The Structure of Industry in Britain*, p. 181. He cites P. Sargant Florence, 'A New Inquiry Into Ordinary Share Ownership', *The Times*, 12 August 1959. Prof. Sargant Florence marshals his evidence more fully in his well-known study *The Ownership, Control and Success of Large Companies*, London, 1961.

those of the Pearson family which included a great merchant bank, a large insurance company, a combine of famous ceramic firms and other businesses; or the Ellerman fortune behind a great shipping combine and other less easily identifiable enterprises; or the more recently assembled Clore possessions with powerful interests in real estate, retail trade, a boot-and-shoe empire, and shipping. The observers of post-war Germany will include in the same category not only the restored fortunes of the Krupp and Thyssen families and of one of the splinters of the Stinnes family, but also the Friedrich Flick interests in car manufacturing, engineering, and other enterprises, the Klockner interests in steel and engineering, the Gerling interests in various industrial and banking properties, the Springer interests in publicity, the Heckermann hold over retail business, Steigenberger's over hotels, or the miscellaneous industrial and financial concerns of men like Herr Goergen and Herr Hermann Krager of Bremen. The old fortunes and some new ones in Italian industry and commerce are equally familiar. There were the Agnelli family with interests not only in Fiat but also in a number of other enterprises, the miscellaneous interests of the Pirelli family, the holdings of the Pesenti family in cement enterprises, insurance, and other business, the Falck interests in steel and allied industries, the Trepcovich holdings in banking and shipping, or the Bastogi interests in the chemical industry.[1]

The proper verdict on company ownership must therefore remain that passed in a recent study of company structure and ownership in the U.S.A. and the United Kingdom. Authority in companies was mixed. 'Some companies have been manager-led, others large-investor-led and in yet others there is a compromise.' But what, from our point of view, is most important is that the mixture was highly unstable. Its ingredient of manager-led firms, already very large before the war, grew all through this period and had by the 1960s come to represent a clear majority of larger companies.

In no European country did the majority become as over-whelming as it had come to be in the U.S.A. by 1963. In 1929 when Berle and Means for the first time separated owner-controlled companies from manager-controlled ones, their figures showed that

[1] E. Sclafari (as in footnote 1, p. 204 above) *passim*, *The Economist*, 21 November 1964; D. Granik, *The European Executive*, as in footnote 1, p. 266 below.

among the 200 largest corporations some 120 were owner-controlled (i.e. were in wholly private ownership, or had majority or substantial minority of shares in relatively few hands, or were privately controlled by means of a legal device), while some 88 or 44 per cent had no recognizable private owner or group of owners and were, in the Berle and Means sense of the term, 'ultimately' controlled by their executives. A very recent inquiry, however, has revealed that by 1963 not a single non-financial corporation among the largest 200 was any longer in wholly private possession, that no more than 31 were in the various categories of owner-controlled firms, and that 169 or 84·5 per cent were wholly manager-controlled.[1]

In Europe the change-over to management-control was not as dramatic as in the U.S.A.; it was nevertheless very marked. Its course is not equally easy to follow in all European countries. In most of them the main evidence, that of share ownership, cannot be – or at least has not yet been – statistically measured; and a student is thrown back upon indirect signs of ownership and authority in companies. In one country, however, the United Kingdom, the evidence of share ownership is available to students and has lent itself to systematic, even statistical, investigations. These investigations, especially the latest and the fullest of them, that of P. Sargant Florence, leaves no doubt about the great extent and continued spread of managerial control and the corresponding decline in the number of owner-controlled firms before 1952. What is known about the history of individual large firms after that date strongly suggests that the process continued throughout the fifties and the early sixties.

Sargant Florence's test of owner-control is concentration of voting shares to the extent of 20 per cent of total voting stock in the hands of a single shareholder or 30 per cent in the hands of the 20 largest stockholders. Judged by these tests owner-control, already much reduced by 1936, greatly declined between 1936 and 1951.

[1] Adolf Berle and Gardiner Means, *The Modern Corporation and Private Property*, New York, 1932; R. J. Larner, 'The 200 Largest Non-financial Corporations', *The American Economic Review*, CVI, No. 4, Pt. 1, September, 1956. What makes Larner's estimates all the more convincing is that he includes into the category of 'minority-owned' companies those in which individuals or related groups own as little as 10 per cent of the voting capital, compared with Sargant Florence's 20 per cent for individuals and 30 per cent for the twenty largest shareholders.

R

In 1936 single individuals and institutions owned 20 per cent and more of the voting shares in 18 companies Sargant Florence classified as very large (those with issued capital of £3 million and more); but in only 10 of these companies was voting capital thus owned in 1951. Of the 24 very large companies in 1951 which had already functioned in 1936, only 17 answered Florence's test of concentrated personal ownership. As far as we can judge from the subsequent history their numbers were further reduced to twelve or thirteen between 1951 and 1964. An assessment by Florence's broader standard – the ownership of at least 30 per cent of voting stock by the 20 largest stockholders – reveals the same trend. Out of 92 very large companies some 50 were so owned in 1936, but only 35 in 1951. This test is difficult to apply to the ascertainable aspects of company history after 1951. But as far as it is possible to gather, five companies, which figured among Florence's 35 in 1951, may have passed out of that category by 1964. The same evidence suggests that among the somewhat smaller companies – Florence's medium-large – the same changes were under way and that the number of such companies with concentrated ownership was getting smaller, and was probably in the minority by 1964. It was only among companies smaller still that control by owner was still characteristic of the majority of enterprises.[1]

In Germany the structure of company ownership differed from that in the United Kingdom, but, as in the United Kingdom, the proportion of the capital of large corporations in the hands of persons recognizable as their 'owners' was relatively small. If we are to trust the obviously imperfect published information concerning

[1] P. Sargant Florence, *op. cit.*, pp. 71–2. The firms in Florence's sample which may have passed out of his category of owner-controlled firms after 1951, may include the Associated Electrical Industries, the Bristol Aeroplane Company, the Winterbottom Book Cloth Company and possibly also J. and J. Colman Ltd. and Bovril. Several other firms (possibly as many as eight) had in the meantime grown to qualify for inclusion among the 'largest' companies, but the relative numbers of owner-controlled firms among them was, if anything, smaller than in Florence's older sample. Florence also classifies as owner-controlled some six British companies wholly or mainly owned by other, mostly foreign, companies, such as British Match Corporation, British United Shoe Machinery, Consolidated Tin Smelters, F. W. Woolworth, Ford, and possibly also Rootes Motors. Most of these foreign institutional owners were themselves manager-controlled; so had Sargant Florence accepted the Berle and Means definition of 'ultimate' managerial control, he would have reduced his list of owner-controlled firms by at least another five.

the ownership of capital, it would appear that in 1962 out of DM 30,500 millions of equity capital of 2,533 large companies, some DM 7,000 millions were owned by other companies, some DM 4,350 by public bodies, governments and municipalities, about DM 4,000 millions by foreigners, some DM 11,000 millions by unidentifiable 'private' shareholders and only DM 4,000 to 5,000 millions by 'controlling' owners or their families. These figures are, of course, bound to be ambiguous. Large private owners sometimes lurked behind cross-company ownership and behind seemingly dispersed and anonymous shareholding. But even if we were to add to our estimate of 'controlling' holdings, those of all the undeclared share-owners and a proportion – say, 25 per cent – of capital owned by other companies, the holdings representing the anonymous and dispersed ownership by the public would at a rough estimate still represent much more than one-half of the total. Similar information for some 22 companies available with assets of over $500 million – suggests that at the end of 1962 the greater part of the 18,000 to 20,000 million dollars-worth of their combined assets was represented by their own accumulated reserves, or else was owned by the 'public' or by financial institutions in quantities not large enough to confer upon any single owner the controlling powers (as distinct from some influence) in an enterprise.[1]

Lack of evidence would make it still more difficult to form exact estimates for other continental countries, even though on the whole in most of them the proportion of company capital held anonymously by the general public was probably somewhat smaller than in the United Kingdom. In France, where family ownership was more widespread, the proportion of industrial capital in the hands of the general public may have remained fairly small, even smaller than before the war. Yet as far as it is possible to judge, at least thirty out of the 'top 50' industrial firms listed in the recent survey by the journal *Entreprise* possessed no identifiable single owner or groups of closely linked owners, unless it was the State itself.

In Italy we have seen that the State, State-owned companies, above all I.R.I., and the State-controlled financial institutions had a stake in a very large number of enterprises. In estimating the proportion of Italian enterprises and of industrial and commercial

[1] *Statistisches Jahrbuch*, 1962, Tables Xb and XVI 10a.

capital not owned and controlled by private capitalist proprietors we must also take account of the immense industrial and commercial holdings of the Vatican. The Holy See's portfolio of quoted securities all over the world in 1962 has been estimated at the equivalent of over £2,000 million, of which about one-tenth, i.e., £200 million, or about one-fifteenth of the total stock of shares quoted on the Italian stock exchange, were held in Italy itself. In addition the Vatican bank, l'Istituto per le Opere di Religione, like other Italian banks, had acquired a large indirect interest, through loans and advances, in a number of business enterprises. It is not therefore surprising that in spite of the conspicuous case of several great firms owned and controlled by millionaire families (they have been cited elsewhere in this chapter) the greater part of the capital of most larger enterprises should have become public, i.e., not owned by single private owners or by small bodies of shareholders in packets large enough to confer on them predominant influence on the conduct of affairs.[1]

The reasons why ownership of enterprises was becoming increasingly anonymous and control of enterprises increasingly detached from the ownership of their capital are well understood. In the middle ranks of industry and trade, family enterprises suffered continuous attrition. In countries like the United Kingdom death duties frequently compelled executors of deceased owners to dispose of their holdings in businesses they previously owned. Owners of enterprises were also exposed to a combination of pressures and temptations characteristic of post-war business. Some smaller firms were unable to 'keep their end up' in the more competitive and unstable climate of the age. On the other hand, in the buoyant conditions of the fifties and the early sixties some firms did so well that their owners were tempted to make easy capital gains by selling their enterprises to the investing public for a price representing the capitalized value of their high profits. But the most important reason why smaller family concerns were receding from the scene was the higher credit ranking or the more abundant capital of large-scale business. I have already mentioned the tendency towards an increasing scale of enterprises and, in doing so, suggested that post-war

---

[1] Eugenio Sclafari, *Rapporto sul Neocapitalisino, passim*; 'The Vatican's Riches', *The Economist*, 27 March 1965.

increases in the scale of enterprises were frequently – perhaps more frequently than in the inter-war period – produced by mergers, i.e. as a result of larger firms acquiring and digesting smaller ones. Growing firms were also more aggressively conducted; and the propensity to 'takeovers' was one of the hallmarks of aggressive management in the post-war world.

The tendency to 'sell out' was not, however, confined to family firms of lowly or middling rank. Now and again large companies whose capital still happened to be in the hands of single individuals gradually admitted the investing public to the ownership of their shares. Here also, death duties was one of the underlying causes; the need of finance for expansion was another. During the twelve or fifteen years before 1963, a number of large companies, still privately held, were compelled to float public issues or to admit outsiders to the ownership of the existing equity, and thereby to dilute the hold of the majority shareholders over the company capital. In the United Kingdom a recent example of such dilution – very slight to begin with – was provided by the British Cocoa and Chocolate Corporation, the Cadbury family concern. In Germany a more striking example will be found in the series of transactions whereby the holding companies representing the disjointed elements of the Thyssen family fortune reassembled the various Thyssen enterprises and, in doing so, reduced the family holdings in the principal Thyssen concern – the August Thyssen Hütten A.G. – to well below one-half. Even Krupp, after more than a century of exclusive family ownership which overcame the attempt of the occupying powers to dissolve it, took steps in 1964 to invite outside capital to its iron and coal enterprises. Other less striking instances of large family-owned corporations going public could be found in all European countries in the fifties and early sixties.

The processes whereby some companies were ceasing to be owned by men who had founded them, or by their successors and heirs, or by small groups of closely linked shareholders, like the continued concentration of ownership in other companies, does not faithfully represent the actual shifts in the location and distribution of effective rule in firms. It indicates the potentialities of owner-rule or management-rule, not their realities. It may be true that a person who happened to possess more than 20 per cent of a firm's voting shares had it in his power to determine its policy or even its day-to-day conduct. But whether he in fact did so depended on a host of other conditions. Concentrated ownership was compatible with considerable or even full managerial control, especially where the executive heads happened to be powerful men while the owners, through age or for other reasons, preferred the role of sleeping partners. The ageing owner of the Flick business in Germany might still have been in full command of its vast enterprises in 1963; the Pilkingtons and the Cadburys might still have owned the bulk of their firms' capital and wholly dominated their management. But the Agnelli family, commonly regarded as the owners of Fiat (they probably owned no more than 25 per cent of its voting capital), could not lay claim to the topmost formal authority in the firm, to say nothing of its day-to-day management, as long as Professor Valetta was at the head of the enterprise. Even in the Krupp combine, whose capital was, until 1963, wholly in the hands of the family, the reigning Krupp apparently shared effective control with its 'hired' head, Herr Beitz. And in firms ostensibly owned and managed by members of the same family groups, the managerial leaders could sometimes behave as professionals independent of their uncles and cousins who owned the shares.[1]

The distinction between opportunities for control and its actual exercise is of especial relevance to companies classified as 'potentially' owner-controlled, by Florence's main criterion: a large block of voting shares – 30 per cent or more – of capital in the hands of a relatively small number, say twenty, of the largest shareholders. Acting as a concerted group such shareholders could dominate the company if they wished, but they did not always wish to do so and were not always sufficiently united in interests or point of view to act as a concerted group. Some such lack of unity between the owners may account for the highly independent policy of the executive heads of Montecatini and Edison which led to the 1965 decision to amalgamate the two firms. Certain crucial decisions in the affairs of two great British firms in 1965 – the Wallpaper Manu-

---

[1] While this book was in galley proof, the Krupp family, acting under the pressure of their creditors (mostly the banks), decided to 'go public', i.e. to part with the exclusive family ownership of the Company's capital and its directorial board (*Aufsichtsrath*). A similar change was announced by Solvay et Cie, the great Belgian chemical firm.

facturers and the British Printing Corporation – showed how difficult it was, in spite of concentrated ownership, to get the owners to act as a concerted group.

On the other hand, it was also possible for a family firm to perpetuate family rule or family connexion long after the family itself had ceased to own a controlling block of the shares. In the United Kingdom the rule of the Nelsons, father and son, in the English Electric Co., of the Clarks, father and sons, in Plesseys, and possibly that of Sir Eric Bowater in Bowater Paper Co., owed much more to the personal qualities of the men, or to some of the other advantages they enjoyed, than to their ownership of voting stock.[1]

Unfortunately, the true relations of power in most firms lie concealed from the gaze of a mere historian who is compelled to go by other, and more superficial, signs. Of these signs the one we have followed here, that of share ownership, is perhaps the most relevant and reliable. And judged by it the overall change in the ownership of enterprises was unmistakable.

However, in the eyes of some students the significance or the novelty of this pattern of ownership was greatly reduced by the increasing hold of 'financial' powers over enterprises. It is possible to argue that the mantle of private owners frequently descended on institutions of every kind. We have seen that in most continental countries banks exercised a very great influence in the affairs of corporate companies. Their influence was, moreover, far greater than their direct holdings of company shares would measure. In Germany representatives of banks filled a quarter of the 3,014 seats on the boards of 577 public companies recently surveyed; yet their direct industrial holdings may have been very small. In 1960 the investment of German banks into company shares formed only 1·25 per cent of their total assets and represented no more than 8 per cent of the companies' capital, and even this proportion included shares which banks held in their function of stockbrokers. Direct holdings of equity, however, were not the sole source of the banks' authority over firms. They had in their hands large blocks of shares deposited with them as collateral security for loans; and these, being bearer shares, conferred on them most of the powers of ownership, including those of voting. Above all, they provided a great deal

[1] *Vide* Appendix Note 17, p. 369 below.

of fixed capital for industry and commerce by buying fixed-interest bonds and above all by means of advances and revolving loans. The outstanding total of long-term loans by banks approached, by the end of 1962, DM 9,000 million. A large proportion of the loans, perhaps as much as one-half, may have gone into government and municipal loans and into advances to individuals; but even then immense financial involvements with industry and commensurate influence over it were bound to result. A more recent development, mostly post-1957, sponsored by the great banks, were investment trusts which by the end of 1963 had come to hold some 8 per cent of German shares in circulation.[1]

So great was, in fact, the authority which German and most other continental banks were often able to exercise over firms that at first sight it may appear to have restored in a new guise the old links between ownership and control. A similar authority could also be acquired by banks and institutions in other countries. Contrary to their pre-war policies British clearing banks (the 'Big Five') tied up vast funds in several industries, mainly in iron and steel, and were therefore compelled to keep a watchful eye over the affairs of debtor firms. As a result of their industrial and commercial investment British insurance companies, investment trusts and pension funds sometimes found themselves possessing blocks of shares in individual companies sufficient to entitle them to seats on the boards of directors and to a voice in major decisions on policy.[2] In most European industries, but especially in the heavy industries and in the chemical industry of France and Germany, cross-ownership of capital by companies could confer on the directors of some firms full powers of both ownership and control over other firms. In such cases directors of insurance companies, banks or just large holding companies might appear to reincarnate the conventional type of the capitalist owner-entrepreneurs.

---

[1] The European country where banks were by law precluded from holding shares of companies was Sweden; and their role in providing industry with fixed capital was, accordingly smaller than in Germany or even the United Kingdom. They nevertheless played some part in providing industrial finance, especially Stockholm's Enskilda Bank and the Svensk Handelsbanken: *The Economist*, 26 December 1964.

[*Vide* Appendix Note 16, p. 368 below.]

[2] For the investments of institutions in the United Kingdom, see J. G. Blease, 'Institutional Investors on the Stock Exchange', *District Bank Review*, 1964.

For this and other reasons it is possible to argue that the growing holdings of capital by institutions should not be considered, as I have considered them here, as evidence of increasing dispersal and anonymity of company ownership or of further separation of ownership and control. This argument must not be pushed too far. However great the influence of institutional shareholders, it was bound to be far short of the powers of the owner-managers old-style. Most institutional investors held shares not in order to acquire or to secure their hold over enterprises but for investment purposes in the narrow sense of the term, as one of the methods of holding funds and as a source of profits. When we find that in the early fifties the Prudential Insurance Company held blocks of shares in at least 47 out of the 98 United Kingdom companies with more than £3 million of issued capital, and that the Pearl Insurance Company had shares in 33 such companies, we must take it for granted that these holdings did not involve the two insurance companies in the control of the enterprises. Such influence as they derived from their holdings they held in reserve, and was often very difficult to mobilize or to bring to bear on the conduct of directors.

This character of institutional holdings is underlined by their distribution. In the United Kingdom, in companies popular with institutional investors the number of such investors was as a rule quite large – too large to enable any of them individually to establish itself in a controlling position, even if in combination they often held more than the 30 per cent, which, had they combined (this they hardly ever did), could easily have delivered the rule of the firms in their hands. The same is true of typical bank holdings. Outside Germany, and perhaps Italy, banks very frequently held shares in their own names or in that of their depositors for the same purposes and in the same manner as the British institutional investors.[1]

The managerial – as contrasted with the proprietary – character of typical cross-company links is exhibited most clearly in Germany, the one country which throughout its recent history has provided historians with the most conspicuous examples of 'financial capital-

[1] P. Sargant Florence, as in footnote 1, p. 249 above. *Vide*, Appendix Note 17, p. 369, below. Oliver Mariott and Roy Mackie, 'Time for Institutions to Move In', *The Times*, 13 Feb. 1967.

ism'. It may be true that nearly one-third of the directorships in a representative sample of Germany's largest companies were filled by bankers, and that half of the places were held by the 'big three' German banks. But we have seen that the representation of banks on boards of directors was not based on ownership of shares, even counting voting proxies of which they disposed. It may also be true that as much as one-quarter of all the directorships in the sample were held by representatives of the eleven largest banks. But then all the larger banks had on their boards representatives of large industrial firms: and fifty such representatives could be identified on the boards of the better-known German banks. The Deutsche Bank may have been represented on the boards of several – fifteen to twenty – of the largest industrial firms, but many of these firms (between five and eight) had their representatives on the board of the Deutsche Bank. If so, what kind of an economic system do the ubiquitous bank directorships exemplify – 'finance-capitalism' wherein banks replaced the capitalist owner-manager, or the rule of an all-pervasive managerial élite occupying the commanding positions in banks and industrial firms alike?

What may at first sight also appear to run counter to the apparent tendency towards the separation of ownership and control is the ownership of shares by directors. In a number of firms in all countries directors, or at least some of them, held blocks of shares sufficient to give them control. In a number of companies the U.S.A. practice of remunerating executives by 'options', i.e. rights to acquire on favourable terms specified quantities of shares, appeared to open the way to gradual transfer of ownership into their hands.

No doubt share-owning directors blurred somewhat the neat distinction between owners and managers, but not to the extent of materially reducing it. To begin with, the relative number of large director-owned companies apparently declined. It formed 35 per cent of Sargant Florence's sample in 1936, but only 27 per cent in 1951, and may have formed a still smaller proportion in 1962. This decline, moreover, appeared to reflect the shrinking of the owner-management sector of the economy. Sargant Florence's investigation suggests that in the United Kingdom, companies in which directors held controlling blocks of shares were family-owned firms, and that in these firms directors were as a rule themselves members of the owning families. If so, director-owned companies were not a category different from, or additional to, that of owner-controlled companies. In the great majority of other companies directors' holdings were too small to confer control.[1]

As for 'options,' the practice in European countries was not as widespread as in the U.S.A. (it was rather rare in the United Kingdom and France) and even in the U.S.A. it hardly ever enabled directors to build up controlling holdings in their companies.

However, the ownership of capital by directors and the influence of banks and institutions were sufficiently widespread to create in the minds of some commentators a great deal of doubt about the nature of the changes resulting from the separation of ownership and control. The latter has so generally and so unquestioningly been accepted as an established historical fact and is so well-worn as a sociological thesis that some recent writers have shown signs of recoiling from it. The recoil is not wholly due to contempt born of familiarity, but may represent a natural reaction against popular simplifications. In text-books and journalistic writings the separation is often presented not as a trend but as a completed historical transformation. Innocent readers are sometimes given the impression that not only in U.S.A., but in Europe as well, all great companies, indeed all large-scale enterprises, were in the course of recent years wholly removed from the control of owners or the latters' families, and that private wealth no longer conferred on individuals the power of directing business enterprises. We have seen, however, that this was not the case, and that although in most great companies the ownership of capital had by the end of our period been dispersed among anonymous owners, and managerial powers were detached from the possession of shares, considerable areas of business still continued to be dominated by owner-managers of every kind. And I shall have another occasion for pointing out that the post-war extension of company ownership and increasing disassociation of ownership and control did not put an end to economic inequality or disestablish all positions of power based on inherited

[1] P. Sargant Florence, *op. cit.*, pp. 124–5. Florence lists thirteen large British companies in which directors owned in 1951 controlling amounts of capital. Of these at least ten were companies in which directors belonged to or represented owning families.

or acquired wealth. The reaction against the simplified version of the separation thesis is therefore understandable and even welcome.

Some of the reaction, however, has been carried over to the very notion of separation, its reality and importance. James Burnham, a publicist, whose writings are responsible for most of the popular notions of the separation of ownership from control, has presented the rise of the managerial class as a stage in a Marxist dialectic movement whereby classes succeed each other in positions of power based on the ownership of means of production. According to this version of the story, the managerial class had even before the war been acquiring the control over ('access to') the capital of companies and using this control to appropriate the products of industry. Mr Burnham's implied prophecy is that when this appropriation has been completed, both the ownership and the management of industry will have come into the hands of the new ruling class and 'the most powerful will also be the wealthiest'.[1]

This prophecy has been used by other writers to imply that the separation of ownership and control in our period was largely superficial and fictitious and that what was really happening was that a class of owner-controllers was recreating itself in the guise of a new élite composed of wealthy executive heads of companies and big shareholders with controlling voices in the affairs of companies. They were the people who were able to use their 'access to' the means of production to obtain 'preferential treatment' in the distribution of company profits, and thereby to consolidate wealth and power, *ergo*, ownership and control in their hands.

This thesis has an obvious relevance to the social changes of our period and will be brought up again in that connexion. Its relevance to the problem of industrial ownership and control is more questionable and owes such credence as it now commands to a certain ambiguity – accidental or contrived – of terms. What does the executives' 'access to' the means of production mean? Is it to be taken as equivalent to capitalist owners' power of disposal over the capital they own? And what is meant by 'preferential treatment' in the distribution of profits? Does it mean that during the last twenty-

---

[1] James Burnham, *The Managerial Revolution*, N.Y., 1941, esp. Ch. VIII; I. C. McGivering, D. G. J. Mathews, W. H. Scott, *Management in Britain*, Liverpool, 1960, Ch. I.

five or thirty years persons or institutions holding large blocks of shares received proportionately higher income on their shares than smaller shareholders, or that professional executives in manager-controlled enterprises were able to use their position for their personal profit in the same way and to the same extent as the owners of family enterprises and of 'close' firms? Or does it mean that the economic interests of executive directors determined the firms' price policies, their profit margins, and their allocations of profits?

Taken at their face value these implications are difficult to reconcile with historical facts, especially in so far as they concern the allocation of profits between dividends and reserves. In the United Kingdom and Germany – the two countries in which the distribution policies of firms' profits have been studied at all closely – the policies appeared to differ very greatly from firm to firm and from period to period. But Professor Sargant Florence and others have demonstrated that in the United Kingdom manager-controlled firms tended to distribute in dividends smaller pro-portions of profits than owner-controlled firms. It also appears that larger, more highly capitalized and progressive firms distributed smaller proportions of their profits than smaller, less capital-intensive and more conservative firms. For all these reasons the proportions were apt to differ from industry to industry and were high in the brewing and distributive trades, but low in engineering. But as I have already shown elsewhere, the proportions also changed over long periods, and in countries like Germany they also fluctuated over short ones. How can the executives' 'access to means of production' or their 'preferential treatment' in respect to dividends come into this complicated picture is something of a mystery.[1]

We must therefore conclude that the firms in which the separa-tion went far differed sufficiently from typical capitalist enterprises and were sufficiently numerous and important, to lend a new and different colour to the economic system as a whole. This colour may not have been lurid enough to influence the vision of some com-mentators, especially of those who happen to dislike 'capitalism' too ardently to want it to die a non-violent death. It is, however, signifi-cant to note that in his later years Marx himself foresaw the fun-damental transformation which the Joint Stock Company with its

---

[1] P. Sargant Florence, *op. cit.*, pp. 41–57.

anonymously owned capital and professional executive was destined to bring about in the very principle of the economic system. In passages in Vol. III of *Das Kapital* he drew attention to the significance of the transformation of the active capitalist 'into a mere director, an administrator of other men's capital' and of the owners of capital into 'mere money capitalists' divorced from directing functions. He went as far as to define company-owned enterprises as forms of enterprise in which 'capitalist production is abolished within the capitalist mode of production itself.'[1]

However, the profundity of the change and above all its social implications can and have been exaggerated. The mere fact that the manager-ruled corporation was so different from a typical capitalist enterprise did not by itself enable it to bring about a wholly new social order with class relations and a pattern of power wholly different from those of the nineteenth century. How much the economic system was in fact transformed and what the social implications of the transformation were cannot be decided without first considering the changes which had come over the two main human components of the industrial system – the managers and the managed.

[1] K. Marx, *Das Kapital* (German Edition of 1953), Berlin, 1953, III, pp. 477–80. It has not been sufficiently noticed how much the need to allow for corporate ownership stimulated the endeavours of latter-day Marxists to identify and to define the differences between 'late-capitalism' or 'monopoly capitalism' and the classical image of capitalist economy. For a recent and a far-reaching endeavour of this kind, see the opening chapters in Paul Baran and Paul M. Sweezy, *Monopoly Capitalism*, N.Y., 1966.

CHAPTER 11

The Managers

The rising importance of the men at the head of firms followed naturally from the growing anonymity of industrial ownership and its separation from managerial control. This importance has sometimes been represented as the triumph of the firm itself. That corporate firms to a large and growing extent financed themselves and that so many of them behaved as self-perpetuating entities may lend conviction to this picture of an economy made up of and dominated by the institution of the firm. But impersonal as corporate firms may appear to be, their powers were exercised by groups of men representing and conducting them. It would, therefore, be simpler, as well as more accurate, to speak not of independently functioning firms but of the growing power and authority of professional directors and managers at their head.

Their power and authority were also older than the post-war era. In the more advanced countries of the West, and more especially in the U.S.A., the numbers of professional managers of enterprises and the numbers of enterprises controlled by them had by the 1930s become sufficiently large to justify some economists and lawyers in regarding them as a new ruling group, the 'managerial' class, typifying a new economic and social order. As early as 1908 Henri Fayol was able to announce the coming age of entrepreneurial government. The announcement echoed the lingering traditions of French Saint-Simonism, and was as yet little more than a wishful prophecy. Even later, the American recapitulations of the Fayol theme, by Berle and Means and others, were also somewhat ahead of events. But in view of subsequent changes in the high ranks of management, the earlier forecasts have turned out to be prophetic. In the inter-war period, and more still after the war, the invasion of the topmost ranks of industry by professional executives proceeded at an even greater speed than before and over a constantly widening front.[1]

Behind this invasion it is possible to discern a number of converging impulses, such as the increasing size of firms and establishments and the growing complexity of products and processes. But the main impulse obviously was the spread of the joint stock, or corporate, ownership. The connexion between corporate forms of organization and the new type of professional leadership was not automatic or instantaneous, and was not equally close in all European countries. In most countries, company laws made it possible and convenient for family firms to don the outward garb of corporate business. Numerous family firms functioned as 'private' companies, in which none or very little of the capital was owned by the general public. And we have seen that in addition a number of companies wholly public in form continued to be conducted by their founders or their families, who owned the controlling component of the companies' capital. In general, however, it remains true that genuinely corporate types of company ownership spread at the expense of private firms, and, in doing so, extended the hold of professional executives over an ever-greater proportion of nations' enterprises.

This movement may have gone farthest in Germany, the country in which it happened to be observed sooner than elsewhere. From its earliest days, in the second half or the last quarter of the nineteenth century, German industrial and commercial leadership contained a larger proportion of professional executives. Needless to say, an historian of German pre-war industry will find among its leaders a large number of self-made men, pioneers of humble

---

[1] The data in the next five or six paragraphs comes partly from current periodical publications, from personal interviews, and from some recent books and articles, such as H. Hartmann 'Die Akademiker in der Heutigen Unternehmerschaft', *Tradition*, 1959; idem, *Authority and Organisation in German Management*, Princeton, 1959; H. W. Ehrman, *Organised Business in France*, Princeton, 1951; M. Drancourt (as in footnote 1, p. 248 above); D. Granik, *The European Executive*, N.Y., 1960; and from more specialized studies quoted in footnote 5 on pp. 266–80 below. The only historical study of the origins of entrepreneurial class in the United Kingdom is confined to two industries and ends in 1950: C. Ericson, *British Industrialists: Steel and Hosiery, 1850–1950*, London, 1959. Tentative historical guesses can be derived from R. V. Clements, *Managers: a Study of Their Careers in Industry*, London, 1958; and *Management Succession*, Acton Society Trust Publication, 1956.

origin, or members of founders' families. Men like Stinnes, Haniels, Siemens and Thyssen were to be found at the head of the largest industrial and commercial complexes in Western Germany as late as 1920, or even 1940. But the characteristic industrial leader of the very large firm at the turn of the century was an employee of the firm, selected for his position or risen to it by virtue of his technical or business qualifications. This type of industrial leader so commonly taken to be the product of twentieth-century U.S.A. was until recent times as characteristic of German business as of the American. Though by no means forming the majority of the business community, he was to be found in the seats of power of most of the greater German enterprises.[1]

If the preponderance of professional executives were to be considered beneficial, Germany could be said to have derived some benefit from the shortage of privately owned capital and from the reluctance of its owners to commit it to industrial investment. Banks were called to step in where the private investors feared to tread. From the very beginning they got involved with financing and hence also with the conduct of industry; and in order to carry out their responsibilities and to watch over their interests they often had to take a hand in the selection of the directors and managers and sometimes imposed their own representatives upon firms. In this way, under the aegis of what some German economists have described as 'finance capitalism', German industry provided itself at an early stage with large, frequently cartelized, firms, headed by professional executives.[2]

[1] This view of German business is, however, challenged by D. Granik, *The European Executive*, N.Y., 1962, pp. 61–7 and Heinz Hartmann, *Authority and Organisation in German Management*, Princeton, 1958. The writers draw a distinction between 'entrepreneurs' in full exercise of supreme authority and managers in control of routine operations, and relate the powers of the former to their ownership of capital. It may be true, as Mr Heinz Hartmann argues (in F. Herbison and Charles A. Meyer, *Management in the Industrial World*, New York, 1959, p. 274), that 94 per cent of all German businesses were managed by owners, but the figure is somewhat irrelevant. Well over 90 per cent of the businesses to which the figure presumably applies were artisan establishments employing on the average fewer than five persons.

[2] J. Riesser, *The German Great Banks and their Concentration*, U.S.A. Senate, National Monetary Commission, Washington, 1911, pp. 721, 725 *seq.*, and Appendix IV.

S

French changes in the entrepreneurial personnel are more difficult to assess, largely because the history of individual French firms
is as yet less known than that of English or German ones, and partly
because much of the recent writings in French industrial leadership
have been mostly concerned with political or socio-political
attitudes – an aspect of the problem which is not strictly relevant to
this part of our story. The tendency in most economic histories of
France has been to treat the French business undertakings taken
en masse as a classical example of traditional family ownership.
These histories sometimes neglect certain important changes in the
French *patronat*, mainly because the changes were very recent and,
on the whole, confined to undertakings in the *grandes industries*.
In these undertakings managers of the modern-type were not
altogether newcomers. Even before the effects of the war, the
Liberation and the Plan revealed themselves, some great firms,
including family firms, recruited into their upper ranks men brought
up and capable of operating as professional managers. But what in
the late thirties and forties was the practice of a very few up-to-date
firms spread in the following years to a wider range of industry and
finance.

Even by 1964 these changes had not yet spread so widely as to
transform the composition of French *patronat* in its entirety. More
than in Germany and the United Kingdom, small firms still remained
in the hands of their owners who managed them. Moreover, in
France, as in other countries, family ownership was still to be found
behind the corporate façade of many a great undertaking. But
generally speaking, in most large firms in France, even the firms
whose capital was still in the hands of very few owners and whose
control still nominally resided in the hands of the men or families
who owned them – such as the Michelin-Citroën combine or the De
Wendel iron and steel combine – the actual direction of the firms
was in the hands of their professional heads.

In the United Kingdom, in spite of the different chronology of its
economic development and its much earlier experience of corporate
forms of business, the changes in the character and composition of
managerial leadership differed little from those of Germany or
France. As elsewhere, small enterprises changed little; but as elsewhere, enterprises directed by professional leaders were becoming

more numerous. On the other hand, banks and other institutional providers of capital did not, until very recently, exercise as important a part in the affairs of British companies as they did in the affairs of German ones. Professional executives, placed in their positions as nominees of financial institutions, were not therefore to be found in comparable numbers; and, where they were so placed, they, as a rule, held no more than a watching brief.

The broad similarities in the historical roots of this new managerial class may obscure certain national differences in its composition and the somewhat disparate effects it had on the post-war economy and society in different European countries. The reason why the features making up the physiognomy of the managerial epoch were as yet very disparate is that the new managerial class was itself highly heterogeneous and that its heterogeneity imprinted itself on the conduct of firms.

Unfortunately, what historians are able to say about heads of enterprises must of necessity be imprecise and seldom more than impressionistic. Historical and sociological studies of industrial and commercial leadership are few, and are fewest of all for Germany, the Netherlands and the Scandinavian countries. Many of them take the form of individual business histories which for all their importance, will not support anything approaching quantitative estimates. The more general studies capable of yielding quantitative conclusions have frequently tended to deal with the managerial class *in toto* and have not always discriminated between the men at the head of enterprises and the echelons in the intermediate and lower ranges of management. The quality of the latter, their recruitment and behaviour, were, of course, highly relevant to the record of post-war entrepreneurship. As we shall see presently, a large number of professional heads of businesses rose from the lower ranks of management. Moreover, the quality of the topmost leaders was very often reflected in the manner in which they recruited, promoted and organized their managerial 'cadres'. The story of the entrepreneurial *élite* is therefore closely involved with that of the managerial class as a whole, and the latter will have to be brought into our story. But, at this stage of the story what matters are the changes at the higher levels, among top managers and their immed-iate subordinates or would-be successors and among the active members of directional boards. And it is on changes at this level that we shall have to focus our attention.

To repeat, the composition and the behaviour of leaders of enterprises were very varied, and their variety to a large extent reflected the occupational sources from which they were recruited. These sources were many. In all the Western countries the method of recruitment alleged to be the commonest was by promotion from lower ranks. Even in some of the largest British firms – Shell, I.C.I., Unilever, the 'Big Five' banks, and the principal insurance companies – this was the road by which some of the leaders travelled on their way to the topmost posts.[1] Several inquiries into the recruit-ment of managers in the United Kingdom revealed that nearly half the men in managerial positions in the mid-fifties had 'come up from the bottom'. In Germany so much of the mystique continued to cling to the prevailing conception of industrial directorate, that boards of directors in charge of policy (*Aufsichtsräthe*) were clearly set apart from managerial boards charged with the daily conduct of business. Promotion to directorial boards from the ranks should therefore have been more difficult than, say, in Britain or in the Netherlands or in Sweden. It is also possible that the upper ranks of German business had been renewed so recently that promotions – a slow process at the best of times – had not yet left clear marks on the composition of the highest entrepreneurial ranks. It has never-theless been claimed that in Germany the way to the highest posts in industry also led up the rungs of the managerial ladder. The same claims have been made for some of the great Swiss and Belgian firms.

[1] The patterns of recruitment of managers in the Manchester area have been exemplified in R. V. Clements, *Managers: A Study of the Careers in Business*, Chs. I–VIII; and D. G. Clark, *The Industrial Manager, His Background and Career Pattern*, London, 1966, Ch. V. For recruitment and promotion from the bottom, see R. V. Clements, *op. cit.*, pp. 64 *seq.*, and D. G. Clark, *op. cit.*, pp. 72–80. Also references to recruitment of managers in I. C. McGivering and others, *Management in Britain* and *Acton Society Trust: Management Succession*, as in footnote 1, p. 282 below. In Joan Woodward's sample of Essex firms, 30 per cent promoted their managers from inside, 5 per cent recruited them wholly from outside and 65 per cent made use of both methods of recruitment: Joan Woodward, *Industrial Management* as in footnote 1, p. 277 below.

Detailed investigations of firms' histories from this point of view have as yet been too few to justify or to refute this claim, but the information which has so far been assembled suggests that this method of recruiting heads of firms became less widespread in recent times. The store which most larger firms on the Continent set by university degrees may have impeded promotion from the lowest managerial ranks. According to some recent reports the proportion of top managers and directors in British firms promoted from the lower ranks of employment may also have declined in recent years, as educational qualifications for managerial posts rose.[1]

The alternative routes, especially in France, but also in England and elsewhere, led across the managerial hierarchy rather than along it, i.e. by direct recruitment of outsiders into commanding positions in firms. On occasions the entrants to the 'top floor' – which is the 'ground floor' in English parlance – might be scientists or technicians brought in from other firms or from universities or from research posts within firms. In general, professional scientists and technicians, as distinct from men who had merely obtained university degrees in science, were more numerous and most influential not in the topmost ranks of industrial and commercial leadership but at its penultimate heights: among the various grades of intermediate management, and more especially among technological experts in charge of design and development. Before 1939 the occasions on which men of this type were able to penetrate the commanding positions in enterprises were still relatively rare, and rarest of all in the United Kingdom. During our period, however, they multiplied fast, particularly in modern science-oriented industries. In Germany, where scientists were always to be found on the boards of great firms, their numbers may have grown after the war, when such men as Professor Kurt Hansen of the Bayer chemical group, or Professor Karl Wurster of the Badische Anilin, or Professor Karl Winnacker of the Hoechst chemical group, were to be found at the head or in important positions on the directorial boards of German chemical, electrical and electronic industries.[2] After the war

---

[1] D. G. Clark, *op. cit.*; also R. V. Clements, *ibid.*
[2] For large numbers of scientists and engineers among German managers, see D. Granik, as cited in footnote 1, p. 267 above, and works of H. Hartmann, *ibid.* For British managers who started as technicians, see D. G. Clark,

'professors' may have also made further inroads into similar positions in the United Kingdom. The federated board of Imperial Chemical Industries and to a smaller extent the boards of firms like Shell or Unilever had come to contain scientists and engineers and themselves became recruiting grounds for other firms on a look-out for scientifically oriented directors. By 1964 erstwhile research scientists and engineers had come to occupy commanding positions in some of the largest firms in man-made fibres, e.g. Courtauld, or heavy electrical engineering, such as the English Electric, or in aircraft groups, such as Hawker Siddeley and British Aircraft Corporation. In most countries with large nationalized industries men of this type were frequently placed in charge of State-owned undertakings.[1]

In France, where their arrival and their predominance in high managerial ranks has been observed and commented upon more openly than elsewhere, they have been admired or blamed, as the case might be, for having imposed their 'technocratic' outlook, mechanistic and science-proud, on the industry as a whole. The fact that in France large numbers of these men had passed through the same educational machine (mostly the École Polytechnique) is perhaps the reason why their 'technocratic' attitude appeared to be more conspicuous than elsewhere. But in a manner somewhat less uniform and articulate the attitude also made itself felt in other countries. In them as in France, its human carriers were not only the young graduates of engineering and scientific faculties, but also recruits from the scientific and technical personnel of universities, research institutes and research departments of firms.

Yet when it comes to the 'top management' and to active directorial positions in firms – their commanding heights – entrants from the civil service were perhaps more characteristic of the post-war trends. In the United Kingdom the movement from the civil

as on p. 270 above. In France, in 1954, the ratio of university-trained engineers to other industrial employees was 1 to 165, compared with 1 to 70 in the U.S.A. Cf. Jean Fourastié's report of the *Commission de la main d'oeuvre du Commissariat Général au Plan* in *Revue Française du Travail*, 1954, No. 3 and 1956, No. 3. Cf. also E. W. Burgess in F. Herbison and Charles Myers, *Management in the Industrial World.*

[1] On small proportions of technicians promoted to directorships or top management in the United Kingdom, cf. D. G. Clark, *op. cit.*; also C. F. Carter and B. R. Williams, *Scientists in Industry*, London, 1959, pp. 33 and 67.

service into industry had begun very recently and had not gone as far as, say, in France; but it had made some headway during our period. Members of the administrative grade of the civil service had for generations maintained their ethos of a public service and a vocation impervious to the attractions of profits or high business salaries. After the war, however, translation from the higher ranks of the administrative civil service to seats of power in private firms became more frequent, and by 1964 a number of great firms had ex-permanent heads or ex-deputy-heads of ministries on their boards. In varying degrees the same interpenetration of higher civil service and business could be observed in Belgium, the Netherlands, Switzerland, and Sweden.

It was again in France that a movement from the civil service into the higher ranks of business became sufficiently conspicuous to earn for itself a nickname. For a number of years, but more especially after the war, the type of career irreverently described *pantouflage* became fairly common among younger public servants. The typical pattern was for graduates of the great schools, frequently the top-rankers (*les bottiers*) of the École Polytechnique as well as those of the École des Mines, the École des Ponts et des Chaussées, and also for young men who had passed through the great administrative corps such as the Conseil d'Etat or the Cours de Comptes, to go into private business after a number of years in State service. Among these men the young Inspecteurs des Finances had by 1960 become the most numerous as well as most prominent. Michel Drancourt has culled from the 1963 Annuaire de l'Inspection the names of at least fifty ex-inspectors of finance in leading positions in at least thirty-five large enterprises. If to those were to be added the names of recruits from other branches of the civil service and the army (the latter became quite numerous after the end of the Algerian war) we might be better able to understand why so much attention has been paid by French writers to the spreading practice of *pantouflage*.[1]

Yet another source of professional business leadership was provided by professions ancillary to business. So great was the effect of taxation on company profits in the United Kingdom that

[1] H. W. Ehrmann, *Organised Business in France*, Princeton, 1957. On *pantou-flage*, see M. Drancourt, *op. cit.*; cf. also Alain Girard, 'La réussite sociale en France, ses charactères, ses lois ses éffêts': *Travaux et Documents de l'Institut National des Etudes Démographiques*, Cahier 38.

between the wars taxation specialists, mostly accountants, played an indispensable part, and found permanent lodgement, in the directorial ranks of many British enterprises. A similar part was played by lawyers in German, Dutch, Austrian and Scandinavian firms. In Germany bankers sat on many boards not in their capacity of owners of capital or providers of credit but in that of financial experts and advisers.

Finally, at the cost of what may appear to be a paradox I must recall what I have already said about recruitment of top managers from among the families of founders and owners of firms. Names of old-established families, some of them belonging to great business dynasties, still stare one in the eye from company accounts, prospectuses, and directories in all European countries. There were still Krupps presiding over their firms in Germany; Boveris in Switzerland; Summers, Rowntrees, Cadbury's, Pilkingtons, and Hambros in the United Kingdom; and Agnellis, Pirellis and Falcks in Italy. Many of the French names of business leaders recall the great entrepreneurs of the early nineteenth and even eighteenth centuries: Wendel, Gramont, Vogüe, Dolfus, Lebon, Rothschild, Worms, Verné, Mirabeau.

These conspicuous signs of ancient family connexions may in some cases represent the surviving hold of rich men over industrial capital. But as often as not they also bear witness to the manner in which the *grande bourgeoisie* of Europe adapted itself to the demands of the managerial age. In the course of the last generation it became quite common for a great family firm to be headed not by its members nearest in the line of family succession or commanding the best claim or the largest share in a family fortune but by members best trained and otherwise best qualified for the position of leadership. In some of the great firms in the United Kingdom, most typical of family ownership – Cadbury, Pilkington, Summers – as well as in some of the greatest brewing firms and banking houses, the men in leading positions bearing their firms' names had come to be chosen from among large numbers of relatives on the strength of their professional qualifications for the posts. In some great business families in France and Italy, certain of their members had been pre-selected for the training and education required of the occupants of directorial posts; in others, new members were recruited into the family circle by marriage and adoption to enable the firms to possess themselves of professional leaders without losing their private family character.[1]

It is because the occupational sources of recruitment were so many and because some of them continued to be disguised under old family names or continued to be fed by recruits from the upper-middle classes and privileged schools, that recent changes in industrial leadership have failed to impress themselves on the mind of the public as fully as they deserve. The man in the street, helped and abetted by some sociologists, is still inclined to think of the typical modern firm as a species of private property at the disposal of the few individuals who happened to own it, and may still fail to recognize the ubiquity and the authority of the new industrial bureaucracy in the post-war period for what they were. What were they?

In assessing the significance of post-war changes in industrial leadership it is important to distinguish their economic effects from their purely social repercussions. For they may turn out to have had a far greater impact on the behaviour of the economy than on class structure and class relations. Needless to say, their impact was most direct where it was also easiest to observe: on the conduct of individual enterprises. For it would not be a bold or indeed an altogether novel generalization to suggest that the professional entrepreneurs brought to the conduct of affairs a more rational and probably also a more adventurous spirit, and *eo ipso* a greater propensity to innovate, than was common in owner-managed family businesses. The role which the quality of entrepreneurs and

---

[1] On 'co-option' of outsiders into German business families, see D. Granik, *The European Executive*, pp. 278–9, 283. François Bloch-Lainé in his *Pour Une Réforme de l'Entreprise*, Paris, 1963, pp. 14–16, argues that the 'technocratie des dirigeants' also established itself in certain family firms. 'Les directeurs, même quand ils sont parents des actionnaires se rendent independants d'eux.' Observers familiar with the history of firms in the United Kingdom and Germany can easily cite instances of family firms managed professionally and independently by members of the owning families. In general there is much to be said for differentiating the various types of patrimonial control, somewhat in the manner in which this has been done by Franco Ferratori in F. Herbison and Charles A. Myers, *Management in the Industrial World*, pp. 237 *seq.*, and place in a category all its own the family firms Ferratori classifies as 'democratic-participative' in which families do not automatically provide the ruling members of the executives, or in which the heads of the firms behave as independent professional managers even when they happen to belong to the owner families.

managers played in expanding and innovating the industries of Western Europe has been repeatedly referred to in earlier chapters of this study. Yet the underlying implications that innovating and expansive entrepreneurs were in the main to be found among the professional executives and that their proliferation was somehow linked with the increasing size of firms and with corporate ownership, may seem to run counter to some of the oldest and fondest traditions of industrial sociology: Schumpeter's and Weber's. In these traditions the professional executives of large and growing corporations typify industrial and commercial bureaucracy; and bureaucracy holds a high place in Weber's and Schumpeter's social demonology. Weber defined hierarchical bureaucracy by various, mostly disfunctional, characteristics, while Schumpeter taught us to associate professional management of large corporate firms with elaborate hierarchies of functions and with strict definitions of rank and duty – both inimical to innovating entrepreneurship. This fiend of bureaucratic inertia was contrasted with the Faustian image of the adventurous pathfinders at the head of personally owned enterprises.

Fortunately this sociological tradition no longer dominates the discussion of economic organization. In some recent writings, such as Mr Tom Burns's, it is still possible to detect a lingering tendency to associate rigid and unresponsive ('mechanistic') conduct of business with elaborately organized hierarchies of management. But even in these writings hierarchy is not presented as an inescapable characteristic of large company-owned business. Joan Woodward's much-cited inquiry into some firms in South Essex also notes the existence in the late fifties of complex, presumably hierarchical, structures of management, characterized by numerous levels of authority and separate departments in charge of specialized functions. She contrasts these managerial structures with others less elaborate or less formal, but relates the distinction not to differences of ownership or even to size but to the nature of products and of corresponding methods of production. 'Mass' or 'continuous flow' outputs of standardized goods called for 'line' or 'military' organization of managerial command or else for 'line-staff' pattern of organization combining hierarchical systems with some functional specialization. On the other hand, 'unit' outputs usually those of complicated products or of products designed and made 'one of a kind' went together with non-hierarchical and undifferentiated bodies of managers. Similarly, the managerial structure appropriate to 'process' outputs, such as those of chemicals, plastics, or petroleum products, was apt to be run more informally and elastically and not be strictly differentiated by function or even by grade.[1]

Other distinctions between types of managerial structure have been suggested by numerous American students of the subject, and their classifications, like the British ones, do not bear out the Schumpetrian juxtaposition of inert management of business corporations and adventurously conducted enterprises owned and managed by individuals. The prevailing tendency in most recent studies is to assume that, if the twentieth-century managers were more rational in the conduct of enterprises and more prone to innovate, this was not only because their establishments grew in size or because their products and processes were getting increasingly complex, but also because they were professional executives and not owner-managers of the traditional kind. Some such assumption lurks behind the demarcation lines drawn by Professors Carter and Williams between firms 'parochial' and 'rational', and it also underlies the earlier references in the present study to the role of entrepreneurs in post-war growth.

In recent studies of managerial structures, however, this assumption is seldom laid bare or discussed; and as long as they take it for granted, they cannot throw much direct light on our problem. The essence of the problem posed here is what was the effect of professional entrepreneurship on the performance of the European economy in our period, and how much credit should be given to it for the increasingly rational conduct of European firms and for their heightened ability to expand and to innovate. These are not the questions to which recent studies of management could yield relevant answers. Most of the firms investigated by them were well within the Carter–Williams 'rational' group. Joan Woodward's

---

[1] J. Woodward, *Industrial Organization: Theory and Practice*, London, 1965, pp. 17–19, 37–8; *Management and Technology, Problems of Progress in Industry*, No. 3, D.S.I.R., H.M.S.O. 1960, *passim*, and pp. 17–18. For the distinction between 'mechanic' and 'organic' systems, see Tom Burns and G. M. Stalker, *The Management of Innovation*, Tavistock Publications, London, 1961, Ch. 5, 6, esp. pp. 119–25 and pp. 237 *seq.*

sample is largely made up of modern establishments corporately
owned at the time of the inquiry and containing very few enterprises recognizable as 'traditional' or 'parochial', and so are also
the other firms figuring in the Liverpool University inquiry.[1]

For somewhat similar reasons the manner in which most recent
studies of managerial structure approach the problems of innovation is frequently irrelevant to the problems of technological progress as it emerges at this point of our study. Capacity for innovation, observed and commended in recent studies, concerns mostly
the use of existing equipment and modifications in current outputs
and in established products. It, as a rule, boils down to the manager's ability to respond easily and quickly to piecemeal changes in
demand, in specifications, in costs and prices. On the other hand,
innovations which figure in Schumpeter's argument and are implied
in our discussion of technological progress after the war, are of a
rarer kind and of a higher order. They entail decisions to launch
wholly new products or to introduce wholly new processes and lead
to the setting up of new industries, or at least the renewal of entire
lines of production. They require for their study an historical perspective and cannot be appropriately dealt with in managerial
studies restricted to the situations as they found them at the time
of writing. Such suggestions of trends as can be read into them must
be very uncertain, highly speculative, and but remotely relevant to
important historical problems. It is thus possible to deduce some
hypothetical history from Joan Woodward's distinction between the
managerial structures of quantity outputs and process outputs. On
her showing, process industries represent a more advanced form of
production and belong to the same category as the 'automated'
industries. If so, the gradual spread of automatic controls to
entire production lines characteristic of quantity industries of the
sixties should have shifted their managerial structures in the
direction represented by Joan Woodward's process type.[2]

---

[1] J. Woodward, *op. cit.*, pp. 7–10. Some of her firms had apparently undergone radical technical changes in their recent past (*ibid.*, pp. 31–6). The main preoccupation of her inquiry, however, is not so much with the effect of managerial
structure and personnel on technological change but rather with the effects of
technology on the structure of management.

[2] J. Woodward, *Industrial Organisation*, refers to and discusses radical changes
in technology involving the transition from one production method to another.
The change-over most relevant to our discussion is that from batch production

However, this and other similar historical extrapolations from managerial structures of the present day are bound to be so hypothetical and, as a rule, so loosely related to significant historical issues that we must regretfully forgo them. In our search for information about changes in managerial behaviour after the war, we shall have to employ other, more oblique but less speculative evidence, such as the observed changes in the composition of managerial personnel; or else rely on deductions from the more general historical movements which we know or can assume to have influenced the make up and the behaviour of industrial management.

The change in the personal composition of industrial management most likely to have influenced the rationality and innovating aptitude of managers was the general, even if gradual, rise in its educational levels; above all, the increasing proportions of managers with university degrees and with scientific and engineering training. Curiously enough the trend was least noticeable in Germany, where the proportions of graduates in society at large had always been high. But it was most pronounced and easiest to follow in France and the United Kingdom. A recent inquiry by Nicole Delefortrie-Soubeyroux has revealed that in the period between 1952 and 1955, from which her evidence comes, over 72 per cent of a sample of some 5,000 French industrial leaders (*les dirigeants de l'industrie*), mostly top managers, members of boards of directors and owner-managers of enterprises, held university degrees; and that of those latter more than one-half came from engineering faculties. That these proportions must have been on the rise for some time is reflected in their distribution by generations. Whereas in the oldest age group of managers – those born before 1890 – the proportion of university graduates was 67 per cent, their proportion in the age groups born after 1910 exceeded 72 per cent. This might appear a modest rate of increase, but it must be remembered that even the managers in the youngest age group had come from a generation

---

to process output. One such change is discussed in the same author's *Management and Technology*, as in footnote 1, p. 277 above; one of the author's conclusions is that a large proportion of manufacturing firms in the future are likely to be process firms, *ibid.*, p. 13. The prognosis can, of course, be inverted to suggest that a proportion of firms engaged in process outputs in the 1960s had begun as manufacturing establishments.

which had not yet benefited either from mounting demands of firms for university-educated staff or from the much better provision of university education after the Liberation. In so far as the more recent history of certain individual French firms – such as Renault, or the main petroleum and chemical firms – allow us to judge, the proportions of young managers with university degrees and with scientific and engineering training rose steeply in the ten years following the Delefortrie inquiry.[1]

Other evidence brought up by the inquiry indicates that, even though improvements in the educational standards of managers were most marked in industries in which large company-owned establishments predominated, they had of late also begun to affect the traditional owner-managed firms. Thus in the same sample of industrial leaders, those at the head of the tradition-dominated textile firms in the North, a far larger proportion continued to enter family firms directly from school. But even among them the recent trend towards better-qualified management showed itself in a variety of ways. Above all, the firms had begun to discriminate more than before in favour of the better-trained and qualified members of the family circles from which their managers were habitually recruited. If, as the same inquiry shows, the proportion of top managers in the petroleum industry without university degrees was also higher than in French industry as a whole, this was equally symptomatic of the underlying trends. For in 1952 the petroleum industry in France was still sufficiently young to be largely run by men of the generation which pioneered and staffed it in its earlier days. The composition of its management showed signs of changing in the sixties, and the changes mirrored, within the span of a single generation, the more protracted course of the

[1] Nicole Delefortrie-Soubeyroux, *Les dirigeants de l'industrie française*, Paris, 1961, pp. 54 *seq.*, and 100 *seq.* None of this data is more recent than 1955. The subsequent ten years witnessed not only further changes in the ownership and concentration of French industry but also a spread of university education, and above all the retirement of the bulk of the generation of managers born before 1890. Comparable Belgian evidence will be found in *Les Cadres Supérieurs des Enterprises*, Pub. of Université Libre de Bruxelles, Brussels, 1959. We are told that the proportion of graduates active in German business before 1914 was very low (14 per cent): H. Hartmann in F. Herbison and Charles Meyers, op. cit., p. 274, but that the proportions grew thereafter in more progressive firms. Moreover, the figures, like those cited in footnote 1 on p. 267 above, apparently include small family businesses.

historical changes in the quality of leadership of French industry as a whole.[1]

The numbers of university-trained and similarly qualified men increased more markedly (mainly because they had been much lower to begin with) in the United Kingdom. In a sample of 102 large companies investigated in 1964 by the National Economic Development Council, each with not less than 2,000 employees, 69 per cent of top managers and 58 per cent of managers of middle rank possessed university degrees or equivalent academic or professional qualifications.[2] The proportions were much lower than in U.S.S.R., or France, but represented a very considerable advance over those a decade or two earlier. A series of regional inquiries confined mainly to Lancashire enables us to compare the qualifications of managers in the late fifties and a decade earlier and also to analyze their distribution by age groups. D. G. Clark's inquiry relating to the early sixties shows that at the later date 37 per cent of all managers in private industry (or 35 per cent if nationalized undertakings were included) possessed university degrees. But an earlier study by R. V. Clements, reflecting the position in approximately the same area ten years earlier, puts the figure of graduates in managerial positions much lower – at little over 25 per cent. A marked improvement over time is also shown by Clark's figures if analyzed by age. The proportion of university-trained managers in the youngest group, that of 39 years and younger, who represented more than one-half of the sample, was 47 per cent, whereas in the oldest group, that of 55 years and more, their proportion was only 11·4 per cent. The trend was obviously rising, and other studies, such as a study of a steel works by W. H. Scott's team, suggest that the trend had begun to rise long before the 1950s. The proportion of graduates among the top managers at the steel works rose from 15 per cent in 1935 to 27 per cent in 1954. In all these samples the lowest proportion of graduates were to be found in age groups most likely to be reduced in the immediate future by death or retirement; so that at the date of the inquiry a further change in overall averages

---

[1] Delefortrie-Soubeyroux, *op. cit.*, pp. 248 *seq.* (textiles), pp. 198–200 (petroleum).

[2] N.E.D.C., *Management Recruitment and Development*, H.M.S.O., London, 1965, pp. 11–12, and Appendix III, Table 11.3.

of graduates could be anticipated through the action of mere time.[1]

Moreover, all these figures underestimate the increase in the numbers of qualified men in managerial ranks, since they do not include men who received their training by part-time 'further' study while already on the managerial ladder. The latter multiplied very greatly after the war. According to D. G. Clark's evidence, not less than 75 per cent of managers in the firms he investigated attended at one time or another part-time courses of further education. As a result, in the early sixties some 33 per cent of the managers could claim qualifications – presumably certified – acquired by them while in employment. If the numbers so qualified were added to those of graduates it would appear that only 21 per cent of the sample possessed neither a degree nor a qualification by 'further education'. What is more, by far the largest proportion of the degrees were not, as is commonly assumed, in arts subjects, but in engineering and, to a somewhat smaller extent, in sciences.[2]

All this data bears strongly, if indirectly, on our problem of the changing quality of entrepreneurs. Increasing proportions of graduates among managers doubtless reflected the general spread of university education in twentieth-century Britain or France and the obvious increase in the proportion of graduates in the age groups from which managers were recruited. To some extent, however, the higher proportions of qualified men must also have reflected the changing standards of industrial leadership. For there is little doubt that the relative numbers of university-trained and similarly qualified men among younger managers grew because their

[1] D. G. Clark, *The Industrial Manager, His Background and Career Pattern*, cf. earlier figures in *Acton Society Trust's Management Succession*, London, 1956, p. 8, Table 3; p. 24, Ch. VII, Appendix 3, p. 93; R. V. Clements, *Managers: A Study of their Careers in Industry*, London, 1958, Appendix 2, Tables 4 and 28; cf. also I. C. McGivering, D. G. J. Mathews, W. H. Scott, *Management in Britain*, Liverpool University Press, 1960, pp. 65 *seq*. For the managers, see W. H. Scott, J. A. Banks, A. H. Halsey, and T. Lupton, *Technical Change and Industrial Relations*, Liverpool University Press, 1956, pp. 88–7. For graduates among members of boards of directors in the early fifties, see G. H. Copeman, *Leaders of British Industry*, London, 1955, p. 102, and *The Director*, January 1965. The last two studies show that the proportions of graduates on boards of directors was lower and increased less than among top managers. It must, however, be borne in mind that the average age of directors was higher and that many of them sat in purely representative or decorative capacities.

[2] D. G. Clark, *The Industrial Manager: His Background and Career Pattern*, London, 1966.

recruitment was now favoured by the older men whose business it was to do the recruiting. There is equally little doubt that, whatever its cause, the invasion of the managerial ranks by men who had gone through several years of intellectual training and testing at university levels was bound to impart into the conduct of their firms higher standards of rationality and literacy than those characteristic of the darker ages in the history of European enterprises.

The reference to darker ages brings us to the connexion between the composition of the managerial ranks and the more general history of our period. The connexions were close and fairly obvious; they were, however, so relevant to our story that they must be retraced here.

Viewed from the point of view of quality and behaviour of entrepreneurs and managers, the British story of the pre-war period, though dark, was gradually getting brighter. It is now an accepted generalization of economic history that before 1914 industrial leaders, whom Schumpeter and Carter would unhesitatingly classify as 'parochial' or 'traditional', had by degrees established themselves as the predominant type in most of the older British industries. The fact that by that time most British industries had long passed the pioneering period of their history may have been partly to blame, since in the newer industries even at that time entrepreneurs, men like Leverhulme, Cadbury, Parsons, or Courtauld, were introducing new processes and new products. But in cotton, linen, wool, coal, steel, shipbuilding, and a host of other old-established trades it was possible to conduct business and make profits without venturing into new attitudes and methods.

For all the doubts which some historians have recently voiced about this generalization, it remains generally true and relevant that at the turn of the century the conduct of many firms in older industries had come into the hands of men in the second, third, and fourth generations of the founders' families. Most of these men (though not, of course, every one of them) had acquired the tastes and attitudes of the leisured classes and were prepared to leave the day-to-day conduct of the firms to shop-floor managers, who were

T

frequently promoted foremen, themselves workmen brought up in the existing methods of production and wedded to them. Underlying these attitudes of the men who owned and managed the firms was the general anti-intellectual bias of the late Victorian age: the attitude of exaggerated empiricism disdainful of first principles, distrustful of scientific rationalizations and insistent on 'learning the job while doing it'. Historians studying industrial problems firm by firm should, of course, be able to cite instances of firms in every generation, even at the end of the Victorian era, which were still led by adventurous, enterprising and scientifically minded men. These men were, above all, to be found in the few young industries which were springing up at the time, or in newer branches of engineering or textiles. But placed against the general background and the prevailing temper of the age they were neither numerous nor representative.

After 1914, and still more after 1939, both the composition and the attitudes of English entrepreneurial personnel began to alter. The wars, and especially the second, shook up the ranks of top managers in leading firms drawn into munitions production. This happened partly because wartime products were not the peacetime goods to which they were accustomed, and partly because efficient managers attracted more government orders than the inefficient ones. But sometimes this also happened because in certain critical situations, i.e. in dealing with certain aircraft and air engine firms after 1942, government departments were compelled to force upon firms changes in their management. The process was continued for some time after the war in industries where nationalization brought new men to the top of the managerial ladder and sometimes even to its lower ranks. Needless to say, opinions differ as to whether the new men, if measured by rigorous standards, were in every respect better than the men they replaced. In the group of Lancashire firms investigated in 1958, older men had during the war replaced the younger men on national service, and the average quality of management probably declined. But in the upper ranks of management in the larger firms drawn into munitions production the average quality of new managers was clearly superior to that of the men they replaced. They were certainly not entrepreneurs of the traditional type wedded to the traditional methods and attitudes they inherited from their parents or learned from their foremen.[1]

As we have seen, the composition of the managerial class in that period was also exposed to certain influences of a more general and permanent kind. Private firms were declining in numbers and the size of firms and enterprises grew with the general movement of industrial concentration. Products and processes were also becoming more complicated. Above all, the changes within industries and firms were accompanied by changes in the scope and character of industries' contacts with government. The new contacts required men capable of responding to government pressures and proddings, of availing themselves of such favours and facilities as the State could now offer and of cushioning the effects of the regulations and taxes the State now imposed. These new circumstances required the presence at the head of affairs of men more articulate and better informed than the men who appeared to suffice a couple of generations earlier.

Equally important were the changes in the intellectual climate of the age – the newborn respect for rational expertise, for university-trained specialists and for intellectual ability in general. And we have seen that these climatic changes affected not only the choice of managers in public companies but also the choice and education of leaders and managers in family-owned and family-run businesses – a fact which explains why sons and nephews at the head of firms still bearing the names of the men who founded them and still led by members of the founders' families – Pilkingtons, Cadbury's, Sainsbury's, Whitbreads, Plessey's, and a score of others – conformed in their outlook and methods to the new managerial standards and proved able to modernize their enterprises as drastically as the most innovating of the professional executives.

These were all changes on the bright side of Britain's industrial record. The latter was, however, also marked by dark patches, especially at the point where it touched the firms' innovating record. Some such patches were, of course, to be found in all countries, and the British patches may have been only marginally larger or darker than the foreign ones. But the margins were still sufficiently wide to keep unfilled the gaps between the United Kingdom's rate

---

[1] R. V. Clements, as in footnote 1, p. 282 above, pp. 156 *seq.*; M. M. Postan, *British War Production*, pp. 314–15 and Chs. VI, VIII, and IX *passim*.

of innovation and growth and that of, say, Germany or Sweden. For this marginal deficiency in British entrepreneurship nobody has as yet been able to provide a wholly convincing explanation. It may well be that the modernization of management since 1939 did not go far or long enough to transform the entire entrepreneurial personnel. In spite of the increases in university-trained managers and specialists, the numbers of men so trained was still lower than in some other countries. The large numbers of heads of firms who, as the Richardson inquiry of 1963 revealed, were unable to understand and to avail themselves of tax-allowances for replacements, might have represented the lingering irrationality and illiteracy of the business community. That in a number of smaller firms the methods of recruiting and promoting leaders should have remained what they had been in Edwardian times is not surprising. But in certain fields (mostly those of finance) and in large firms within them, privileges and preferences based on family, class and school, immune from the intellectual and educational changes of the time, may even have consolidated themselves after 1939. It may also turn out that some of the effects of the great shake-up of the war had gradually evaporated; and that not all the major firms in private industry in Britain had as yet developed the metabolic mechanism by which the leading personnel could renew itself periodically as it did in politics and the universities.

In most of these respects, the history of British entrepreneurship differed somewhat from that of German industrial leadership. The contrast should not be exaggerated. Looked at in detail, the organization of German industry and of individual firms within it may turn out to have been not much unlike their British and even their French counterparts. Most of the smaller and middle-sized firms were family firms and were family-managed. Like most firms so managed they were more tradition-bound and more timid in their investments and their technological plans, than larger professionally managed enterprises.

It was in the latter that professional management found its lodgement; and, on the whole, professional heads of firms, even if and when recruited from the families of owners, were to prove more rational in their conduct of business, less bound by industrial tradition and hence also more prone to innovate, than the owner-managers of older type. That this managerial *élite* was always favourable and receptive to technological innovation was to some extent due to certain enduring features of the German social and intellectual scene. In the past, such was the German respect for university learning and science, so exalted a place did universities and professors occupy in social life, and, above all, so high were the standards of technical education (especially at university level) that the links between the laboratory and factory formed earlier and more easily in Germany than in most other European societies. It is therefore not surprising that when the development of electricity and organic chemistry prepared the ground for the so-called new industries, Germany should have been better able to take fuller advantage of them than the United Kingdom.

Since the last war German entrepreneurs continued to profit from some of their country's disadvantages. Her defeat and the utter dislocation of her industry on the morrow of peace and the compromising record of so many of her industrial leaders under Hitler, produced an even greater disturbance of her economic leadership than in the United Kingdom. A brand-new race of entrepreneurs appeared on the morrow of the war – mostly younger men compelled and determined to rebuild their own and their firms' fortunes from scratch. They set about working systematically and rationally; that they also worked harder than ever was almost certainly due to the tribulations of war and the challenge of defeat.

Political and economic challenges of the time also helped to change the composition and the managerial methods of larger enterprises in France. These undertakings, like their counterparts in Germany and the United Kingdom, were bound to be affected by the spread of corporate ownership and the march of industrial concentration. But some of the changes had been made necessary by political events and the international situation after the war. There was the creative response to defeat and to occupation; there were the subsequent responses to the opportunity presented by the European Economic Community; and there were also benign effects of the French Plan.

In some enterprises important changes resulted from their nationalization by the State. We have seen that after the war the bulk of the railways, most of the aircraft industry, the entire electrical and gas industry, some of the banks and several large individual firms like Renault, passed into the hands of the State, and their managing personnel were accordingly renewed. But the renewal was by no means confined to nationalized industries. The collaborationist record of some of France's industrial leaders during the Occupation compelled some of the firms to equip themselves (the compulsion sometimes came from the State) with new sets of leaders. Even more effective were the economic and technical compulsions of the Plan. We saw that the overall Plan was made up of investment plans and corresponding forecasts of output agreed between the planning authorities and individual industries. This system of industry-by-industry agreements not only gave the officials of the Plan great influence over the conduct of individual industries, but also compelled the leading firms to consider their resources and the organization of their production with a higher degree of rationality. This, in its turn, had its effect on the personnel of larger enterprises in the leading sectors of the economy.

France's new international position also had its effects. The formation of the European Coal Iron and Steel Community and of the Common Market confronted a number of French companies with new opportunities and challenges, such as greater exposure to competition from across the Eastern frontier or the possibility of combining with firms in the same industries in Germany and Benelux. The new confrontation often brought with it changes in organization, and change in organization often required a new type of man to lead it.

The number of these men and the range of activities they influenced must not be exaggerated. Small and middle-size industry continued to be run as heretofore. Professional and fully qualified executives were mostly to be found at the head of larger firms in the 'great industry'. That these men were able to contribute as powerfully as they did to the modernization of the country and to the expansion of its industrial output may to some extent have been fortuitous, for it was their good fortune that in the late fifties the economic weather in the country turned fair. Yet even if the balance of historical circumstances were shown – as it well can be – to have tipped in France's favour, her economic record since the war will defy a wholly material explanation. Her industrial investment grew almost as slowly as in the United Kingdom and Belgium and did not grow at all in the early sixties. If so, whence came France's remarkable industrial progress? Some of it can perhaps be derived from the working of the Plan; some could be considered as an 'overspill' of the great technological advances in other countries. But no allocation of credits will be right if it does not give full weight to the conduct of great firms by their professional managers of the *nouvelle vague*.

Our story of the 'new wave' of business leaders and of its effect on the conduct of business has been confined to the United Kingdom, France, and Germany since, with the possible exception of Belgium, the relevant experience of other European countries has on the whole been neglected by industrial sociologists and historians. Yet even if their experience had been investigated and been fully written up, our story and its moral would in all probability have remained the same. As far as we can judge, the managerial class taken as a whole continued in all Western countries after the war to enlarge the hold it had established over industry and commerce in the preceding generations. In doing so it apparently brought to the conduct of enterprises a greater degree of rationality and professional expertise and a greater proneness to innovate than those characteristic of owner-managed enterprises also taken as a whole.

However, much more than this has been claimed for professional managers. A number of writers, both those who approve and those who disapprove of the managerial régime, have read into it an historical significance far transcending its immediate effect on business enterprises, and have credited it with some fundamental social transformations. Even the more moderate claims on behalf of the new class frequently assume that it cut across the older social demarcations and thereby helped to bring down economic and social hierarchies. According to a more extreme view, their impact on society and social destiny went still farther. They ushered in a social revolution in the Marxian sense of the term, since they replaced or were about to replace the owners of property both in their command over personal wealth and in their possession of economic and social power.

How far are any of these claims justified? Did the rise of the managers alter the inherited order of inequalities in the distribution of wealth, income, status, and power? Above all, did the professional executives form a new social layer wholly distinct from the existing ranks of society? And did they take over or were they about to take over the plenitude of economic power and of political influence from older ruling classes? In short, did the spread of professional management to ever-wider ranges of industry and trade represent a new social order and a new phase in the development of the Western world?

The answer to these conundra very largely depends on which of the features of the old order we choose to focus our attention. If the main feature of the old order, its hallmark, were taken to be its inequality, then the growth of the new executive class would obviously not present itself as a revolutionary departure. All over Western Europe economic and social differences were narrowing down in response to a great variety of pressures. Inequalities in the distribution of property were being somewhat reduced (we shall see later that these particular reductions were neither radical nor rapid) as a result of higher popular savings, inflation, death-duties and taxes on high incomes which compelled some of the rich to live on their capital. The levelling of incomes, as distinct from property, went somewhat farther, but it was also the result of progressive taxation and of lower incomes from property as well as of full employment, social services and narrowing differentials between the earnings of unskilled and skilled or clerical employees. In this array of converging factors the post-war advances in the numbers and authority of professional managers and the underlying changes in the structure of enterprises figured hardly at all.

This should not be taken to mean that no social changes of any kind resulted from the greater size and importance of managerial personnel. We shall see further that, as the numbers of men in managerial positions grew, so the structure of industrial employment and possibly the mutual relations of industrial employees outside their places of employment also altered. These alterations did not, however, transform the social condition of the upper ranks of management itself. Neither the sources from which these ranks were recruited nor the stations of life at which their more successful members arrived, differed much from what they had been in previous generations.

In Western countries all managerial ranks continued to be recruited mainly from the different layers of the middle classes, to a smaller extent from among the technical, clerical and other skilled employees, and to a very insignificant extent from the families of unskilled or semi-skilled manual workers. So marked was the middle-class origin of the new managerial class that hardly any recent sociological study of industry fails to bring it out. Indeed, the ability and willingness to demonstrate it are so manifest that they threaten to become the recognition call of the industrial sociologist.

The call has come clearest from the United Kingdom mainly because British sociologists happened to be more sensitive to class differences than sociologists of most other countries. In their opinion the social origins of British managerial personnel, viewed as a whole, changed little. If results of a recent inquiry into managerial recruitment (mostly relating to Lancashire) are to be trusted, at least 43 per cent of managerial personnel in the early sixties came from the two highest occupational groups in the Registrar-General's classification, which formed only 15 per cent of the population. Moreover, the figures indicate an underlying tendency for recruits from the middle and upper-middle classes to become relatively more numerous. At first sight these figures would, by comparison with those revealed by inquiry into managers of Lancashire firms a decade earlier, appear to reveal a decline in the proportion of managers from the topmost grade in the Registrar-General's classification. But the figures of the later inquiry, when analyzed by age, suggest that in fact the proportion of managers (especially of top managers) drawn from better-off families was on the increase. Whereas in the over-55 group little more than 40 per cent of managers came from the top-income groups, about 48 per cent of the under-39 group came from this source. On the other hand, the numbers of recruits from the lowest of the Registrar-General's classes – that of unskilled or semi-skilled manual workers – which had always been small, suffered some further decline after the war.[1]

[1] R. V. Clements, *Managers*, Appendix 2, Tables 27 and 38, pp. 184 and 189; D. G. Clark, *The Industrial Manager*, pp. 24–36; also Acton Society Trust,

These two trends were facets of the same economic and social process; and, paradoxically, the process itself was part and parcel of what in other contexts is often presented as the post-war movement towards higher efficiency and greater social justice. The proportions of recruits from manual workers' families declined for the same reasons for which promotion to upper, and indeed to any, ranks of management from the shop floor became difficult. Industry required better-schooled cadres; and I have already dealt with the effect this requirement had on numbers of graduates in managerial posts. But educational requirements and standards were also rising at the lower points of entry into salaried employment, and education of grammar-school standard came to be expected from most new entrants. What with these expectations and with the actual increases in the output of grammar schools, the numbers of men with grammar-school education in managerial ranks grew during our period and appeared to be especially high among the managers in the youngest age group. The social corollary of this educational uplift was to reinforce the middle-class – be it even the lower-middle class – component of the managerial personnel. For in post-war Britain as before the war, the intake of grammar schools consisted mostly of boys and girls from the various layers of the middle class, including clerical and skilled manual employees of industry. In this intake the numbers of children of unskilled or semi-skilled workers grew somewhat, but not sufficiently to upset the overall preponderance of the middle-class offspring.[1]

The reasons why the working-class entry into grammar schools was so small and expanded so slowly are very many; and in so far as they were connected with the organization of British secondary school education, or with the cultural and psychological milieu of manual workers' families, they lie outside the scope of this study. But some of the causes were inherent in the very economic changes we have dealt with here. The decline in the proportion of recruits from manual workers' families may to some extent have followed

---

Management Succession, Table 5, pp. 8 and 22; G. H. Copeman, *Leaders of British Industry*, London, 1955, p. 101; *The Director*, January 1965, pp. 86–91.

[1] D. G. Clark, op. cit., Ch. IV; also A. Little and J. Westergaard, 'The Trend of Class Differentials in Educational Opportunity in England and Wales', *British Journal of Sociology*, vol. XV, December 1964.

from the decline in the relative numbers of such families in society at large.[1] Full employment and high earnings of juveniles may have strengthened the traditional eagerness of working-class families to turn their children into earners at the earliest possible date and the equally traditional reluctance to contemplate for them careers dependent on better or further education.

It is also possible to find post-war causes behind the one phenomenon which most observers would unhesitatingly identify as a manifestation of the inherited, and purely British, class distinction, i.e. the high and increasing proportion of public-school boys among managers, especially among their upper echelons. According to an Acton Trust inquiry, ex-public-school boys formed 10 per cent of the upper-managerial ranks and 25 per cent of the Boards of Directors in their sample of firms. Their proportion was also high and rising in the sample of firms covered by the Lancashire studies cited above. The implication of persisting powers of snobbery which these figures carry is undeniable. The men who selected and promoted younger managers obviously continued to share the traditional regard for the manner of speech and deportment imparted by public schools and for the qualities of leadership and decision which these schools were reputed to develop. The relatively large numbers of public-school boys in high positions also betrays the continued influence of nepotism at its widest, i.e. of family links and social connexions, in appointments and promotions.

Yet the surviving manifestations of class would not explain why the numbers of public-school-educated young men in higher managerial positions should have grown, since nobody has suggested that class distinctions and snob values were greater after the war than before 1939. Other, more recent influences must have been at work. In the first place, the output of the public schools had grown (it had been growing since the inter-war years). But what was even more important is that a far larger proportion of public-school boys sought business careers after the war than a generation or two earlier. Openings in occupations which in the past would have attracted most public-school boys – the army, civil service, and church – were not to the same extent restricted to the offspring of the upper-middle and upper classes, and for many other reasons

[1] pp. 302–3 below.

were no longer as attractive to such offspring as they had once been. The attractions of business careers of every kind – from bill-broking to bookmaking – for young men from the top drawer was a secondary characteristic of the change that came over English society after the war.

However, this, like the other explanations of persisting social inequalities in the recruitment of managers, will not and must not be allowed to, explain it away. The fact remains that the managerial personnel of industry, commerce and finance continued as hereto-fore to be drawn mainly from the middle classes, and that the proportion of men of middle-class origin was higher at the top of the managerial hierarchy than at its lower levels.

The British evidence of the persisting middle-class 'bias' of managerial recruitment has been recited at some length mainly because it has been more fully studied and more conspicuously displayed than continental evidence. But it would be wrong to conclude from this, as is very often done, that it was an exclusive peculiarity of Britain's class-ridden society. The same social bias will be found in all other countries (and not in Western Europe alone) in some of which it stood out more prominently and was slower to recede than in the United Kingdom. In France the sources from which top managers were drawn continued to be confined to the *bourgeoisie*, more particularly to families of businessmen, civil servants, and members of professions. The post-war improvement in educational opportunities may have raised the level of literacy and technical competence of managerial recruits, but could do very little to alter their middle-class provenance and composition. Some French commentators have recently pointed out that the entry into the higher ranks of business bureaucracy continued to be regulated by competitive examinations in subjects, such as Latin and mathe-matics, best suited to children from cultivated *bourgeois* families. So closely were the French educational requirements fashioned to suit middle-class environments that when, after the war, the École Nationale d'Administration was set up with the intention of attracting recruits from lower social ranks than heretofore, the bulk of entrants still came from better-off families.[1]

That the recruitment and social composition of managers in

[1] P. Drancourt, as in footnote 1, p. 248 above.

Belgium should have been at least as *bourgeois* as in France is perhaps not unexpected. What at first sight is more unexpected is that the entry into managerial ranks should have been marked by the same social stigmata in Scandinavian countries. In Sweden, in the forties and fifties, only 1 per cent of a sample of managers investigated by Carlson were sons of manual workmen, whether skilled or unskilled, and only 7 per cent were sons of farmers, while 92 per cent were drawn from families of businessmen, civil servants, and members of professions. Changes since the early fifties have been little studied, but indirect evidence suggests that they were very small; if anything smaller than in the United Kingdom. As far as we know, the situation and the historical evaluation were similar in Denmark.[1]

The social bias in the composition of business leadership and recruits to it, its strength and its persistence in the post-war world, appear to be curiously unrelated to what we are told of class divisions in individual European countries. What is even more curious, and offers unpalatable food for idealistic thought, is that a somewhat similar bias should during our period also have existed in the 'classless society' of the U.S.A. and in the Communist society of the U.S.S.R. Our information about the managers of Soviet enterprises is, of course, very scanty and not very reliable. But such as we possess leaves little doubt that the proportions of directors and top managers who had themselves begun as manual labourers, or were sons of manual labourers, though higher than in the West, was far from overwhelming and was, moreover, declining.

The mid-thirties witnessed important changes in U.S.S.R., both in education and in management, as a result of which the proportions of managers with degrees rose from about 26 per cent in 1934 to 46 per cent in 1936; and the proportions apparently continued to rise thereafter. (In metallurgical and defence industries they apparently reached 80 per cent as early as 1939.) As in the West,

---

[1] Sune Carlson, *Företagsledning och företagsledre*, Stockholm, 1941, pp. 99–105, 150–57; idem, *Executive Behaviour*, Stockholm, 1951, pp. 53–4; Gösta Carlsson, *Social Mobility and Class Structure*, Lund, 1958, pp. 49, 131–7, deals mostly with social origins of entrants to higher education required for economic and social promotion. The middle-class bias appeared to be if anything more pronounced than in the United Kingdom. Similar conclusions emerge from the Danish study by Kaare Svalastoga, *Prestige, Class and Mobility*, Copenhagen, 1959, p. 348; also pp. 212–13 and 368.

rising educational requirements appear to have made the entry into managerial ranks and promotion within them easier for children of skilled and clerical workers, and, above all, for children from families of managers and members of professional occupations, than for the offspring of peasant and unskilled workers. As a result of successive educational reforms and increased differentiation by profession and status, children from peasants' and labourers' homes were finding it increasingly difficult to qualify for places in the more sought-after university institutions. This trend was further stimulated by the Khruschev reorganization of education of 1958. Under the 1958 system, two years' work in industry or on farms were required from entrants into university institutions, but the requirement could apparently be waived in the case of better pupils. And local inquiries into educational standards in Soviet secondary schools reveal that the academic performances of children from better families were far higher than those of children from peasants' and unskilled labourers' homes. In other words, as in the West, the rising educational requirements for managerial posts, made it easier for the groups in Soviet society corresponding to the lower-middle classes and professional groups in the West to strengthen their hold over the managerial recruitment.[1]

We must not therefore exclude the possibility that stubborn persistence of what appears to be a social bias in the recruitment of managerial personnel may, to some extent at least, have been inherent in the very nature of managerial function. That the rising educational requirements for managerial positions in our period should have made it more difficult for men to ascend the managerial ladder underlines this 'functional' – as distinct from purely social – bias in the recruitment. Where social bias appears to have come in more directly is in the predominantly middle-class entry into schools from which managers were drawn. But we must not exclude the

[1] W. Lloyd Warner and James C. Abegglen, *Occupational Mobility in American Business and Industry*, Minneapolis, 1955; Mabel Newcomer, *The Big Business Executive*, N.Y., 1955; David Granik, *The Red Executive*, N.Y., 1960, Ch. III; H. H., 'Education and Social Mobility in the USSR', *Soviet Studies*, Vol. XVIII, No. 1, July 1966, pp. 57 and 59, and the Soviet authorities cited therein; A. Inkeles, 'Social Stratification and Mobility in the Soviet Union', in R. Bendix and S. M. Lipset (eds.), *Class, Status and Power*, N.Y., 1953; Gregory Bienstock, S. M. Schwarz, and Aaron Yugow, *Management in Russian Industry and Agriculture*, N.Y., 1954.

further possibility that even here – in the social selection of pupils for better schools – a 'middle class' or 'white-collar' bias was built into the very nature of the educational process. However, the educational process and its social factors lie outside the scope of this study and must, for our purposes, be taken for granted.

So much for the inequalities at the point of entry. In all European countries these inequalities persisted, and may even have got more pronounced past the entry point and showed themselves clearest in the standards of life and in the social affiliations of business leaders. French sociologists have made great play with the ease with which the executive leaders of businesses, whether they came from the wealthy middle-class families or not, merged with the French *haute-bourgeoisie*, shared its pattern of life, mixed with it and married into it. In the early years after the war some French sociologists entertained the idea – or was it a hope? – that the new executive class might form a social group wholly distinct in motivation and mode of existence from the capitalist *bourgeoisie* of old. Later studies have repudiated this belief root and branch.

The belief was never shared by English writers, but had it been avowed it could also have been easily repudiated. The relevant evidence has not been properly analyzed and written up, but it can be clearly observed and leaves little room for misunderstanding. The top layers of the British managerial class entered into the upper layer of society and shared the mode of life of all the other groups which made it up.

So when all is said and done, and all the exceptions and allowances for post-war changes are made, there still remains the fundamental fact of persisting inequality of incomes, social rank and status which the rise of the managerial class did not and could not overcome, and into which it, in fact, easily fitted. Our answer to the question put at the beginning of this argument must therefore be in the negative. As long as the old economic order is defined solely by the incomes and social demeanour of industrial and commercial leaders, then the new order was anything but a radical departure from the old one.

On the other hand, it can be argued that the definitions of the 'old order' need not be based solely on differences of income and on superficial marks of status. The top men's attitudes and outlook and the sources of their power, the circumstances of their rise, or their professional behaviour in their jobs, might well be more significant as demarcations of social systems than income levels or even the personal associations of men in their leisure hours. If so, we should be justified in attaching greater weight to the functional characteristics that distinguished the topmost executives from the general mass of wealthy men and, more especially, from capitalist 'bosses' of traditional kind. From the latter they differed as profoundly as their American prototype is said to differ from the conventional image of the industrial tycoon. In an attempt to reappraise the recent change in the economic system ('monopoly capitalism') two well-known Marxist writers – Sweezy and Baran – have, in spite of their ideological loyalties, taken pains to underline the fundamental difference between a leader of corporate business and a mere tycoon. The extent to which his activities were focused on the firm, the success and failure of the firm itself determined the career of a typical executive, his behaviour and his motives. The latter were, of course, strongly imbued with the pursuit of personal gain; and the firm's ability to earn higher profits and to grow were to a large extent appreciated and fostered because rising profits and growth brought higher managerial incomes. But allied with this pursuit of personal gain and sometimes over-riding it, were the concern with the success of the firm itself. Much as wealth was sought it was of secondary importance in determining the power and authority of the executive leader in his firm. In Sweezy's and Baran's view, wealth and membership of a wealthy and well-connected family helped a man to enter high managerial ranks; but they were no more than tickets of entry, not a means whereby an executive, once he entered a firm, could go on exercising his influences within it.[1]

Moreover, in European countries, perhaps more in the United Kingdom and in France than elsewhere, the managerial class had come to harbour a group of men who departed even farther from the typical image of capitalist owner than the average executive heads

[1] Paul A. Baran and Paul M. Sweezy, *Monopoly Capitalism*, N.Y., 1966, pp. 15 and 30.

of American business and, in fact, differed from most upper-class Britishers or Frenchmen in their general outlook, their attitude to economic and industrial problems and often also in practical and intellectual affiliations. In the United Kingdom it was possible in 1964 to name a considerable number of business leaders who regarded themselves as public servants and behaved accordingly. In France of 1964 they were frequently men whose ambition was to fulfil some very great task (*de réaliser une oeuvre de grandeur*). One would include into this category the then head of Renault, the head of the Caisses des Dépôts et Consignations, the Director-General of the Plan, and numerous other, mostly younger, men in positions of authority in great enterprises. For all the ease and comfort of his life, a man of this type would speak, write and appear to be motivated in a manner which set him apart from the conventional members of the *haute-bourgeoisie*, whether they be ship-owners of Marseilles, or cloth manufacturers of Lille, Champaigne-cum-steel magnates of the eastern provinces, or bankers of Paris. Judged by his income, his power in the city, or his leisure occupations, a Frenchman or a Britisher of this type was a fully fledged member of the upper-middle classes. Yet his presence and his influence in society and the features which singled him out from the general mass of the well-to-do were both new and unmistakable.[1]

Alternatively the economic systems could be classified in the old-fashioned Marxist way. If the old order were accordingly defined as a social and economic system wherein the 'ownership of the means of production' conferred on the owners individually the supreme authority in their firms and invested all of them collectively with the power to determine the volume and the course of economic activity and a near-monopoly of social prestige and political power, then the rise of the new entrepreneurs must also mark the end of one phase in economic development and the beginning of another.

The words 'end' and 'beginning' must not, of course, be taken too literally. The coming of the new economic order did not, and may never, bring about the wholesale takeover of authority by professional heads of large firms. Even if the control of all great enterprises had been completely separated from the ownership of

---

[1] Cf. F. Bourricaud, 'Le jeun patron', *Revue Economique*, 6, 1958.

U

their capital – and we have seen that this was not the case – professional executives might still have failed to acquire the monopoly of power in industry or an overwhelming influence in society and the State. Within individual enterprises their authority over the men they employed was limited by the powers of organized labour; their freedom of directing, planning and otherwise disposing of the use of material resources was circumscribed by the ever-present and omnipotent State and its planning bodies, by the corporate structure of companies, by the hierarchical organization of the management, and by the latent powers of shareholders, bankers and other providers of capital. In State and society their influence was very considerable, but as yet far from wholly supplanting the influence of other powerful groups, including those of the owners of great wealth.

Yet however much we deflate the 'new' managerial class we must not explode it altogether. Those who deny it on the ground that it did not displace the old capitalist *élite* but merely merged with it, disregard the inescapable heterogeneity of the ruling sectors of society. The literature on this subject has been growing very fast and is by no means unanimous; but for all its built-in discordances, it accepts, as it must, that the 'power *élite*' was always more mixed and more finely subdivided than the vulgar notions of capitalism or feudalism seem to imply. Was there ever a time when the possession of power in economy, society and State was as fully monopolized by the owners of the means of production as Marx is – mistakenly – reputed to have believed? The ruling ranks of European societies always were a composite group – an 'establishment' – composed of all their *élites*: the leaders of political groups, the more illustrious members of the professions and universities, inheritors of aristocratic names and positions, possessers of great wealth, successful entertainers, and of late years, also leading members of great trade unions. The fact that in the past, especially in the British past, the members of the 'establishment' were as a rule well-to-do, i.e. shared in the 'ownership of the means of production', is not very relevant. They did not all rise to their positions by virtue of their ownership; their ranking within the establishment was not determined by the size of what they owned; and above all they did not all participate in the control over the use and management of productive wealth. From all these points of view the 'establish-ment' was always a disparate mixture. Its true history, if written, would assign different weights to the different social ingredients within the mixture, and may also record how from time to time some ingredients weakened and others gathered strength. If so, the fact that the executive *élite* of business firms shared its authority and power with other ruling groups does not make its massed arrival on the scene any less significant. If, in recording its arrival, an historian does nothing more than note, as I have done, the great increases in the relative weight of executive leaders of firms and the correspond-ing decline in the relative weight of owner-industrialists, he will have every reason to notch up on his tally a further step away from the economic and social order of nineteenth-century Europe.

CHAPTER 12

The Managed

The changes at the top, in the commanding positions of industry and trade, were accompanied by changes in the lower ranks of employment. In general, industrial employment tended to rise less than the national product; and, considering the higher productivity of labour, this is not surprising. What may appear more surprising is that the numbers of wage-earners in the narrow sense of the term should have grown even less than industrial employment as a whole.

The two tendencies, but especially the second, ran counter to some of the most firmly held expectations. It was a commonplace of social forecasting in the early nineteenth century, by French socialists of the Saint-Simonist school and later by Marx and the Marxists, that the industrial wage-earning classes were destined to grow so incessantly as eventually to absorb the entire mass of humanity. The belief that all mankind would in the end be 'proletarized' underlay not only the Marxian expectation of eventual social revolution but also the fears of such anti-socialist doctrinaires as the statesmen in charge of Russian economic policy before 1890, or the conservative and romantic anti-capitalists of the Oastler–Sadler–Belloc tradition in Britain.

Both these hopes and these fears were to be belied by changes in the social structure and occupations since the late nineteenth century. As we have seen, some sections of the working population in traditional occupations, i.e. artisans and to a smaller extent petty traders, did not disappear as fast as they were expected to do. In addition, the numbers of those who could not possibly be classified as capitalists, and yet stood outside the wage-earning classes, were swollen by ever larger drafts of men and women in so-called 'tertiary' occupations: state functionaries, office clerks, teachers, or members of professions. As a result, the relative proportions of workers in so-called 'secondary' occupations, mainly in manufacturing industries, gradually declined, except in such countries as Italy or Denmark, which were rapidly industrializing during our period.

These reductions in the relative weight of the industrial labour force were matched by changes in its internal structure. In the early phases of the factory system, the industrial proletariat appeared to possess a number of characteristics clearly differentiating it from other working people. Less skill may have been required from factory 'operatives' than from mechanics and handicraftsmen unconnected with factories or employed in them in supervisory capacities as foremen and charge hands. But such skills as they possessed and, above all, their concentration in factories set them apart from labourers in wholly unskilled and casual occupations both within and outside the new industry.

The contemporaries, and in the first instance Karl Marx, noticed these demarcations very clearly; perhaps too clearly. The Communist Manifesto of 1848, in proclaiming the industrial proletariat as the carrier of the world's destinies, proceeded to exclude from its ranks both the foremen and the masses of unskilled 'lumpenproletarians'.

For a long time after 1848 this view of the proletariat and its composition continued to be held not only by Marxists but also by their opponents: the Russian 'populists', the German revisionists, the French and Spanish anarchists and the German academic advocates of the Welfare State (*Kattedersozialisten*). They may have disagreed with Marxist forecasts about the doom awaiting the peasants and artisans or about the 'proletarian' character of socialism or the socialist revolution, but they accepted the view of the industrial proletariat as a single group of partially skilled workers bound together by common conditions of work, similar functions in the economy and identical status in society.

It is highly probable that even in the early phases of British, Belgian, or French industrialization this image of the industrial proletariat did not wholly correspond to facts; and that even at that time the industrial labour force was composed of a number of groups and grades differing in skills, status and function. These differences were, however, becoming more pronounced, or were perhaps better observed, in the twentieth century. Historians were able to note and to record several deep-seated changes – some in the composition of the labour force in factories and shops, others in the position of the working classes in society at large.[1]

Let us begin with the composition of the labour force. A faithful historical record reflecting the variety of ways in which employment of labour changed in individual industries and plants has not yet been composed. Even when composed it may fail to reveal any overriding trends common to the labour force as a whole. But in a bird's-eye view appropriate to a general and purely preliminary study like this, two such trends can be vaguely discerned. One would be that of 'polarization': the process whereby employment increased at the two poles – the wholly unskilled and the skilled – at the expense of the intermediate ranks. The most obvious and most easily discernible signs of this process were to be found in those lower reaches of employment where semi-skilled workers were being replaced by wholly unskilled labour. The other tendency was confined to the upper ranks of labour. Man in these ranks not only grew in numbers but in doing so sometimes arranged themselves along a ladder of skills, functions, and status – longer and perhaps less steep than of old.

The changes at the lower levels of employment are better known than those at the higher levels. Further polarization of the labour force came as a by-product of the continued spread of 'quantity' or 'flow' outputs. As industry after industry turned over to mass production, its operations were subdivided, simplified, and standardized, and the modicum of skill required from its semi-skilled labour was reduced. The process was by no means recent. It was as old as the factory system itself, and was part and parcel or that subdivision of labour which Adam Smith described and eulogized in his example of the pin factory. In the early twentieth century it culminated in Henry Ford's conveyor-belt assembly

[1] E. P. Thompson, *The Making of the English Working Class*, London, 1963, *passim*: a treatise in the socialist tradition which, however, assumes the mixed composition of the British proletariat in the early nineteenth century. Similar assumptions underlie references to labour in S. G. Checkland, *The Rise of Industrial Society in England, 1815–1850*, London, 1964, Ch. 7, esp. pp. 216–19, and Sidney Pollard, *The Development of the British Economy, 1914–1950*, London, 1962, pp. 129–31.

and in the various systems of 'scientific' management: Taylor's, Bedaux's, and others. In industries so organized the main body of manual labourers were put to greatly simplified operations requiring from them little beyond the ability to perform fast and regularly a narrow range of movements and to fit into the pre-set rhythm of continuous production lines.[1]

Indeed, so far gone was this process by 1945 that in the subsequent twenty years it may well have exhausted itself. In some industries, such as the making of shoes and clothing in Germany and France, where mass production made its first rapid advances after the war, skilled and semi-skilled labour was still being replaced by narrowly specialized 'hands' engaged on repetitive operations. But in most of the industries which had gone over to mass production with modern methods at an earlier period, such as clothing and shoe manufactures in the United Kingdom or the manufacture of nuts, bolts and ball-bearings, cigarettes or stationery in the United Kingdom, Germany, France and Sweden, and in some branches of light electrical engineering, the subdivision and standardization of labour had by 1950 proceeded as far as the economics of quantity production required, and may even have shown signs of slowing down.

By that time experience, mainly American, revealed that in a number of industrial establishments further subdivision of operations might not bring additional economies, and that in some factories employers would have been well-advised to enlarge the cycle of operation performed by individual workmen. In the United Kingdom, inquiries into the effects of repetitive labour were conducted after the war by a number of academic and official bodies, and in the first place the Department of Scientific and Industrial Research and the Medical Research Council. They showed that some factories would have benefited from lengthening the 'unit of work cycle', i.e. from making work less specialized and monotonous.

There is, of course, hardly any evidence to show that these findings had as yet any marked effect on prevailing practice. In European countries very few firms engaged in conscious experiments in 'job-enlargement' comparable to those carried out in the

[1] G. Friedmann, Le Travail en Miettes, Paris 1950, passim, pp. 12–23.

U.S.A. by firms like Sears Roebuck, I.B.M., or Edison (Detroit). But if deliberate experiment and reform by precept were as yet rare, the belief in the virtue of unlimited subdivision of labour and the desire to extend it no longer appeared to be as widespread as hitherto. Among the managers of some sixty mass-producing firms covered by British inquiries very few were not aware of the economic and human limits of specialization, or not anxious to draw back from the limits already reached.

This new awareness was not, however, the sole reason why the trend towards extreme forms of standardized labour appeared to have slowed down. Some part, however small, must have been played by the new opportunities for automation; or by the related transformation of 'quantity' or 'line' outputs into 'process' production.[1] As electronic computing devices and transfer equipments became available or as a greater share in the 'value added' was assigned to plant and machines, many highly subdivided and standardized operations were, or could be, taken over by machines. The actual progress of automation during our period was still very slow. It has been estimated that even in the U.S.A. in 1952 not more than about 8 per cent of industrial employment was ripe for replacement by automatic machinery, and in Europe ten years later the proportion of output flowing from fully automated plant was probably little higher than that. The more gradual transformation of quantity outputs into 'process' outputs may have been somewhat more widespread. But however small turned out to be the numbers of men and women in 'specialized' employment replaced by automatic machines, they were probably large enough to hold back this employment or at least to prevent it from expanding very fast. Many a standardized line of production would, with further advances in the subdivision of labour, have toppled over into a wholly automated set-up or ripened for process methods of production. In this way the arrival of mechanical automata may have helped to slow down the proliferation of human ones.

Repetitive labour was, however, merely one component, albeit the most important one, of the unskilled labour force. In some industries, notably in steel, but probably also in construction, civil

---

[1] Cf. Solomon Barking in *O.E.C.D. Observer*, February 1965.

engineering, shipbuilding, or heavy engineering, numbers of unskilled workers were engaged in occupations demanding little more than hard physical exertions, such as digging and shifting of earth, or moving, loading and otherwise manhandling heavy materials or pieces of equipment. Of late years, however, the use of unskilled labour of this kind was being reduced by the introduction of mechanized equipment, such as bulldozers, excavators, cranes and fork-lifts, or else absorbed into the direct production lines. This process was under way in all Western countries during our period and has been described at some detail with reference to the steel industry. In a large French steel works where between 1955 and 1957 a new rolling mill replaced an old one, large numbers of unskilled labourers were eliminated. The total employment of unskilled men engaged on heavy manhandling tasks formed only 14 per cent of the labour force in the new mill, compared with 34 per cent in the old one.[1]

Considered summarily and as a whole, the changes at the lowest level of employment could thus be presented as one of continued polarization slowed down by an incipient tendency to reverse the movement and to reduce the numbers of the unskilled. Somewhat more recent than polarization, less reversible and more characteristic of the post-war era were certain transformations in the upper ranks of employment. Numbers in these ranks had been on the rise long before 1945, but the rise apparently gathered speed after the war. It was compounded of several ascending movements. The one best reflected in statistics of employment was the increasing proportion of salaried workers – supervisors and inspectors of every kind on the shop floor, office clerks, technicians, draughtsmen and salesmen, outside it. The change may not have gone as far in European countries as in the U.S.A., where the proportion of white-collar employees was estimated to rise from 31·1 per cent of the total labour force in 1940 to 43·1 per cent in 1960. Yet in most European countries, the numbers moved in the same direction. In the manufacturing industries in the United Kingdom, total employment between 1948 and 1962 increased by about 1,105,000, but of this

[1] Jacques Dofny, Claude Durand, Jean-David Reynaud, Alain Touraine, *Attitudes of Steel Workers to Technical Change*, C.E.P.A. Project 164, Institut des Sciences Sociales du Travail, Paris 1957, pp. 47–56.

increase 745,000 were represented by 'salaried' workers, mainly the technical and clerical personnel of industry, and only 360,000 by manual labourers of every grade. In 1948 the clerical, technical and supervisory grades accounted for about 16 per cent of total industrial employment, compared with 23·1 per cent in 1964. In Germany the 1961 census of occupations revealed that in that year salaried employees in trade and industry formed 23 per cent of total employment. Compared with the returns in the previous census, that of 1950, the numbers of wage-earners had risen by 47 per cent, and that of salaried employees by 95 per cent.[1]

These figures cannot, of course, be accepted as a precise measurement. In most of the statistical series available to us, clerical and supervisory and even the lower managerial grades are identified by the manner in which they were paid – monthly or annual salaries; and in some industries manual labour not usually classified as skilled could also be remunerated on a monthly or even annual basis, even if actual payments were made weekly or daily. At the time of writing, certain categories of manual workers in the United Kingdom – engine drivers, certain grades of manual employees in chemical works and in electric power stations – were offered 'staff' status which might result in their translation to salaried ranks. Similar translation had taken place much earlier on German railways or in municipal employment in Scandinavian countries. In general, however, these statistical distinctions are more likely to underestimate than to exaggerate the post-war increases in the non-operative ranks of industrial employment, since they do not take account of the men and women in administrative and supervisory grades who still continued to be classified and paid as 'operatives'.

[1] *Occupational Trends in the United States, 1900 to 1950*, U.S. Department of Commerce, Bureau of Census, pp. 6–7 (with projection to 1970): Manpower Report to the President. United Kingdom, C.S.O. *U.K. Annual Abstract of Statistics*, vol. 99, 1962, Table 154; vol. 102, 1964, Table 138. Cf. tabulation in D. G. Holland, 'Costs, Productivity and Employment of Salaried Staff', *Bulletin Oxf. Inst. of Statistics*, vol. 25, no. 3, 1963. For Germany, see *Wirtschaft und Statistik*, 1963, Heft 11, pp. 676 *seq.*, esp Tables 1 and 2. For France, see returns and projections to 1970 in Claude Vimont, 'Methods of Forecasting Employment in France, etc.', *Economic Aspects of Higher Education*, O.E.C.D., 1964, p. 233 (based on data of the Second Sub Commission of the *Commissariat Général au Plan*). For somewhat earlier Swedish figures Fritz Kroner, *Die Angestellten in der Modernen Gesellschaft*, Frankfurt, 1954, pp. 120–1.

The rising numbers of salaried employees were obviously related to most of the industrial changes described elsewhere in this study – in the scale of outputs, in the industrial organization and in technological standards. Increases in the scale of output and in the size of individual establishments often led to more than proportionate increases in office staffs to deal with costs, accounts, sales, and the planning and administration of production. Special provision for centralized planning and administration of production also followed from the more rational attitudes of modern management. Expanding firms, especially those embarking on quantity or flow methods of production, frequently detached the functions of planning and administration of production from the competence of foremen and shop-floor managers, and transferred them to separate services run from the centre and staffed by a specialized body of men. Establishments which happened to be enlarging their operations and going over to quantity production as a rule appointed specialists for the duties of inspection, storekeeping, or control over the progress and quality of output. Technologically advanced firms, especially in science-oriented industries, also found it necessary to equip themselves with research departments. And nearly all the modern or modernized firms in the engineering, shipbuilding, electrical, aircraft and motor industries had to maintain and to enlarge their design offices. In most of these new sections, offices, departments and new shop-floor functions the work was as a rule done by salaried employees, mostly clerks and technicians.[1]

This process, and the consequent growth of clerical and technical staffs, can easily be followed in the post-war record of all the expanding and modernizing firms whose history we happen to know. In one instance, that of Renault, the process has been traced

[1] *The Place of Foremen in Management*, National Institute of Industrial Psychology, London, 1957, p. 23; W. H. Scott, J. Banks, A. H. Halsey, and T. Lupton, *Technical Change and Industrial Structure*, Liverpool, 1956; Jacques Dofny and others, op. cit. p. 307 above, footnote 1, pp. 22–6 and 57. However how excessive this proliferation of clerks and supervisors could sometimes become is illustrated by the I.C.I. inquiry cited in the *Financial Times*, 18 November 1966. In this particular case the greater number of supervisors in I.C.I. plants, compared with some similar plants in U.S.A. were apparently responsible for the relatively higher productivity per employee in the latter.

back to the end of the nineteenth century, when the whole of the staff in intermediate positions between the employers and their 400-strong labour force, were three foremen. On the eve of the First World War the 6,000 workers were manning a 'Taylorized' production line, with developed planning and administrative sections. By the 1960s employment in the firm had undergone all the structural transformations we have listed here – a decline in unskilled occupations, and large additions to the number of operatives classifiable as skilled, but above all great increases in clerical and technical personnel.[1] Similarly most of the firms in Joan Woodward's Essex sample (both those which happened to have been engaged in quantity production and those in 'process' production) found it necessary to establish specialized sections in charge of production planning, inspection and other functions not hitherto differentiated from the general duties of foremen and shop-floor managers. In a sample of Scottish firms studied by a Glasgow team of industrial sociologists, the steel firm engaged in modernizing its plant was similarly enlarging its clerical, technical and supervisory personnel in response to the same requirements as the larger firms in Joan Woodward's sample.[2]

It is therefore not surprising that the numbers of white-collared employees should have increased more rapidly and been higher in the modern industries, the up-to-date branches of general engineering and in some of the services, than in the economy as a whole. In Germany in 1961 salaried employees formed between 15 and 18 per cent of total industrial employment, but 27 per cent in the chemical industry and 24 per cent in electro-chemical and engineering industries, compared with 15 per cent in textiles and 11 per cent in mining. In the United Kingdom administrative, technical, and clerical employees accounted for some 23·1 per cent of total employment in industry in 1964, but more than 35 per cent in the chemical industry, nearly 30 per cent in engineering and

---

[1] Alain Touraine, *L'évolution du travail ouvrier aux Usines Renault*, Paris, C.R.N.S., Paris, 1955. Similarly with the French steelworkers studied by Alain Touraine's team the increase in production required large, and apparently more than proportionate, additions to numbers of office workers and white-collared employees in workshops. There was more form-filling on the floor, and some foremen's jobs were subdivided: Jacques Dofny and others, *op. cit.*, pp. 21–3.

[2] J. Woodward, *op. cit.*, pp. 55–9.

electrical industries and 42 per cent in services, but only 13·5 per cent in textiles.[1]

Changes in the higher ranks of employment were not, however, confined to supervisory, clerical, or technical grades: they were to be felt well down the ladder of manual or 'operative' labour. Needless to say, the relative numbers of operatives in skilled occupations did not necessarily grow in every major industry or firm. They changed relatively little in such older industries as cotton and wool, railways, building, or the older branches of the distributive trade. What happened in a number of industries is that some types of skilled labour were replaced by others without altering the relative proportions of skilled and unskilled. With the reconstruction of the coal-mining industry in the Netherlands and West Germany before the war, and still more with the drastic mechanization of coal-mining in the United Kingdom since the war, mechanics, maintenance men and electricians replaced the older types of skilled miners at the coal-face. Similar substitutions but on a smaller scale took place in foundries and even in shipbuilding, where, with the arrival of welding and prefabrication, new skills replaced some older shipbuilding and boiler-making crafts without radically changing the overall proportions of skilled and semi-skilled operatives.

Even in 'modern' industries the relative numbers of operatives in skilled grades did not increase equally fast in every establishment. The numbers in these grades depended not only on the progress of modernization, mechanization, or concentration but also on the nature of the productive processes. On purely *a priori* grounds it appears probable that in firms going over to standardized quantity production the relative proportion of operatives on skilled jobs may not have increased and may even have declined. Whether these *a priori* expectations were borne out by experience we shall not know

[1] Cf. Solomon Barking 'Manpower and Management in Automated Age', *O.E.C.D. Observer*, no. 14, February 1965; *Statistisches Jahrbuch*, 1962, Table XI Ab (*b*). For the increasing numbers of salaried *cadres* in French industry and their sectoral distribution in the fifties, see 'Répartition du personal dans les établissements industriels et commerciaux etc.', *Revue Française du Travail*, No. 2, April–June 1959 (the largest rise was in chemicals), and *Wirtschaft und Statistik* as in footnote 1, p. 308 above; for the United Kingdom, see C.S.O.: *U.K. Annual Abstract of Statistics*, vol. 102, 1964. Table 138.

until the post-war evidence of such firms has been made available to students. Better known is the contrary trend in industries such as steel, where the introduction of modern methods almost invariably raised the relative numbers of skilled operatives, or rather of operatives classified and paid as skilled. The French study of the steel works, which we have cited elsewhere, makes it clear that in that particular case modernization resulted in increased employment of men in skilled categories. Whereas in the old mill the proportion of these men did not exceed 11 per cent, in the new mill it rose to 43 per cent of the total labour force. Apparently the same is true of the British steel works modernized after the war, even though the labour-hoarding proclivities of some British steel firms may have preserved more of the old structure of employment than the economic and technical requirements of new plants would have justified. The proportions of skilled labour possessing or claiming the same type of qualification as the skilled workers in the French new rolling mill were also higher in modern chemical, plastics, and petroleum plants. In general, the proportions of labour in positions classifiable as skilled was higher in modern industries, and especially in process industries, than in other branches of manufacturing production.[1]

However, post-war transformations in the higher ranks of industrial and commercial employment were not confined to their rising numbers. The very nature of skilled employment, the jobs to be done and the qualities of men doing them, were changing. The skills of skilled employees were not necessarily greater than before.

---

[1] In the United Kingdom the numbers of males classifiable as skilled in manufacturing industry in 1964 was 567,890, compared with 253,230 semi-skilled and 229,270 unskilled, and the proportion of skilled was highest in the three main 'growth' industries – chemicals, engineering and electrical and vehicles, in which it was considerably higher than that of the semi-skilled and amounted to more than a third of total manual labour. C.S.O.: *U.K. Annual Abstract of Statistics*, no. 102, 1965, Table 131. For skilled labour in individual establishments, see C. Durant, 'L'évolution du Travail dans les Laminoirs', *Revue Française du Travail*, XIII, 1959, p. 16, n. 1; Jacques Dofny and others, *op. cit.*, pp. 47, 22, 96; cf. also the article on 'Répartition du Personnel etc.' in *Revue Française du Travail*, no. 2, 1959, p. 48. In view of these figures it is significant to find that in the seventy-six firms in Joan Woodward's sample, mostly modern firms in new industries, unskilled operatives formed a smaller proportion of the labour force than in the national sample, but the author finds that the skilled were still in the majority. Why still?: *Industrial Organisation*, p. 129.

They were, however, frequently different: more specialized and departmentalized, more technologically informed, less practical and less rooted in tradition and routine. That new-fangled qualifications appropriate to technologically advanced and advancing industries should have been possessed by men whose job it was to apply and to design the new techniques – draughtsmen, chargehands and section-leaders in design shops or even fitters and erectors of machines – was not unexpected or remarkable. What was remarkable and characteristic of the trend was the extent to which new skills had come to be expected of men in supervisory and administrative posts, and in the first place of foremen.[1]

The changing character of foremens' duties has been studied somewhat more fully than most other aspects of employment. In my earlier references to salaried personnel I argued that the numbers in clerical and other office posts often increased because supervisory jobs were being redefined and because specialized planning and administrative services were budding off the erstwhile undifferentiated duties of foremen. From a foreman's point of view the change often meant a reduction in the scope of his functions and a greater degree of specialization. But it also required from him different personal qualifications and a different course of training and preparation. In the past, or in smaller and more traditionally organized establishments in our period, most supervisors and foremen were men risen from the ranks of manual labour by a long process of promotion. As a rule they received such training as they had by apprenticeship within the factory. Few of them possessed or had much opportunity for acquiring any general knowledge of the technological principles of their trade. Shipbuilding firms, the larger motor manufacturers and aircraft firms, some larger firms in civil engineering, some makers of railway equipment or of prime movers always employed draughtsmen and other technically trained men; but before the war even in these industries the numbers of men so employed were small, and none of them functioned as shop-floor foremen.

After the war the situation showed every sign of changing. In the

---

[1] The discussion of foremen here is largely based on *The Place of Foremen in Management*, National Institute of Industrial Psychology, London, 1957, *passim*, esp. e.g. pp. 59, 70, 131–7.

older industries the salient characteristics of skilled industrial employment were, in the main, the same as before the war. Even in the large and efficiently run wool works with 1,200 employees, investigated in the mid-fifties by the National Institute of Industrial Psychology, the ranks above those of shop-floor operatives consisted entirely of foremen with traditional craft qualifications and training. The foremen in the blending, warping and weaving departments, though no longer in the carding and dyeing departments, had received no general technical education and owed their expertise to what they had learned in the long years of their employment as apprentices and craftsmen. On the other hand, in another large firm investigated by the Institute at the same time, a modern steel-making establishment with 3,000 employees, the selection of supervisory staffs and their qualifications, was being radically reformed. The shift foremen and the sample passers in the melting shop and the foreman in charge of gas-cleaning plant in the blast furnaces were still of the old type: they had received next to no technological education and possessed very little general technical knowledge. But in the other departments, even where the foreman was still a craftsman of the traditional kind, the assistant foreman was a younger man versed in the technological principles of his operations and initially trained in the firm's laboratories. The general policy of this partciular firm was to make the lower supervisory posts into starting rungs in the managerial ladder and, with this object in view, to replace all their foremen old-style by younger men with good technical preparation and high standards of general education.

Other changes in the function, position and training of foremen and supervisors were linked with the same factors which were responsible for the proliferation of clerical posts. In yet another establishment investigated by the Institute – a firm of electrical engineers – the newly established planning and progressing sections took over from foremen the main decisions on the sequence of operations and the methods of production. With these functions, so to speak, put into commission, the calls on the foremen's expertise were reduced, but the numbers of skilled and technically trained men required for them probably went up.

Of these three firms cited in the Institute's study, most characteristic of the post-war trend in the United Kingdom were obviously the steel-makers and the electrical engineers. But towards the end of our period the more traditional set-up of the supervisory and sub-managerial ranks exemplified by the woollen firm was on the way out even in the textile industries. At the time of writing the main body of the British cotton industry was in the process of being reorganized and re-equipped under the aegis of three or four great combines. And, as far as the available information enables us to judge, the re-equipment of the spinning mills and weaving sheds was accompanied by a wholesale change in the management and supervision, such as a much enlarged planning, processing, costing and engineering sections with their preponderantly skilled personnel. On a smaller scale and in a less conspicuous manner similar changes were also taking place in the better-run firms in such conservative British industries as building and furniture making.

Changes in the nature of skills did not stop at the foreman's grade, and were also to be observed on the higher levels of manual or 'operative' labour. The new operative skills might not be always recognized and classified as such by traditional criteria. The qualities required of skilled operatives in the shearing, rolling, and finishing shops of the new French mill were rare and exacting, and justified the operatives' view of themselves as being skilled workers and the skilled rates of pay they commanded. Yet they might not have been regarded as skilled in the sense in which this term is applied to a fully qualified craftsman. As a rule they demanded the ability to watch a large number of automatic controls, to interpret accurately a whole series of abstract signals and to carry out rapidly and precisely multiple adjustments (there were sixteen of them per station in the shearing section) and, in doing so, to take responsibility for instantaneous decisions of great importance to the quality of the product and to the flow of output. These qualities, taken by themselves, were inherent in the personal, mostly psycho-motor, features of personality; they were not acquired by much specialized training. In the new mill the new skilled workers were mostly young men, who had received brief theoretical instruction in Training Centres (seldom lasting longer than one month), but had at the same time been subjected to exacting psychotechnical tests. As far as we can judge, these were also the abilities required of

x

skilled workers monitoring the equipment of fully automated plant in process works. All these men rose to their positions largely by virtue of their personal qualities rather than by the virtue of their acquired qualifications.

Largely but not wholly. In spite of the brevity of their specialized preparation the operatives of the new French mill, like the monitoring operatives of process works, had to be more lettered, possess a fuller understanding of technical processes and be better able to follow written and printed instructions than the operatives, even skilled workers, in more traditional plants. For this they needed, and had as a rule received, a superior general education. In the words of operatives cited in the French report – the qualities of skill had previously been derived from experience, but 'today they are obtained first of all from books.'[1]

Those requirements were even more essential for the mass of skilled workers in industries in which the function of the operatives was not confined to monitoring automatic plant or watching process dials. In a large majority of manufacturing establishments producing bespoke equipment – 'one-of-a-kind' – as well as in most large firms in the engineering and electrical industries – in fact, over what was the main area of industrial employment – skills were still the product of much acquired knowledge and dexterity. The knowledge and the dexterity were, however, likely to be different from the craft skills of old, and would in other periods or in traditionally run establishments still be regarded as hallmarks of white-collar occupations, such as the ability to read blueprints, to follow work-manuals, to understand and to use delicate instruments and to work to very fine tolerances.

These qualifications assumed both a higher level of general education and a higher standard of technical training. Educational

---

[1] S. Mallet, *La nouvelle classe ouvrière*, Paris, 1963; Jacques Dofny and others, as cited on p. 307, footnote. 1, pp. 34–40, and 76–83. Some 44 per cent of the skilled operatives in the new mill had been subjected to the aptitude tests or had passed through the *Centres d'Apprentissage Professionnels*. Seniority was no longer the main basis for promotion. Also *ibid.*, pp. 102–8. For comparable German and British experience, cf. Popitz and others, *Gesellschaftsbild der Arbeiters, passim*, and p. 44 *seq.*; W. H. Scott and others, *Technical Change etc., op. cit.*, p. 309, footnote 1, pp. 56–63; Olive Banks, *The Attitude of Steelworkers to Technical Change* Liverpool, 1960, pp. 44–8, 104–5. However, in the latter work the changes in the character of new skills is not directly brought into discussion.

levels were, in fact, rising in all western countries after the war, but their history lies outside the scope of this study. What concerns us more in this story are the more direct adjustments which were made – indeed had to be made – in the training of skilled labour to meet the increasing demand for skills and the changing contents of the skills themselves.

In all countries and in most industries within them the main road to skilled occupations lay through the apprenticeship system. In some countries apprenticeship had been extended to wider ranges of industry than hitherto. But in almost every European country it was rationalized and systematized. Provisions for formal instruction in technical schools or in part-time courses, whether in conjunction with apprenticeship or in substitution for it, were introduced or extended everywhere, and some such instruction had become an essential condition of entry into skilled industrial employment.

If the larger European countries alone were considered, the pre-war apprenticeship in Germany would appear more adequate than elsewhere. A period of training was required of new entrants in more industries than in the United Kingdom or in France, and com-pulsory apprenticeship of three years' duration was obligatory in most skilled occupations. Vocational schools and technical courses were also more numerous, were probably better run than elsewhere and were compulsory for most apprentices. Yet even in Germany some changes in the system had to be introduced. On the eve of the war the duration of compulsory apprenticeship was reduced, pro-bably in order to speed up the flow of new skilled labour, and further piecemeal improvements were made after the war. Full-length apprenticeship (*Lehrberufe*) was still required in some industries; but a shorter period of training was deemed sufficient for a large number of trades (*Anlernberufe*). Training in factories, combined with technical courses, was on the whole preferred to technical schools, even though the network of the latter was enlarged and improved. Training was, as a rule, wound up and crowned by exam-inations and diplomas, and in some cases led to further education in universities. In some go-ahead firms, such as Siemens-Schuckert, the entry into skilled ranks was also accompanied by elaborate psycho-technical tests.[1]

[1] 'Utilisation et développement des méthodes psychotechniques en Allemagne

The reform of old apprenticeship and its merger with newer methods of technical training was most far-reaching in France, though it did not result in a system as uniform and streamlined as in Germany. In France, the apprentice system with its roots in old guild organization, survived till the very eve of the war. After the Liberation the system was swept away in the wave of the more general economic and educational reforms. The technical section of the Ministry of Public Instruction established a network of Centres d'Apprentissage providing full-time courses, mostly of three years' duration, for would-be entrants into industry. They were, as a rule, conceived and run as a cross between technical schools of the conventional type and factory workshops. In addition, training centres were also set up by the firms, and some technical training of use in civilian life was provided by the army to recruits serving in its technical branches. Not counting the latter, the number of youths thus trained had by the end of the fifties come to exceed 200,000, and the bulk of younger industrial employees in skilled and technical grades would have passed through a training centre. As a result, observers of French industry in the late fifties were able to note great improvements in the quantity and quality of skilled and technically trained recruits compared with pre-war – improvements which were somewhat obscured from view from a continuing shortage of skilled labour.[1]

The corresponding changes in the United Kingdom were less systematic; they were, nevertheless, not as negligible as they are sometimes represented to be. By the end of our period the training of entrants into skilled occupations differed little in organization from the system operating in Germany and was not much inferior to it in scale. Before the war, the entry into most industrial crafts rated as skilled were either through protracted (commonly seven years') apprenticeship, as in engineering, shipbuilding, woodworking, building and printing; or else, as in the paper industry,

---

Fédérale', *Revue Française du Travail*, October–December 1959, pp. 38–40, 45; E. H. Marriott, 'Technical Education in West Germany', *B.A.C.I.E. Journal*, September–October 1953; *idem.*, 'Industrial Training and Education in West Germany'; *ibid.*, June 1954; Gertrude Williams (as in footnote below), pp. 185 *seq.*

[1] C. H. Dobinson, 'Technical Education in France', *B.A.C.I.E. Journal*, 1954; Gertrude Williams, *op. cit.*, p. 185; 'Utilisation et développement, etc.,' *Revue Française du Travail* as above.

the textiles and boot-and-shoe manufactures, through somewhat shorter and more loosely organized periods of 'learnership', during which the youths were expected to pick up their skills by observing the adults in whose company they worked. In both cases the conditions of employment and the quality of training left much to be desired; such as it was, the training benefited a relatively small and declining proportion of juvenile recruits to industry. In the mid-twenties it was reckoned that three-fifths of juvenile workers had not been apprenticed or formally enlisted as 'learners'. The stream of youths prepared for junior technical posts in technical schools increased (the numbers enrolled in them in the thirties probably approached 40,000, of which rather more than one-half were in junior technical and trade schools), but not on a scale that would have met post-war needs.

These needs were to some extent met by a general educational reform and by a number of piecemeal measures to improve the supply of skilled and technical labour. In these changes the main signposts were the Education Act of 1944, the setting up of the Youth Employment Executive in 1946 and the Education and Training Act of 1948. As a result of these provisions and in response to the demands of industry, some 40–45 per cent of youths entering employment at the end of the fifties were either apprenticed or otherwise trained for skilled jobs, compared with less than 20 per cent before the war. In engineering they were said to exceed two-thirds of the total number of entrants. The throughput of technical schools and courses also increased. The secondary technical schools established under the act of 1944 may not have achieved what was expected from them, since by late fifties they drew only 5 per cent of the school-leavers. On the other hand, the various provisions for 'further education' in technical subjects attracted large numbers of youths – more than a quarter of a million in the late 1950s.

By that time the larger establishments in engineering, metal-working, electrical, electronic and chemical industries not only took in much higher proportions of technically prepared entrants, but also provided them with improved training facilities while employed – frequently by means of part-time courses outside the factories 'sandwiched' into their working week. The White Paper on Technical Education of 1956 may have been over-sanguine in its claim that 90 per cent of youths under 18 employed in engineering industry were undergoing part-time instruction in technical courses. There is, however, little doubt that between 1945 and 1960 both the quantity and the quality of the technical training offered to industrial recruits, and the numbers availing themselves of it, were much greater than before the war. These supplies helped to feed the voracious appetite of post-war industry for skilled and technical personnel.

Shifts in the structure of employment and the choice and training of employees were bound to affect the ranking of men and women by status, authority, and estimation in factories, and they may also have affected their position in society at large. But what precisely these effects were is as yet difficult to say. Within factories authority, and still more status, were partly linked with earnings and functions, but were also charged with subjective valuations. They were, therefore, difficult to define, impossible to measure, and bound to differ not only from country to country but also from industry to industry and from establishment to establishment. All we can hope to do at this stage is to distinguish some of the more obvious ways in which changes in the labour force, considered as a factor of production (these are mostly the changes we have so far dealt with), were reflected in the layers of status and authority within factories and outside them.[1]

These reflections might at first sight appear both unexpected and contradictory. Thus on *a priori* grounds, with the continued polarization of industrial employment in establishments recently gone over to mechanized mass production, the traditional dichotomy of industrial employment – that of 'hands' *versus* 'bosses and managers' – should have become more pronounced. Yet in most British investigations such establishments were, as a rule, associated with an extended hierarchy of management and administration. The establishments in Joan Woodward's sample engaged in quantity or mass production frequently enlarged the cadres of their lower management and their office staffs, multiplied technical and specialized posts of every kind, and in doing so not only added to the

[1] *Vide*, Appendix Note 18, p. 369 below.

numbers of their salaried employees but also extended their chain of command. The study suggests that in large up-to-date establishments making bespoke, individually constructed equipments, and also in large modern establishments in process industries, the numbers of employees on non-manual jobs also increased; but at the same time the distinctions of authority, and presumably also differences of status, were less hierarchical than in mass-producing establishments. Yet in the French case of the new rolling mill, hierarchies of function of authority were not so much reduced as recast on a different scale. Whereas in the old rolling mills the unit of hierarchy was the team led by a foreman, in the new mills, with their centralized and specialized controls of production, the whole mill became a single unit of hierarchy. Within this enlarged unit the relations of authority and function became less clear-cut and more complicated than of old.[1]

The distinctions of status within factories were further complicated by post-war changes in wage structure. A couple of generations earlier men in managerial and supervisory ranks, even at the lowest, were paid considerably more than the men they supervised, men in clerical jobs more than manual workers, and skilled operatives more than the semi-skilled and unskilled ones. In more recent times, however, these payment differentials were narrowed by the effects of full employment, trade union action and the growing difficulty of recruiting labour for the less-pleasant unskilled jobs. In the United Kingdom the general trend between 1914 and the mid-fifties was for the differentials between skilled and unskilled rates of pay to become progressively smaller. On the eve of the war of 1914–18 the rates of pay of the unskilled were between 44 and 66 per cent of those of the skilled; by 1950 the rates of the unskilled rose to between 80 and 90 per cent of the skilled. In the late fifties and the sixties the narrowing down of differentials appeared to stop; in fact, the difference widened slightly in such occupations as engineering and building. Still, in 1965, the wage rates of the skilled and the unskilled were still little more than one-half the distance at

[1] J. Woodward, *Industrial Management*, pp. 200–1, 234; Alain Touraine and others, *Workers' Attitude to Technical Change*, O.E.C.D., 1965, fn. 10, p. 8: 'plant-hierarchy replaced the job-hierarchy'; J. Dofny and others, *op. cit.*, pp. 23–6; Ferdinand Zweig, *The Worker in the Affluent Society*, London, 1961, pp. 80–3.

which they stood at the beginning of the century. In Germany the corresponding indices moved in a similar way: approaching each other before the early or mid-fifties and parting slightly again after 1954. The changes were equally marked in the Scandinavian countries, but were somewhat more irregular in France. The French differentials, like the British ones, narrowed between the wars, widened between 1945 and 1950, largely as a result of legislation (the Parodi Law of 22 September 1945) and narrowed again under the collective agreements of 1950–51. Until the mid-fifties the rates of pay of white-collared employees also failed to keep pace with those of manual labourers. Their earnings also suffered from fewer opportunities for overtime and bonus payments. The same was also to some extent true of supervisory grades – foremen, overseers, and chargehands – as recent British and German studies have brought out.[1]

In fact, what recent studies have shown is that the most important differentials of grades which continued to set the clerical and supervisory ranks above the others (and, in steel works studied by Popitz's team, also the skilled operatives above the semi-skilled ones) were the symbolic marks of status and esteem – the prestige of being classified as 'staff', greater security of tenure, membership of pension schemes, longer holiday leave, pleasanter physical conditions or work, separate provision for eating and washing. Yet in the more up-to-date establishments even these marks of status were in the process of being whittled down by agreements conferring staff status and long-term contracts of employment on manual employees (this was done long ago on most continental railways, in post offices and municipal employments and, at the time of writing, was proposed

[1] K. G. J. C. Knowles and others, 'Differences between the Wages of Skilled and Unskilled Workers, 1880–1950', *Bull. Oxford Inst. of Statistics*, vol. 13 (1951), no. 4; K. G. J. C. Knowles and E. M. F. Thorne, 'Wage Rounds, 1948–1959', *ibid.*, vol. 23 (1961), no. 1; S. W. Ostry, H. P. D. Cole, and K. G. J. C. Knowles, 'Wage Differentials in a Large Steel Firm', *ibid.*, vol. 20, (1958), no. 3; D. J. Robertson, *Factory Wage Structure and National Agreements*, London, 1960, pp. 172–3. For comparisons reaching to Baxter's 1867 classification and beyond, cf. G. D. H. Cole, *Studies in Class Structure*, London, 1955, pp. 51–8. For United Kingdom differentials after 1955, *Ministry of Labour: Statistics on Incomes, Prices, Employment and Productivity*, 1964, no. 16, Tables B.1, B.7a and B.16. For the movement of French differentials, cf. F. Jacquin, *Les Cadres de l'Industrie et du Commerce en France*, Paris, 1955, pp. 116–17. For Germany, cf. *Statistisches Jahrbuch*, 1962; Tables XXI A (p. 517), XXI B.1, *a* and *b*, and B.2 (pp. 534–6).

by the electricity concerns and by the chemical industry in the United Kingdom), by company pension schemes, by longer allowances for annual holidays, by more generous redundancy schemes and by striking improvements in cleanliness, lighting, and ventilation in modern industrial plants.

Thus no single or simple picture appears to emerge. Yet the few snapshots of labour at work we possess display at least one common feature. We have seen that, except in establishments going over to standardized mass-production, the relations of men to masters, or of operatives to foremen in charge of teams, were gradually ceasing to be those of direct subordination. In factories, in which the controlling functions were broken up and distributed among a multiplicity of intermediate supervisors and functional specialists, a thick intermediate stratum formed between masters and men, the top managers and the main body of operatives. The intermediate stratum could itself be made up of several super-imposed layers of status and command; or else, as in Joan Woodward's example of plastics and chemical works, it could be a somewhat formless body of men sharing approximately the same technical qualifications and not clearly differentiated in function or status. In both cases, however, the intermediate ranks were much more numerous than the foremen and supervisors had been in the older establishments.

In other words, larger numbers of men could now regard themselves as being above the unskilled and semi-skilled ranks and attach high subjective valuations to their jobs and persons. The increasing numbers in more highly regarded ranks may explain why in so many of the establishments so far investigated an unexpectedly large proportion of men in manual jobs rated highly their prospects of rising through promotion: some 40 per cent of the younger face workers in the British coal-mine investigated by W. H. Scott's team, and comparable proportions among the German workers in the rolling mill investigated by Popitz and his colleagues, and workers in French and British steel works described by Olive Banks and Alain Touraine's colleagues. What makes these numbers unexpected is that their proletarian outlook, as conventionally interpreted, is supposed to carry with it the fatalistic acceptance of existing positions and status. This fatalistic mood may or may not have prevailed in the past; it may or may not have affected the attitude of working-class families outside factories (and more will be said about this presently); but it appeared to be far from universal among operatives (especially the younger operatives) in modern industrial establishments.[1]

Somewhat similar consequences may have flowed from the increasing numbers of men trained for skilled employments. We have seen that the 'new skilled' may not have possessed the qualities of high craftsmanship and practical expertise characteristic of skilled operatives in older industries and establishments; but they were often selected by stringent tests of personal aptitudes and also benefited from elaborate schooling of a technological kind. It is not therefore surprising to find that, whenever these men were questioned about their view of themselves and their position, they almost invariably revealed a highly developed sense of self-importance. As most of them were also younger than the average, their heightened self-esteem often went with disparaging attitudes to the older generation, to promotion by seniority, or to length of service as a test for redundancy.[2]

These attitudes may not have gone far enough, or spread to numbers large enough, to alter the valuations of status and personal self-esteem of the average industrial employee. For all we know, the men marked by these attitudes were still a minority and were, moreover, confined to the most modern or modernized establishments in large-scale industry. To this extent they were no more than marginal and premonitory; but as I shall have to repeat presently, this makes them historically all the more significant.

[1] H. Popitz and others, *Der Gesellschaftsbild des Arbeiters*, 1961, p. 273. Out of a sample of 600 workers interviewed 40 per cent (mostly skilled and of younger age groups) believed in the possibility of being promoted. Among re-rollers (*Umwälzer*), the percentage was 60 per cent. Nevertheless, in his conclusions Popitz insists, without citing figures, on the unshaken consciousness of proletarian solidarity derived from the difficulty of rising in the world (pp. 241–2). For the attitudes to promotion and estimates of its chances in some United Kingdom establishments, cf. Olive Banks, *The Attitude of Steelworkers to Technical Change*, Liverpool University Press, 1960, pp. 45–6, 51–3; W. H. Scott, Enid Mumford, I. C. McGivering, and J. K. Kirkby, *Coal and Conflict: A Study of Industrial Relations: Collieries*, Liverpool, 1963, p. 70. Cf. also Elisabeth Bott, *Family and Social Network*, Tavistock Publications, London, 1957, p. 172.

[2] Olive Banks, *The Attitude of Steel Workers*, etc., op. cit., pp. 105–7.

So much for the changing relations and attitudes on the shop floor. Whether the changes in function, status and self-evaluation at work were carried over into men's attitudes and relations outside their working hours and affected social ranks and relations at large is difficult to say. It is equally difficult to be certain that the connexion between social rank and status on the shop floor, where it existed, was one of direct concordance and not one of conflict and compensation. At least one British investigator has drawn a distinction on status 'conferred' on men by their role in their factories and the status 'assumed' by them in the social milieu in which they moved. In this view there was no direct relation between the two valuations, since men could strive for and achieve positions of importance outside the factories in order to compensate for their subordinate position and their inability to assert themselves at work.[1]

However, this argument, and the example on which it is based, may not be strictly relevant to the social problem which concerns us here. It relates to individuals in leading positions in new communities, not to the order in which entire groups arranged themselves in the hierarchy of social rank. And when it comes to the ranking of social groups, there is a near consensus among recent investigators that men in white-collar occupations, skilled operatives, the semi-skilled and unskilled workers continued to form recognizable layers of post-war society.[2] These demarcations were, however, bound to be affected by the post-war prosperity of all workers, by larger numbers in the higher ranks and by the narrowing differentials of earnings. On *a priori* grounds we could expect these post-war changes to reduce social differences within employed population, and above all, to narrow the gap between the families of men ranking as lower-middle class and those of manual workers. At least two other developments should also have worked in this direction. One was the higher and more uniform standards of schooling in all levels of employment below that of managers; the other was the somewhat greater importance of cultural

[1] G. Duncan Mitchell and Thomas Lupton, 'The Liverpool Estate' in *Neighbourhood and Community*, University of Liverpool, 1954, pp. 44–8; cf. Mark W. Hodges and Cyril S. Smith, 'The Sheffield Estate', *ibid.*, p. 138.

[2] Tom Burns and G. M. Stalker, *The Management of Innovation*, London, 1961, p. 149.

standards in determining the deportment and self-evaluation of families.[1]

These multiple changes were all inter-related and may have composed themselves into a veritable historical trend: a general uplift of people in manual employment, and an increase in the relative numbers of men likely to be thus uplifted. This composite trend has been noted by most observers, though it has not always been interpreted in the same sense. To some it appears as a movement of 'convergence' between different groups composing the working class: a convergence reinforcing the fundamental unity of the proletariat. To others the trend signifies the gradual absorption of manual workers into middle classes – their *embourgeoisement* or *Verkleinbürgerlichung*.[2]

Unfortunately, this difference of opinion has obvious ideological implications which have confused the debate and somewhat obscured the issues. On one side of the ideological divide will be found ranged the optimistic writers and politicians, who approve of the existing economic order and believe that economic and social changes in post-war Europe and the U.S.A. came near to resolving the main social conflict of the Western civilization. Their arguments may differ in detail, but all agree on several main propositions. The whittling away of the simple dichotomy of 'bosses' and 'hands' in employment led to corresponding reductions in the social distance between the middle classes and men and women tradition-

[1] F. Zweig, *The Worker* etc. (as in footnote 1, p. 321 above), p. 211; Colin Rosser and Christopher Harris, *The Family and Social Change; A Study of Family and Kinship in a South Wales Town*, London, 1965, p. 113; also A. H. Birch, *Small Town Politics*, Oxford, 1959, p. 39. The two last books emphasize the cultural preferences distinguishing working-class from middle-class households, some of which (brass bands *v.* serious music, bowling *v.* tennis) were traditional; others 'mild,' *v.* 'bitter', I.T.V. *v.* B.B.C.) were ephemeral. Newer and more significant differences in 'cultural' preferences among working-class families were those based on differences of education.

[2] John H. Goldthorpe and David Lockwood, 'Affluence and the British Class Structure', *Soc. Rev.*, XI, no. 2, 1963, represent the belief in the persistence of traditional differences of class and status tempered by some convergence between the lowest levels of white-collared employees and the topmost levels of manual workers. Cf. *idem.*, 'Not so Bourgeois At All', *New Society*, vol. I, no. 3, 1962. For a somewhat more uncompromising view of class demarcations, see J. W. Westergaard in *Towards Socialism*, London, 1964, pp. 79 *seq.*

ally considered as members of the lower classes. This hopeful proposition derives further support from what is believed to have been the post-war changes in standards of life and social values of the working classes. As their real incomes rose, so their patterns of consumption approached those of the middle classes. Hence the so-called *embourgeoisement* of workers, their assimilation to the values and the modes of behaviour characteristic of the *bourgeoisie*. The assimilation, on its part, could be expected to generate middle-class yearnings for social stability and corresponding political allegiancies.

On the other – the pessimistic – side of the ideological divide will be found the various groups of the radical left, mainly British and French, who of recent years have been endeavouring to rehabilitate Marxian theory from its failure to predict the evolution of modern capitalism. The burden of their argument is that post-war changes in industry and society did nothing to remove the fundamental social differences between capitalists and workers. The new executive class – so the argument runs – diverged little in its interests and attitudes from the capitalist employers of the classical type. The collateral changes in inferior ranks did equally little to transform their position in society. Above all, manual workers did not prosper and did not react to their prosperity in the manner implied by the term *'embourgeoisement'*. Great as may have been the improvement in average standards of working-class lives, it did not do away with fundamental inequalities of wealth and did not abolish poverty among the old and the sick. Even those workers whose standards rose highest, were not thereby lifted into higher social spheres. Manual labourers, however prosperous, did not abandon the modes of behaviour characteristic of the working classes; nor were they able or willing to mix with the middle classes on terms of social equality. As often as not, *bourgeois* tastes merely sharpened the sense of deprivation in families whose requirements were rising faster than the means of satisfying them.

The ideological difference thus appears to be very wide. Fortunately, it does not require more than the average dose of critical sense to observe and to dismiss the exaggerations on both sides of the divide. The 'optimistic' exaggerations are too obvious to delay us unduly. The commentators who subscribe to the *embourgeoisement* thesis frequently lump together two distinct social processes: the increasing proportion of the working population in categories traditionally classified and still classifiable as middle class, and the changes in the standards of life, values, and social relations of the categories of the working population still remaining in manual occupations. Obviously the former is easy to observe and difficult to misunderstand; but the latter, i.e. the changing social affiliations of manual workers, easily lends itself to wishful or simply unhistorical thinking. The discoverers of *embourgeoisement* sometimes imply that in the course of the past two decades the condition of manual workers in their mass came so close to that of the middle classes as to obliterate the old class distinctions. Any such implication would obviously be too wholesale and too premature to be true. Even if real, and however real, the post-war *embourgeoisement* of manual workers could be nothing more than a trend, a process still in its initial stages. What makes it significant to the social historian is the direction to which it points. But the actual transformation it brought about or could have brought about in the post-war decades could be no more than partial, and was, moreover, bound to be less in evidence within the main body of working-class humanity than on its more sensitive margins.

In the 'neo-Marxist' argument the lumping together of the two processes is more, so to speak, selective, but is perhaps equally misleading. Sociologists of this persuasion make every allowance for marginal changes among white-collared classes. They accept that the numbers of white-collared workers grew but insist that the clerical ranks were not thereby freed from the disabilities of proletarian life; on the contrary, they came to be subjected to new disabilities from which they had previously been immune. The difference between their incomes and those of the manual workers were being narrowed down; the mechanization of clerical work in counting-houses and the introduction of computers into the design offices and planning branches of firms was gradually reducing the men working in them to the position of routine operators of machinery, similar to that of the semi-skilled workers on the shop floor.

This argument, even if true, focusses solely on changes at the one layer of salaried employment – the lowest – where the objective conditions of white-collared lives may have approached those of the upper ranks of manual labour. It does not touch upon the ever-growing number of employees in better-paid clerical posts: technicians of every kind, public servants, men in the lower and middle ranks of professions. Families in these ranges approached, in their patterns of life, ambitions and self-evaluation, the prevailing *bourgeois* standards at least as closely as the lower-grades of clerical labour are said to have approached the proletarian standards. But what is perhaps even more important is that statistically these middle and upper ranges of white-collared workers may turn out to have grown faster than the clerical employees threatened with proletarization.

Where the neo-marxist argument is most insensitive to marginal changes and thus least historical is in its treatment of the social relations and attitudes of manual workers. This treatment carries most weight in so far as it implies a clear distinction between material well-being and social relations. A neo-marxist should have no difficulty in showing how naïvely determinist is the hope that increased prosperity of manual workers would necessarily and immediately transform their social values and attitudes. Where his argument appears to be more questionable is in its insistence on the immutable peculiarities of working-class society and of customary deportment of families within it. This insistence obviously follows from the traditional Marxist definition of the proletariat (of which, we are now told, Marx was himself wholly innocent) as a largely uniform social mass set apart from the rest of humanity. Its unity and its 'apartheit' are supposed to derive from its subordinate place in production, from its divorce from the ownership of capital and from its inability to share in the direction of the capitalist economy and of capitalist enterprises. It is not within the powers of working-men to lift themselves by their personal efforts from the condition in which every one of them individually and their class collectively find themselves. Such improvements in their conditions as they can hope for are possible only as a result of improvements in the common lot of all proletarians, and could be achieved only by collective class action. Hence the sense of common class interest and common destiny, which is further reinforced by the presence of a common antagonist in the shape of the capitalist owner-boss and the *bourgeois* State. Hence also the essential sameness of social attitudes in all the grades and layers of the working classes.

These primary characteristics of proletarian physiognomy are supposed to reveal themselves in a number of secondary features of proletarian deportment. We are told that working-class families lead existences at once more communal and more so-to-speak 'atomized' than those of middle-class families. Political and trade-union organization in defence of class interests, and neighbours and relatives for companionship and for succour in time of need are the two typical and only forms of proletarian association. A working-class family does not readily form or join clubs or associations through which middle classes prefer to organize their leisure. They do not 'visit' or 'entertain', do not share in cultural pursuits of the middle classes, do not try to excel each other in visible signs of success, prosperity or comfort.

The image thus conceived is, as it is meant to be, an idealized construction; and this may be one of the reasons why it has not been found fully reproduced in any of the working-class environments so far studied. But another reason is that it is so over-generalized as to fail to reflect the action of recent social and economic change. It appears to be highly insensitive to phenomena on the historical margins. One or two recent studies have gone far in admitting that during our period the middle-class modes of existence and even middle-class values made great inroads into some sections of the manual workers. At the same time, however, they tell us that these inroads were not of great social significance, since they affected most, or were perhaps confined to, the younger, more skilled, better-paid and better-housed families of workers in more progressive industries. They characterized not the average manual worker, not manual labour *en masse*, but only its marginal elements.

A directly opposite view would, however, make better sense. Historians in search of social trends and tendencies may find some of the 'marginal' changes more revealing than the 'representative samples', 'modes' or 'medians' appropriate to the static study of society. From the point of view of historical changes the disturbances on the social peripheries directly exposed to historical forces are more significant than the conditions in the main mass of humanity so far unaffected by them. Historians will therefore do well to focus their attention on those very fringes which so many writers are inclined to dismiss. For it is on these fringes that incipient transformations indicative of recent trends are most likely to be found.

One such incipient change appeared to occur on the demographic margin, i.e. in the social position of the younger generations in salaried and wage-earning employments. The post-war change characteristic of the younger generation of workers which a casual observer would find easiest to notice was that of superficial deportment of the youngest age groups: their dress, hair-styles and favourite pastimes. Judged by these superficial signs, a large proportion of urban youths of working-class affiliations and a somewhat smaller but still considerable proportion of middle-class youths appeared to merge into a single mass of 'modern youth'. Within that mass, the traditional class demarcations seemed to be overlaid by similarities of outward appearance and conduct. And what is perhaps even more significant is that most of the manifestations of the new deportment spread not from the middle-class downward but originated in the working-class milieu of large cities.

The upward spread of behaviour patterns may to some extent have been due to the remarkable rise in material standards of young workers. In all European countries young men and women in manual occupations were very much better off than their opposite numbers had been before the war, and perhaps also better off than manual workers in older age groups. European 'juveniles', unlike their American contemporaries, were fully employed; such unemployment as there was, hit mainly the over-forties. The 'participation rate', i.e. relative numbers in gainful employment, was very much higher among the unmarried women than among married ones. Above all, the burdens of maintaining families weighed less, or not at all, upon the younger generation. As a result, young working-men and women, even in the age groups and occupations in which juvenile wages were lower than those of adult workers, had more than their elders to spend on those conspicuous inessentials in which the new deportment found its material expression: clothes, cigarettes, records, entertainments and travel. Their needs and tastes had come to dominate the large and growing supply of goods serving young consumers of all classes.

Y

The *rapprochement* in outward patterns of behaviour between the very young of different classes may also have sprung from less material causes. The radical change in accoutrements of the young may have symbolized their wish to set themselves apart from their elders more definitely and conspicuously than in the past; and the wish, common to the young of all classes, brought also a common pattern of conspicuous behaviour.

However, great as may have been the symbolic significance of outward appearances and patterns of conduct, we must be careful not to attach too great an historical importance to them, for we are not yet in a position to know how enduring they were and how important were their social consequences. From the point of view of younger workers, much more permanent and more deeply rooted appear to have been the effects of the post-war changes in education. The spread of education to ever-widening ranges of operatives and its effect on demarcations of grades within factories has been noted by most students of modern industry and has been described in an earlier part of this chapter. It is because high standards of schooling and literacy were expected of skilled workers and supervisors that the better-educated men among them were getting more numerous and that the average age of skilled workers was getting considerably lower in modern and modernized factories than in the older ones. They were more frequently than before 'youngsters with certificates'. What is even more significant is that their ranking as skilled labour depended not so much on their official classification by wage scales or functional categories but on their own estimation of their worth as individuals and workers.

This estimation and the qualities of personality and education on which it was based were bound to have a corrosive effect not only on the inherited social distinction in factories but also on class divisions in society at large. That their working-class parents should have helped to educate their children for advancement in life could perhaps be in itself be regarded as a breach in what we are told is a traditional working-class view of life's prospects and of a proper preparation for them. But still wider breaches in traditional class attitudes were bound to result from relayed effects – the 'feedback' – of improved education and of changed character of training for skilled occupations.

One of the most obvious 'feed-back' effects of improved education followed from the promotion of the better educated young offspring of working-class families (mostly those of skilled workers) into stations above those of their parents. Though well observed, this movement of promotion has not yet been sufficiently studied or analyzed. So far sociologists have discussed it merely to account for the changes in the post-war *élite*; and the discussion of the latter has been largely concentrated on the prospects and threats of meritocracy, i.e. the arrival at the top positions in society of men propelled upwards by intellectual tests and academic records.

The prospect or the threat of meritocracy is supposed to have been that of deepening class cleavages. In swelling the flow of working-class youths into superior occupations, promotion by educational test threatened to deplete the working classes of their abler and more ambitious elements. Some commentators have construed an even more awesome threat – that of personal deterioration in the human quality of families remaining in manual occupations. By draining away all able and ambitious youths from these families educational progress may have begun to create new class distinctions based on fundamental differences of intellect and character; and may even threaten to convert social differences into genetic ones.[1]

Fortunately, in our period these threats did not loom very large. That opportunities of promotion into skilled and white-collared occupations were bound to reduce the intellectual level of those who had not made use of these opportunities is not borne out by some recent statistics of the I.Q.s of children of middle-class and manual workers' families. On the whole, it appears most unlikely that the differences in human quality between social classes now discernible in Western Europe could have been brought about by recent promotions across class frontiers. The permanent effects of these promotions must be judged in relation to the entire reservoir of ability in the working classes; and we are told that this reservoir was probably too large to be depleted by such recruitment into higher groups as took place in the twenty years between 1945 and 1965.

[1] An early and a moderate attempt to sketch the meritocratic prospects of society will be found in Michael Young, *The Rise of Meritocracy*, London, 1961. For some figures of promotions (especially of sons of skilled workers), see F. Zweig's sample (*op. cit.*, pp. 143–4).

Above all, the promotion of abler recruits into manual occupations must not be judged unrelated to other social trends. Even if it could be shown that, measured in absolute numbers, the flow of abler boys and girls into manual occupations declined, this would not necessarily signify that the relative number of abler youths entering into these occupations in fact altered. For we have seen that the proportion of manual occupations in the employed population as a whole was itself on the decline.

Moreover, in society, taken as a whole, the levelling action of social mobility was probably great enough to compensate for the polarizing effects of meritocracy. This action could manifest itself in many forms, but the forms most familiar to unprofessional observers were, first, the proliferating numbers in the intermediate class layer, i.e. in the lowest white-collar and the topmost operative grades; secondly, the increasing recruitment into most levels of employment of men trained for their jobs by school-based and book-fed methods; and finally, the formation of mixed families with members in both manual and middle-class occupations. The first two manifestations have already been dealt with; the third is implied in them and need not detain us too long.

If literary sources, as well as the few sociological surveys so far available, are to be trusted, a belt of mixed families had always lain along the inter-class frontier. The belt was not wide enough to cover the higher levels of middle-class families; but in the lower reaches of the middle classes mixed families were always to be found. Some of the 'mixed' families resulted from mixed marriages: those of young men and women on both sides of the class line. Whether such marriages became more frequent after the war we are not told. But what with the greater uniformity of educational standards and the larger numbers of skilled workers' children in grammar schools and the spread of common tastes and pastimes among the young of all classes, young people of different class origins should have been thrown together, and presumably married, more frequently than before the war.[1]

---

[1] Jerzy Berent, 'Social Mobility and Marriage', in D. V. Glass (ed.) *Social Mobility in Britain*, London, 1954, pp. 324 *seq.* esp. p. 337; Josephine Klein, *Samples of English Culture*, London, 1965, vol. II, pp. 550; Colin Rosser and Christopher Harris, *The Family and Social Change* (as in footnote 1, p. 326 above), pp. 98, 245–6. According to a French survey cited by Alain Touraine, the increase

Superior education and social promotion resulting from it could, moreover, add to the numbers of mixed families irrespective of the cross-class marriages. Highly impressionistic as the evidence is, it strongly suggests that young men and women of working-class origins who entered into the lower ranks of the civil service, the clerical personnel of factories and the junior technical occupations in industry and were thereby socially promoted, maintained some ties with their parental families. And in view of the rising numbers of men and women in these employments, it would also be reasonable to assume that mixed families with personal contacts across class lines were also on the increase.[1]

The other 'marginal' changes were sectoral. They were to be observed mainly in the new and renovated industries and to some extent in the service occupations. We have seen that in these industries and occupations the structure of employment changed most radically, and that white-collared or salaried employees were most numerous. The few surveys so far made also leave the impression that the more highly paid, better-housed and, as a rule, more highly skilled employees of modern and progressive firms moved furthest away in their manner of life and perhaps also in their social values from proletarian standards.

In addition, we are told that the position of junior technicians and supervisors in some of the more advanced establishments frequently deviated from that typical of other large establishments. Joan Woodward draws a clear distinction between the duffle-coated administrators and managers in the 'process' firms (we have seen that these were the technologically most advanced establishments in her sample) and their black-suited counterparts in 'batch' production. Among the former, similar educational background, common experience in training and the absence of a clearly stratified functional hierarchy prevented the emergence of social distinctions corresponding to different levels of management. Hence the prevailing sense of social homogeneity and free and equal contacts outside

in tertiary occupations in France also led to a corresponding decline in the relative numbers of families composed entirely of manual employees of industry: 'Management and Workers', *Daedalus*, March, 1962, p. 316.

[1] Michael Young and Peter Wilmott, *Family and Class in a London Suburb*, London, 1960, pp. 142–3; Colin Rosser and Christopher Harris, *op. cit., passim*; Elisabeth Bott (as in footnote 1, p. 324 above), p. 144.

working hours. But, according to Joan Woodward, the greater harmony and equality were not confined to supervisory and managerial ranks. In establishments engaged in process outputs and in other forms of automated output wage policies were as a rule so liberal, the ratio of manual workers to managers, technicians and supervisors so low and communications on the shop floor so informal, that personal relationships between the managers and the managed blurred 'the edges of role relationships' and thereby prevented the functional inequalities and conflicts in personal and social relations.[1]

By implication most neo-Marxists recognize the special characteristics of employment in the technologically advanced industries. But in their eyes this concentration of 'deproletarized' workers in new and progressive establishments disqualified them from being considered as fully representative of their class. Why this should be so is difficult to understand. In view of the role which new and innovating industries played in the economic and technological advances in post-war Europe, historians in search of characteristic social trends should have addressed themselves to these industries first. That manual workers in these industries were less numerous than the mass of manual employees in the older and traditional occupations is from this point of view immaterial. Their relative numbers grew after the war, and the prophets are probably right in expecting their relative numbers to grow still more in the foreseeable future.

The third factor of deproletarization was residential. Like the other two factors it was most effective and easiest to recognize on the margins of society, among those members of the working classes who moved after the war into new and superior homes, more especially in new towns or up-to-date housing estates. The social effects of modern housing may at times be difficult to distinguish from those of higher incomes or younger age structure, since a large proportion of the inhabitants of better working-class quarters in Germany or the new towns in the United Kingdom belonged to the more highly paid younger workers in modern industries. However, some of the characteristic features of new housing estates stand out

[1] J. Woodward, *Industrial Organization*, pp. 49, 198–201, 229, 236.

quite clearly and have as a rule been taken for granted by most observers and students.

Unfortunately, the resettlement and rehousing of working-class families in continental countries have not been studied in much detail. Moreover, in most continental countries a large proportion of people on new housing sites were foreign immigrants; and for these reasons the social consequences of rehousing, even if known and understood, might turn out to be too complex to illuminate the problems of social change which occupy us here. We are, therefore, thrown back on such little information as can be obtained from the small number – a mere baker's dozen – of recent British studies of working-class neighbourhoods, old and new. And as the scope, chronology, and character of British housing history are markedly different from those abroad, the conclusions emerging from British evidence may not apply to recent social history of other European countries, especially that of France and Italy.

As it is, even taken by itself, the British evidence will not support any categorical verdicts. In analyzing it, we must distinguish the effects of mere migration, i.e. of the moving of families out of their old environment, from those of better housing in new locations. In most of the United Kingdom studies the two phenomena are apt to be confused; and the confusion makes the passing of verdicts all the more difficult.

The effects of actual removal and resettlement were to a large extent negative, since the most immediate result of transferring a family was to break the links which hitherto bound it into the network of working-class society. Moreover, in so far as families in older working-class neighbourhoods were frequently related by birth or marriage to other families in the vicinity, the removal to new habitations often disrupted not only the communal ties of neighbourhood but also the kinship ties of the extended family. The working-class household on the new sites, shorn of all its ancient links with larger social groups, was thus turned in upon itself.[1]

These purely negative consequences of resettlement may have been somewhat overdramatized. Some later studies suggest that the

[1] M. Young and P. Wilmott (as in footnote 2, p. 335 above), pp. 97 *seq.*; Colin Rosser and Christopher Harris, pp. 57–8.

process of disassociation was neither universal nor long-lasting. Where neighbourhoods were removed whole, or in large groups (this happened in slum clearances, as on the 'Sheffield Estate', or in wartime evacuations, as on the 'Liverpool Estate') the families of new settlers soon retied in their new habitations the links with neighbourhood and kith. But what is even more important was the effect of time. Some of the earlier sociological inquiries caught the new settlers in their initial stages of resettlement, long before they had taken root in their new communities. As Raymond Williams has pointed out, their position at that time was not much different from that of the working-class families in the first half of the nineteenth century soon after they had moved to the newly industrialized and urbanized areas. Observed after an interval of several decades, the new, i.e. twentieth century, communities of working-class families, such as Dagenham, bore few signs of that disassociation which Young and Wilmott found among Bethnal Green families recently settled in the green belt. Even kinship ties – much as they may have suffered from the distances which now separated related households – were not wholly broken. And in any case, in the course of time, sons and daughters, who had grown up, married and settled in the new localities, created fresh kinship ties in replacement of the old.[1]

Against the purely disruptive effects of migration, great or enduring as they may have been, we must set the positive effects of new housing. The most obvious effects were those of the material and largely external characteristics of the new houses and the lives led in them. Working-class families on the new housing estates in the United Kingdom, in Germany and in Scandinavia frequently created for themselves a material framework and a superficial design for living – furniture, appliances, arrangement of rooms and styles of decoration – which resembled the material background of families on the *bourgeois* side of the class frontier. Both appeared to follow the same post-war standards of refinement and to conform to the same patterns of comfort and propriety. In British, Scandinavian or German suburbs and housing estates the homes of young

---

[1] Peter Wilmott, as in footnote 2, p. 340 below, *passim*; Mark W. Hodges and Cyril S. Smith, 'The Sheffield Estate', in *Neighbourhood and Community*, Liverpool, 1954, pp. 79 *seq.*; Raymond Williams, *The Long Revolution*, London 1961, pp. 337 *seq.*

marrieds in clerical, technical and skilled manual occupations would often boast of the same accoutrements, the same type of furniture, the same range of new-fangled appliances.

We cannot, of course, assume that these cross-class similarities of house-and-garden were closely woven into the social fabric. As some sociologists have rightly insisted, the possession of identical hardware, and even the adherence to the same domestic routines, could not by themselves submerge the other distinctions of class and status. On the other hand, a change in the outward and purely material equipment and arrangement of homes may have resulted from changed family relations, or made such changes necessary. In some cases it may also have signified a willingness and an ability to assimilate the mode of life hitherto characteristic of other, somewhat higher, social ranks. In these cases, the levelling of the external and material patterns of existence may have helped to overcome, or at any rate to lower, the barriers preventing mixture and communication across the older class frontiers.[1]

It would, of course, be an exaggeration to conclude that the new working-class families beautified and equipped their homes in the middle-class manner mainly in order to lift themselves into middle-class positions. Tidier and prettier homes could be appreciated for their own sake. As for appliances, it is important to remember that they were of some practical use. In Mr Lockwood's words, a washing machine was after all a washing machine. At the same time, it would be wrong to neglect the changes in the inner core of the family, which new homes symbolized, and the social effects they could produce. Several recent observers have noted the changed husband-wife relation in better-educated and more prosperous young working-class families on new estates. The wife was no longer the household drudge and conscripted child-bearer; the husband was no longer a mere bread-winner leading a largely absentee, pub-centred existence. The characteristic pattern of newer and younger households was the husband-wife companionship in which the wife, frequently

---

[1] Dennis Chapman, *The House and Social Status*, London, 1955, Ch. VII and *passim*. On the causative pattern of social contacts and the quality of accommodation, see Winifred M. Whiteley, 'Littletown-in-Overspill', in Leo Kuper (ed.), *Living in Towns*, London, 1953, p. 211; Mark Hodges and Cyril Smith, *op. cit.*, p. 137. However, cf. J. W. Westergaard (as in footnote 2, p. 326 above), p. 54.

herself a bread-winner, had a position not much different from that of her husband, and shared in some of his after-work interests and company. On his part, the husband spent more time at home, not only on various do-it-yourself chores but also in obedience to the daily routine of the household, be it watching television or the tending of the garden. In this way, the trim and well-kept-up home on the modern housing estate could reflect some of the changed shape of the family itself.[1]

The house may also have expressed the new view of the family's position in society. Middle-class appearances could represent not so much the hankering after a higher social status, but a higher assessment of the actual status, material, cultural and social, of the working-class household. And this new assessment tallied well with the young skilled workers' high self-evaluation at work. It explains also why these families did not appear to find social contacts with neighbours classifiable as lower-middle class as difficult or as unpalatable as they were (or are said to have been) to the members of older and more traditional working-class households.

This does not mean that these cross-class contacts were very frequent, even among the younger families in the new neighbourhoods. The reason for this was the uniform social composition of the new housing estates and new towns in which the overwhelming majority were drawn from among manual operatives. Now and again, the reluctance to mix was evinced most clearly by the few superior middle-class families anxious to keep their distance. But in nearly all the new communities so far surveyed a considerable proportion of working-class families shared some of their activities and concerns with the few younger middle-class families in their midst.[2]

[1] Michael Young and Peter Wilmott, *Family and Kinship in East London*, pp. 3–14: 'In place of the traditional working-class husband as mean with the money as he was callous in sex has come the man who wheels the pram on Saturday mornings.' C. Rosser and C. Harris, *op. cit.*, pp. 183–4. Even pubs adjusted their character to the new family; *ibid.*, p. 185.

[2] J. H. Nicholson, *New Communities in Britain* (National Council of Social Service), London, 1961, p. 29 and *passim*; Peter Wilmott, *The Evolution of a Community: A Study of Dagenham after Forty Years*, London, 1963, pp. 55–7; M. W. Hodges and C. S. Smith, *op. cit.*, pp. 85–9. On reputedly class-conditioned traditions and those formed in old and unchanged surroundings, see Josephine Klein, *op. cit.*, pp. 631 *seq.*; also Richard Hoggart, 'Challenge of the Working Class Scholar', *The Observer*, 11 February 1962.

The occasions for such sharing and the machinery for it was still to be found in associations of every kind – committees representing the householder's interests, functional societies of every kind, social clubs. Indeed, so considerable was the working-class participation in these bodies that it must either throw doubt on the alleged aversion of working classes from clubbable activities or else indicate a significant change in the post-war attitudes.

The doubt is prompted by all we know of working-class lives in the nineteenth century. From the very early years of the industrial revolution, British working-men associated for a variety of objects: politics, industrial action, mutual-aid, sports and pastimes. Some of the most characteristic national organizations of the twentieth century, from friendly societies and co-operative organizations to football associations and cycling unions, originated in working-class clubs and societies. In this respect the British working-man was no different from the German working-man with his *Vereine* of every kind: convivial, musical and political. If British working-men, unlike their Scottish counterparts, did not form or join golf clubs, or did not belong to fox hunts, and until recently were not very numerous in tennis clubs, this was due not to any dislike of associations, but to considerations of cost or to differences of taste (these were sometimes regional in origin) which made working-men prefer some pursuits to others: bowls to golf, soccer to rugger, brass bands to chamber ensembles. But whatever was or was not in the past the working-class propensity to club, or their choice of club-worthy pursuits, in more recent times they appeared to approach more closely those of other classes. Such little information as we possess of post-war associations in British working-class areas, mostly in new towns and housing estates, suggests that in some of them the proportions of working-class families belonging to associations of various kinds was not strikingly lower than the proportion of middle-class families belonging to associations in middle-class or mixed areas. It also appears that in those towns or housing estates in which middle-class families took a disproportionately large part in local associations, this did not prevent the working-class families from belonging to the associations and even from playing leading parts in them. In Crawley at the end of a decade of the new town's existence some 45 per cent of all married men belonged to societies of every kind functioning there; in Harlow the proportions were very nearly the same.[1] These proportions were probably much larger than those in older working-class neighbourhoods.

If so, the clubs and associations in some new localities either belie the fundamentalist belief in the working-class aversion from pursuits and occupations channelled through voluntary associations, or else suggests the possibility that the younger and better-off working-class families did not find it difficult to establish for themselves the same machinery for 'getting together' which, we are told, was a characteristic facility of middle-class lives.

The impression recent studies then give, whether they intend it or not, is that 'respectable' working-class families in the new communities had grown less sensitive of difference from the middle-class families in their midst than the older working-class families in older localities. This reduced sensitiveness may have reflected a variety of recent changes. Earnings on both sides of the frontier were now near equal; education was often similar; the social class of the parents was sometimes identical. Frequently and importantly, homes and lives in them were also similar.

Nothing underlines more clearly the growing equivalence of self-esteem along this particular social frontier than the wholly different position of the lowermost ranks in working-class communities. For most observers agree that the sharpest lines of demarcation, across which few contacts took place or were encouraged, were those which divided respectable working-class families from the rough families of unskilled, uneducated, or casually employed men and women. The 'respectable' and the 'superior' elements in new communities represented the same sandwich layer in society which was

---

[1] J. H. Nicholson (as in footnote 2, p. 340 above), pp. 140–1; Janet H. Madge, 'Some Aspects of Social Mixing in Worcester', in Leo Kuper (ed.), *Living in Towns*, London, 1953, pp. 273–5; Winifred Whitely, ibid., pp. 229–30; G. D. Mitchell and T. Lupton (as in footnote 1, p. 325 above), pp. 31–9; but cf. contrasts in N. Elias and J. L. Scotson, *The Establishment and the Outsiders*, London, 1965, pp. 51 seq., and Peter Willmot, *op. cit.*, p. 85. But even though in Dagenham membership and attendance in clubs is smaller than in Woodford, the social composition of those who belonged and attended was drawn from among both clerical and manual employees. However, cf. M. Stacey, *Tradition and Change: A study of Banbury*, 1960, Ch. V seq.

represented in factories by the white-collar clerical, lower super-visory and the skilled manual workers.[1]

This reference to the skilled must not be allowed as it often is to detract from the importance of the new trend. One of the charac-teristic and unfortunate propensities of some sociologists writing about the working classes, more especially in the United King-dom, is to include the skilled operative into the working classes in a few contexts and to exclude them from others. He is commonly excluded from current generalization of class bias in school entries, in recruitment into universities and into white-collar and managerial ranks. For some purposes and in some contexts such exclusions are justifiable. But in considering the movements along and across the class divisions, the fortunes, the attitudes and the modes of life of the skilled operatives are highly significant of the post-war world. Their significance derives from their being themselves a marginal sector of society. They were marginal not only because they happen to be located on the social periphery of the working classes, or because their numbers were growing faster than those of any other section of the manual workers, but also because the growth in their numbers occurred in response to the economic changes most characteristic of the post-war epoch and most indicative of things to come.

To conclude – the notion that the structure of the labour force and its position in society were no longer the same as in the nine-teenth century is no mere figment of wishful political thinking. What appeared to change most conspicuously was the numerical weight of industrial labour narrowly defined. In the economy at large the relative numbers of workers in industry and mining declined, while the relative numbers in non-industrial occupations had grown and was growing. Within industry this numerical shift had for its corollary an equally significant increase in non-manual ranks. But at the same time the old distinction between operatives,

[1] N. Elias and J. Scotson, *The Establishment and the Outsiders*, London, 1965, pp. 107, 122; Mark Hodges and Cyril Smith (as in footnote 1, p. 338 above), p. 122; J. H. Nicholson (as in footnote 2, p. 340 above), p. 29; Josephine Klein (as in footnote 1, p. 334 above), p. 631.

on the one hand, and clerical and technical employees, on the other, was probably getting fainter. In a number of industries the proportions of skilled men grew; and the very character of their skills and their training brought them closer to the men in technical, clerical and supervisory positions. And as the demarcations of function and status on the shop floor were being redrawn, the working-men's mode of life and the social relations in the urban areas they inhabited were taking on a new colour. That the new colour was not evenly spread and was clearly visible only on the margins of employment and on fringes of society may justify some historians and sociologists in toning it down. But those historians – and the present writer is one of them – to whom social evolution is not a pantomime, a disjointed sequence of spectacular transformations, but a continuous current of detailed and local responses to historical forces, would not expect the responses to have been any less piecemeal and peripheral than they turned out to be.[1]

[1] *Vide*, Appendix Note 19, p. 369 below.

CHAPTER 13
Cui Bono

The manner in which the social and economic history of Western
Europe has been told here is open to the obvious charge of inhu-
manity. I may have demonstrated how the European economy succeeded in growing faster than ever before and how at the same time
profound changes took place in industrial ownership and employment and perhaps also in social relations. But I have said little
about the difference which economic growth and its attendant social
changes made – or failed to make – in the condition of persons. Did
a larger product per head in fact bring greater material bounty to
humble men and women? And if it were shown that this is in fact
what higher national outputs brought about, it would not necessarily
follow that they also resulted in corresponding increases of welfare.
As for social changes, how much did it matter to the well-being of
the vast majority of men that industries were now differently owned
and administered, or that distinctions of rank were now more gently
graded, or that the numbers of skilled and better-trained employees
had grown?

What makes social study so frustrating is that its most important
problems, the ones most relevant to moral judgments and political
actions, are as a rule the most difficult to define and worst served by
evidence. From this frustrating rule the questions posed here are no
exception. Their very meaning eludes us for the simple reason that
economic welfare, its existence as a quality capable of being object-
ively assessed, is subject to philosophical doubt. And in the absence
of objective standards of economic welfare, the student of the
economy must make do with superficial measurements which veil
the fundamental issues to the point of obscuring them altogether.
All he is able to record and to measure is the flow of material
goods and services, not the satisfactions they are supposed to produce; quantities of foods grown, in lieu of hungers assuaged or

pleasures of the table dispensed; the cubic room space per person in lieu of the true qualities of homes; the numbers of schools, of children and masters, or the age groups served by them, in lieu of what they do to form personalities, to improve minds, characters, or skills. And even this measurable flow of material goods and services does not include either objects or services, equally material but as a rule unpriced and therefore unmeasurable, such as the purity of air and water, the pleasures of unspoilt nature or the blessings of privacy.

Still farther beyond these insufficiencies of academic standards of welfare lies hidden the great ambiguity of the very pursuit of satisfaction. Are the benefits of economic and social change fully measured by their ability to meet humdrum needs and to provide petty comforts? And if they are not, what are the higher benefits we must take into account in striking the balance of economic gains and losses?

The superficialities and evasions inherent in academic treatment of economic welfare have been acknowledged here mainly as an excuse for the all-too-obvious substance of the discussion to follow, and especially of its opening moves. As elsewhere in this study, I must begin my exposition with several facts obvious to the point of truism. What can be more obvious than the conclusion that the increasing national products represented a larger flow of goods and services catering for the material needs of individuals? This conclusion, however, may turn out to be less obvious when viewed historically. An increase in national product could be expected to enhance the economic welfare of individuals, and more particularly that of men and women of modest means, only as long as the distribution of national product remained the same or changed in favour of the lower incomes. The two main patterns of distribution – the fiscal, i.e. that between the State and private individuals, and the 'social', i.e. that between different income groups and occupations – can be assumed to remain the same over very short sequences of years, but the assumption need not hold good of periods even as short as the post-war epoch. In fact, both patterns of distribution, the fiscal and social, changed quite considerably in the quarter-century after 1939, and these historical changes must be allowed for before we can gauge how far the rises in national products after the war affected the material well-being of the mass of ordinary men and women.

Historical allowances for the distribution of national product between the richer and the poorer members of society have of late become somewhat easier to make than they were only a few years ago. Simon Kuznets and his associates have been able to offer tentative estimates showing that during the nineteenth century national products in most European countries were being gradually reapportioned in favour of incomes from employment (wages and salaries) at the expense of the incomes from property (interest, profits, and rents). These estimates have been confirmed by the results of still more recent inquiries summarized in Table 24 below.

The reapportionment of incomes proceeded very fast in the earlier phases of industrialization, e.g. in France and Germany in the second half of the nineteenth century, when small independent enterprises were being rapidly replaced by factories employing ever-increasing numbers of wage labour. In most European countries this process slowed down or ceased altogether at different points of time in the first half of the present century. After 1945, however, the share of labour in the national product began to increase again; and increased faster than in any other period since the nineteenth century.

There should not be any need to labour the meaning of these figures. It may, however, be worth pointing out that in most countries, but more especially in the United Kingdom, the real share of national product available to working-men and women was somewhat greater and grew somewhat faster than the table indicates. The figures for the United Kingdom, and to a somewhat smaller extent those for Germany, underestimate the actual incomes of employed classes compared with the incomes of owners of capital and other forms of property. What they measure is not the division of national product between social classes, i.e. between the actual recipients of wages and salaries, on the one hand, and those of profits, interest and rents, on the other, but its division between the two institutional sources of income which happen to be conventionally labelled as 'employment' and 'property,' and, somewhat less directly, its division between labour and capital considered as material 'inputs'. However, neither of these categories – sources of

z

income and material inputs – corresponds at all exactly with labour and capital as social classes. The income of labour as a social class cannot be wholly identical with the share of national income accruing to employment or to labour inputs; similarly, the incomes of capitalists as a social class were not identical with incomes from capital and property.

Table 24 *The Distribution of Income between Employment and Property*[1]

| | Year | (as percentage of National Income) | | |
		Employment	Property and Enterprise	Balancing Items
United Kingdom	1910–14	55·3	44·7	
	1925–29	66·4	33·6	
	1935–38	67·1	32·9	
	1946–49	73·0	27·0	
	1960–63	78·6	26·4	
France	1938	51·4	47·7	0·9
	1949	53·5	41·0	5·5
	1953	56·5	37·5	6·0
	1958	58·3	36·0	5·7
	1962	60·6	33·7	5·7
Germany[2]	1950	58·6	41·4	of which 2·3 public sector
	1953	58·7	41·3	of which 3·8 public sector
	1958	60·5	39·5	of which 4·5 public sector
	1963	64·8	35·2	of which 4·8 public sector

At what point and for what reasons the two sets of concepts, the economic and the social, deviate emerges quite clearly from the nature of the concepts themselves. The statistics of incomes from

[1] The table is derived from reports to the Conference of the International Economic Association on Distribution of National Income held in Palermo in September 1964. The figures for the United Kingdom come from the report of C. H. Feinstein; those for France from the report of Monsieur Jacques Lecaillon; and those for Germany from that of Herr Albert Jeck. At the time when this was written the reports were still unpublished, and were made available by Mr Feinstein's kindness.

[2] In the pre-war German Reich the share of employment in national income rose from 46·5 per cent in 1913 to 61 per cent in 1925 and 66·1 per cent in 1931, but declined in the thirties to 43·7 in 1939. Albert Jeck as (above) Table 4.

employment, as a rule, include the earnings of members of liberal professions and the salaries of managerial heads of firms who in any realistic social classification would be grouped with the well-to-do owners of property. But what is equally important and applies to all three countries in our table, is that by no means all incomes from property and capital accrued to persons who in any realistic social discussion would be considered as members of the property-owning classes. These incomes included interest on savings (and we have seen how important were popular savings in capital formation after the war) and rents of owner-occupied houses (and we know that a large proportion of these belonged to men and women classified as workers). Moreover, a great variety of institutional owners, claiming a large share of aggregate income from capital (in the case of the United Kingdom, colleges, charities, Ecclesiastical Commissioners, and above all, pensions funds, mutual insurance companies, friendly societies, co-operatives and trade unions), must be considered as owned by the mass of their humble members or policy-holders, who received the bulk of their profits directly in the form of dividends, or indirectly in the form of services or delayed benefits.

For all these reasons our figures of shares of labour and capital in the national product cannot, without major corrections, be translated into social terms, i.e. into incomes of labouring classes, on the one hand, and propertied classes, on the other. The share of national product assigned in current statistics to labour must be corrected by the addition of working-men's income from savings and property, while the share assigned to property owners must be increased by the addition of salaries of highly-paid employees.

Needless to say, an exact estimate of these corrections has not yet been made and perhaps cannot be made, but approximate orders of magnitude can be assessed, however sketchily; and these magnitudes bring out even more forcibly the extent to which the share of the employed classes grew between 1950 and 1964. Estimated very roughly, in the roundest of figures, the 'unearned' income of recipients of wages and salaries in the United Kingdom amounted to c. £1,360 million in the early fifties and c. £1,860 in 1963/4; whereas the aggregate 'earned' income of recipients of high salaries – say those over £2,000 per annum in the early fifties and £3,000

Z2

in 1963/4 – was probably less than £800 million at both dates.[1]

These facts must be borne in mind in assessing what is often written and said about the income of labour and about the economic welfare of working-men. Their bearing on the ancient Marxian prediction that the capitalist's share in the aggregate product of industry would grow as the total value of fixed capital increased need not at the present moment detain us; nor need the associated notion that the aggregate incomes from wages were fixed by a static 'wage fund'. This proposition, like its companion proposition of the 'iron law of wages', does not necessarily follow from Marxian conceptions of capitalist economy and is no longer held in its original form even by the most literal of Marxists. On the other hand, the notion that labour's share in the national product remained constant is still to be encountered in some highly respectable theoretical models of economic growth and in some recent essays of political sociology. Their validity in the economic context is highly questionable. In most economic models labour is defined as wage-earners and excludes recipients of salaries. Similarly incomplete, and to that extent irrelevant, is the treatment of income of labour in some recent socio-political discussions, since it almost invariably fails to take account of the income of members of the wage-earning and salaried groups from property and savings.

In estimating the economic welfare of these groups and the changes it underwent after 1945 yet further corrections must be made in the United Kingdom figures, and to a smaller extent also in the German ones, to allow for the second – the fiscal – pattern of distribution. It is now generally understood, and has in fact been stressed elsewhere in this study, that the State claimed a large proportion of the national product and that, in some countries, the proportions grew after the war.

These appropriations by the State, and to a smaller extent the appropriations by social service funds, bore upon the material

---

[1] The savings of the working classes in the United Kingdom have been assumed to be equal to two-thirds of personal savings: see above, p. 234. They were, however, considerably lower in France. According to M. Lecaillon's computations the combined savings of all the categories of wage and salary earners formed rather less than 10 per cent of total personal savings: J. Lecaillon (as in footnote 1, p. 348 above), Table XI. For the United Kingdom estimates *Vide* Appendix Note 20, pp. 370–3 below.

Table 25 *Taxation as Percentage in 1962 of G.N.P.*[1]

France	41·0
Germany	41·0
United Kingdom	34·3

well-being of men and women in two ways – by the burdens they imposed and by the benefits they conferred. Of the two, the burdens, i.e. the weight and incidence of taxes, had a distributive effect which was much less significant than the distributive effects of the benefits they financed. In most countries during our period direct personal taxes fell more heavily on the individual incomes of the well-to-do than on those of poorer men, even if the aggregate burden of direct personal taxes falling on smaller incomes (say those below £1,000 in the United Kingdom) was only a little – if at all – lighter than their aggregate weight borne by the well-off. At the same time indirect taxes fell mainly on the multitude of humble consumers. And as in most countries about as much was collected by indirect taxes as by direct ones, the fact that a higher share of the former were borne by small incomes means that in the aggregate the relatively poor bore a somewhat higher proportion of taxes than the relatively rich. In other words, however great may have been the equalizing effect of taxation on individual incomes, its total effect in the United Kingdom, as in most other countries, was to reduce slightly labour's portion of the national product.

These higher burdens were, however, fully outweighed by what wage-earners and the mass of salaried employees received from various state disbursements. In the United Kingdon, in an average post-war year, as much as about 75 per cent of the 'divisible' State expenditure, i.e. of State disbursements capable of being considered as direct additions to personal incomes, may have gone to persons with incomes which in 1950 stood below £2,000. As in an average year 'divisible' expenditure of the State may have absorbed at least 50 per cent of the revenues of public authorities, the small incomes must have got back from the State rather more than the equivalent of what they paid out in taxes. On the other hand, persons with incomes of £2,000 and above could not have received back in

[1] *Report of the Committee on Turnover Taxation, 1964,* Cmnd 2300, p. 9.

social benefits the equivalent of more than 10 per cent of what the State had taken away from them in taxes.

The United Kingdom figures are cited here not only because they happen to have been better studied but also because they represent State disbursements at their lowest. In a number of other European countries, considerably higher proportions of national income were collected by the State and distributed in the form of social services. According to an I.L.O. report of 1957 public expenditure on health, pensions, family allowances, and assistance, but excluding expenditure on education or housing, formed 20·8 per cent of the national income in Germany, 18·9 per cent in France, 12·1 per cent in the United Kingdom; and their comparative levels changed little between 1957 and 1965. In the United Kingdom expenditure on social services, inclusive of education and food subsidies, rose from 2·6 per cent of national income in 1900 to 11·3 per cent in 1938 and to between 17 and 18 per cent in the early 1960s. Needless to say, the bulk of these disbursements went to the men and women classified as recipients of wages and salaries. Computed as a proportion of wages and salaries, these social benefits formed 4 per cent of French wages and salaries in 1938, 10·5 per cent in 1949, 12·7 per cent in 1956, 13·8 per cent in 1962. They formed an almost equal proportion of wages in Germany, and an even larger one in Italy.[1]

The history of these accretions cannot be discussed here in proper relation to the purposes and methods of individual social services. But their cumulative progress in the age of economic growth was an essential element in that growth and must form part of its story. It is, of course, well known that social services of every kind had been in existence in most European countries long before the war. As early as 1889 Bismarck's Germany had equipped itself with a system of compulsory and contributory social insurance covering old age, sickness, and invalidity; and by the first decade of the twentieth century there were to be found in almost every European country social insurance schemes, mostly local or indus-

---

[1] *Report on Turnover Taxation*, as on p. 351 above. According to Lecaillon's estimate for France (as in footnote 1, p. 348 above) Table X social benefits, social insurances, and tax-free transfers formed 4 per cent of national income in 1938, 10·5 per cent in 1939, 11·6 per cent in 1953, and 13·8 per cent in 1962. These disbursements are, however, included in his estimates of the share of incomes from employment.

trial, to say nothing of the various poor law provisions like the German *Fürsorge*, or the French *aide sociale*, or provisions for municipal relief.

On these foundations all European countries had by 1939 erected a structure of social services, as a rule contributory and comprehensive and designed to provide assistance or minimum subsistence in cases of sickness, old age, invalidity, maternity, and, sometimes, also in cases of unemployment.[1] It was, however, left to the post-war era to extend social services to a height at which they could be claimed to have come near to solving the problem of poverty and insecurity and, in doing so, to bring about massive transfer of income in favour of lower income groups. The turning-point in the United Kingdom came with the publication of the Beveridge Report of 1942 and its adoption by the National Government of the day and by the Labour Government which succeeded it in 1945, as a basis for the universal system of social welfare. The comprehensive system of insurance it introduced had for its object 'security' defined as freedom from want and, more particularly, from the penalties of unemployment, old age, widowhood, and disability. The act was followed in 1948 by Bevan's National Health Scheme. The latter was also conceived as an insurance subsidized by the State; its object, however, went beyond the minimum standards of subsistence secured by other social insurances, since it was designed to offer to all as full a health service as the medical and financial resources of the country permitted.

This conception of the British National Health Service was in keeping with the scale and purposes of the social services as they were taking shape at the same time in continental Europe. The benefits under them, especially under the various pension schemes, gradually came to be cast on a scale and conceived in a spirit in many cases far removed not only from those of the old poor laws but also from those of social services in the early stages of their developments. The new conception and the new scales came to France by a series of consecutive steps – the various pension schemes introduced in 1946 including a most generous system of

[1] The account of social services here largely follows that in T. H. Marshall, *The Social Services*, London, 1964, but has been supplemented from various other sources.

family allowances; a series of health measures based mostly on the principle of reimbursement of private expenses on medical care (these measures culminated in the reforms and amendments of 1955, 1958, and 1960); and finally, the somewhat belated housing subsidies and schemes of the late fifties and sixties. Unemployment remained, perhaps, the only social problem unprovided for by national insurance. It continued to be treated as part of the wage contract, but was made universal and enforceable under the collective wage agreement introduced in 1958.

In Germany the post-war escalation of social services terminated in the great social insurance act of 1957, which not only extended it to the entire population but also related benefits and pensions more realistically to earnings. In doing so, it placed Germany ahead of all the other Western countries with regard to the cost of the social services, the scale of some of the benefits and the size of public disbursements they required.

Social services on their post-war scale were bound to bring economic and social consequences beyond the mere additions to income as measured in our tabulation of aggregate shares of national products; and their most obvious consequence was that of greater economic equality. For without them, the higher aggregate share of national income accruing to wages and salaries would not always have been sufficient to equalize the actual distribution of incomes as between average working-men and average members of the well-to-do groups. The equalizing effects of labour's growing share in the national product could sometimes be nullified by other economic trends. There is thus some evidence for the view that in the one country in which the share of labour grew most rapidly after the war, i.e. in Germany, the numbers of men and women in the wage-earning and salary-earning classes increased so greatly that the average incomes of working families rose more slowly than the average incomes of families in professional and entrepreneurial groups. As a result, inequalities in German society may have widened between 1950 and 1960 (but probably not after 1960), even though the material standards of working-class lives rose well above their pre-war levels. In this respect, however, the German experience may have been exceptional, since in most other European countries not only did the aggregate incomes of wage-earners

and salary-earners rise relatively faster, but the difference between incomes of individual families also appear to have narrowed
down.[1]

Moreover, increases in real wages and salaries and additions
made to them by social services and various other transfer payments,
could, and most probably did, enhance the material welfare of
ordinary men and women more than even the statistics of individual
incomes can measure. It is an elementary proposition of welfare
economics that the same addition to income would bring a greater
increment of material welfare to a poor man than to a richer
one. From this proposition it also follows that in transfers of incomes from wealthier taxpayers to poorer beneficiaries of social
services the latter could generally be expected to derive material
benefits greater than the benefits the taxpayers would have derived
from the income with which they were made to part.

Like most postulates of welfare economics, this one is so general
and abstract as to run counter to the private experience of some
individuals; but in its general abstract form it follows inevitably
from the logic of marginal utility and from the ethical postulates
of Western civilization. To that extent it need not be – indeed,
cannot be – exhibited statistically. Somewhat more open to argument, but as a rule accepted as self-evident, is the paternalistic
view that it is in the nature of some social services, such as education or public health, to add more to the well-being of their
beneficiaries than what their money-worth could yield to the taxpayers were it to remain in their hands, and also greater than the
benefits it could procure for the beneficiaries were it made available
to them in the form of higher purchasing power.

What does not follow quite so obviously from welfare theories or
from conventional ethics is the effect of public expenditure in fields
other than social services. In our period, as in all periods, public

---

[1] Whereas between 1950 and 1962 the aggregate incomes from employment in
Germany rose by 324 per cent compared with 226 per cent from profits and
entrepreneurship, the relative position of average individual wage and salary
earners, compared to other Germans, appeared to decline. The rise in average
incomes of individual employees was 172 per cent, compared to 269 per cent for
individuals in self-employed and professional classes. However, in the sixties the
average incomes of individual wage and salary earners began to rise again in
step with other incomes: Albert Jeck (as in footnote 1, p. 348 above) Tables
8 and 9.

expenditure was not entirely confined to social services, but went into traditional public disbursements, such as administration, enforcement of law and order or national defence. In strict logic some of these activities could also claim to be in the nature of transfers, since they had an obvious value to individuals and would have had to be paid for somehow if not provided by the State. Yet even if this claim could be made for some public outlays, it could not in equal measure be made for all of them; and for some the measure would be very small indeed. Most ordinary people might reject the claim altogether for armaments scaled up beyond all reasonable needs of security or serving the aggrandizement of rulers or their ideologies. Judgments of this nature are, of course, bound to be highly subjective, uncertain and unstable. But in the eyes of most men sharing the elementary assumptions of Western ethics, the utility of expenditures of this kind would be insufficient to justify the corresponding retrenchments in private expenditure of individuals.

These distinctions between public outlays which can, and those which cannot, be justified in comparison with private expenditure they replace, imply a shifting frontier between public and private outlays. The ideal position for this frontier is of course indeterminable, but there is little doubt that in some historical situations the actual frontiers were drawn nearer to, while in other positions they ran farther away from, what reasonable people would now consider their 'optimum' positions. By modern humanitarian standards, as well as by the more artificial standards of welfare economics, there would be no difficulty in condemning the division of national product between public and private uses in Pharaonic Egypt, where slave labour and poverty was the lot of common humanity, while the Pharaohs could indulge in the building of pyramids. *Mutatis mutandis*, most modern economists and moralists might agree in condemning the division of national product in places and at times when most families lived in abject poverty while the state indulged in immensely costly space rocketry – the flying pyramids of our civilization.

How are we in that case to adjudicate on the position and the shifts of the frontier in Western Europe after the war? Did it move towards its optimum position or away from it? Professor Galbraith believes that in the fifties the frontier in the U.S.A. was wrongly positioned, and that American life, as a result, suffered from public squalor amidst private affluence. Would this also be our verdict on Western Europe after the war?

Most students, however partial and subjective their judgment, would probably answer the question in the negative. The frontiers in Europe after the war were much nearer to what Professor Galbraith would recognize as the optimum position than they were in the U.S.A. or had been in most European countries at earlier periods. Indeed, with regard to public outlays, the criticism was that in Western Europe in the early sixties frontiers between public and private outlays had moved too far State-wards.

Even the critics did not as a rule question that in most European countries after the war there was still much poverty and privation, and that further extensions of education, health services, or pensions were desirable. But the opinion that public outlays had gone far enough and that private outlays and private choices should be given greater scope could be heard more often than in the honeymoon years of the Beveridge Report. The note began to be sounded in discussion of housing policy: whether the object of the subsidy should be the houses as heretofore, or the budgets of families inhabiting them. The same note entered into the proposals for universal old age insurance linked to earnings, but combined with private superannuation schemes. It entered the proposals to facilitate the increases in various social benefits by restricting them to those in need.

The practical impact of these criticisms and questionings was not very great. They mostly came from conservative quarters; none of them were as yet able to influence the actual practice in 1965. Moreover, in some European countries major social services requiring greater public outlays were still at their inception in the 1960s: the health service in Belgium, comprehensive housing policy in France, universal social insurance in Sweden. But generally speaking, it could be argued that in most countries the public share in the provision of education, social security, housing and health had grown to a height as great as national products could sustain; and that, failing a drastic, perhaps revolutionary, redistribution of wealth and income, further large increases in national products would be required to support further additions to social benefits.

The same record of high aggregate utility resulting from State-ward shifts of the frontier can be read into the history of the other, less material, benefits financed by public authorities: arts, sciences and amenities of urban and rural life. In such countries as Germany, where princes, States and municipalities, had since the Middle Ages devoted large resources to the arts, the post-war increases in public expenditure on cultural amenities, large as they were, did not perhaps appear out of the ordinary. In such fields as higher education or facilities for pure research, post-war Germany, the cradle of modern university culture, may even have lagged behind some other European countries. The countries in which the post-war facilities in arts and sciences increased most markedly were probably the United Kingdom and France, where in the past public expenditure in these fields had been lower than in many other European countries. Expressed in absolute amounts or even as pro-portion of the national product, the sums devoted to these objects in these two countries after the war were still lower than in the U.S.A. or the U.S.S.R.; within Europe they may still have been outstripped by comparable outlays in Austria or Sweden. Yet they were suffi-ciently high and had grown fast enough to have succeeded by 1964 in affecting the quality, and still more the potentialities, of people's lives.

Thus, Britain, the 'country without music', had by the early sixties become one of the world's largest centres of musical activity. What a German businessman who settled in England in the middle of the nineteenth century could at that time describe as a 'cultural desert' justly boasted in 1965 of the largest number of newly published books per head of the population, and sustained the most lively and adventurous theatrical activity in its history since the seventeenth century. Somewhere on the borderline of improved social services, of measures to foster economic growth and of the new concern for arts and sciences, there sprouted the post-war ambitions and plans for higher education, culminating in the Robbins Report of 1962. As a result, the numbers of university students, of institutions for higher education and learning, and expenditure on pure research – and presumably its products – had grown between 1946 and 1964 about threefold.

The post-war improvements in culture and additions to gracious living were somewhat less conspicuous in France. But since the late 1950s, State subvention of sciences, State patronage of plastic and theatrical arts and public expenditure on the beautification of cities increased sufficiently strongly and sufficiently fast to leave an almost immediate imprint on the face of the country.

The culture-fostering deeds of public authorities remain unsung and of course unmeasured. But both their costs and their benefits were very substantial and added more to the credit balance of European growth after the war. Needless to say, there was also a debit side to the balance. There was the inflation; and the penalties of inflation were not confined to the purely material effects of unstable prices, commercial insecurity, and latent threats to continued expansion. Inflation was costly in human terms since it hit hardest the men and women who benefited least from economic growth – the aged, the sick, the recipients of fixed incomes, the poorest-paid workers.

Captious observers would also add to the debit balance some of the direct consequences of growth itself. They would list the over-crowding in the cities and the consequent decay in the most essential urban amenities, congestion on the roads, destruction of peace and privacy on sea-coasts, mountains, and rivers, pollution of waters and of air, decline in the quality of services and goods, debasement of arts by new mass media. These critics would even deny the worth of some of the most obvious and tangible symbols of the new affluence. In their view economic growth in its latest stages did not bring with it anything finer and better than what it had, in fact, been bringing for years in the U.S.A. without greatly improving the quality of American life and civilization – a more abundant flow, hence a faster obsolescence and a quicker turnover, of the more ephemeral implements and gadgets which economists so inappro-priately describe as 'durable' consumption goods. And Professor Galbraith would add to this indictment the artificial promotion of new and unnecessary needs created by big business to support the expanding capacity of its monopolistic enterprises.

Responses to this indictment, like the indictment itself, must be largely personal; and personal attitudes of observers vary not only with their psychological make-up but also with their income. It cannot be a mere accident that the men most inclined to spurn the material gifts of economic growth are frequently those who need them least. They would be, as a rule, found in professions and income groups first to have benefited from the fruits of new abundance, and first to have reached the state of comparative satiety. Our answer to the indictment need not, however, be entirely involved with individual biases. There are objective reasons why a rational European should refuse to spurn the blessings of economic growth; and the most objective reason of all is that modern societies, including all the European societies in the post-war period, were still were very far from that universal condition of satiety which would justify the rejection of past economic growth or of its further promise. I have already admitted that even at the end of our period there still remained some residual poverty and deprivation in all Western countries. Their social services and public amenities had not yet reached by 1964 the point of diminishing returns beyond which Western humanity could no longer benefit from further diversion of resources to public outlays. And, *horribile dictu*, even the current flow of gadgetry and hardware had not yet grown so far as no longer to be able to add, and to add greatly, to the ease of average lives. And beyond all the relief which economic growth brought, and could continue to bring, to men and women in Western Europe, there still were the deprived multitudes beyond Europe's pale, to whose growth Europe probably could not, and certainly would not, contribute more than it did in the past unless it itself continued to get richer by growing.

Appendix Notes

NOTE 1

The United Kingdom's figures in Table 2 and the references to them in the text agree with the estimates in P. Dean and W. A. Cole, *British Economic Growth 1688–1959; Trends and Structure*, Cambridge, 1962, p. 313, that the average annual rate of growth of *per capita* income between 1938 and 1958, at 2·4 per cent, was twice that of the previous thirty years. The figures and the conclusions drawn from them may, however, appear to run counter to some of the long-term estimates derived from W. G. Hoffman's *British Industry 1700–1950*, Oxford, 1951, which suggests that manufacturing output in the century between 1813 and 1913 grew at the average annual rate of 2·7 per cent, or about the same rate as after the Second World War. Mr H. D. Willey, *Growth of British and German Manufacturing 1951 to 1962* (Ph.D. thesis in Columbia University, 1966), pp. 81–4, argues from these figures that the United Kingdom rates of growth after 1945 were 'in line' with Britain's historical record. A somewhat similar conclusion also appears to emerge from comparison between post-war figures and the estimates for the inter-war period in K. S. Lomax, 'Production and Productivity Movements in the U.K. since 1900', *Journal of the Royal Statistical Society*, 122, Pt. 2, 1959, which indicate an average annual rate of growth of labour productivity between 1924 and 1938 at 1·8 per cent, compared with Mr Willey's 1·9 per cent for 1951–62. The differences between pre-war and post-war figures would, however, be wider if not restricted to manufactures. Moreover, Mr Willey concedes that appropriate allowances for rising employment rates in the thirties would make it necessary to scale down the inter-war figures. These figures would also be lowered if the dates were shifted to include the years between 1920 and 1924 or to exclude the rearmament years of 1935–8. Mr Willey also brings out (*op. cit.*, pp. 61, 65, and Table 7) the accelerated pace of increases in output within the post-war period: from 2 per cent per annum in 1951–4 to 3·4 per cent in 1959–62.

NOTE 2

The Caisse des Dépôts et Consignations disposed not only of the resources of the Caisses d'Epargne but also the funds of pension funds and unspent balances of taxes. The Crédit National acted as the discounter of bills, which were the chief instrument of short-term finance. These could be rediscounted at the Banque de France and thus become instruments of medium-term finance if and when the transaction they financed was for an activity provided for in the Plan and not opposed by the planning authorities. Issues of bonds – the preferred instrument for long-term investment – were subject to the approval of the Treasury division of the Ministry of Finance, which in its turn required the planners' *fiat*.

NOTE 3

On the whole, the tendency in most of the papers at the conference was to make light of the difficulties of adapting recent immigrants from the countryside to the requirements of modern industry. The most, however, that any paper claims for rural immigrants is that their potentiality for productivity and successful absorption into the labour force was not appreciably lower than that of average industrial employees. The reports do nothing to dispel the prevailing view that 'turnover' is relatively high among immigrants from the countryside, partly because they tend, to a larger extent than other workers, to concentrate in building industry and public works, and partly because of an innate 'inadaptability' (*ibid.*, p. 74). See also a study of French automobile workers in the Paris region in A. Touraine: 'Les ouvriers d'origine agricole', *Sociologie du Travail*, 1960, no. 3.

NOTE 4

As a percentage of labour force British *net* immigration was lower than in most European countries, though higher than that in the Netherlands and Scandinavian countries. From the point of view of the effects of 'new' immigrant labour on productivity it is, however, the figure of *gross* immigration that is most relevant, and for the United Kingdom it is higher than for most countries except France, Germany, and Switzerland. Contrary to some current assumptions the contingent of foreign immigrants after 1958 was of the same order of magnitude in the United Kingdom and Germany. The cumulative total of foreign (non-German) immigrants into Germany between 1958 and 1964, i.e. the years when the flow of East Germans ceased, was estimated at 800,000. The cumulative numbers of resident coloured immigrants into United Kingdom, who had arrived in approximately the same period, varied between 500,000 and 800,000, though the latter figures included dependants non-gainfully employed.

NOTE 5

A statistical argument against any close long-term correlation between growth of G.D.P. and investment has been developed by S. Kuznets, 'Quantitative Aspects of Economic Growth', *Economic Development and*

Cultural Change, ix, pt. 2, July 1961, pp. 55–6. The absence of clear correlation between rates of economic growth and rates of investment in individual countries emerges clearly from the facts and the argument in U.N.O., *Economic Survey of Europe in 1961*, pt. 2, U.N.O., Geneva, 1964, pp. 18 *seq*. This is also the main preoccupation of R. C. O. Matthews' study cited on pp. 117–18 above, and of most other studies of 'technology' as an input. In all of them capital and labour are assigned a relatively modest share in economic growth. In a recent comparative study by E. Domar, 'Economic Growth and Productivity in the United States, the United Kingdom, Germany and Japan in the Postwar Period', *Review of Economics and Statistics*, February 1964, the contribution of the 'residuary' factor, i.e. technology in the broad sense of the term, to rates of growth is assessed at 50 per cent for Germany and 25 per cent for the United Kingdom. These figures are lower than those of most other assessors, but one of their features is that they assign to the 'residuary' factor the highest value in countries where investment also happens to be high. The issue and the method of these inquiries go back nearly a decade to R. Solow's 'Technical Change and the Aggregate Production Function', *Review of Economics and Statistics*, vol. 1, August 1957, and the earlier Cobb-Douglas attempt to assess the combined contribution of material inputs to national products. For a recent exposition and criticism of the formula, see *Some Factors*, Ch. III, pp. 34–5; cf. also Solow's later 'Investment and Technological Progress', *Mathematical Methods in Social Sciences*, Stanford, 1960. Although Solow's studies deal ostensibly with technological change, the term technological is used in the more general sense of a 'residual factor', i.e. inputs other than capital and labour; and the studies are mainly concerned with the relative contribution of labour and investment to economic growth.

NOTE 6

P. J. Verdoorn, 'On the Empirical Law Governing the Productivity of Labor', *Econometrica*, XIX, April 1951, argues that rate of productivity growth went together with the rate of output growth, so that industries which expanded most also increased their productivity fastest. The 'law' does not fit agriculture or industries with large fixed capital of mixed vintage, such as European coal or textiles or even iron and steel, where increases in productivity could and were achieved by reducing capital stock and aggregate output. Direct causal connexion implied by the Verdoorn 'law' should be sought and will probably be found in manufacturing industries in which increases in total output could be achieved mainly by increases in the 'scale' of enterprises. But most of the observed connections, and hence also the correlation, between output and productivity are probably coincidental and reflect the simple fact that adventurous and expansive firms and entrepreneurs pursue both increased outputs and higher productivities, and invest with this double object in view.

NOTE 7

Some recent studies appear at first sight to show that 'sectoral' differences in rates of investment, increases in productivity, etc., between countries like the United Kingdom and Germany were not statistically significant (cf. H. D. Willey, *op. cit.*, pp. 69–71). This argument owes much to the somewhat misleading classification of statistical material in official series which group together 'new' man-made-fibre industries with other textiles, the very modern paper industry with more traditional printing industry, and treat different branches of engineering as a single statistical category. Mr Willey suggests, however, that differences in 'vintage structure', which on his showing are not great enough to correlate with the order in which manufacturing sectors rank in productivity, may nevertheless be sufficiently important to account for international differences in productivity. For the age structure of capital in different sectors of the United Kingdom's manufacturing industry, cf. G. Dean, 'The Stock of Fixed Capital in the United Kingdom in 1961', *Journal of the Royal Statistical Society*, Series A, 127, 1964, pp. 348–9.

NOTE 8

On *a priori* grounds wide variations of I.C.O.R.s between nations and periods can by themselves be taken as evidence that rates of investment were not the decisive influences behind differences in rates of growth of national products. If the rate of growth of capital stock were equal (and in the cases where it happened to be near-equal) to the rate of growth of gross investment into fixed capital, differences in I.C.O.R.s would represent contributions to economic growth of factors other than the rate of increase of fixed capital: *Some Factors*, Ch. II, p. 18. That I.C.O.R.s in fact reflected factors other than investment also underlies Mr Matthew's argument in his *Some Historical Aspects of Post-War Growth*, p. 11. As differences in I.C.O.R.s were the significant factor behind different rates of growth in post-war Europe but as, in his view, economic growth in the United Kingdom responded mainly to higher investment (or as he prefers to term it, high savings ratio) he comes to the 'non-surprising conclusion' that 'the reasons why the British economy has grown faster in the post-war period than earlier are unlikely to . . . be the same as the reasons why other countries grew faster than Britain in the post-war period'. Another look at factors other than saving ratios in different phases of British growth might perhaps make this conclusion less self-evident than it appears. However, the probability that the contribution of investment and other inputs (so-called 'technological' factors) were somewhat different in the United Kingdom than elsewhere is suggested by the figures in *Some Factors*, Ch. III, p. 36, Table 18. The difference is, nevertheless, merely one of degree, since even in the United Kingdom the figures, for whatever they are worth, estimate the contribution of 'technology' at 1·1, compared to 0·9 for investment.

NOTE 9

A general discussion of the issues involved in the treatment of education as 'investment into human capital' will be found in *Residual Factor of Economic Growth*, O.E.C.D., Paris, 1964, more especially in Denison's paper and the following discussion; in Bruce W. Wilkinson, *Studies in the Economics of Education*, Economics and Research Branch, Department of Labor, Ottawa, Occasional Paper 4, 1965, and in W. G. Bowen, 'Assessing the Economic Contribution of Education: an Appraisal of Alternative Approaches', *Economic Aspects of Higher Education*, O.E.C.D., Paris, 1964. Both studies, and especially W. G. Bowen's (*ibid.*, pp. 177 *seq.*) emphasize the pitfalls of simple correlations of G.N.P. with expenditure on education, and the difficulty of inter-country and long-term comparisons. For the importance of accumulated 'stocks' of educated people, and not only their current flow through educational channels, see T. W. Sollity in *Education and Economic Growth*, pp. 64 *seq.*

NOTE 10

It has been argued that high prices of capital goods in the United Kingdom accounted for the steep rise of the United Kingdom capital–output ratios between 1938 and 1958. These ratios did not, however, rise to the same extent in most other continental countries when relative prices of capital goods were approximately as high in the United Kingdom. Cf. R. C. O. Matthews 'Economic Growth in the U.K., Historically considered'; p. 10–11.

NOTE 11

The authorities cited in footnote 1, p. 196, use different standards of measurement – employment, assets, output, etc. These differences in measurement do not, however, make much difference to results as the different standards of size happen to be closely connected: see P. E. Hart, *Studies in Profit, Business Saving and Investment in the United Kingdom*, Liverpool, 1965, Ch. VIII, esp. p. 149; J. M. Samuels, 'Size and the Growth of Firms', *Review of Economic Studies*, Vol. XXXII (2), No. 90, 1965, p. 106. What is, however, more relevant is that concentration ratios, expressed as the combined share of the industry in the hands of the largest firms or establishments, cannot fully measure the international differences and the historical changes in the 'scale' of enterprises and plants. These differences and historical changes were reflected not only in the different concentration ratios but also in what Bain terms the dispersion ratios, i.e. the distribution by size of units other than the largest. Measured by the simple indices of concentration many Italian industries might turn out to have been more concentrated than corresponding industries of other European countries, and some industries in all European countries more concentrated than the corresponding industries in the U.S.A. But in most European countries industries were as a rule more dispersed than in the U.S.A.; and the changes in their dispersal were as characteristic of their post-war development as the changes, or absence of changes, in their concentration. Cf. James S. Bain, as in footnote 1, p. 196 above, pp. 36–96.

NOTE 12

Even with regard to innovations resulting from substitution of capital for labour it is important to bear in mind that the willingness and ability of industries and firms to substitute could be imperfect. K. J. Arrow, H. B. Chenery, B. S. Minhas, and R. M. Solow in their 'Capital-Labor Substitution and Economic Efficiency', *Review of Economics and Statistics*, XLIII, August 1961, have come to the conclusion that the so-called elasticity of substitution between capital and labour in manufacturing may be less than unity. Some recent attempts to measure these elasticities for different industries put them at levels varying between 0·62 and 0·83. The bearing of these measurements on empirical, above all historical, study of investment and innovation is difficult to assess. They are open to the same statistical criticisms as other econometric aggregates. In addition, they share the conceptual difficulties which attach to other derivatives of the 'production function', more particularly the difficulty of differentiating between capital and labour or treating substitution as a continuous process. The present writer, however, does not believe that these shortcomings deprive the measurements of all relevance; and in so far as these measurements are relevant to historical experience what they signify is that changes in relative prices of factors could not have had as great an effect on the relative proportions of labour and capital actually employed in production as that assumed by some earlier writers.

NOTE 13

J. Riesser, *The German Great Banks* (as in footnote 2, p. 267 above), pp. 705 *seq.*, deals approvingly with the part German banks played in creating the great combines at the turn of the century. Herman Levy's study *Monopolies, Cartels and Trusts in British Industry* (English edn), London 1927, is not wholly confined to the United Kingdom experience. The British cartels and mergers formed before the First World War included several groupings of large and medium-sized firms, such as Wall-Paper Manufacturers, Fine Cotton Spinners and Doublers, Bradford Dyers' Association, Wool Dyers' Association. Small and medium-sized firms were also well represented in such inter-war combines as Allied Iron-founders or Textile Machinery Manufacturers. Trade combination and price agreements also embraced numerous units of every size. Herman Levy in his classical study, while agreeing with the view that formation of monopolies was made easier by the concentration of production in the hands of few large firms, quotes several instances of enduring cartels combining numerous firms of moderate size.

NOTE 14

In the United Kingdom official estimates of fixed capital formation in the public sector put it at 40 per cent of the total. In 1962 it was £1,812 million out of a gross domestic fixed capital formation of £4,441 million: *The British Economy: Key Statistics*, 1900–64, Table E. The share of publicly owned fixed capital in total capital stock of the nation was probably of the same order. But these estimates do not as a rule include the British Government holdings of shares of companies which functioned wholly as private enterprises. On the borderline between true and absentee national ownership was the British Petroleum Company in which in 1964 the Government held 51 per cent of equity: about £100 million ordinary stock worth at the time £400 to £500 million. The Exchange Equalization Account owned dollar securities worth at 1964 prices about $1,250. In addition, the Government held a large amount in securities in a fund established under the Export Guarantees Act of 1949. It also possessed small miscellaneous holdings in some twelve other enterprises; cf. *The Times*, 28 January 1966.

NOTE 15

In Germany corporate savings stood in 1960 at DM 5,910 million compared with DM 1,470 million in 1950, and absorbed about 32 per cent of net company profits: *Statistisches Jahrbuch*, 1962, XXIII, pp. 561–2. They receded somewhat in 1961, but were high in 1962. As a result of changes in taxation, but partly also because of decline in profits and investment, retained profits fell to 19 per cent in 1963: *The Times*, 23 April 1965. According to the computations of Mr M. C. MacDonald of Econtel Research, retentions (including investment allowances) rose in 1960s. Their rate of growth was 0·9 per cent per annum in 1955–60 and 1·2 per annum in 1960–5: *Financial Times*, 9 August 1966. However, the proportion of corporate savings may have risen in 1961–2 in Sweden in

AA

relation to total savings to G.N.P., O.E.C.D., *Survey for Sweden, 1961–2*. In general, retained profits in Sweden and Norway were enhanced by the exemption from taxation of a proportion of profits set aside for reserve investment funds to be drawn on in years in which special stimulus to investment was in official view desirable: O.E.C.D., *Survey for Norway and Sweden, passim*.

NOTE 16

In France the private Banques d'Affaires, such as Banque de Paris et des Pays Bas, la Banque d'Indochine, Banque de l'Union Parisienne et l'Union Européenne Industrielle et Financière played a greater part in the affairs of enterprises than the main deposit banks owned by the State, important as the latter were in managing the current balances of individuals and enterprises, and of late also in financing small enterprises. The influence of private banks in industrial and commercial enterprises was not, however, rooted in their ownership of large packets of shares (*paquets de contrôle*) but in personal links of cross-ownership and of multiple directorships. The links created close associations between certain banks and industrial enterprises, the control of which was shared by largely the same groups of men. In the United Kingdom merchant banks continued after the war to play their traditional role in financing individual transactions and in organizing the flotations of new capital issues. After the war, however, the great merchant banks acquired an ever greater influence in their capacity of financial advisers to firms, especially in connexion with mergers and take-overs or with reorganization of company capital. Links based on ownership of shares or on membership of holding groups were less important except, as in the case of a bank such as Lazard Bros, which happened to form part of the Pearson interests.

NOTE 17

However, in his 'Size of Companies and other Factors of Dividend Policy', *Jour. Roy. Stat. Soc.*, vol. 122, 1959, Sargant Florence draws attention to smaller influence of substantial shareholders in large companies. In general, the tendency to underestimate the influence of large shareholders in companies is more than matched by the tendency to overestimate it. As a recent Marxist study has pointed out, 'stock ownership by itself does not nowadays enable a man to exercise great influence on a giant corporation from the outside': Paul A. Baran and Paul M. Sweezy, *Monopoly Capitalism*, pp. 15 *seq*. This point received a recent corroboration in the failure of a combined group of its largest shareholders to make the directors of the Legal and General Insurance Company change an important policy decision with regard to the 'with profit' policies, and the similar failure of Mr Stutchbury, the head of a group of unit trusts with a large stake in another large company, to revoke certain, much criticized, arrangements for remunerating their directors.

NOTE 18

Some German sociologists have read into the record of changed relations on the shop floor a wholly new pattern of power and authority, both in factories and in society at large. The argument is that the extended hierarchy of industrial functions was reducing the prevailing relations of authority to material relations of production (*Versachlichung der Herrschaft*). This notion derives from Max Weber's view of the historical relations between *Macht* and *Herrschaft* (cf. Ralph Dahrendorf, 'Aspekte der Ungleicheit in der Gesellschaft', *Archives Européennes de Sociologie*, Vol. I, No. 2, 1960, pp. 229–30). In spite of all temptation to join in this socio-philosophical exercise, I have decided to confine my discussion of relations between organization of the labour force in factories, on the one hand, and social patterns outside the factories, on the other, to those superficial phenomena which lend themselves to direct sociological observation and historical study.

NOTE 19

Dr Lockwood, in marshalling his argument against the advocates of the embourgeoisement thesis complains that the latter are apt to compare the 'least socially distinctive sections of the working class of today with the least prosperous and most socially distinctive section of the working class of yesterday' (D. Lockwood, 'The New Working Class', *Annales Européennes de Sociologie*, I, No. 2, 1962, p. 251). This complaint has been sympathetically re-echoed by several recent writers even when they do not happen to subscribe to the whole of Mr Lockwood's argument (e.g. R. Dahrendorf, 'Recent Changes in the Class Structure of European Society', *Daedalus*, 1964, p. 257); but is it justified? I presume that in the Lockwood context the term 'socially distinctive' designates sections of the working class most clearly demarcated from other social classes. If so, the advocates of the embourgeoisement are not at fault in citing them as evidence. The essence of their argument is that the old class demarcations were losing their sharpness and were doing so precisely because the 'most prosperous and the least socially distinctive sections' of the working classes were proliferating at the expense of the 'least prosperous and most socially distinctive ones'. From this point of view, the technical, clerical and skilled employees of modern industries were no less representative of the labour force of post-war Europe than the industrial proletariat of the Communist Manifesto was of the working classes of the nineteenth century (they were certainly not its least prosperous section). Both must be considered as social groups characteristic of the economic transformations of their time. And it would also be a tenable Marxist argument that in the post-war world the semi-skilled operatives in the older branches of industry were, as the lumpen-proletarians of the Communist Manifesto, social ingredients of a departing economic system.

NOTE 20

The object of this note is to explain the procedure by which the estimates of shares of labour and capital in national income, considered as factors of production, have been modified to serve as estimates of shares of 'workers' and 'capitalists' as social groups. For the purposes of the conversion, the official figures for aggregate 'earned' incomes, i.e., those from wages and salaries, have been reduced and the aggregates of 'unearned' incomes augmented by the equivalent of salaries of top-managerial ranks. Corresponding additions and deductions have also been made to allow for the earnings of wage and salary earners from property, i.e. from investments and rents of houses they owned. The estimates, on which these additions and subtractions are based, are of necessity very imprecise and are not offered as anything more than rough indications of the relevant orders of magnitude.

1. Earned incomes of 'workers'. It has been assumed that all recipients of incomes of £2000 and above in 1954/55 quinquennial survey represented the 'non-labour' element among the salary earners; and that allowing for the rises in prices and increases in the subsequent decade, the corresponding group in 1963/64 was that with incomes above £3,000. In actual fact the groups in the borderline income layers in both cases – those in receipt of total incomes between £2,000 and £3,000 in 1954/55 and between £3,000 and £5,000 in 1962/63 – derived about 30 per cent of their incomes from investments at both points of time. The total earned incomes of £2,000 and above in 1954/55 quinquennial survey (a) came to £795 million, and of those of £3,000 and above in 1963/64 (b) came (approximately) to £790 million. Total *earned* incomes of all income levels at these two points of time were £10,380 million (c) and £15,934 million (d), respectively. By deducting (a) and (b) from (c) and (d) we arrive at our first approximation to incomes of wage and salary earners as social groups: £9,585 in 1954/55, £15,144 million in 1963/64. [Source: C.S.O.: *Annual Abstract of Statistics*, No. 102, 1965, Table 322.] As these are 'assessable' incomes only and exclude incomes below the exemption limit (£155 in 1952/55 and £275 in 1963/64, the latter includ-

ing the National Insurance allowance of £22), the estimated aggregate of incomes thus exempt – £45 million and £63 million respectively – must be added to these totals. Thus corrected the total earned incomes of 'workers' at these dates came to ca. £9,630 and ca. £15,207, respectively.

2. Investment incomes of wage and salary earners. The official income tax statistics make it possible to compute directly the investment income of all persons within our wage and salary limits. Investment incomes of individuals whose taxable incomes were below £2,000 in 1954/55 quinquennial survey was £570 million. The corresponding figure for persons with taxable incomes below £3,000 in 1963/64 was approximately £680 million. Those figures, however, contain the incomes from investments of persons not employed in any wage- or salary-earning capacity – retired persons, widows, and juveniles dependent solely on investment incomes; to this extent it exaggerates the investment income of employed workers. On the other hand, it does not include the accruing interest of insurance or pension funds. These profits can, however, be assumed to be eventually paid out in various benefits included in the recorded totals of incomes. In so far as the benefits took the form of pensions or payments to widows or children, they largely account for the 'unearned' incomes of low-income groups and compensate for the overestimate mentioned above. But in so far as these benefits were not thus paid out they must be assumed to cause a small over-all underestimate in our figures of 'workers' income from investment (*ibid.*, Table 322).

3. Rents of owner-occupied houses. The estimates are built up in two stages. The first stage is concerned with the number of houses owned by recipients of wages and salaries within income limits defined in paragraph 1. The second stage is concerned with the rental value of houses so owned.

(*a*) Owner-occupied houses. The official estimates available are those of totals of occupied dwellings (DT = 16,273,000 in 1964); the aggregate output of new dwellings in 1948–64 (DC = 4,886,000) divided into that of dwellings for local housing authorities and those of dwellings for private owners (DCO = 1,897,000). I have assumed that all the houses constructed for housing authorities were rented, and all the houses built for private persons were owner-occupied. The former assumption involves a slight underestimate and the second a slight overestimate of the owner-occupied housing completed during this period. There are also two further assumptions. The *first* is that no owner-occupied houses were owned by persons in income groups below £300 of taxable income in 1954/55 and £500 in 1963/64. The *second* is that above these income levels, ownership of houses was equally distributed among different income groups so that the houses owned by recipients of incomes higher than those of wage and salary earners (i.e. above £2,000 and £3,000 at our two dates) formed the same proportions of total stock of dwellings as recipients of these incomes formed in the total numbers of income earners, or $2\frac{1}{2}$ per cent. Thus computed $DT \times \dfrac{DC}{DCO}$ minus $2\frac{1}{2}$ per cent $=$ 6,350,000. [Source: *ibid.*, Tables 55, 293.]

(*b*) Rent. The simplest way of computing average rents is to divide the National Income estimates of total annual consumers' outlays on housing (£2,246 million in 1964) by the number of occupied dwellings in that year. This would suggest £140 as an annual rent of a dwelling. This figure includes the costs of maintenance (estimated as £365 million for income tax purposes in 1962/63), but excludes the cost of annual housing subsidies and the effects of rent-controls. The two resulting errors very largely cancel out. On the other hand, some allowance must be made for the considerably higher value of dwellings owned by persons with incomes higher than those of wage and salary earners. I have accordingly reduced the estimate by £20 per dwelling or about 12 per cent; which probably overallows for the possible errors. An alternative way is to deduce the annual rent from the capital cost of a local authority ('Council') house. A sample of five local authorities in England and Wales suggests that the capital cost of a 'Council' dwelling was £1,900 in 1954 and £2,800 in 1964. To allow for the higher cost of most privately built dwellings I have taken £2,500 and £3,600 to be the average cost of dwellings (at current prices) at the two dates. Private inquiries from a group of estate agents in Cambridge, London, Liverpool, Newcastle, and Ipswich from a housing charity in London, and some recent returns of building societies appear to corroborate these figures. At 5 per cent interest the annual rent of a dwelling would in that case be £125 and £175 at the two dates. Multiplied by the estimated number of dwellings owned by wage and salary earners this figure suggests £790 million and £1,080 million as the total income of wage and salary earners from owner-occupied dwellings at the two dates. The corresponding rent incomes of the group above our wage and salary levels, if computed on the same basis, should be £11·8 million and £16·2 million. Information from estate agents, however, suggests that the values of houses occupied by recipients of highest (i.e. non-'workers'') incomes, as defined here were so very much higher than the average values of 'workers'' houses that the doubling of these figures would produce a more realistic approximation of the rent value of the dwellings they occupied. The sums of £22·5 million and £33 million would therefore represent their incomes from houses they occupied. A considerable proportion of this income, however, was in the fifties assessed to income tax under Schedule A and included in the totals of assessable incomes. These sums have not, therefore, been added to the totals of taxable incomes in our calculations.

4. The incomes of the two groups thus corrected work out as follows:

	1954/55 quinquennial survey *£ millions*	*1963/64* *£ millions*
(*a*) All earned incomes of wage and salary earners	9·630	15·207
(*b*) 'Workers'' incomes from investments	570	680
(*c*) Rents of 'workers'' houses	790	1·080
Totals	£10·990	£16·967

The figures include employers' contribution, but do not include National Insurance benefits and other current grants from public authorities. They include profits of companies only in so far as they are paid out in dividend and interest to investors; nor do they include personal incomes from abroad. Incomes from 'self-employment' have been left out of the calculations altogether. [Sources: *ibid.*, Tables 293, 294, 319, 322.]

Index